BY THE SAME AUTHOR

China, Pakistan, Bangladesh, 1950-1976
Detente in Europe: Implications for Asia
Japan's Postwar Peace Settlements
Soviet-South Asian Relations, 1947-1978: Volume 1 and 2
China-South Asian Relations, 1947-1980: Volume 1 and 2
China and Japan, 1949-1980 (2nd rev. ed.)
The USSR and Japan, 1945-1980
US-South Asian Relations, 1947-1981: Volume 1 and 2
  (forthcoming)

CHINA AND JAPAN
1949-1980

R K JAIN

*Thoroughly revised and
expanded second edition*

HUMANITIES PRESS
ATLANTIC HIGHLANDS, N.J.

First edition 1977
Second revised edition 1981
First Published in 1981 in the United States of America by
Humanities Press Inc.
171 First Avenue
Atlantic Highlands
N.J. 07716
(by arrangement with Radiant Publishers, New Delhi)

ISBN 0 391 0234 7

Printed in India

Contents

List of Documents

List of Tables

List of Appendices

Preface to the Second Edition

Since the book was first written in 1976, the power configuration in Northeast Asia has undergone significant changes. Sino-Soviet confrontation has become more intense and Chinese fears of Soviet encirclement in the wake of the Soviet-Vietnamese Friendship Treaty and intervention in Afghanistan have increased. In the early 1970s, Japan had adopted an even-handed approach towards China and the Soviet Union. But after the MIG-25 affair of September 1976, Soviet-Japanese relations, which had remained strained because of the unresolved territorial issue, have steadily declined and Japan has become increasingly concerned about the growing Soviet build-up on the Northern Territories. Sino-Japanese relations, on the other hand, have shown a marked improvement as witness the signing of the Peace and Friendship Treaty and the broadening and expansion of economic relations. Close economic and political relations between China and Japan have altered Japan's equidistance approach towards the neighbouring Communist giants and a tilt in favour of China is apparent. At the same time, Japan, while maintaing its security alliance with the United States and confident of its defence capabilities which have been substantially increased under American pressure and Chinese encouragement, has recently acknowledged the desirability of an appropriate division of roles with the US for peace and security in the Far East region and the defence of Japan. Moreover, the normalization of Sino-American relations and the recent US decision to sell arms to China reflect "parallel strategic interests" of the two countries. These developments seem to confirm Soviet fears about a triangular Sino-Japanese-US relationship or "axis."

This thoroughly revised, mostly rewritten, and updated second edition analyses the economic, political, and strategic dimensions of Sino-Japanese relations from 1945 to 1980 in the context of Sino-Soviet rivalry, Sino-US *rapprochement*, and the emerging new alignment between China, Japan, and the United States. The book contains six new chapters, which deal with the significance and implications of the Sino-Japanese Peace and Friendship Treaty, the Senkaku Islands dispute, economic relations in the seventies, cooperation in the development of energy resources, political relations since the signing of the Peace and Friendship Treaty in August 1978 and outlook for the future. Earlier chapters have also been thoroughly revised and to a great extent rewritten.

The analysis is followed by a reference collection of 87 documents bearing on the subject. These include full texts or relevant extracts of bilateral treaties, agreements, joint communiques, important interviews and statements by government dignitaries, articles, commentaries and editorials in the Chinese Press. Of the 82 documents included in the first edition, this new edition omits 37 documents, most of them relate to the repatriation of POWs and unofficial trade agreements. This second edition includes 42 new, currently more relevant documents. Of these, 33 relate to the period 1977 to 1980.

I have greatly benefitted from the very perceptive comments of Dr J. P. Jain who read the revised manuscript of the edition with painstaking care.

15 July 1981   R. K. JAIN

Preface to the First Edition

Ever since the establishment of the People's Republic of China in 1949, the Peking leadership has pursued a policy of hostility and suspicion towards Japan centring mainly on the latter's early military alliance with the United States and close ties with Taiwan. (In 1952 Japan signed a Peace Treaty with Taiwan; in 1969 Premier Sato went to the extent of committing Japan to Taiwan's security in his anxiety to recover Okinawa from the United States).

During 1953-57, China adopted a soft line towards Japan by concluding a number of non-official trade agreements and engaging itself in "Cultural Diplomacy." However, after the Nagasaki Flag Incident (1958), Peking suspended all its business dealings with Japan and reverted to a hard line, which continued throughout the 1960s. Peking made a determined, but unsuccesful, bid to oust Premier Kishi for his renewal of the US-Japan Security Treaty and his invitation to President Eisenhower to visit Japan. The great internal turmoil which engulfed the whole of China in the second half of 1960s had its adverse spillover effects on Sino-Japanese relations. Peking continued its vehement attack, even after the so-called "Great Proletarian Cultural Revolution," against Eisaku Sato for his revival of Japanese militarism and for publicly identifying Japan's security interests with that of Taiwan and South Korea.

In the early 1970s, however, the pattern of international politics began to change and Sino-Japanese relations were normalized. Among the factors that contributed to the normalization of Sino-Japanese relations were flexibility in Chinese policy towards Japan in the post-Cultural Revolution period, President Nixon's visit to China, the exit of Premier Sato, the ruling Liberal Democratic Party's eagerness to resolve a highly explosive domestic issue and open the Chinese market to Japanese trade, and Tokyo's quest to regain its role in world politics.

The normalization of relations, which resulted in the abrogation of the Japan-Taiwan Peace Treaty, opened broad prospects for the development of good neighbourly and friendly relations between the two countries. By the middle of 1975, all the four administrative agreements envisaged in the September 1972 Joint Communique on the normalization of relations, *viz.* a trade, civil aviation, shipping, and a fisheries agreement, had been concluded. However, the Peace and Friendship Treaty between the two countries, also envisaged in 1972 Communique, has not yet been signed—because of Chinese insistence that an "anti-hegemony" clause be included in the Treaty and Tokyo's reluctance to ignore Soviet susceptibilities and apprehensions in the matter. . . .

While the two countries are likely to continue to maintain and develop their normal, good neighbourly relations, an *entente cordiale* does not seem in sight in the near future. . . .

I am greatly indebted to Dr. J.P. Jain for reading the manuscript and for his valuable comments and suggestions. However, the views expressed in the book are entirely mine.

New Delhi   R.K. Jain

Pinyin Equivalents of Chinese Names

From the beginning of 1979 the Chinese State Council decided to go over wholly to the pinyin method of 'romanising' Chinese characters. Pinyin equivalents of Chinese names are as follows.

Chang Tsai-chien	Zhang Caiqian
Chi Peng-fei	Ji Pengfei
Chiang Kai-shek	Jiang Jieshi
Chiao Kuan-hua	Jiao Guanhua
Chou En-lai	Zhou Enlai
Chungking	Chongqing
Han Nien-lung	Han Nianlong
Hsinhua	Xinhua
Hua Kuo-feng	Hua Guofeng
Keng Piao	Geng Biao
Ku Mu	Gu Mu
Kwangchow	Guangzhou
Li Hsien-nien	Li Xiannian
Mao Tse-tung	Mao Zedong
Paoshan	Baoshan
Peking	Beijing
Peng Chen	Peng Zhen
Pohai Bay	Bohai Bay
Taching	Daqing
Teng Hsiao-ping	Deng Xiaoping
Teng Ying-chao	Deng Yingchao
Yu Chiu-li	Yu Qiuli

1. Introduction

China and Japan, the two prominent countries of East Asia, are geographically close to each other, separated only by the East China Sea. Japan's southern islands are situated approximately 216 miles east of the coast of the Chinese Mainland and are about seventy miles north-east of the island of Taiwan. There is also close cultural, linguistic affinity between the peoples of the two countries, who are of the same racial stock and belong to a common civilization—the Sinitic civilization.

Historical Perspective

Both China and Japan were closed to foreign intercourse early in the seventeenth century, and both were forced open by the colonizing nations of the West in the middle of the nineteenth. The two, however, reacted quite differently to Western imperialism. China disintegrated as a social system and suffered untold humiliation at the hands of the "foreign devils." Japan, on the other hand, not only modernized itself quickly along Western lines, but it also endeavoured to expand its influence in the weaker adjacent areas and soon become a Power to reckon with. A strong Japan, thus, embarked on asserting its control over the neighbouring areas which brought it into conflict with the other major Powers of the region, viz. China and Russia.

As early as 1871, following the signing of a bilateral treaty of friendship and commerce between the Meiji government in Japan and the Ching dynasty in China, the "Wa dwarfs" (as Chinese called the Japanese) attempted to subject China to an unequal treaty, one similar to the treaties China had concluded with the Western Powers under pressure. China stoutly resisted the attempt and the Japanese abandoned the idea, for the time being at any rate.

Towards the end of the 19th century, Japan placed the highest strategic value on the Korean Peninsula partly because of its growing imperial aspirations and partly because of its commercial interests in central and south China and to gain control over the sea approaches to the home islands. In 1895 Japan inflicted a defeat on China. By the Treaty of Shimonoseki, China ceded to Japan the Liaotung Peninsula containing Ports Arthur and Darien as well as the island of Formosa and the Pescadores. This meant that Japan had gained the beachhead for further expansion on the continent. However, Japan was compelled by France, Germany, and Russia to return the Liaotung Peninsula to China Three years later, Russia acquired that Peninsula for itself.

After unsuccessful attempts to regulate the conflct of interest between Japan and Russia over Korea, Japan waged a successful war against Russia in 1904-5. As result of the Portsmouth Treaty (5 September 1905) Japan acquired complete and absolute right of control in Korea and established special interests in Manchuria alongside that of Russia. Thus Japan had expelled Russian influence from Korea and acquired a strong foothold on the Asiatic continent. Subsequently, Japan and Russia sought to demarcate their respective spheres of interest in Northeast Asia in order to prevent any third Power, especially the United States, from penetrating the region and excercising political domination over China. By 1910 Korea became a Japanese colony. The Japanese sought to take advantage of the internal turmoil that shook China in the immediate aftermath of the 1911 Revolution as well as of the preoccupation of the European Powers with the global engagements of the First World War. In 1915, they tried to impose their stringent Twenty-one Demands on China. This made both the Yuan Shih-kai regime and the revolutionaries feel that the Japanese were only intent on humiliating their country. In the twenties, under Chiang Kai-shek, the Kuomintang government succeeded in unifying China. This posed a threat to the Japanese rights and interests in Manchuria. In September 1931, therefore, the Japanese army in the Kwantung Leased Territory fabricated what become well known later as the Mukden incident. Japan seized Manchuria and established the puppet regime of Manchukuo. In 1936 the Japanese government issued a decree, declaring that the five provinces of north China should be made "autonomous".

After the Marco Polo Bridge Incident of 7 July 1937, the Japanese army gradually usurped the powers of the Foreign Ministry, so much so that the Ministry came to be called the "foreign affairs bureau of the army." Throughout the years 1937 to 1945, the Japanese government kept up its efforts to subjugate the Jiang Jieshi (Chiang Kai-shek) regime, if not to to liquidate it altogether, and continued their war of aggression against China.

China and a Peace Treaty with Japan

After the defeat of Japan in World War II, the Chinese people felt deeply concerned about the nature and content of a peace treaty with Japan as the Japanese militarists had inflicted on China "a loss of more than 10 million lives and the destruction and burning of property worth at least 50,000 million US dollars."[1]

As early as 23 September 1947, an article in the pro-Communist *China Digest* asserted that China should have a "a decisive role informing Japan's future" sinceit had been a victim of Japanese aggression and had fought Japan the longest. China, it added, should veto anything detrimental to its interests "no matter whether it comes from America or is agreed by majority."[2]

Commentaries in the pro-Communist Press criticised the United States policy of building Japan into a military ally and "a strong, American-controlled military, political and economic bulwark in the Far East to be the bastion of an anti-Bolshevism crusade and a secure base for American expansion."[3]

By the middle of 1949, the Chinese Communist views on Japan had crystallised in a policy framework which included: advocacy of an early peace treaty with Japan; emphasis on demilitarisation and democratisation of Japan; and apprehension about the US policy in Japan, which favoured release of war criminals, cessation of payment of reparations, and preservation of the *Zaibatsu*.[4]

Bejiing opposed US attempts to conclude a separate peace with Japan without the participation of China and the Soviet Union. An article by Li Chung·ching in *World Culture* in March 1950 expressed concern about the conclusion of a United States-Japanese military alliance upon the conclusion of a peace treaty which "may possibly be developed into a 'Pacific Pact'."[5]

The official Chinese attitude on a peace treaty was spelt out in a statement of Premier Zhou Enlai on 4 December 1950,[6] his letter to the Soviet Ambassador dated 22 May 1951,[7] his statement on the US-British draft dated 15 August 1951[8] and his statements on the San Francisco treaty dated 18 September 1951,[9] and 5 May 1952.[10] The salient points stressed in these statements were: (1) an overall treaty should be concluded with the participation of Communist China and all other countries which had fought Japan; (2) Taiwan and the Penghu Islands (Pescadores) should be restored to China in accordance with the Cairo Declaration; (3) the Kuriles, the southern part of Sakhalin, and all islands adjacent to it should be returned to the Soviet Union; (4) the peace treaty should guarantee the genuine independence and sovereignty of Japan; (5) all foreign troops should be withdrawn from Japan; (6) there should be an assurance against the revival of Japanese militarism by limiting the size of the armed forces, which should not exceed the requirements of self-defence; (7) Japan must not join any alliance aimed at any of the Allied Powers; and (8) no restrictions should be imposed on the development of a peacetime Japanese economy and trade with other countries.

These Chinese demands were generally in line with the Soviet stand in the matter. Premier Zhou Enlai also asserted his country's right to claim reparations from Japan and said that any treaty with Japan in the preparation, drafting, and signing of which China did not participate would be considered "illegal" and "null and void" by his government.[11]

American plans for a peace treaty with Japan, Zhou Enlai argued, was a flagrant violation of the common war aims of the Allied Powers. They utterly disregarded the fundamental interests of the Chinese people as well as the aspirations of the the Japanese people for the future. Moreover, the United States draft treaty with Japan, Zhou Enlai stated on 22 May 1951, provided no guarantee at all for preventing the revival of Japanese militarism, nor did it place any limitation upon the size of the armed forces. The aim of the United States Government, he stated, was clearly not to eliminate, but to revive, militarism in Japan and, with its territory as war base and its people as cannon fodder, to make Japan a tool of the United States in continuing and expanding aggression in Korea, China, and other Asian countries.[12]

Zhou Enlai pointed out that the provisions in the joint Anglo-American draft treaty concerning the disposal of the property and rights or intrests in Japan of the Allied Powers and their nationals during the war completely ignored the period before 7 December 1941 when the Chinese people were carrying on war against Japan single-handed. In his statement of 15 August 1951, Zhou Enlai reiterated China's right to claim reparations from Japan and asserted his country's inviolable sovereignty over Nansha and Hsisha Islands in the South China Seas.[13]

The United Kingdom and the United States were divided in their opinion as to who truly represented China—whether it was the Mao regime on the mainland or the Jiang (Chiang) regime in Taiwan. It was, therefore, decided not to invite either of them to the San Francisco Conference. This was how in the absence of any Chinese representative the San Francisco Peace Treaty was signed on 8 September 1951. On the same day, the United States signed the US-Japanese Mutual Security Treaty which was later modified and renewed for a period of ten years in January 1960 and extended indefinitely in June 1970.

When the peace treaty with Japan became effective, Zhou Enlai denounced it as a "forcible imposition on the Japanese people" which in no way restored sovereignty and independence to Japan and did not change its status as an occupied country. He also expressed his firm opposition to the Yoshida-Jiang treaty, which he described as "an open insult and act of hostility to the Chinese people."[14]

The San Francisco Peace Treaty, signed on 8 September 1951 by 49 nations, was basically an American document which reflected Cold War considerations and American interests. In fact, George F. Kennan, the chief architect of the treaty, shared the belief of many ranking officials in the United States that Japan's strategic position, human resources, and industrial potential must somehow be denied to China and the Soviet Union.[15] The Korean War and the Chinese intervention in it further enhanced the value of Japan as an indispensable military base and source of military supply for the United Nations forces in Korea. Besides, Japan, Korea, Okinawa, Formosa, and the Philippines were seen as forming a defence ring against Communist expansionism.

A defenceless Japan struggling to bring the American occupation to an end as speedily as possible was hardly in a position to either exploit the Anglo-American differences on China or to contemplate going against American wishes in the matter lest such an attitude should jeopardize its negotiations with the Allies for a peace treaty as well as with the United States for a security treaty. With the outbreak of the Korean War and the conclusion of the Sino-Soviet alliance, Japan began to share the post-war American world-view and the overwhelming need to "contain" communism. Yoshida felt that in the face of the Sino-Soviet alliance, which was specifically directed against Japan, it was dangerous for defenceless Japan, which was marked as "special prize" by the Communists, to remain exposed to the Communist "war threat."[16] The Korean War, Shigeru Yoshida pointed out, was proof of how real and close the Communist danger to Japan was.[17] To what extent Yoshida was moved by this consideration of Japan's national security is difficult to say, but the fact remained that the treaty allowing US forces to be stationed in Japan became "the unavoidable quid pro quo for the non-punitive peace settlement—a concession to irresistible American pressure."[18]

For a while Japan seemed reluctant to proceed with any China treaty. The Yoshida Government, however, eventually decided under US pressure to negotiate a treaty of normal relations with Nationalist China. The consensus among the American legislators and people that prior to final Congressional action on the San Francisco treaty, Japan should conclude a peace treaty with the Nationalist government of China, stemmed from fears of the possibility that, after the return to independence, Japan might move closer to the Beijing regime. If American wishes were not met, Shigeru Yoshida felt that "ratification of the Japanese peace treaty by the U.S. Senate would be difficult and might well be delayed or rejected."[19] In a letter to John Foster Dulles on 24 December 1951 Premier Yoshida made it clear that the "terms of such a bilateral treaty shall, in respect of the Republic of China, be applicable to all territories which are now, or which may hereafter be, under the control of the National Government of the Republic of China."[20] Yoshida at the same time asserted his government's desire *"ultimately* to have a full measure of political peace and commercial intercourse with China, Japan's close neighbour." Yoshida had no illusions about the reality of Communist control over the mainland. In fact, he clearly hinted that Japan would seek to achieve peace with the Beijing Government in future.

Meanwhile Yoshida sought to justify establishing relations with Taipeh by stating that its government "has the seat, voice and vote of China in the United Nations. . .exercised actual government authority over certain territory and. . . maintains diplomatic relations with most of the members of the United Nations." The Chinese Communist regime, on the other hand, Yoshida argued, stood condemned by the United Nations as an aggressor. He also accused Beijing of seeking, through its support of the Japan Communist Party (JCP), to overthrow the Japanese government and constitutional system by force. Moreover, the Mao regime, he pointed out, had entered into a military alliance with the Soviet Union aimed at Japan.[21] These arguments, though plausible, could not obliterate the fact that the Conservative government of Japan, in a period of national weakness, had "acquiesced definitely in America's China policy and had to live with the consequences of that policy."[22] This acquiescence was the price Japan paid for regaining its independence in 1952 after seven years of US occupation. Diplomatic recognition of the government in Taiwan, Richard Storry writes, hardly represented the true wishes of the Yoshida Cabinet. What Yoshida had in mind was a simultaneous *de facto* working arrangement with both Beijing and Taipeh. But he was not allowed to make the experiment and US pressure compelled him to recognise Taipeh.[23]

On the same day (28 April 1952) that both the San Francisco Peace Treaty and the US-Japanese Mutual Security Treaty came into force, under intense US pressure, signed a peace treaty with the Republic of China at Taipei.[24] The peace treaty with

Taiwan was strongly criticized by Chinese leaders. It remained a stumbling block in the normalization of relations between China and Japan for two decades.

Conclusion

The important features of China's policy towards Japan during 1949-52 were, firstly, to seek early conclusion of peace with Japan in order to end the US occupation of Japan. Secondly, China sought to make common cause with the Japanese people in their struggle against the American occupation of Japan. To that end, the *People's Daily* editorial of 17 January 1950 supported Cominform criticism of the Japan Communist Party and exhorted the Japanese people to wage a determined revolutionary struggle against American imperialism and against the reactionary forces in Japan."[25] This reflected Peking's expectation of a revolution in Japan.[26] The criticism of the Soviet and Chinese Communist Parties had the desired effect on the Japanese Communist Party as it soon abandoned its moderation; for it became violently anti-American and started a nation-wide agitation for a general peace settlement and for peace and national independence. The Statement of the Central Committee of the Chinese Communist Party on the situation in Japan, issued on 12 June 1950, denounced the action taken by the Yoshida Government of Japan, "under orders from Mac-Arthur," against the Japanese Communist Party and its members. The Chinese Party statement also expressed sympathy and support for the struggle of the Japanese Communist Party and "the patriotic Japanese" against the American "aggressors and the Japanese traitors, with the aim of achieving an early all-inclusive peace settlement with the Allied Powers and liberation for the Japanese people."[27]

The Chinese felt greatly concerned about possible Japanese rearmament[28] and the establishment of American military bases in Japan. This concern found expression in the conclusion of the Sino-Soviet Treaty of Friendship, Alliance, and Mutual Assistance of 14 February 1950. The preamble of the Treaty spoke of preventing jointly "the revival of Japanese imperialism and repetition of aggression on the part of Japan or any other state that may join in any way with Japan in acts of aggression." Under Article 1, China and the Soviet Union agreed to take all necessary measures to prevent "a repetition of aggression and violation of peace on the part of Japan or any other State that may directly or indirectly join with Japan in acts of aggression." Should either of the two states be "attacked by Japan or States allied with her and thus find itself in a state of war," the other contracting Party "shall immediately render it military and other assistance with all the means at its disposal."[29]

In the immediate aftermath of the Second World War, it was not possible for Japanese leaders to improve relations with the People's Republic of China because of domestic and international factors. Japan was under US military occupation from 1945 to 1952. Its foreign policy, therefore, was merely an integral adjunct of US policy. The conclusion of the Sino-Soviet alliance, the outbreak of the Korean War, and incessant US pressure led Japan to more closely align itself economically, militarily, and politically with the United States. This was evident from the conclusion of the San Francisco Peace Treaty, the US-Japanese Security Treaty, and the Japan-Taiwan Peace Treaty. Even with the resumption of Japan's political independence in 1952 United States policy continued to influence Japan's China policy.

NOTES

1 *Renmin Ribao (People's Daily)*, 10 May 1960, as translated in *China Reconstructs*, June 1960, Supplement, 7.
2 *China Digest*, 23 September 1947, 3.
3 Ibid., 24 February 1948, 10-1. Also see *Wen Hui-Pao* and *World Culture* of 1 July 1949 in *China Weekly Review*, 2 July 1949, 109 and ibid., 9 July 1949, 127.
4 See Xinhua News Agency, 21 June 1949 in *China Degest*, 28 June 1949, 14-5. Also see a joint statement of various parties and people's organizations of China on the occasion of the 12th anniversary of the war of resistance against Japan. *China Weekly Review*, 16 July 1949, 151.
5 *China Weekly Review*, 25 March 1950, 68.
6 *People's China*, 16 December 1950, Supplement, 17-9.
7 Ibid., 1 June 1951, Supplement, 3-5.
8 Ibid., 1 September 1951, Supplement, 3-6.
9 Ibid., 1 October 1951, 38-9.
10 Ibid., 16 May 1952, 4-6.

[11] Ibid., 1 October 1951, 38-9.

[12] Ibid., 1 June 1951, Supplement, 3-5.

[13] Ibid., 1 September 1951, Supplement, 3-6.

[14] See Zhou Enlai's statement of 5 May 1952, in ibid., 16 May 1952, 4-6.

[15] For Kennan's views, see US, Department of State, *Foreign Relations of the United States* (hereinafter cited *Foreign Relations 1947*), *Vol. VI, The Far East* (Washington, D.C., 1972), 537-43 and *Foreign Relations, 1948, Vol. VI, The Far East and Australasia* (Washington, D.C., 1974), 691-6 and 712-9.

[16] Statement issued by the Japanese Foreign Office for the purpose of clarifying Japan's position in the Korean conflict, 19 August 1950. See *Contemporary Japan*, July-September 1950, 463-9.

[17] Shigeru Yoshida, "Japan and the Crisis in Asia," *Foreign Affairs*, 6 January 1951, 174.

[18] Martin E. Weinstein, *Japan's Post War Defence Policy, 1947-1968* (New York, 1971), 50, 55 and 63. The Japanese appeared willing to tolerate US troops in their midst, but only for a very short time and as a matter of necessity. Roger Dingman, "Reconsiderations: The United States-Japan Security Treaty," *Pacific Community*, July 1976, 478.

[19] Shigeru Yoshida, *Japan's Decisive Century* (New York, 1967), 85, also see Anthony Eden, *The Memoirs of Anthony Eden, Full Circle* (Cambridge, 1960), 20-2.

[20] *Department of State Bulletin*, 28 January 1952, 120.

[21] Ibid.

[22] Lawrence Olson, *Japan in Postwar Asia* (London, 1970), 75.

[23] Richard Storry, "Options for Japan in the 1970s," *World Today*, August 1970.

[24] For a detailed discussion of Nationalist China's attitude towards the Peace Treaty, see R.K. Jain, *Japan's Postwar Peace Settlements* (New Delhi, 1978), 57-64.

[25] *Soviet Press Translations*, 1 March 1950, 151-2.

[26] Shinkichi Eto, "Pastwar Japanese-Chinese Relations," *Survey* (Autumn 1972), 58.

[27] Xinhua News Agency, June 1950, 80-1.

[28] A resolution on the Japanese question, unanimously adopted in the Peace Conference of the Asian and Pacific Regions held in Beijing from 2 to 12 October 1952, demanded an end to the remilitarization of Japan and withdrawal of all foreign troops from Japanese territory. The Peace Conference also resolved to send a peace delegation to Japan and favoured exchange of regular visits between the organizations of the Asian and Pacific countries and those of Japan. *People's China*, 1 November 1952, Supplement, 6-7.

[29] *New Times* (Moscow), 22 February 1950, Supplement, 3.

2. People's Diplomacy, 1953-1957

During the period from 1953 to 1957, China initiated "people's diplomacy" in order to develop good-neighbourly relations with Japan and facilitate normalization of relations between the two countries. This policy also sought to wean Japan away from the United States and Taiwan, put pressure on the ruling Liberal Democratic Party to change its policy towards China, and strengthen the Leftist, democratic forces in Japan with a view to build public opinion in favour of improved relations with China. To that end, China entered into non-governmental agreements on trade and fishing, exchanged numerous goodwill and cultural delegations, repatriated a large number of Japanese nationals, released Japanese war criminals, and stopped capturing Japanese fishermen. Beijing's soft line towards Japan during this period coincided with a general relaxation of tension in the region, as witness the signing of the armistice agreement in Korea in 1953, the peace settlement Indo-China in 1954, and the convening of the Bandung Conference of Asian, African countries in 1955. Beijing's more pragmatic policy was also partly due to the failure of the violent struggle of Japanese Communist Party (JCP) in Japan.

A major instrument of "people's diplomacy" was the exchange of cultural delegations. Usually private citizens belonging to the opposition or to business circles were invited to China and after being treated well were enticed into signing a joint statement denouncing American imperialism and Japanese monopoly capitalism.[1] Thus a large number of Japanese groups—"peace" groups, Diet Members, youth and women's groups, local groups, religious groups, labour unions, "friendship" groups, fishery and agricultural groups, professional groups,

and others were invited to visit China during 1954-57. Thus,
while only five Japanese delegations had visited China from
1952 to the end of 1954, their number rose steadily thereafter.
In 1955, it was nine; in 1956, fifteen; and in 1957, twenty. The
number of Japanese visitors increased from 100 in 1954 to 847
in 1955; 1,243 in 1956; and more than 2,000 in 1957. A small
number of Chinese also visited Japan. There were ten Chinese
visiting Japan in 1954; 112 in 1955; and 142 in 1956.

By the end of 1957, more than thirty non-governmental
agreements and joint statements had been signed by the various
"people's organizations" of China and Japan. Thirteen such
documents were signed in 1956 alone. These agreements and
joint statements covered a wide range of subjects. Some dealt
with technical problems of trade, fishery, and repatriation of
nationals. Others were concerned with cultural and scientific
exchanges. Yet others were quite political. All, however, called
for the strengthening of mutual friendship and the "normalization" of relations between Japan and Communist China.[2]

China launched a vigorous campaign to normalize relations
with Japan. In his conversations with Professor Ikuo Oyama,
member of the House of Councillors and Chairman of the
Japanese National Peace Committee, on 28 September 1953,
Premier Zhou Enlai expressed China's desire to establish normal relations with all countries of the world, particularly Japan.
The soft line towards Japan also found clear expression in the
joint Sino-Soviet Declaration of 12 October 1954 in which the
two Communist states categorically stated that they stood for
the development of broad trade relations and the establishment
of close cultural ties with Japan. They also expressed their
readiness to take steps to normalize their relations with Japan.[3]

Japan was blamed for "creating obstacles to the possibility
of her concluding a peace treaty with new China and establishing normal diplomatic relations."[4] Zhou Enlai alleged that by
continuing to act as a tool of United States policy, by continuing to maintain diplomatic relations with the Jiang Jieshi
(Chiang Kai-shek) clique, and by adopting a policy of hostility
towards China, Japan was becoming day by day "a factor of
unrest" in the Pacific.[5] The Chinese Press echoed these views.
For example, a long editorial in the *People's Daily* of 30
October 1953, described Japan as "a satellite and war base of

the United States in the Far East." The editorial criticized
Tokyo for signing a separate peace treaty with United States,
the US-Japanese Security Treaty, and the so-called peace treaty
with Jiang Jieshi (Chiang Kai-shek) and also for being a party
to the US policy of imposing an "embargo" on trade etc. with
Communist China. It stated that normal relations with Japan
could be established and developed if that country would
severe its relations with Taiwan, free itself from the position of
"a satellite and follower of the US aggressors," and become a
peaceful and independent state. It felt that if these conditions
were fulfilled even a non-aggression pact between the two countries might be considered. Finally, it expressed the hope that
good neighbourly relations could be established between China
and Japan "on the basis of mutual respect, non-aggression,
peaceful coexistence, equality and friendship, trade freely carried
on, and cultural exchange."[6]

Subsequently in his speech before the Conference of Asian
countries held in New Delhi in April 1955, the leader of the
Chinese delegation, Kuo Mo-jo, observed that the obstacles in
the way of the normalization of Sino-Japanese relations came
neither from China nor from Japan but "from the pressure
imposed upon the Japanese Government by the Government
of the United States." He, therefore, expressed the opinion that
"when the Japanese people shake off the shackles of foreign occupation and regain their political and economic independence,"
they would establish friendly relations with other Asian countries and that the "vicious" attempts being made by certain
Western Powers to revive Japanese militarism and to use Asians
to fight Asians would be frustrated and defeated.[7]

China continued to criticize the Japan-Jiang peace treaty
and called for its abolition. However, on 17 August 1955 while
answering written questions submitted by a visiting Japanese
Press delegation, Zhou Enlai did not specifically insist on its
abrogation as a pre-condition for normalization of Sino-
Japanese relations. He also stated that the San Francisco Peace
Treaty, though opposed by China, did not constitute an obstacle to the normalization of relations or to the conclusion of a
peace treaty between China and Japan."[8] On the same day the
Chinese Consul General at Geneva Shen Ping in his secret
reply to his counterpart, Keiichi Tatsuke, proposed that in

order to promote normalization of Sino-Japanese relations and contribute to further relaxation of international tension the Japanese Government send a delegation to Beijing to discuss trade, exchange of persons, status of overseas residents, and "other important problems" of mutual interest. The Japanese did not respond to Shen Ping's offer. As a result, in another secret note dated 4 November 1955 Shen invited a Japanese Government delegation to Beijing and argued the time was ripe for the restoration of diplomatic relations between China and Japan.[9]

On several other occasions Chinese leaders reiterated their desire to normalise diplomatic relations between China and Japan. These include the joint statement which Peng Chen signed with a visiting Japanese Diet delegation on 17 October 1955[10] and the statements of Kuo Mo-jo of 20 November and 1 December 1955.[11] In a statement on 30 January 1956, Premier Zhou Enlai referred to the proposals made by the Chinese Government on 17 August and 4 November 1955 and proposed to the Japanese Government, for the third time, that consultations for promoting normalization of Sino-Japanese relations should be held.[12]

Japan did not respond favourably to Chinese overtures for improved relations because the ruling Liberal Democratic Party was convinced that even after the restoration of independence Japan's security and economic prosperity entirely depended upon the United States. Japanese leaders, therefore, described co-operation with free nations, especially the United States, as "the key-note of Japan's foreign policy."[13]

Though Premier Hatoyama (December 1954-1956) could restore Japan's diplomatic relations with the Soviet Union, he did not succeed in normalizing relations with China. He maintained that "the normalization of diplomatic relations with Communist countries is one thing and the acceptance of communism is another" and that Japan would adhere to its attitude of anti-communism and adopt every available means in defence of the cause of democracy.[14] "Readjustment of relations with our continental nieghbours," Japanese Foreign Minister Mamoru Shigemitsu felt, was a question that required 'delicate consideration." This was to be achieved "on mutually acceptable terms with the free nations."[15] Besides, Japan had misgivings about the "actual conduct of Beijing's diplomacy," as witness the Formosan Straits crisis of early 1955. Shigemitsu described the fighting across the Formosa Straits as "a threat to peace and security in East Asia" and deprecated the tendency towards having recourse to force."[16] Nevertheless. Tokyo lifted restrictions on Japanese wishing to travel in China and permitted Chinese delegations to visit Japan.

Foreign Minister Shigemitsu spoke of the inability of his Government to recognize the Beijing regime but expressed his desire "in the light of the fact of the existence of the latter" to continue to pursue the policy of increasing Japan's trade with China "within the bounds of our international commitments."[17] He denied having received any official proposals from China about restoration of diplomatic relations. The Chinese Foreign Ministry, therefore, published the full texts of all the documents exchanged in 1955 between the Chinese and Japanese Consul-General at Geneva on 11 February 1956.[18] Consequently, Shigemitsu admitted that a further check had revealed that Japan had received China's formal proposals. He, however, emphasized that the time was not yet ripe for the restoration of official ties between the two countries.[19]

While Premier Hatoyama did not favourably respond to Chinese overtures he endeavoured to normalize Japan's relations with the Soviet Union in order to open up a channel for direct discussion with a view to an early solution of the problem of repatriation of prisoners-of-war and a speedy settlement of the fisheries and territorial questions. Normalization of relations with the Soviet Union, it was felt, would also enable Japan to secure Soviet support for its aspiration for admission to the membership of the United Nations so that it might join the international society and seek to raise its international stature and prestige.[20] Thus Hatoyama's preoccupation with the Soviet Union precluded his quick response to Chinese overtures. Besides, Hatoyama's conciliatory approach towards China encountered growing opposition within his own cabinet (led by Foreign Minister Shigemitsu) and among Conservative Dietmen (led by Yoshida's adherents). Since his Democratic Party did not command a majority in the National Diet, Hatoyama had to take into account the Liberal Party's strong anti-Beijing orientation. Even after the Liberal-Democratic merger in

November 1955, he was invariably sensitive to the recalcitrant Yoshida faction.[21]

Despite the inability of Hatoyama and his successor, Tanzan Ishibashi, to achieve normalization of political relations with China, they encouraged the expansion of economic and cultural exchanges between the two countries. Many agreements were concluded, e.g. fisheries agreement in April 1955 and the third unofficial trade agreement in May 1955. The volume of trade between China and Japan reached the postwar peak of $ 150.9 million. Chinese commercial exhibitions were held at Tokyo and Osaka in the fall of 1955; in return, a Japanese exhibit was held in Beijing and Shanghai the following year.

Meanwhile, the Soviet Union normalized diplomatic relations with Japan on 19 October 1956. *Renmin Ribao* (21 October 1956) welcomed this and felt that it would prove beneficial to Japan's independent development and strengthen Far Eastern peace.

With the coming into power of the staunchly pro-American and pro-Taiwanese Premier Nobusuke Kishi in February 1957, prospects for the improvement of Sino-Japanese relations did not seem too bright. Nevertheless, the Japanese Socialist Party (JSP) energetically sought to improve economic and political relations with China.

A goodwill mission of the Japanese Socialist Party, headed by Inejiro Asanuma, held extensive discussions with Zhou Enlai (on 15 April 1957) and with Chairman Mao Zedong (on 21 April) and issued a joint statement with Chang Hsi-jo, President of the People's Institute of Foreign Affairs, on 22 April. Throughout the talks, the Chinese leaders emphasized that Beijing would not tolerate the concept of two Chinas and that Japan should "de-recognize" the Nationalist Government in Taiwan if it wanted to establish diplomatic relations with Communist China. The Japanese delegation affirmed its policy of not recognizing two Chinas and described Taiwan as an internal question of China in the joint statement.[22] Zhou Enlai suggested a step-by-step establishment of Sino-Japanese diplomatic relations through a peaceful settlement of the Taiwan issue.[23] Mao Zedong expressed his willingness to conclude a treaty of friendship and non-aggression between China and Japan after normal relations had been restored. The existence of the US-Japanese Security Pact he, added, was no bar to the conclusion of such a non-aggression and friendship treaty between China and Japan. Both Zhou Enlai and Mao Zedong assured the Japanese Socialist Party delegation that if Japan abrogated the US Security Treaty and if Washington removed its military bases and withdrew its armed forces from Japan, Beijing would be willing to revise the provisions of the Sino-Soviet Treaty of Friendship, Mutual Assistance, and Alliance of February 1950 aimed at guarding against the revival of Japanese militarism and its use by others.[24]

Premier Zhou Enlai was favourably impressed by the enthusiastic friendship and co-operative spirit shown by the JSP mission. Given its recent gains in the National Diet, he wished to use the JSP, in addition to the JCP, as an institutional device to penetrate into Japan's political processes and to influence the Japanese Government's China policy. His strategy was to mobilize and form the broadest possible united front among all Japanese forces that were sympathetic to China's interests. Hence he asked the JSP to enlighten the Japanese people about China and to assume "leadership" in Japanese diplomacy.[25]

The main motivations of the JSP towards China were to restore peaceful and friendly relations with China; to demonstrate its capability in conducting external affairs and thereby to exert political pressure upon the Japanese Government for a change in its China policy; and to articulate and mobilize those elements in Japanese society which were favourably disposed towards China and critical of the ruling Liberal Democratic Party's foreign policy.[26]

Under the strongly anti-Communist Kishi Government relations with Taiwan were further consolidated. During his visit to Taipei in June 1957, Kishi resolved to further strengthen his country's economic and cultural co-operation and "friendly relations" with Taiwan. Soon thereafter he visited the United States. In his address before the National Press Club, Washington, D.C., on 21 June 1957, he stated that Japan had no intention of extending political recognition to China "at the present time" and that Tokyo would not act in that regard "except in and through the United Nations." He affirmed that as a free nation Japan would continue to observe international controls over the shipment of strategic goods to China. Japan, he added, asked only that "the restrictions be made practical and reasonable." Although because of sheer economic necessity Japan was seeking increased trade with mainland China, Tokyo would not, Kishi assured his American audience, do anything "that would weaken the solidarity and security of the free world."[27]

China was visibly concerned about the "plot" to create two Chinas. Thus, Kishi's visits to Taiwan in 1957 and again in 1961 were vehemently criticized by Beijing. In a long editorial on the Kishi Cabinet's China policy, the *People's Daily* (30 July 1957) criticized the Japanese Premier for following a policy "opposed to the national interests of Japan, hostile to the Chinese people, and subservient to the US policy of aggression." It accused Kishi of hindering the signing of the fourth Sino-Japanese trade agreement, of blocking mutual exchange of trade delegations between the two countries, and of preventing the opening of a Chinese Commodity Exhibition in Japan and the signing of a Sino-Japanese payment agreement. During his visit to Southeast Asia in May 1957 Kishi was accused of trying to disturb relations between the various Southeast Asian countries on the one hand and China on the other and broadcast the "benefits of US aid." It declared that in contrast to Kishi's hostility to China, the Japanese masses and the popular organizations, including the Japanese Socialist Party, had a friendly attitude towards China.[28] Five Chinese organizations and a delegation of the Japan-China Friendship Association also issued a joint statement on 28 October 1957 severely condemning the "plot" to separate Taiwan from China and calling for diplomatic relations and cultural and economic exchanges between China and Japan.[29]

Foreign Minister Aiichiro Fujiyama reiterated on 29 January 1958 that his Government was not thinking of recognising Communist China "at this time." The relaxation of the ban on trade with China, he said, was aimed at promoting Japan's foreign trade "while pursuing the policy of co-operation with other free nations."[30]

Repatriation of Japanese Nationals and War Criminals

During 1949-50 China insisted that any decision regarding the

release of Japanese war criminals taken without the consent
and endorsement of the Chinese people was "illegal and
invalid."[31] Thus, Beijing protested against General Douglas
MacArthur's announcement on 24 December 1948 to release
nineteen Japanese war criminals. The Central Committee of the
Chinese Communist Party criticized the "arbitrary" release
and repatriation of Neiji Okamura and 260 other Japanese war
criminals by the Chinese Nationalist Government in Nanking
in February 1949. It reserved to itself the right to demand
re-trial of those who had been allegedly responsible for the
Japanese aggression on China.[32] In February 1950 Chinese
Vice Foreign Minister Li Ke-nung expressed full support for
the military tribunal of the Khabarovsk Military Area trying
those Japanese who were reported guilty of bacteriological
warfare. He complimented the Soviet Union on meting out due
punishment to the Japanese war criminals who had endangered
humanity, and said that it had lived up to its great responsibility of protecting the interests of humanity and peace.[33]
Subsequently, on 15 May 1950, Premier Zhou Enlai issued a
strong statement criticizing MacArthur's "illegal Directive
No. 5" of 7 March 1950 concerning the release of major war
criminals already sentenced by the International Military
Tribunal for the Far East.[34] In another statement issued on
23 November 1950, he criticized the "premature" release of
Shigemitsu and other Japanese war criminals.[35]

   However, in keeping with its "people's diplomacy" China
adopted a lenient policy in regard to the repatriation of
Japanese nationals and release of Japanese "war criminals"
towards the end of 1952. Thus, China announced on 1 December
1952 that it would be willing to assist in the repatriation of
about 30,000 Japanese residents in China and a few Japanese
"war criminals" awaiting trial there if Japan would provide ships.
Beijing rejected the idea of government-to-government negotiations and instead invited the Japan Red Cross Society, the Japan-
China Friendship Association, and the Japanese Peace Liaison
Committee to send a delegation to Beijing to negotiate with the
Chinese Red Cross Society. This provoked officials of the
Japanese Foreign Ministry to comment that the Chinese Communists were "trying to achieve some political gain through
negotiation with pro-Communist organizations in Japan "[36]

The three Japanese organizations readily accepted the
Chinese offer and formal talks began on 15 February 1953. On
this occasion, Liao Cheng-chih the leader of the Chinese Red
Cross Society, described all the peace-loving people of Japan
"as our friends" and made a distinction between them and the
Yoshida Government. He offered the use of three ports—
Tientsin, Chinwangtao, and Shanghai—as exit ports for
Japanese nationals returning to their homeland.[37] As a result, a
total of 26,026 Japanese nationals were enabled to return home
in a series of seven repatriation sailings from China.

Mrs. Li Teh-chuan visited Japan in October-November
1954 as leader of a delegation of the Chinese Red Cross
Society. Speaking on her arrival in Japan on 30 October 1954,
she stated that she had brought a roster of Japanese war
criminals "now still in China" and said that "another group of
Japanese nationals will return home by the end of this year or
the beginning of the next year." The majority of these war
criminals, she added, "will receive speedy lenient consideration
by the Chinese Government." She further stated that a group
of Japanese nationals in the Democratic Republic of Vietnam
was wanting to return home and that the Red Cross Society of
China would assist it to do so via Shanghai.[38]

Between September 1954 and March 1955—i. e. shortly
before and after Li Teh-chuan's visit—2,934 Japanese, including 417 "war criminals," were further repatriated from
China in four separate groups. It was stated that the 417 war
criminals had committed only "minor" crimes and that they
had, therefore, been spared and sent back to Japan.[39] The
Chinese Red Cross Society provided the Red Cross Society of
Japan with a list of names containing 1,069 names of alleged
war criminals and information concerning their conditions.

On 16 August 1955 a spokesman of the Chinese Foreign
Ministry officially stated that by the end of March 1955, out
of the original total of about 35,000 Japanese civilians, about
29,000 who desired to return to Japan had been repatriated.
The remaining 6,000 were said to have expressed their desire
to reside in China permanently or for the time being. "Should
any of them change their mind and apply for returning to
Japan," he declared, "the Chinese Government will still provide
them facilities" for repatriation.[40]

In accordance with a decision taken by the Standing Committee of the National People's Congress in April 1956, the Supreme People's Procurator of China took immediate steps to pardon the majority of Japanese "war criminals" in custody and brought to trial only a few "who [had] committed serious crimes." As a result, out of the 1,062 Japanese still detained, 1,017 were released and repatriated in three groups in the summer of 1956. The remaining forty-five were convicted however, and given prison terms. None of them were sentenced to death or life imprisonment, and some of them were subsequently released either because of ill health or by way of reward for good behaviour.[41]

The Consul-General of Japan in Geneva, Keiichi Tatsuke, requested his Chinese counterpart on 15 July 1955 to facilitate repatriation of the 6,000 Japanese civilians and other detainees still remaining in China. He also asked for investigation about some 40,000 Japanese "who apparently have been in China but whose whereabouts or death have never been ascertainded."[42] Inreply, a Chinese Foreign Ministry spokesman denounced the Japanese Government's position as "completely groundless . . . unilateral and unreasonable". On the other hand, he alleged that there were "tens of thousands of Chinese civilians residing in Japan whose legitimate rights and interest have not been properly cared for . . . and who have no facilities to return to China." He referred to the massacre of tens of millions of Chinese to the loss of property suffered by both the Chinese State and private citizens worth tens of billicrs of US dollars during the Japanese war of aggression against China, and said that the Chinese people had the right "to claim compensation for the enormous loss they sustained." He concluded with a stress on the common desire of the Chinese and Japanese peoples for normalization of Sino-Japanese relaticns, the promotion of contacts between the Chinese and Japanese peoples, and the development of normal trade between the two countries.[43]

In reply to the Chinese Foreign Ministry Statement of 16 August Keichi Tatsuke again wrote to Shen Ping on 29 August 1955 maintaining that 40,000 Japanese nationals were in China whose situation was unknown and requested the Chinese Government to investigate their situation.[44]

On 13 May 1957, the Japanese Government again sought, through Geneva, the co-operation of the Chinese Government in order to secure repatriation of all the Japanese nationals in China. It sent a list of 35,767 unrepatriated nationals comprising all the data available as on 1 January 1957 and requested Beijing to determine whether the persons on the list were alive or dead and, if alive, to ascertain whether they wished to return. The Chinese Government reacted by repudiating the problem of missing Japanese. It said that there was not a single Japanese national whose whereabouts could be described as unknown. It reiterated that there were only 6,000 Japanese nationals in China and that these wanted to stay on in China.[45]

According to Chinese reports, 422 Japanese nationals left China for home via Tientsin on 19 April 1958 on board the Japanese ship *Haku-an Maru*. This meant that, since 1953 more than 30,000 Japanese had been repatriated from China. The Japanese Government, it was pointed out in the Cninese Press, had taken an entirely contrary stand with regard to Chinese residents in Japan" and had placed many obstacles in the way their return home.[46] China released two Japanese war criminals, Hiraku Suzuki and Hideya Iyake, on 6 April 1963 before the expiry of their term in view of their good behaviour.[47] With the release of Yoshida Saito, Juntaro Tominaga, and Hiroshi Jono on 6 March 1964, it was stated on the Chinese side that all the Japanese war criminals detained in China had been released. Of the last three, the first two had been sentenced to a term of imprisonment of twenty years and the third to a term of imprisonment of eighteen years.[48]

Conclusion

Ever since its establishment in 1949, the People's Republic of China had been very apprehensive of the revival of Japanese militarism and the implications of the US-Japanese Security Treaty for itself. Moreover, Beijing did not accept the Japan-Taiwan Peace Treaty as valid. Besides, the problem of reparations, which Jiang Jieshi (Chiang Kai-shek) had waived, was by no means a small matter.

China realized that it was no easy task to either loosen Japan's economic and military ties with the United States or dissociate Japan from Taiwan. These objectives, China thought, could be achieved by encouraging sentiments of independence, peace, and neutrality within Japan and against entanglement in any military alliance with the United States and against any strengthening or expansion of Tokyo's self-defence forces. To that end, it made use of pacifist sentiments within Japan and gave support to Communist, Leftist and Socialist elements and the opposition parties in their struggle against the ruling Liberal Democratic Party.

Furthermore, China was prepared to accept an independent, peace-loving, and democratic Japan maintaining armed forces to safeguard its own independence. China declared in 1957 that it would be willing to modify the provisions of the Sino-Soviet Alliance of 1950 directed against Japan in the event of Japan abrogating the US-Japanese Security Treaty and securing the removal of American bases and forces from its soil.

In its trade dealings, Beijing gave preference to the so-called "friendly firms", i.e. the ones that were favourably inclined towards China. However, China's "people's diplomacy" towards Japan succeeded only in limited measure. Barter trade increased somewhat between 1955 and 1957, but Japan's exports to China never exceeded 3 per cent of its total exports. Japan's imports too, remained in the 3 per cent range. Japan's trade with China was more "a hope than a reality, and the conditions surrounding it were abnormal."[49]

The Chinese sought to highlight the achievements of "people's diplomacy." It had led to the exchange of friendly visits between the Chinese and Japanese people. Moreover, there were no fewer than thirty non-governmental agreements relating to trade, fishery, cultural, and scientific fields between representatives of the trade unions, the Members of Parliament, and the leaders and workers of the political parties of the two countries.[50] In his report on foreign policy to the National People's Congress on 7 February 1958 Zhou Enlai noted that contacts and trade relations had developed to a great extent, showing the common desire of the Chinese and Japanese peoples for peace and friendship.[51]

24 *China and Japan*

NOTES

1 P.A. Narsimha Murthy, "Japan's Changing Relations with People's Republic of China and the Soviet Union," *International Studies*, July 1965, 6-7, footnote 11.

2 Shao Chuan Leng, *Japan and Communist China* (Kyoto, n.d.), 32-3.

3 *News Bulletin* (Embassy of China, New Delhi), 20 October 1954, 4-5.

4 Ibid., 21 October 1953.

5 Ibid.

6 *Renmin Ribao*, 30 October 1953, as translated in *People's China*, 16 November 1953, 3-7.

7 *Conference of Asian Countries*, New Delhi, 6-10 April 1955, 16.

8 *People's China*, no. 17, 1955.

9 Xinhua News Agency, 14 February 1956.

10 Xinhua News Agency, 17 October 1955. See also *Survey of China Mainland Press*, no. 1151.

11 See *News Bulletin*, 1 December 1954, 3-4 and ibid., 14 December 1954, 5-6.

12 *People's China*, 16 February 1956, 5.

13 See Prime Minister Nobusuke Kishi's policy speech in the Diet, 30 September 1958. *Contemporary Japan*, March 1959, 715.

14 See his statement to the Diet, 25 April 1955. *Gaimusho Bulletin*, 25 April 1955.

15 *Gaimusho Bulletin*, 11 December 1954.

16 Shigemitsu's speech, 5 February 1955. Japan, Ministry of Foreign Affairs, *Major Policy Speeches of M. Shigemitsu* (Tokyo, n.d.), 17. Also see statement by Foreign Minister Aiichiro Fujiyama in the United Nations General Assembly, 18 September 1958. *Contemporary Japan*, March 1959, 711-5.

17 Statement in Diet, 30 January 1956. *Information Bulletin* (Embassy of Japan, New Delhi), vol. 3, no. 4, 4-7.

18 *Renmin Ribao*, 14 February 1956.

19 See Kyodo, 3 February and 16 February 1956, cited in Leng, n. 2, 95.

20 See R.K. Jain, *The USSR and Japan, 1945-1980* (New Delhi, 1981), 27.

21 Chae-Jin Lee, *Japan Faces China: Political and Economic Relations in the Postwar Era* (London, 1976), 33.

22 Xinhua News Agency, 22 April 1957.

23 See *Asahi Evening News*, 17 April 1957; *Japan Times*, 23 April 1957; and *Yomiuri Shimbun*, 22 April 1957.

24 Zhou Enlai's interview with Japanese delegation, 25 July 1957. Xinhua News Agency, 30 July 1957.

25 Lee, n. 21, 36-7.

26 Ibid., 37.

27 *Information Bulletin* (New Delhi), 15 July 1957, 6-9.

28 Ibid., 30 July 1957.

29 Xinhua News Agency, 28 October 1957.

30 *Information Bulletin* (New Delhi), 15 February 1958.

31 *China Digest*, 11 January 1949.

32 Ibid., 22 February 1949, 8-9.
33 *China Monthly Review*, October 1950, Supplement, 11-2.
34 Ibid., 12.
85 *Pravda*, 25 November 1950, as translated in *Soviet Press Translations,* 15 December 1950, 693-4.
36 Leng, n. 2, 73-4.
37 *News Bulletin*, 12 March 1953.
38 Ibid., 10 November 1954, 10.
39 Shen Ping's letter to Keiichi Tatsuke, 4 November 1955. Xinhua News Agency, 14 February 1956.
40 Statement of the Spokesman of the Foreign Ministry of China, 16 August 1955. Ibid.
41 Leng, n. 2, 81.
42 Letter from Keiichi Tatsuke to Shen Ping, 15 July 1955. Xinhua News Agency, 14 February 1956.
43 Statement of the Spokesman of the Foreign Ministry of China, 16 August 1955. Ibid.
44 Xinhua News Agency, 14 February 1956.
45 See Statement by Ichiro Kawasaki, Japan's Chief Delegate to the 7th session of the UN Ad Hoc Commission on Prisoners of War, 2 September 1957. *Information Bulletin* (Ministry of Foreign Affairs, Tokyo), 15 September 1957, 9-11.
46 *Peking Review*, 29 April 1958, 20.
47 *Hindustan Times*, (New Delhi), 8 April 1963.
48 *Peking Review*, 13 March 1964, 4-5.
49 Lawrence Olson, *Japan in Postwar Asia* (New York, 1970), 81-2.
50 Xinhua News Agency, 30 July 1957.
51 *China Today* (Embassy of China, New Delhi), 25 February 1958.

3. Economic Relations, 1949-1958

Before the Second World War, Sino-Japanese trade played an important part in the economies of both countries. This was especially true after the 1930s when Japan vigorously pursued an imperialist policy towards China which greatly increased its trade and investment penetration of the latter. China occupied the first position as a market for Japanese exports and, as a source of Japanese imports, was next only to the United States and Korea in terms of total volume. Japanese industry was greatly dependent upon raw materials from China. From 1934 to 1936, the mainland of China supplied 34 per cent of Japan's imports of iron ore, 38.6 per cent of salt, 68.4 per cent of coal, 71.3 per cent of soyabeans, and 100 per cent of tung oil. From 1930 to 1939, the China trade became increasingly important to Japan's economy, accounting for 21 per cent of Japan's total exports and 12.4 per cent of its total annual imports.[1]

Sino-Japanese Trade, 1949-1952

After the Second World War Sino-Japanese trade was minimal because of the near collapse of the Japanese economy at the end of the war, the civil war in China, and the surrender of Japan's trade autonomy to the Supreme Commander of the Allied Powers (SCAP).

In August 1949 even before the establishment of the People's Republic of China, a four-man trade mission representing the Chinese Communists arrived in Japan to negotiate the purchase of Japanese rail equipment for the railroads in North China. It was believed that once order and stability was restored on the Mainland, trade would increase. The Japanese Communist

Party especially advocated the growth in trade between China and Japan.[2]

Japan also appeared keen to develop trade relations with China. In May 1949 some members of the Japanese National Diet, conservative and progressive, set up a nonpartisan Diet-men's League for China-Japan Trade Promotion. The League helped in organizing a civilian China-Japan Trade Promotion Council in August.[3] During 1949 Japanese exports amounted to only $3.1 million and Japanese imports stood at $21.8 million. The climate seemed to improve with the United States State Department officially permitting Japan to trade with China in March 1950. Next month, the Japanese House of Councillors adopted a resolution introduced jointly by several political parties calling for further promotion of Sino-Japanese trade. Commenting on this, the *China Weekly Review* (13 May 1950) recalled that the resolution called upon the Government of Japan to "exchange economic missions with new China and to reopen direct trade speedily." It described resumption of trade with China as a "fundamental solution to the serious domestic depression and the unsatisfactory progress" of Japan's foreign trade, argued that the Government should not be bound by "political or ideological issues but should regard the question from a purely economic standpoint."[4] As compared to 1949, Sino-Japanese blateral trade more than doubled to $58.9 million in 1950.

In the wake of the embargo being imposed on the shipment of goods to China in the course of the Korean War, however, the trade between China and Japan declined sharply both in terms of the variety of commodities exchanged and in terms of its total value. The rigid system of "categories" which grew out of the CHINCOM trade restrictions and the conduct of trade on an individual barter contract basis led to delays and de-faults. As a result, the Sino-Japanese trade declined in 1951 and the lowest point was reached in 1952, when Japan's trade with China amounted to only $15.5 million. In September 1952 Japan joined the China Committee (CHINCOM), which was set up to control and regulate exports of strategic goods to the Communist bloc. In order to counter the harmful effects of the embargo imposed by the Western Powers, China adopted the barter trade system in March 1951 and expanded its trade relations with the Socialist countries of Europe.

The Chinese sought to induce Japan to desist from stringently following the United Nations embargo by emphasizing that it had led to an "artificial" diminishing of exports to China. They also highlighted the "heavy losses" to the Japanese economy since Japan had to purchase industrial raw materials at comparatively higher prices from the United States and other countries, which had created difficulties for Japan's economic advancement."[5]

Addressing the Moscow International Economic Conference on 4 April 1952, the leader of the Chinese delegation to that conference, Nan Han-chen, referred to the "extremely unfair and irrational phenomenon" which prevented Japan from buying coal from China even though it "costs less."[6] Lei Jen-min, another member of the Chinese delegation, stated that the embargo deprived Japan of supplies of cheap and excellent ores and raw materials. Besides, the price of coal shipped to Japan from China was "about twenty US dollars cheaper per ton than the price Japan has to pay for coal imported from the Western Hemisphere."[7]

The Japanese Government had sought to prevent any Japanese from attending the Moscow Conference, but a member of the House of Councillors, Mrs. Kora Tomi, managed to reach Moscow in time. Two Members of the Diet, Haashi Kei and Miyagoshi Kisuke, arrived just after the conference had ended. All three were very much impressed by the possibility of increased trade with China and expressed concern that unless Japanese businessmen acted quickly the important Chinese market would be preempted by Japan's old competitors from Western Europe.[8]

Non-Official Trade Agreements

During the 1950s several Japanese groups and the China Committee for the Promotion of International Trade (CCPIT) (set up on 4 May 1952 under the Chairmanship of Nan Han-chen) signed several Sino-Japanese non-official trade agreements which contributed to the development of modest trade. China was apparently keen to gradually upgrade the status of this arrangement and give it an official colouring.

The first Sino-Japanese non-official (but considered semi-official by the Chinese) barter trade agreement was signed on 1 June 1952. Subsequently, three more private trade agreements were signed on 29 October 1953, 4 May 1955, and 5 March 1958. The first three agreements envisaged a total trade turnover of £30 million for each side while the abortive fourth unofficial trade agreement expected exports and imports on each side to reach a total of £35 million. But none of the trade agreements was wholly fulfilled although the validity of the first agreement was extended twice—first in January and later in June 1953—and the validity of the third one was extended for one more year, i.e. up to 4 May 1957. The first agreement (June 1952-October 1953) was fulfilled upto only 5.05 per cent; the second agreement (October 1953-December 1954) up to 38.8 per cent; and the third (May 1955-May 1957) upto 75.12 per cent.[9] The fourth agreement was never carried out.

The trade agreements could not be fulfilled because of the problems of embargo and the barter arrangement, which classified exports from each side into different categories and limited exchange of goods only within the same class. The chief problems, S.C. Leng remarks, was that most items of Japanese exports under Category "A" were on the embargo list and therefore couldnot be freely sold to Communist China in exchange for Category "A" imports like iron ore, coal, and soyabeans. This not only affected the volume of total trade but prevented Japan from getting key industrial materials in large quantities from the nearby mainland.[10]

Beijing always attributed the non-fulfilment of the trade target envisaged in the private agreement to the Japanese Government's adherence to the "American-dictated" trade restrictions and to Japan's non-cooperative attitude as regards normalization of relations. For instance, in his statement on the occasion of the second extension of the first trade agreement on 30 June 1953, Nan Han-chen observed that all goods to be exported by Japan under Category "A" and the great majority of the goods under Category "B" had, from the beginning, been under "embargo". The scope of Japanese exports goods, he stated, "have been reduced to very narrow limits and the full carrying out of the agreement has been rendered impossible." This, he added, was "the greatest obstacle to the development of Sino-Japanese trade at present." He declared: "The facts in the past year have shown that Sino-Japanese trade cannot be developed smoothly unless the 'blockade', 'embargo', stalling, sabotage, and scheming of the American and Japanese reactionaries are smashed." He hoped that the Japanese people would make further efforts to eliminate these barriers to Sino-Japanese trade.[11]

Sentiment in the Japanese business community was almost unanimous in favour of greatly increased trade with China. China was looked upon both as a market for Japanese goods and as a source of cheap raw materials.[12] The American Ambassador to Japan, Robert D. Murphy, tried to caution those Japanese who still thought of the China trade in terms of the old days. He advised them to consider how "today in Communist countries everything goes through some government agencies and immediate political objectives often outweigh economic considerations."[13] His advice, however, cut little ice with the Japanese people. Facts spoke louder than words. It was common knowledge that the United States was replacing China as the source of supply of key commodities to Japan and that Japan was importing them from the US at prices much higher than those of the Chinese products. In 1934-36, for instance, Japan had not imported iron ore, coal, soyabeans, or salt from the US. It was China which had supplied to Japan 34.0 per cent of its import of iron ore; 68 per cent of its import of coal; 71.3 per cent of its import of soyabeans; and 38.6 per cent of its import of salt. In 1951, in contrast, the United States was supplying to Japan 33.6 per cent of its import of iron ore; 70.9 per cent of its import of coal; 97.3 per cent of its import of soyabeans; and 10.6 per cent of its import of salt. Japan's imports of these key commodities from China dropped to 1.3 per cent, 1.1 per cent, 2.6 per cent, and 0.2 per cent respectively. By 1956, the United States share in Japan's imports of these four commodities was 12.1 per cent, 80.1 per cent, 74.7 per cent, and 2.3 per cent respectively; and the share of China was 0.1 per cent, 15.1 per cent, 23.1 per cent, and 37.1 per cent respectively. The prices that Japan had to pay in 1956 for its imports from the United States were: $26.5 per ton for coal; $20.3 per ton for iron ore; and $18.1 per ton for salt. The prices it paid for the import of the same commodities from China were: $12 2 per ton for coal; $13.7 per ton for iron ore; and $9.4 per ton for salt.[14]

A number of organisations to promote the China trade sprang up in Japan, including the Conference for the Promotion of Sino-Japanese Trade, the Diet Members League for the Promotion of Sino-Japanese Trade (established in December 1952 and consisting of members of both Houses of Japanese Diet, with a voluntary membership by 1958 of about 360, representing approximately 50 per cent of the total membership of the Diet) and the Local Assembly Members League for the Promotion of Sino-Japanese Trade. These were in addition to the already existing Sino-Japanese Trrde Promotion Society. The movement became so strong, and cut across Party lines so conspicuously, that on 24 July 1953 the Japanese House of Representatives passed a resolution calling for the promotion of Sino Japanese trade. On 30 July House of Councillors followed suit.

Meanwhile, with the armistice in the Korean War, the Japanese Government began to remove many items from the embargo list. On 2 August 1952, textile machinery, woollen goods, paper, and dyestuffs were freed. Two days after the Korean armistice, the Japanese Diet passed a resolution calling for the efforts by the Government to promote trade with China, to relax export restrictions, and to liberalize travel regulations.[15] In the middle of October 1953, the Japanese Government published five more lists, freeing more than 250 additional items from the embargo list. The Japanese Ministry of International Trade and Industry announced the seventh relaxation of the ban on the China trade as from 18 January 1954. As a result, rubber and rubberized piece-goods, airplane cloth, etc. were deleted from the embargo list.[16] Late in 1954 the Japanese Government began to employ the special "exceptions" procedure of the NATO China Committee (CHINCOM) regulations to export certain embargoed goods to China. In September 1956, it decided to utilize that procedure to the same extent as West European countries.[17] The Japanese White Paper of 1956 recognized that the embargo posed a most serious problem for Japan, especially because of the frequent, wide-ranging fluctuation in Japan's internationl trade. On 16 July 1957, following the British lead in the matter, it

announced its decision to relax the embargo against Communist China and bring the level of the controls applied in the
case of the Soviet Union and Eastern Europe.[18] Thus, 207 items
on the CHINCOM list and 65 items on the COCOM list were
removed from the embargo list, thereby lifting restrictions on
iron, steel, machinery, items on the embargo list.[19] These
measures led to a modest increase in Sino-Japanese Trade.

It was against this background that a 23-member Japanese
trade mission was invited to Peking and the second unofficial
trade agreement was signed.[20] The Foreign Minister of Japan
Katsuo Okazaki, considered this trade agreement and the
repatriation of Japanese nationals from China as "something
of deep significance." He expressed the intention of his
Government "to continue its efforts to the extent that the ties
with the free nations are not broken and in the direction of
the purport of the resolution adopted by the previous Diet on
the question of promoting trade with Communist China."[21]

The movement to expand trade with China continuously
grew stronger. In September 1954 the Japan Association for
the Promotion of International Trade was formed. In the same
month the Japanese Government made thirteen more downward revisions of the embargo list. On 17 December 1954, the
Japanese House of Representatives approved a resolution jointly
sponsored by both Houses urging the Government to invite a
Chinese trade delegation to Japan to open negotiations for a
third agreement.

In January 1955, China invited Murata Shozo, President
of the newly-formed Japan International Trade Promotion
Association (JITPA) and others to Peking. The Japanese delegation was received upon its arrival by Premier Zhou Enlai and
Minister of Foreign Trade Yeh Chi-chuang.

Subsequently Japanese businessmen succeeded in persuading
Japanese officials to permit the JITPA and the Diet Members'
Union to invite a Chinese delegation to Japan. On 29 March
1955 a 14-member Chinese delegation, headed by Lei Jen-min,
acting Chairman of the CCPIT and Vice-Minister of Foreign
Trade, arrived in Tokyo.

The *People's Daily* wrote a long editorial on the significance
of the first visit of a Chinese trade delegation to Japan in the
wake of the favourable situation created by the February

1955 elections in Japan and the formal inauguration of the Hatoyama Cabinet. It referred to the geographical nearness and the historically close economic relations between the two countries and drew pointed attention to the US machinations designed "to undermine peaceful coexistence and economic and cultural cooperation between Japan and other Asian countries" and impede normalization of Sino-Japanese relations. It called upon the new Japanese Government to stand up to "US pressure and coercion" and behind-the-scenes manoeuvres and tread the road of independence and self-determination and development of Sino-Japanese trade relations.[22]

In the month-long difficult negotiations that followed, the Chinese delegation tried hard but in vain to get the Japanese Government's approval for its proposal that China and Japan should establish permanent trade missions in each other's capitals. China also made unavailing efforts to promote a trade payments agreement between the People's Bank of China and the Bank of Japan. It was thus obliged to content itself with an unofficial trade agreement. Under this agreement, which was the third such unofficial agreement to be signed between China and Japan, the two sides agreed to exert themselves in the direction of obtaining a payments agreement and of establishing permanant trade missions in each other's capitals. The trade agreement also contained a provision for the holding of Chinese trade fairs in Tokyo and Osaka in 1955 and of Japanese trade fairs in Beijing and Shanghai in 1956. The joint communique on Sino-Japanese trade talks, issued on 4 May 1955, declared that it was a matter of "paramount importance" to find fair solutions for questions concerning payments and accounts clearance and exchange of permanent trade missions as they had a significant bearing on the development of trade between the two countries.[23]

China agreed to extend the third Sino-Japanese trade agreement in May 1956 for one more year even though there had been no significant progress in the direction of finding a solution for the question of a payments agreement between the two countries and the proposal for an exchange of commercial representatives had also not been accepted. In 1956 it extended invitations to the office-bearers of the Japan-China Importers and Exporters Association (JCIEA) (formed in November 1955), another 36-member delegation of Japanese industrialists and businessmen, and a delegation of the Diet Members' Union. In the joint statement issued by the CCPIT and the unofficial Japanese trade promotion delegation on 15 October 1956, the two sides once again agreed to make efforts to bring about the exchange of permanent civilian trade representative organizations and to promote the conclusion of a trade agreement between the two governments.[24]

China's efforts to remove "artificial obstacles" imposed by the embargo and to promote Sino-Japanese trade relations met with considerable success. Successful trade fairs were organized in the two countries between 1955 and 1956. Trade between the two countries also registered appreciable growth during 1953-55. Chinese exports to Japan increased from $29.7 million in 1953 to $80.8 million in 1955. Chinese imports also grew almost seven-fold from $4.5 million in 1953 to $28.5 millon in 1955. However, trade between the two countries still remained far below the pre-war level. Chinese Minister of Foreign Trade Yeh Chi-chuang considered this to be due to the Japanese Government's adherence to the embargo policy of the United States which, he said, could not "but be detrimental to Japan's economic development."[25]

Fourth Non-Official Trade Agreement, March 1958

A fourth non-official trade agreement was signed by the China Committee for the Promotion of International Trade on the one side, and the Diet Members' Union, the Japanese Association for the Promotion of International Trade and the Japan-China Importers and Exporters Association (JCIEA) on the other, on 5 March 1958. It envisaged a trade turnover of £35 million (about $198 million) each way, an increase of £5 million or $12 million over the third agreement. The classification of commodities was simplified by reducing the number of categories from three to two. The method of payment in pound sterling, hitherto effective only through London, was replaced with that of direct business transactions between the foreign exchange banks of the two countries. The agreement thus contained a provision for settling accounts for trade transactions "through the conclusion of a payment agreement . . . between the Bank of Japan and the People's Bank of the People's Republic of China."

The two sides agreed to "reciprocally establish a permanent civilian trade representation" in Tokyo and Beijing. A Memorandum also signed on the same day, i.e. 5 March 1958, which was attached to the agreement and which constituted an integral part of the trade agreement, *inter alia*, stated that the civilian trade representation in each other's capitals "shall have the right to fly its national flag over its building" and that "there shall be no finger-printing required of the personnel of the civilian trade representation and their families."[26]

The fourth Sino-Japanese private trade agreement also stipulated that the two countries should endeavour to promote technical exchange and co-operation. This provision was considered important in view of China's Second Five-Year Plan for economic development. It was believed that serious negotiations would be opened shortly, case by case, in respect of factory equipment, high-efficiency machinery, and agricultural technique so urgently needed in China. Shigeyoshi Takami, Director of JCIEA, observed that the new items for export would open a new field in Japan's trade with China.[27]

The signing of the fourth non-official trade agreement seemed to brighten prospects for the expansion of Sino-Japanese trade as it entailed both a qualitative and a quantitative improvement in trade relations between the two countries. Japanese policymakers, however, urged caution and felt that undue hope should not be placed in regard to trade with China in view of the changes in the economic structure and the financial and economic policies of Communist China.[28] Moreover in an effort to placate Taiwan, which strongly objected particularly to the provision allowing the Chinese trade mission to fly its flag in Japan,[29] Tokyo refused to recognize the "right" of the Chinese trade representation to fly its national flag in Japan and to proffer protection to the flag. This attitude on the part of the Japanese Government was considered by Beijing as tantamount to a denial of reciprocal offer of guarantee for the facilities. In a long letter to the three Japanese organizations on 13 March 1958, therefore, Nan Han-chen, Chairman of the China Committee for the Promotion of International Trade, took the view that the refusal of Premier Kishi to recognize the "right" of the Chinese trade representation to hoist its national flag on grounds of Japan's "internal laws," "international environment," and "non-recognition" had made the implementation of the fourth trade agreement "an impossibility." Nan's letter concluded by saying that the trade agreement could not be implemented unless the obstructions imposed by the Japanese Government were removed.[30]

Nagasaki Flag Incident

While Japanese businessmen were engaged in finding a way out of the difficult situation, an incident occurred at Nagasaki. On 2 May 1958 two Japanese youths pulled down one of the Chinese flags at a stamp show in a departmental store in Nagasaki.[31]

Beijing retaliated by unilaterally cancelling the fourth Sino-Japanese trade agreement on 13 April 1958 and by suspending all business dealings worth $330 million with Japan on 10 May 1958. China suspended all import and export licenses for Japan, discontinued the on-going commercial negotiations with the Japanese at the trade fair in Guangzhou and recalled the steel mission of the Chinese National Metals Imports and Minerals Corporation holding talks with the Yawata Iron Steel Company for the import of 158,000 tons of steel. Japanese businessmen lost 650,000,000 Yen reshipping exhibits from the Wuhan and Canton fairs then being held.[32] Forty Japanese businessmen left Peking for home. Approximately 300 foreign trade firms were involved in this trade suspension and about 2,000 other enterprises, mainly manufacturers and transporters, were affected. Beijing cancelled general permission for Japanese vessels to enter Chinese ports and cabled to the Japan-China Fishery Association in Japan that the fisheries agreement would not be renewed.[33] China also seized fourteen Japanese fishing boats about a hundred miles north of Taiwan.

Fishery Agreement of 1955

Initially, China opened a few of its ports to Japanese fishing operations. This was followed by a marked decline in the number of cases entailing seizure of small fishing vessels and detention of their crews. As long as Prime Minister Shigeru Yoshida (1948-1954) was in power hardly any progress was made in furthering co-operation in fishery matters between the two countries.

"People's diplomacy" led China to adopt a more concilia-tory attitude in fishery matters as well. Chinese seizure of Japanese vessels nevertheless continued unabated. In 1951, China seized fifty-five Japanese vessels with 671 fishermen; in 1953, twenty-four ships with 311 men, and in 1954, twenty-eight ships with 329 men, but with Yoshida's departure from power at the end of 1954 the number abruptly fell. In 1955, China seized only one ship with ten men; in 1956, two with twenty-four men; and in 1957, none at all.[34]

The fishery negotiations which began in Beijing in early 1955 lasted for ninety days. Eventually on 15 April 1955 a non-official fishery agreement was signed between the China Fishery Association and the Japan-China Fishery Association of Japan. This Agreement demarcated fishing areas in the Yellow and East China seas and set up regulations for Chinese and Japanese fishing boats entering those waters. It divided the fishing grounds in the Yellow Sea and the East China Sea into six fishing areas and provided for the measures needed to enable the two sides to maintain harmony and order in fishing operations. It also contained provisions for dealing with fishing vessels in distress and for exchange of fishery data and techni-ques. Furthermore, the two parties indicated their willingness to try to persuade their respective Governments to enter into fishery negotiations promptly at a governmental level. The area covered by the agreement did not include the patrolled areas near the Bohai Bay, the military areas near the Bohai Bay, the military areas near the Chousan Islands (in which navi-gation was forbidden), and the military operation areas south of 29°N., which were concerned with the liberation of Taiwan. Nor did it include the "area forbidden to motor trawler fishing" established by the Chinese Government for the protection of fishery resources. The two sides exchanged letters embodying the understanding that Japanese fishing motor boats would not fish in that area.[35]

On 8 May 1956,[36] the fishery agreement was extended upto 30 June 1957. In May 1957 it was again extended for another year.[37] In the wake of the Nagasaki flag incident of May 1958, when China broke off trade relations with Japan, the China

Fishery Association announced that the Fishery Agreement would not be extended any further but would be allowed to expire on 12 June 1958.[38]

In December 1956, a delegation of the China Fishery Association visited Japan. On 19 December it signed a joint communique with the Japan-China Fishery Association. The two sides pledged to exchange fishery experts and technicians and to campaign for the conclusion of agreements between their Governments. Five months later, in April 1957, a Japanese Socialist goodwill mission also visited China. On this occasion an agreement was reached with the Chinese on the exchange of private fishery missions. A private ship rescue agreement was also concluded under a guarantee by the Governments of the two countries.[39] Further, in the middle of October 1959, China reached an agreement with the Japanese non-official organization on emergency shelter for fishing boats.

Conclusions

Although little progress could be made in the improvement of political relations in the fifties, the Japanese Government endeavoured to expand trade between China and Japan by adopting a policy of separating economic and political matters. Japanese leaders advanced several arguments to justify this policy. Thus, it was pointed out that the results of Japanese efforts to develop economic relations with Southeast Asia, Central and South America, and the Middle and Near East as dependable suppliers of raw materials to Japan and promising markets for Japanese exports had not been satisfactory enough to induce Japan to give up Communist China. Moreover, boycotts against Japanese exports in the United States and discrimination against Japanese goods in many West European countries were said to have given a fresh impetus to the popular demand for "more trade with Communist China."[40]

Japanese leaders were careful lest their trade policy towards China created any misunderstanding amongst Americans. Thus, Prime Minister Nobusuke Kishi assured American critics that Japan would seek to expand trade with China as much as possible within the framework of maintaining harmony with other free nations. But as regards non-economic matters, he stated, "a careful study will be continued as they involve a variety of complicated problems of international politics."[41] Foreign Minister Aiichiro Fujiyama emphasized that it was purely from the point of economic necessity that Japan sought to expand trade relations with Mainland China. Trade with China assumed importance because it could help Japan improve its balance of payments position by increasing its exports as well as enable it to disperse its export markets on a global scale. Fujiyama added that while his government had recently decided to relax the embargo against China, it had not altered, nor had it any intention to alter in the future, its policy to maintain the existing export ban on commodities of strategic importance."[42]

On the contrary, China did not consider trade and politics to be inseparable. Trade was viewed and used as an instrument to persuade and pressurize Japan to recognize Beijing and modify its China policy. However, Chinese efforts to use economic means to achieve political goals were not very successful largely because of American pressure on Japan, Tokyo's marginal dependence on the China market, and the geopolitical situation in Northeast Asia. China's unilateral suspension of trade failed to arouse a nation-wide public outcry in Japan against Prime Minister Kishi's China policy.

The Chinese asserted that if trade was to develop between China and Japan, it was necessary to eliminate two "incorrect viewpoints." The first, viz. the "imperialist viewpoint" of "an industralised Japan, raw material China",[43] was said to be a thing of the past. The idea of trying to procure Chinese goods of high economic value in exchange of goods of little value not needed by China and falling into line with the US policy of embargo, the Chinese argued, only enabled "US-Chinese reactionaries" to take advantage of it. The second viewpoint was: "China is industrialised; Sino-Japanese trade has no prospects." Zhou Enlai sought to dispel this belief by stating that Chinese requirements would grow as China became industrialised.[44]

China stepped up its criticism of Japan when it found that overtures failed to evoke a sympathetic response from the Japanese. It also began to "dump" its goods in Hong Kong and "particularly in Southeast Asia to spite Japan, and sabotage arrangements with the West which seeks to provide an outlet for Japanese industries in this region."[45] Zhou Enlai in his report to the first session of the Second National People's Congress on 18 April 1959, described that allegation as a "rumour." He said that because China had an immense domestic market and because its trade with the capitalist countries and Southeast Asian nations was minimal, it had no need to resort to such tactics.[46]

Theoretically, Sino-Japanese trade relations had developed on the basis of "separation of economic from political affairs". It was a useful smokescreen for China engaging in such trade as it deemed it beneficial to import steel, fertilizers, agricultural chemicals, and machinery in return for coal, iron ore, corn, soyabeans, salt, and tin. At the same time, it did not preclude exerting pressures for political purposes.[47]

NOTES

[1] George P. Jan, "Japan's Trade with Communist China," *Asian Survey*, December 1969, 900. See also Shao Chuan Leng, *Japan and Communist China* (Kyoto, n d.), 39.

[2] As early as October 1949, in an article entitled "Sino-Japanese Trade and Japan's Future" published in *Hyoron* and reproduced in the pro-Beijing *China Weekly Review*, Sanzo Nozaka, Member of the Politbureau of the Japanese Communist Party and leader of the 36-man Communist parliamentary delegation in the Japanese Diet, felt that Japan and China, for better or for worse, had constituted an economic whole. Nozaka added that Sino-Japanese trade in future would be different than that of the past in the following four ways:

  (i) Japanese exports will be such commodities as will help China to industrialize herself . . .

  (ii) The future Sino-Japanese trade must be organized. The Chinese Government certainly will not permit unregulated transactions between individual merchants. . . very probably in the future, the government itself or associations of traders will engage in trade with Japan. . .

  (iii) China will trade with Japan on a barter basis. New China will not turn out commodities for export purposes only, but will produce and import what is necessary for her economic development and improvement of the livelihood of her masses. . . Of course barter will not be the exclusive means for China to settle her trade accounts, especially at the present time. . .

(iv) China will call for such a trade as will benefit both China and Japan. China wants to help Japan's recovery and to be helped by Japan in her industrialization. See *China Weekly Review*, 17 December 1949, 37-8.

3 *Nitchu Kankei shiryoshu, 1945-1971* (Tokyo, 1971), 155-7, cited in Chae-Jin Lee, *Japan Faces China: Political and Economic Relations in the Postwar Era* (London, 1976), 135-6.

4 *China Weekly Review*, 13 May 1950, 193.

5 *Renmin Ribao*, 6 October 1956.

6 *People's China*, 1 May 1952, 31.

7 Ibid., 16 May 1952, 33-4.

8 James W. Morley, *Soviet and Communist Chinese Policies towards Japan 1950-1957 : A Comparison* (New York, 1958), 3.

9 *Renmin Ribao*, 16 October 1956.

10 Leng, n.1, 46-7.

11 *News Bulletin*, 8 July 1953, 9-11.

12 Chinese coal was cheaper because freight charges were lower. The quality of Chinese coal was inferior to that of US coal, e.g. Kailan coal (North China) contained 20 per cent ash as against mere 6 per cent in US coal.

13 *Mainichi*, 22 April 1953.

14 See the *Oriental Economist*, June 1965, 269; *Monthly Return of the, Foreign Trade of Japan*, January-December 1956. See also Leng, n. 1, 60 and Jan. n. 1, 903-4.

15 Leng, n. 1, 67.

16 *Mainichi*, 17 January 1974.

17 See J.P. Jain, *China in World Politics* (New Delhi, 1976), 234-7.

18 Leng, n. 1, 47.

19 Jan, n. 1, 906.

20 Morley, n. 8, 6.

21 *Mainichi*, 1 December 1953.

22 *Renmin Ribao*, 2 April 1955, as translated in *News Bulletin*, 13 April 1955, 11-2.

23 Ibid., 11 May 1955. See also Zhou Enlai's statement at the Bandung Conference, 13 May 1955. Ibid., 23 May 1955, 6.

24 Xinhua News Agency, 15 October 1956, as reproduced in *Survey of China Mainland Press*, no. 1392, 36-7.

25 Jan, n. 1, 906.

26 *Contemporary Japan*, September 1958, 520-4; also Xinhua News Agency, 5 March 1958.

27 Shigeyoshi Takami, "Prospects for Trade with Continental China," *Contemporary Japan*, April 1958, 210-1.

28 See statement by Japanese Foreign Minister before the Japan-America Society of Yokohama, 7 April 1958. Embassy of Japan, *Information Bulletin* (New Delhi), 1 May 1958, 5.

29 On 7 March 1958, two days after the signing of the fourth Sino-Japanese private trade agreement, Taipeh lodged a protest against the flying of Communist China's flag in Japan. Suspension of Taiwan-Japan trade transactions and trade negotiations was announced in the middle

of March 1958 and on 28 March 1958 Nationalist China's Ambassador in Japan declared that Taipeh would severe its deplomatic relations with Japan, if Tokyo recognized the right of Beijing's trade representation to fly its flag in Japan.

30 For the text, See *Contemporary Japan*, September 1958, 373-8.

31 For Chinese commentaries on the flag incident, see Xinhua News Agency, 6 May 1958 and *Ta Kung Po*, 7 May 1958.

32 *Far Eastern Economic Review*, 23 April 1959, 571.

33 See *Renmin Ribao*, 7 May 1958.

34 Lawrence Olson, *Japan in Postwar Asia* (New York, 1970), 77-8.

35 *Renmin Ribao*, 16 April 1955, as translated in *News Bulletin*, 27 April 1955, 8.

36 See *Renmin Ribao*, 9 May 1956. See also *Survey of China Mainland Press*, no. 1287, 27 and Fa-li Ch'u-pan-hsie, *Chung-hua Jen-min Kung-he-kuo T'iao-Yueh Chi*, Vol V: 1956 (Beijing, 1958), 410-3.

37 *Renmin Ribao*, 7 June 1957. See also *Survey of China Mainland Press*, no. 1548, 35 and *Chung-hua Jen-min Kung-he-kuo T'iao-Yueh Chi*, n. 36, Vol VI: 1957, 330-3.

38 *Peking Review*, 17 June 1958, 19.

39 Leng, n.1, 32-3.

40 See statement by Japanese Minister of International Trade and Industry, Tanzan Ishibashi, in August 1958. Quoted in Leng, n. 1, 61.

41 See his statement of 15 February 1957. Quoted in Leng, n. 1, 63.

42 See his statement of 9 August 1957. Embassay of Japan in India, *Information Bulletin*, 1 September 1957, 2.

43 *Renmin Ribao*, 30 October 1953.

44 Zhou Enlai's remarks during his conversation with Professor Ikuo Oyama, Chairman of the Japanese National Peace Committee, 28 September 1958. *News Bulletin*, 21 October 1953.

45 *Far Eastern Economic Review*, 23 October 1958, 515.

46 *Peking Review*, 21 April 1959, 25-6.

47 Armin J. Meyer, *Assignment to Tokyo: An Ambassador's Journal* (New York, 1974), 126.

4. *Uneven Course, 1958-1971*

China's policy towards Japan in the aftermath of the Naga-saki Flag incident has been in marked contrast to that of the Soviet Union. Since the late fifties the two Communist Powers had apparently begun to act towards Japan as separate entities rather than as members of a "single Socialist bloc" and to adopt separate ways in weighty policy matters like the strengthening or loosening, or severing of economic, political, and cultural ties with Japan.[1] Nevertheless, one also notices a parallelism of interest in so far as the elimination of US influence and the promotion of "neutralist" trends in Japan were concerned.

The People's Republic of China gave consistent and active support to "peace forces" and "pro-Beijing" groups (including the JSP, the JCP, senior members of the LDP, etc.) in Japan and lent a helping hand in the building up of a mass movement against the Government. China also sought to mobilize Japanese business circles, especially those engaged in Sino-Japanese trade, to exert pressure on the Government to revise its anti-Beijing policy.

In the sixties, as Sino-Soviet differences widened China pursued a "dual adversary strategy", i e. opposition to both American imperialism and Soviet revisionism. This approach was reflective of a tough international posture which aimed to forge a world-wide anti-imperialist alliance or broad united front by all the oppressed countries and pecples against the two Super Powers,[2] and to assume a leading role in pressing the cause of anti-colonialism and war of "national liberation" in Asia and Africa.

In August 1958 Premier Zhou Enlai enunciated "three

political principles" for the normalization of Sino-Japanese relations, viz. that Japan should not (1) adopt policies hostile to China; (2) participate in any plot aimed at creating two Chinas; and (3) obstruct the normalization cf relations with China. The acceptance of these conditions also became the prerequisite for any Japanese firm seeking to trade with the Mainland.

From November 1958 onwards China launched a vigorous drive against the signature and ratification of the US-Japanese Security Treaty and in suppoit of the struggle then being waged by "patriotic" Japanese in that regard. Prime Minister Kishi was singled out for denunciation as "the chief culprit" in obstructing normalization of Sino-Japanese relations and "the concentrated expression of latent imperialism in Japan." The Kishi cabinet was described as "the most reactionary of all the cabinets formed since the Japanese surrender in 1945."[3] Such criticism remained a regular feature of articles and commentaries appearing in the Chinese Press and statements of Chinese leaders throughout the sixties.

Most delegations visiting China expressed approval of such Chinese statements. For instance, the Communist Parties of China and Japan issued two statements, cne on 3 March 1959 and the other on 20 October 1959,[4] expressing "concern" about the proposed revision cf the US-Japanese military alliance and the conversion cf Japan into an American war base in the Far East. Inejiro Asanuma, leader of the Japanese Socialist Party delegation, expressed similar views in a joint statement of 17 March 1959 and demanded the withdrawal of US troops stationed in Japan.[5]

In a statement on 14 January 1960, the Chinese Ministry of Foreign Affairs considered the signing of the US-Japanese Mutual Security Treaty "an extremely grave step taken by the Japanese reactionaries and the US imperialists colluding to prepare new aggression and war and menace Asian and world peace."[6] The Chinese Press supported "the nation-wide struggle" of the Japanese people against "the reactionary policy" of the Japanese Government of "openly reviving militarism and integrating Japan into the US aggressive military bloc and atomic war system."[7]

At the second session of the Second National People's

Congress on 10 April 1960, Zhou Enlai reiterated that the
US-Japanese Security Treaty was a treaty of disaster for the
Japanese people in the long run. He said that it threatened the
security of China, the Soviet Union, and above all the countries
of Southeast Asia. He concluded:

> So long as the Kishi Government does not abandon its policy
> of hostility to China, there can be no possibility of im-
> proving Sino-Japanese relations. The responsibility for the
> present abnormal situation in Sino-Japanese relations rests
> entirely with the Kishi Government.[8]

A mass rally of more than one million people was organized
in Beijing on 9 May 1960 to express resolute opposition to the
US-Japanese Security Treaty and extend support to the Japanese
people who had by then "carried through 15 rounds of sweeping
nation-wide united actions" to oppose the signing of the
"aggressive" pact.[9] This rally was designed to raise the morale
of the "patriotic" Japanese people struggling under the direction
of the National Council for the Prevention of the Ratification
of the US-Japanese Security Treaty comprising the Japanese
Socialist Party, the Japanese General Council of Trade Unions
(*Sohyo*). Liao Cheng-chih in his speech particularly recalled the
bloody massacres carried out fifteen years before by Japanese
"militarist" forces in China, Korea, Vietnam, Burma, Indonesia,
Cambodia, Laos, the Philippines, Thailand, Malaya, and
Singapore.[10] Five days later, Chairman Mao Zedong also
described the new US-Japanese Security Treaty as "an aggressive military alliance treaty hostile to China and the Soviet
Union and to the Asian peoples."[11] Zhou Enlai termed the US-
Japanese Security Treaty a "menace to Southeast Asia" which
jeopardized peace in the Far East and Asia.[12]

The Chinese line of unyielding toughness towards Japan
continued even when Hayato Ikeda assumed office as Prime
Minister.[13] Barely a week after Ikeda's assumption of office
as Prime Minister, Chen Yi exhorted a visiting Japanese delegation to wage a resolute struggle against "US imperialism,"
and considered Japan as a good place for "teaching American
imperialism a lesson or two."[14]

Eight Chinese people's organizations and twelve visiting
Japanese delegations issued a joint statement on 3 October

1960 criticizing the Ikeda Government in strong terms for obstructing normalization of Sino-Japanese relations and expressing their determination to defeat the reactionary Ikeda Government of Japan.[15]

The consolidation of US-Japanese relations was also the subject of vehement Chinese criticism. Commenting on the visit of Prime Minister Ikeda to the United States in June 1961, the *Peking Review* described the Japanese Government as a willing ally of the US and made the following points:

1. Kennedy and Ikeda were agreed on the need to increase Japan's military strength. They also agreed to dicuss the question of nuclear weapons for Japan.

2. The USA was determined to keep South Korea as a separate entity. Japan agreed to normalize relations with South Korea and to support the USA in detaching Formosa from China.

3. Japan will increasingly attempt to reassert its old position in both Korea and Formosa. Ultimately, this would lead Tokyo to promote an independence movement in Taiwan against the interest of Jiang Jieshi (Chiang Kaishek.)

4. In Southeast Asia, Japan would try to forestall the rise of Chinese influence in co-operation with Washington. To that end, it would co-operate with China's hostile neighbour, India, confirm Thailand, Malaya, and South Vietnam in their anti-Communist posture, and build links with Burma, Laos, and Cambodia by exporting capital and technology. Tokyo was considering extension of aid, possibly disguised, as reparations, to Burma, Laos, and Cambodia.

5. Although there were still contradictions between the USA and Japan, Ikeda's mission was a success inasmuch as it would enable him to adopt a more active anti-Communist policy. Such a policy would, however, make it easier to mobilize the people of Japan in their struggle against their own Government and the USA.

The above analysis did not go beyond current Chinese propaganda, and did not suggest that a soft Chinese policy might detach Japan from the United States.[16]

Chinese fears of the revival of Japanese militarism were heightened by Japanese rearmament under US encouragement. A Chinese commentator, Chung Hsin-chung, highlighted how the firepower of the Japanese forces was "four times greater than in pre-World War II days" and its mobility "seven times greater." Apprehensions were also expressed about Japan's nuclear industry. Of the seventeen members of the Ikeda Cabinet, twelve were described as "militarists." Under US tutelage and with increased US military aid, Chung concluded, Japanese militarism was "staging a comeback, more powerful and more dangerous than before."[17] Japan, the *People's Daily* said on 8 September 1961, faced a dilemma: Should it follow the path of militarism, monopoly, and subservience to the United States and antagonism towards Southeast Asia? Or should it choose the path of peace and common prosperity with Southeast Asia? The article reiterated the Chinese viewpoint that the establishment of any kind of official friendship or of diplomatic relations with Japan was impossible so long as

> the pro-American, reactionary, and traitorous monopoly capital of Japan and its political spokesmen, the Hayato Ikeda Cabinet, . . . [is determined] to be subservient to the USA and base its foreign policy on the doctrine of "taking the UN as the centre", openly describes itself as a member of the Western aggressive bloc, repeatedly expresses its intention to continue to be hostile towards China and create "Two Chinas", and openly indicates that it would risk antagonising the Asian-African countries in order to toe the line of the USA and keep pace with the Western aggressive Powers.

The *People's Daily* article went on to add that Ikeda's profession of affection for China was nothing but a smokescreen for covering up an attempt to "regain its lost colonies such as Korea and China's Taiwan, so that it may collaborate further with the USA to stage a comeback to China." It referred to the active preparations allegedly being made by Japan to regain Taiwan, and predicted that Japan would first follow the US in creating two Chinas and obstructing the Chinese people's liberation of Taiwan, then overthrow the rule of the Jiang Jieshi (Chiang Kai-shek) clique, later instigate and support the traitorous pro-Japanese element in Taiwan to create a so-called "independent country of Taiwan," and finally establish a so-called "North East Asia anti-communist system including Japan, Taiwan and S. Korea."[18]

When the US Secretary of State, Dean Rusk, held talks

with Japanese leaders in November 1961, Beijing thought that "a sinister plot" was being hatched to form "a new military alliance to be known as NEATO—the Northeast Asian Treaty Organisation."[19] China felt that the talks that took place in the beginning of 1963 between Japan and the Republic of Korea were actually designed to advance the plan for a "Northeast Asian military alliance."[20]

Prime Minister Ikeda's statement in the Lower House of Japanese Parliament that neutralism was an illusion and that Japan could not afford to embrace it was criticized in a joint statement issued on 13 January 1962 by Chang Hsi-jo of the People's Institute of Foreign Affairs and a visiting Japanese Socialist Party delegation. The statement declared that the transformation of Japan into a neutral country and the abolition of the US-Japanese Security Treaty would be "the greatest guarantee of peace in Asia."[21]

The French recognition of Communist China on 19 January 1964 led Japanese leaders to realize that they could not ignore the existence of the People's Republic of China. The Japanese Government expressed its inability to change its policy towards Beijing unless there was a "fundamental change" in the US policy towards China or unless a situation arose in which the Mao regime became "a legitimate member of the United Nations with the blessing of its members."[22]

Chinese leaders deprecated the policy of the Government of Japan of regarding politics and economics as separate. Chen Yi felt that that policy implied "politically, to continue to adhere to the attitude of non-recognition of China and economically to develop Sino-Japanese trade on a limited scale." This, according to him, was not in full accord with the demand for promoting the normalization of relations between the two countries. He also reserved the right of the Chinese people to claim reparations.[23]

Meanwhile, on 21 January 1964 a *People's Daily* editorial enunciated the concept of two intermediate zones—the first part consisting of the independent countries and those striving for independence in Asia, Africa, and Latin America; and the second part consisting of the whole of Western Europe, Oceania, Canada, and other capitalist countries.[24] After stating that Japan was part of the second intermediate zone, the editorial went on to assert:

> Countries in this second intermediate zone have a dual
> character. While their ruling classes are exploiters and
> oppressors, these countries themselves are subjected to U.S.
> control, interference and bullying. They therefore try their
> best to free themselves from U.S. control. In this regard
> they have something in common with the socialist countries
> and the peoples of various countries. By making itself
> antagonistic to the whole world, U.S. imperialism inevitably
> finds itself tightly encircled.

In his conversation with Japanese guests in Beijing on
27 January 1964, Mao Zedong justified the large-scale struggle
of the Japanese people against the entry and stationing of
nuclear aircraft and submarines in Japan, the presence of US
military bases, the US-Japanese Security Treaty, etc. He expressed his conviction that the Japanese people would certainly be
able "to drive the US imperialists from their soil and that their
aspirations for independence, democracy, peace and neutrality
will surely come true."[25]

The Chinese Press continued to express its support for the
Japanese "people's struggle" against the United States—against
the US-Japan Security Treaty of 1960, against the 40-odd US
military bases in Japan, against the stationing of US nuclear
submarines, etc.[26] Beijing made full use of the sessions of the
World Congress against Atomic and Hydrogen Bombs, held
anually in Japan, to condemn the "nuclear war policy of US
imperialism."[27] It also highlighted the appeal issued by twenty-
five prominent public figures of Japan on 13 February 1964.
The appeal issued by the leaders of the Japanese Communist
Party, the Japanese Socialist Party, and the General Council
of Trade Unions, demanded normalization of Sino-Japanese
relations and expansion of trade, economic and cultural
exchanges with China. It also called for the abrogation of the
treaty between Japan and Jiang Jieshi (Chiang Kai-shek),
serverance of diplomatic relations with the Jiang Jieshi clique,
and the restoration to China of its lawful seat in the United
Nations.[28] The appeal was followed by a mass movement to
win greater public support for these objectives.

In the absence of official ties with Japan, China continued to
lay stress on "people's diplomacy" by inviting a large number

of Japanese visitors to China. The Japanese visitors consistently outnumbered all other foreigners invited to China. The number of Japanese visiting China (most of them were from the "progressive" camp) was, according to official reports, 343 in 1961; 596 in 1962; 1,778 in 1963; and over 2,000 in 1964.

Zhou Enlai noted there was some expansion of economic and cultural exchanges between China and Japan but the "extremely unfriendly attitude" of the Sato Government and its support for the United States "two Chinas" policy had created difficulties in the improvement of Sino-Japanese relations.[29]

After Eisaku Sato replaced Ikeda as Japanese prime minister in November 1964 and China launched upon the Great Proletarian Cultural Revolution, relations between China and Japan grew, if anything, worse. Throughout this period, China criticized in strong terms the conservative Sato Government, which, it said, was "more reactionary than any previous Japanese Government."[30] The *People's Daily* editorial of 25 November 1964, written after Eisaku Sato had been in office for just five days, listed a number of "malicious acts" of his Government to undermine Sino-Japanese relations. These included denial of entry visa to a CCP delegation led by Peng Chen to attend the ninth JCP Congress, criticism of China's first nuclear explosion, opposition to the restoration of China's legitimate rights in the United Nations, and the reiteration of the unsettled legal status of Taiwan.[31]

China was critical of the "Republic of Korea-Japan Basic Treaty" signed in June 1965 (effective from 21 December 1965). The Chinese Government statement of 26 June 1965 described the Treaty as "a grave step taken by US imperialism in its attempt to perpetuate the division of Korea and its occupation of South Korea and to enlist Japan and the Pak Jung-hi clique on the service of its policies of aggression and war." China considered that treaty and the related "agreements" as "a grave provocation" not only against the Korean and Japanese peoples but also against the Chinese people and the peoples of other Asian countries and avered that it would never recognize it. The United States was accused of actively fostering the forces of Japanese militarism and deliberately instigating the Japanese and the South Korean reactionaries to collude with each other in its attempt to forge a "Northeast Asia military alliance" with Japan as the nucleus and including the South Korean puppet clique and the Jiang Jieshi (Chiang Kai-shek) remnant gang. The United States was criticized for trying to link this alliance with "Southeast Asia Treaty Organisation" and to bring all its lackeys in Asia into "a unified aggressive military system".[32] In another statement dated 16 November 1965, the Chinese Government stated that the ratification of the Japan-ROK Treaty by the Japanese House of Representatives was "a serious step taken by the Sato Government to accelerate the revival of militarism" and "a serious step taken by the US imperialism to conspire with the Japanese reactionaries in expanding its war of aggression in Asia." China protested against what it considered "an aggressive military treaty" directed not only against China. The American purpose in exhorting Japan and South Korea to conclude that treaty and rig up a "Northeast Asia military alliance" was said to be to drive Japan to renew its aggression against Korea and all of Asia and to send Japanese people as canon fodder to Vietnam and China.[33] An article by Jen Ku-ping in *Peking Review* in December 1965 repeated these charges and observed that the Japan-South Korea Treaty was designed "to block the peaceful reunification of Korea and pave the way for renewed infiltration of Japanese monopoly capital." The Chinese commentator's article entitled "Japanese Militarism on the Road Back" criticized in strong terms both the domestic and foreign policies of Japanese Government and quoted figures about the strength of the Japanese armed forces to prove that Japan's military strength had reached the level attained when the militarists invaded Northeast China in September 1931.[34] It was asserted that Japan's economic and military collaboration with Jiang Jieshi (Chiang Kai-shek) was aimed at building a so-called "Japan-South Korea-Taiwan defence system" as part of the crescent-shaped encirclement of the Chinese mainland.

Impact of the Sino-Soviet Rift

In the wake of the 20th Congress of the Communist Party of the Soviet Union and the Hungarian crisis, Sino-Soviet relations started deteriorating. The Soviet Union had not hesitated to normalize relations with Japan in 1956 much ahead of China and leave China in the lurch. With the worsening of the Sino-Soviet rift, the Soviet Union began to adopt a more conciliatory and flexible approach towards Japan. The Soviets seemed to have realized that Soviet-Japanese relations were not confronted with any intricate problem like that of choosing between two Chinas.

China also initiated a campaign for improving "friendship" between China and Japan primarily to counteract Soviet efforts to step up its propaganda in Japan. This campaign was reported to be in "full swing" in Japan in September 1963. The Japan-China Friendship Association launched a two-month campaign on 1 September 1963 and offered *People's China*, *China Pictorial*, and *Peking Review* for sale in order to acquaint the Japanese people with the situation in China.[35]

Chinese leaders and newsmedia began to exploit Soviet-Japanese differences, especially as regards the Northern Territories issue. In a complete reversal of China's earlier stand[36] that the Kurile Islands were Soviet territory, Chairman Mao Zedong told a group of Japanese socialists on 10 July 1964 of Chinese support for the Japanese claims to Kunashiri and Etorofu.[37] This elicited a long rejoinder in *Pravda*.[38] Zhou Enlai subsequently stated that the Chinese support was not motivated by any desire to damage Soviet-Japanese relations but by what China had consistently believed to be the correct solution to the problem of unjust territorial settlements. The Chinese attempt was clearly aimed at souring Soviet-Japanese relations on an issue which was extremely sensitive and important for the Japanese people.

As Sino-Soviet relations worsened, all Soviet-Japanese contacts came in for severe criticism at the hands of Beijing. Co-operation between Japan and the Soviet Union was described as "a conspiracy against China," and Soviet diplomatic moves in that direction were seen as an attempt on the Kremlin's part "to drive a wedge between China and the countries surrounding it."[39] The Soviets were denounced for "busily" helping the United States in building a cordon around China. Soviet-Japanese "amity" was considered merely "an extension of Japan-US collusion."[40] The Soviet policy towards Japan was stated to be "closely related to the US imperialist policy of accelerating the revival of Japanese militarism" while the attitudes adopted by the Kremlin on Vietnam, India-Pakistan question and towards Japan were viewed as completely conforming to the requirements of US imperialism, especially with the US policy of encircling China.[41] The *People's Daily* on 31 July 1966 referred to the alleged formation of a "holy alliance" between the United States, Japan, and the Soviet Union on the basis of their "inveterate hatred for socialist China and their rabid hostility towards the revolutionary forces in Asia."[42] The Soviet "revisionist clique," it added, was "vainly" attempting to realise its vicious plan for "US-Japanese-Soviet co-operation for the domination of Asia."

Soviet-Japanese discussions on economic collaboration were described as a move meant to toe the US line in Asia, oppose China, suppress national liberation movements in Asia, and undermine the militant solidarity of the Japanese people under the leadership of the Japanese Communist Party. Soviet-Japanese co-operation for the development of Siberia and the Soviet Far East likewise caused much concern to China. While Moscow was criticized for "opening the door wide for Japanese monopoly capital's expansion into the Soviet Union," Japan was cautioned against the "smiling policy" followed by the Soviet leaders towards Japan, which was aimed against China and had "defence and political reasons" behind it. The whole thing was seen as serving the strategy of the United States to encircle China.[43] Thus both Japan and the Soviet Union were depicted as willing tools and accomplices of US imperialism.

The frequent visits, the series of political and economic transactions that took place between Japan and the USSR, and the agreement reached between the Foreign Ministers of the two countries to hold regular consultations each year were considered to be visible instances of "complete collusion" between the ruling circles of the two states. In 1966, the Chinese Press had spoken of Soviet-Japanese amity as an extension of US-Japanese collusion. A year later, the *People's Daily* described the "Soviet-Japanese alliance" as "actually an extension of the Soviet-US alliance." In stepping up its collaboration with the Japanese "reactionaries," it alleged, the Soviet "revisionist clique" was "in reality" seeking to help US imperialism in making Japan serve its policy of aggression and war in Asia. Like the US-Japanese alliance, the paper observed, Soviet-Japanese collaboration was directed primarily against China.[44]

The Soviet Union refrained from strong criticism of Japanese defence and foreign policy. But the Chinese increased their criticism of Prime Minister Sato and his policies. Sato was denounced for reducing Japan to a "military and supply base for the US imperialist war of aggression against Vietnam," for supplying US and South Vietnamese troops with large quantities of war material, and for acting as a salesman for the "peace talks" fraud. Chinese commentators called him "an accomplice in US aggression." It was stated that in doing all that it had done, the Sato Government was prompted by its own need for overseas exansion, by the hope of re-establishing its "colonial sphere of influence in Asia with U.S. backing." The Chinese Press also painted a disheartening picture of the Japanese economy.[45]

As a neighbour of both the Communist giants, Japan could hardly remain unaffected. The business community felt that the withdrawal of Soviet economic assistance to and technicians from China left many projects imcomplete and offered considerable potential for Japanese exports. The Japanese Goverment also noted that the two Communist countries no longer constituted a single monolithic bloc. However, it deemed it inadvisable to either embroil itself in Sino-Soviet rivalry or deviate from American perception of and policy towards these Communist Powers.

Although Japan fully reciprocated the Soviet desire for trade and working political relations, it continued to regard the Soviet Union as much the greater menace than China to its interests. Thus, Japan's vehement denuciation of Soviet intervention in Czechoslovakia was more an expression of this traditional distrust and dislike of the Soviet Union than a sense of moral outrage.

The Cultural Revolution gave rise to further rigidity in Beijing's policy towards Japan. China accused the Japanese Government of further perpetrating "extremely serious anti-China fascist outrages" on 8 and 9 September 1960 by sending policemen and hooligans to assault and injure many members of the staff of the Tokyo Liaison Office of the Liao Cheng-chih

Office, Chinese journalists and other Chinese personnel in Japan.[46] Beijing retaliated by announcing the cancellation of the credentials of the correspondents of three Japanese news-papers—*Mainichi Shimbun, Sankei Shimbun, and Tokyo Shimbun*—and ordered them to leave China within a specified time. It a¹so made it clear that "for the present" it would not consider the possibility of the three papers sending new correspondents to China. It accused the Japanese correspon-dents of printing, on many occasions, stories and cartoons wildly smearing China's Great Proletarian Cultural Revolution and of presenting a distorted picture of China's domestic situation.[47] By September 1970, the number of Japanese correspondent resident in Beijing had been reduced from nine to one (*Asahi*'s Akioka).[48] It was not till January 1971 that the Chinese authorities relaxed some restrictions on foreign reporting in China and allowed two more Japanese correspon-dents representing *Nihon Keizai Shimbun* and *Nishi Nippon Shimbun* to be stationed in Beijing.

The *People's Daily* saw Sato's trip to Taiwan in September 1961 as an intensification on his part of Japan's "political, eco-nomic, and military collusion" with Jiang Jieshi (Chiang Kai-shek) in order "to stretch its tentacles of aggression into China's territory of Taiwan and serve the scheme of the US imperialists and Soviet revisionists for forming a ring round China."[49] Similarly Sato's visit to Saigon next month was inter-preted as further involving Japan in the US war of aggression against Vietnam.[50] Sato's visit to Indonesia, Australia, New Zealand, the Philippines, and South Vietnam in the fall of 1967 was said to have a sinister motive, viz. to facilitate the pene-tration of Japanese monoply capital into Southeast Asia on a large scale, to expand Japan's sphere of influence in a big way in the Asian and Pacific region, to raise a hue and cry about the Chinese "threat," and to build "an anti-China ring for US imperialism."[51] Prime Minister Sato's extensive foreign trips were not only a reflection of his desire for anti-Communist regional solidarity, especially in relation to China and North Vietnam, but also a prelude to his determined negotiations with President Johnson for the reversion of the Ryukyu and Bonin Islands.[52]

The visit of Chiang Ching-kuo, the son of Jiang Jieshi

in November 1967 and the search ordered of the headquarters
of the Japan-China Friendship Association (Orthodox) and the
Japan International Trade Promotion Association and its
Kansai branch were also set down as anti-Chinese activities on
the part of the Sato Government.[53]

China declared that it had no faith in the reactionary Sato
Government's "professions of improving Sino-Japanese relations." It said that in pursuing the policy of "separation
between politics and economics," Sato was trying "to make
economic profits while politically maintaining a hostility attitude towards China." The *People's Daily* sternly told the Sato
Government that its "smug calculations will come to naught."[54]
In other words, it made it clear that Beijing would not engage
in trade relations with Japan as long as Sato remained in power.

The *People's Daily* took the Sato Government to task for
pushing its policy of "industrial Japan, agricultural Asia" and
for speeding up its economic expansion and political infiltration
under the signboard of "economic co-operation" with a view
to realizing its ambition of reasserting its hegemony in Asia
and re-establishing the spheres of influence of Japanese militarism in the Asian region "in a vain attempt to revive their
old dream of "Greater East Asia Co-Prosperity Sphere."[55]

As Sino-Soviet ideological differences deepened, the
Japanese Communist Party (JCP) began to take an "independent" line or to lean on Moscow. Beijing accused the JCP of
flirting with "modern revisionism," the unforgivable sin. A
Red Guard poster that appeared in Beijing on 22 January 1967
criticized the JCP for turning "revisionist." The JCP retaliated.
On 9 February 1967, *Akahata*, the JCP paper, disclosed that
ten JCP members had been expelled in Beijing for following the
doctrine of the "head of a certain foreign country."[56] By early
1968 about 600 members had been expelled from the JCP for
pro-Chinese sympathies.[57] The *People's Daily* editorial on 18
September 1968 urged the Japanese to follow Mao's example.
It said that "the flame of the revolutionary struggle" was the
only way to achieve victory in the "Japanese revolution." It
lashed out at Soviet opportunism and modern revisionism, and
warned the "Miyamoto renegade clique," the ruling faction in
the Japanese Communist Party, against advertising what it
considered "independence."[58]

Premier Eisaku Sato and other Japanese Government leaders in their policy statements recognized the fact of Japan's close relationship with China "both historically and geographically" and expressed a desire for economic and cultural interchange with Communist China on the basic principle of *seikei bunri* (separation of political and economic relations) and without prejudice to their friendly relations with Taipeh.[59] Acordingly, the Japanese Government continued to support the US position that any proposal to change the status of the Chinese representation in the United Nations should be decided by a two-thirds majority.[60] Tokyo felt no urgency about normalizing its relations with China. It watched with concern the various developments within China, such as the formation of the Red Guards and the declaration of the "Great Cultural Revolution." They seemed, in the words of then Japanese Ambassador to the United States, "to negate our hopes that the Chinese will gradually enlarge their contacts with the free world." Advocating a policy of "wait and watch," he pinned his hopes on the liberation of the "masses of Chinese people from their present spiritual serfdom under the doctrinaire dictatorship."[61] Both Prime Minister Sato and Foreign Minister Miki, in their statements before the Diet on 14 March 1967, expressed their anxiety and concern about the tumultous developments within China and stressed the need to watch them carefully.[62] Sato doubted that given the situation then obtaining in China Beijing would orient its foreign policy towards conciliation in Asia.[63]

In other statements, Sato expressed his appreciation of the "sacrifices" the United States was making in Vietnam and his concern over the acquisition of nuclear weapons by China. He also criticized Beijing for trying to influence, "in a dogmatic and selfish way, the domestic and external policies of its neighbouring nations."[64] In short, the Chinese nuclear tests, the Sino-Indian border dispute, the Vietnam War, and the Cultural Revolution—all apparently created difficulties for the Japanese leadership to develop relations with China.

On the other hand, Japan's efforts to gain regional leadership through such organizations as the Asia-Pacific Council (ASPAC) and its hosting of a number of regional conferences early in 1966 were described by Beijing as attempts "to build the so-called 'Asian and Pacific Community," an "anti-China arc stretching from South Korea to Australia and New Zealand."[65] Japan's active economic and political diplomacy in Southeast Asia, which was evident from its participation in the Ministerial Conference for the Economic Development of Southeast Asia (Tokyo, 6-7 April 1966) and the Asian Development Bank and its support for the new Association of Southeast Asian Nations (ASEAN), also created suspicion in the Chinese mind. The Japanese naval cruises in the Southeast Asian waters and the projected return of Okinawa to Japan's political control were interpreted as enhancing Tokyo's military capablity.[66] Japan's rearmament was assessed by Chinese news media in "the omnipresent context of [its] collusive efforts with the United States and Soviet Union."[67] The fact that Soviet, Japanese, and American fleets were all plying in the waters surrounding China made Beijing feel that it was being threatened with encirclement both on land and in the sea.[68]

Following armed clashes between the Chinese and Soviet forces on the banks of the Ussuri in March 1969, Chinese criticism of Soviet-Japanese "collusion" became especially bitter. The Sato Government was accused of playing "an exteremely despicable role of an accomplice in the criminal plots jointly engineered by US imperialism and Soviet revisionism to encircle China."[69] Joint Soviet-Japanese development of Siberian resources was viewed by the Chinese as a Russian "sell-out" to "Japanese monopoly capital." The Soviet Union was also accused of actively assisting the Japanese in their efforts to promote arms expansion and war preparations by making copper and other "strategic materials" available to them. The visit of D.M. Gvishiani, Vice-Chairman of the State Commitee for Science and Technology of the USSR, to Japan in November 1969 was undertaken, it was stated, to aid and abet Japanese arms expansion and to beg Japan to help extricate the Soviet Union from its economic difficulties.[70] Similarly the Soviet-Japanese agreement (November 1969) permitting Japanese aircraft to fly over Siberia on Tokyo/London flights was compared to a territorial invasion by Xinhua.[71]

In his anxiety to recover Okinawa from the United States, Sato went to the extent of committing Japan to Taiwan's security. In a joint communique he signed with President

Nixon of the United States on 21 November 1969, he declared that "the maintenance of peace and stability in the Taiwan area is also a most important factor for the security of Japan" and that Tokyo would do all it can to assist the US fulfil its obligation in regard to "the peace and security of the Far East."[72] Japan's regaining its administrative rights over Okinawa was not to hinder in any way the effective discharge of the international obligations assumed by Washington for "the defence of countries in the Far East, including Japan." The defence of Taiwan obviously formed part of the defence of the countries of the Far East.

In his address before the National Press Club in Washington on 21 November 1969, Premier Sato not only affirmed that the maintenance of peace in the Taiwan area was an important factor for Japan's security, but also declared: "If an armed attack against the Republic of Korea were to occur, the security of Japan would be seriously affected." Should a situation arise in which it became necessary for the US forces to use facillties and areas within Japan, Sato stated, the policy of the Government of Japan would be to decide its position in regard to prior consultation "positively and promptly on the basis of the foregoing recognition." Premier Sato expressed his hope that Beijing would revise its rigid posture and participate in international affairs as a country "that will carry out its responsibilities in a constructive manner in the cause of international peace." For that purpose, he considered it necessary that both the United States and Japan should always keep the door open to Communist China.[73]

The *People's Daily* editorial of 28 November 1969 severely criticized the Sato-Nixon joint communique. It observed that the Nixon-Sato talks had brought the military collaboration between the US and Japanese reacti onaries to a new stage. It said that in the US imperialism's counter-revolutionary global strategy, the Japanese reactionaries had now been made to serve as gendarms in Asia.[74] Next day Premier Zhou Enlai described the newly intensified military collusion between the US and Japanese reactionaries as "a grave provocation against the people of China, Korea, Vietnam, Laos, Cambodia and the other Asian countries." He considered the so-called "reversion of Okinawa" a "fraud" because, according to him, Eisaku

Sato had agreed to turn the whole of Japan into an Okinawa, "into a US base for aggression." He said that abetted by US imperialism and drunk with rabid ambitions, the Sato Government was wildly attempting to step up militarism and realize its old dream of a "Greater East Asia Co-prosperity Sphere." Social-imperialism (i.e. the Soviet Union) was also criticized for "actively wooing" the Japanese Sato Government and for trying to make use of the military alliance between the US and Japanese reactionaries "to oppose China, stamp out the flames of the Vietnamese people's war against US aggression and for national salvation and sabotage the cause of the re-unification of Korea."[75]

The "automatic extension" of the US-Japanese Security Treaty in the middle of 1970 was similarly regarded as another step in the direction of reviving Japanese militarism and committing further aggression in Asia. The existence of the US-Japanese military alliance was described as "a grave threat to the peace and security of all countries in the Asian and Pacific region."[76] Japan was also denounced for harbouring wild designs on African resources,[77] and for its collaboration with South Korea.[78] The *People's Daily* described the Japanese "Draft of the Fourth Military Defence Build-up Plan," which envisaged military expenditure of US $16 billion for 1972-76, as a proof of the revival of Japanese militarism and "a blueprint of the Japanese reactionaries to step up arms expansion and war preparations." Yasuhiro Nakasone, Director-General of the Japanese Defence Agency, was denounced for flagrantly including China's sacred territory Diaoyutai and other islands in "the scope of Japanese defence."[79]

Conclusion

The opposition within Japan to the revision of the US-Japanese security treaty, Chae-Jin-Lee points out, provided the Chinese with a unique opportunity to take part in Japan's dynamic political process. They actively supported the violent anti-treaty movement with extensive propaganda, financial aid, and sympathetic mass demonstrations throughout China. In the process they gained a valuable insight into Japanese policies; while they were impressed by the strength of mass

actions led by progressive parties, trade unions, and radical
student groups, they were also reassured of the importance of
deep factional and policy cleavage in the LDP itself.[80]

During the Memorandum Trade talks China raised political
questions partly because this was virtually the only channel
for direct political discussion and communication in the absence
of normal relations.

In the prevailing international situation marked by American
hostility and competition with the Soviet Union, China enunciated the concept of a second intermediate zone comprising
of Japan and the West European countries in order to cultivate
friendly relations with them. The needs of the Chinese economy which was going through a difficult period of adjustment
also led China to adopt such a course. However, China felt
that Japan was not favourably responding to its overtures as
witness the "Yoshida Letter". During the Cultural Revolution
China adopted an overall rigid foreign policy posture which
precluded any meaningful relations with Japan. Acute US
hostility twoards China and strong American pressure as well
as domestic factors such as the leadership of Premier Sato and
considerable support within the LDP for Taiwan prevented
Japan from taking any initiative regarding improvement of
relations with China.

NOTES

[1] R.K. Jain, *The USSR and Japan, 1945-1980* (New Delhi, 1981), 31.
[2] *Peking Review*, 30 April 1969, 31 and 34.
[3] *Renmin Ribao*, 7 July 1958.
[4] *Peking Review*, 10 March 1959 and 27 October 1958, 15.
[5] Ibid., 24 March 1959, 18-9.
[6] Ibid., 19 January 1960, 8. See also *China Today*, 16 January 1960, 3.
[7] Resolution adopted at a Beijing rally on 23 January 1960. Foreign
Languages Press, *Oppose the Revival of Japanese Militarism* (Beijing,
1960), 130.
[8] *China Today*, 16 April 1960, 5.
[9] Speech by Kuo Mo-jo at the Beijing rally, 9 May 1960. *China Reconstructs*, June 1960, Special Supplement.
[10] Ibid., 13-4.
[11] Foreign Languages Press, *Support the Just Struggle of the Japanese
People Against the Japan-US Treaty of Military Alliance* (Beijing, 1960), 1-2
Also see his statement of 21 June 1960 to a visiting writers delegation.

Ibid., 4-5.

[12] *Peking Review*, 14 September 1960.

[13] See Chen Yi's remarks to a visiting Japanese delegation. Ibid., 2 August 1960. Also see *Peking Review*, 5 October 1962, 13-4.

[14] Ibid., 2 August 1960.

[15] Ibid., 11 October 1960, 22-3.

[16] Ibid., 16 June 1961, 27. See also *Renmin Ribao* 23 June 1961.

[17] *Peking Review*, 8 September 1961, 8-11.

[18] *Renmin Ribao*, 8 September 1961.

[19] *Peking Review*, 24 November 1961, 7.

[20] Ibid., 4 January 1963, 30-1.

[21] Ibid., 19 January 1962, 13-4.

[22] Foreign Minister Ohira cited in Morunosuke Kajima, *A Brief Diplomatic History of Modern Japan* (Tokyo, 1965) 143.

[23] *Peking Review*, 26 June 1964, 10-2.

[24] Ibid., no. 4, 1964, 7.

[25] *China Today*, 30 January 1964, 2-3. See also *Peking Review*, 31 January 1964, 5.

[26] See *Peking Review*, 14 February 1964, 20-1.

[27] Ibid., 28 February 1964, 21.

[28] Ibid., 21 February 1964, 20.

[29] Zhou Enlai's Report on the work of the Government to the First Session of the Third National People's Congress, 21-22 December 1964. *Peking Review*, 1 January 1965, 17 and 19.

[30] *Peking Review*, 22 September 1967, 29.

[31] Ibid., 4 December 1964, 30.

[32] Ibid., 2 July 1965, 7-8.

[33] Ibid., 19 November 1965, 5-6.

[34] See ibid., 10 December 1965, 5-8 and 17 December 1965, 18-20.

[35] Xinhua News Agency, 27 September 1963.

[36] See *Remin Ribao*, 8 September 1961.

[37] See *The Hindu*, 14 July 1964.

[38] See *Pravda*, 2 and 19 September 1964, as translated in the *Current Digest of the Soviet Press*, 16 September 1964 and 23 September 1964. Premier Khrushchov considered Mao's support as an attempt to "sow seeds of strife and enmity". *News and Views from the Soviet Union* (New Delhi), 28 September 1964, 3.

[39] *Japan Times*, 2 August 1964.

[40] *Renmin Ribao*, 4 February 1966; as translated in *Peking Review*, 11 February 1966, 11-3.

[41] *Renmin Ribao*, 2 February 1966; *Peking Review*, 4 February 1966, 11-2.

[42] *Peking Review*, 5 August 1966, 17-8.

[43] Ibid., 28 October 1966, 39.

[44] Ibid., 18 August 1967, 34-5.

[45] Mingko, "Japanese Economy Going Downhill," ibid., 18 and 25 March 1966.

[46] Ibid., 15 September 1967, 33.

[47] Ibid., 22 September 1967, 29.

48 Osamu Miyosi, "How the Japanese Press yielded to Peking," *Survey* Autum 1972, 112-4.

49 *Peking Review*, 15 September 1967, 32.

50 Ibid., 20 October 1967, 38.

51 Commentator's article entitled : "Strip Eisaku Sato of His Disguise," in *Renmin Ribao*, 23 October 1967, as translated in *Peking Review*, 3 November 1967, 27-8.

52 Chae Jin-Lee, *Japan Faces China : Political and Economic Relations in the Postwar Era* (London, 1967), 67.

53 *Peking Review*, 15 December 1967, 30.

54 Ibid., 26 April 1968, 27-8.

55 Ibid., 23 August 1968, 19-20.

56 Kyosuke Mirotsu, "Trouble Between Congress," *Current Scene*, 15 March 1967, 1-12.

57 Lawrence Olson, *Japan in Postwar Asia* (New York, 1970), 125.

58 *Renmin Ribao*, 18 September 1968.

59 See Sato's statement in the Diet, 25 January 1965. *Contemporary Japan*, June 1965, 464. See also Premier Ikeda's statement in the Diet, 28 September 1961. Ibid., March 1962, 374.

60 Speech by Foreign Minister Kosaka in the Diet, 20 January 1962. *Japan Times*, 20 January 1962. See also statement by Japanese representative in the UN General Assembly, 20 November 1967. UN Document A/PV 1600, 20 Noveber 1967, 37-43.

61 Ambassador Ryujiy Takeuchi's Address before Yankton College in the United States, 6 December 1966. See *Japan Report* (Embassy of Japan in USA), 15 December 1966, 3-5.

62 See ibid., 15 March 1967, 3 and 7.

63 *Contemporary Japan*, May 1967, 692-3.

64 Statement in New York, November 1967. *Japan Report* (New York), 20 November 1967, 9-10.

65 *Renmin Ribao*, 26 January 1968.

66 See Xinhua News Agency, 11 July 1969 and *Renmin Ribao*, 23 July 1969.

67 Sheldon W. Simon, "Sino-Japanese Relations in China's Asian Policy," *Current Developments in Mainland China*, 15 November 1969, 2.

68 Ibid., 29 May 1969,

69 Foreign Broadcast Information Service, *Daily Report*, 25 March 1969, A-7.

70 Xinhua News Agency, 1 December 1969.

71 Ibid., 10 November 1969.

72 *Survival*, January 1970, 27-8.

73 *Pacific Community*, January 1970, 335-6.

74 *Renmin Ribao*, 28 November 1969, as translated in *Peking Review*, 5 December 1969, 14-6.

75 *Peking Review*, 5 December 1969, 11.

76 See ibid., 26 June 1970, 24. See also ibid., 24 July 1970, 17-9; ibid., 6 November 1970, 12-3; and ibid., 4 December 1970, 13-4.

77 Ibid., 25 September 1970, 27.

78 Ibid., 7 August 1970, 27-8.

79 Ibid., 25 June 1971, 7-8.

80 Lee, n. 52, 42.

5. Economic Relations, 1958-1971

The severance of all trade relations with Japan in 1958 over the Nagasaki Flag incident led to a severe contraction of trade between China and Japan. Japan's exports to China dropped from $60.5 million in 1957 to $2.7 million in 1960, and its imports from China fell from $80. 5 million in 1957 to $20.7 million in 1960. However, trade between the two countries never came to a complete halt as it continued through Hong Kong or through the mechanism of the so-called "friendly firms" and other non-governmental channels.

In the post-1958 period, China laid considerable emphasis on the principle that politics and economics were inseparable from each other and that in the absence of normalization of political relations, it was futile to hope for a thriving economic intercourse. Zhou Enlai ennunciated "three political principles" for Sino-Japanese relations in August 1958, viz. Japan should not (1) regard China as an enemy; (2) participate in any plot to create "two Chinas"; and (3) obstruct normalization of relations with China.[1] So long as Japan continued to support the Taiwan Government and co-operate with it, it could not hope to expand its trade relations with the People's Republic of China or to establish formal political relations with Beijing.

On 27 August 1960 Zhou Enlai laid down the three principles for Sino-Japanese trade relations as an important supplement to the three political principles. These were: (i) government agreement; (ii) private contracts; and (iii) special consideration in individual cases. The aim of these principles was to establish three stages in the process of restoration of Sino-Japanese relations and to repudiate the legitimacy of the

Taipeh regime. The first stage consisted of individually approved trade transactions. It was made clear that requests for trade deals submitted by Japanese individuals or organizations would be approved by China only on special consideration in case of special difficulties of Japanese small and medium industries. The second stage consisted of the so-called friendly trade. Trade transactions of this category would be limited to those Japanese private enterprises or the so-called "friendly firms" which adhered to the three political principles and the three trade principles enunciated by Beijing. The third stage consisted of Government-to-Government trade. The last stage came only after considerable progress had been made at the first and second stages of trade transactions.[2]

Special consideration trade began in 1959 when the Japanese Socialist Party (JSP) and the General Council of Japanese Trade Unions (*Sohyo*) reached agreement with the All-China Federation of Trade Unions to conduct trade geared to the needs of Japan's small and medium-sized enterprises in commodities like medicinal herbs and sweet chestnuts. This trade was limited (reached only about $1 million) and gradually faded out with the growth of LT and friendly firm trade.[3]

Private trade with "friendly firms" began in late 1960 and early 1961. It represented a marked improvement over the consideration trade. China's sympathetic attitude towards trade with Japan at this juncture was the outcome of the failure of the ambitious Great Leap Forward and poor agricultural production due to a series of natural calamities which began around 1959. More importantly, the growing Sino-Soviet rift, especially the wholesale departure of Soviet experts engaged in the execution of various projects in China and declining Sino-Soviet trade, made it imperative for China to import materials and technology from abroad in order to ensure economic development at home.[4]

Late in 1960, Beijing named fifty "friendly firms" in Japan with which it would be willing to do business. The list of friendly firms grew longer with the passing of time. They numbered 67 in March 1961, 108 in January 1962, and stood at 350 at the end of 1964. More and more Japanese firms accepted the three "political principles". Since the Chinese held the ultimate right to recognize or reject Japan's "friendly

firms", they could easily obtain favourable commercial terms
in such specific arrangements as pricing, inspection, insurance,
arbitration, and shipping. These terms were far more beneficial
to China than what it had gained from the past four private
trade agreements. The Japanese Government also repealed
the principle of maintaining a compulsory barter trade system
on 15 April 1961 and formally approved the one-way cash
settlement formula for imports from China.[5]

The *People's Daily* declared in October 1960 that so long as
the Government of Japan continued to be hostile to China,
connived with the United States in maturing the "two Chinas"
plot, and obstructed the progress of Sino-Japanese relations
in the direction of normalization, it would be impossible for the
two countries to resume trade on a large scale. It, however,
considered private economic contracts on an individual basis
both "indispensable and necessary for the two peoples."[6]

Although Sino-Japnese trade had fallen sharply to $23
million in 1960, it rose to $47.55 million in 1961, and reached
$84.84 million in 1962. Japanese exports in 1962 doubled
over the preceding year largely due to a sharp increase in the
shipments of steel materials to China. Moreover, Japanese
authorization of deferred payments for export of steel materials
and fertilizers in May 1962 also substantially contributed to the
expansion of trade between China and Japan."[7]

LT Trade Agreement, 1963-1967

While the conciliatory Chinese policy had enabled Sino-Japanese
trade to increase almost four-fold during 1960-62, "friendly
trade" proved inadequate to meet the needs of the Chinese
economy. China, therefore, endeavoured to increase its trade
with Japan by approaching influential figures in the ruling
Liberal Democratic Party.

In September 1962 Premier Zhou Enlai held talks with LDP
Dietman Kenzo Matsumura. Zhou suggested that since it
would be difficult at present to conclude a government trade
agreement, China and Japan should proceed for the time being
with private trade with a view to expanding it progressively
in the years to come.[8] Next month Tatsunosuke Takasaki,
former Minister of International Trade and Industry (1958-59)
and also LDP Dietman, visited China. On 9 November 1962

he signed a non-governmental LT Trade Agreement known as such after the initials of its two signatories—Liao Cheng-chih and Tatsunosuke Takasaki. This five-year trade agreement (1963-67) provided for an average annual trade turn-over of £36 million ($100.8 million).[9] The LT Agreement was to be implemented by an annual "Detailed Agreement" specifying the exact quantities of specific products and other terms. Articles to be exported by China under the agreement included coal, iron ore, soyabeans, corn, salt, etc. Japan agreed to export steel (including special steel), chemical fertilizer, farm chemicals, farm machinery, farm tools, plant equipment, etc. The two sides agreed to discuss and settle later on the *modus operandi* as regards deferment of payments on certain commodities which Japan exported to China as well as payment by instalments on industrial plants. On 16 November 1962, the "Japan-China Over-All Trade Liaison Council" was established in Tokyo, with Tatsunosuke Takasaki as its first Chairman, to facilitate implementation of the LT Trade Agreement.

The LT agreement was an important landmark in Sino-Japanese economic relations. The fact that a senior politician of the LDP had signed the agreement gave it a semi-governmental character.

Immediately after the signing of the LT Trade Agreement, Kazuo Suzuki, Director-General of the Japan-China Trade Promotion Association, and Eiichi Shukutani and Ichizo Kimura of the Japan International Trade Promotion Association, visited China and signed an agreement on 27 December 1962 with the China Council for the Promotion of International Trade. The agreement called for the holding of a Japanese Merchandise Fair in Beijing and Shanghai during 1963 and a Chinese Merchandise Fair in Tokyo and Osaka in the following year. It was agreed to promote exchanges of visits between members of economic and trade circles and organizations concerned with a view to the development of friendly economic and trade relations between the two peoples.[10] The idea of promoting technical exchanges found favour with both sides. In order to facilitate trade, they agreed to strengthen relations between Chinese and Japanese banks and to institute direct letters of credit between the banks of the two countries.

The first contract between China and Japan under the five-year LT trade agreement was signed on 11 January 1963. Under this contract Japan agreed to export 250,000 tons of ammonium chloride fertilizer (worth US $8 million) to China, while China undertook to sell 450,000 tons of salt to Japan. Japan agreed to China's settlement for its purchase with a lump-sum cash payment "after an 18-month deferment."

A group of executives of the Kurashiki Rayon Company, leading manufactures of synthetic fibres in Japan, signed a contract on 13 July 1963 to export vinylon plant facilities worth $20 (million (and capable of producing 30 tons of vinylon a day) on a five-year deferred payment arrangement. The Japanese Government approved the contract on 20 August 1963 but insisted that interest rate should be raised from 4.5 per cent to 6 per cent. This was meant to avoid giving the impression that special consideration was being given to the Beijing regime. At the same time, it did not affect China, for the price of the plant was reduced by 200 million Yen (from 7,403 million Yen to 7,200 million Yen), so that the actual amount to be paid by China would remain the same.

On 7 September 1963 formal contracts were signed in Beijing by ten large Japanese steel manufacturers to import 100,000 tons of Kailan coking coal from China in 1963. Five major steel companies (Yawata Iron and Steel, Fuji Iron and Steel, Nippon Kokan, Kawasaki Steel, and Amagasaki Iron and Steel) also signed a barter contract for import of 20,000 tons of Chinese iron ore in 1963 in exchange for 2,000 tons of steel sheet—the first import of Chinese iron ore since the Pacific War. The ore was of exceptionally high iron content.

By this time the Japan Economic Research Council (founded in 1962 by the Federation of Economic Oorganisations, *Keidanren*, the Japan Foreign Trade Council, and other influential economic groups in Japan) had come to the conclusion that Japanese businessmen should move with greater initiative without depending exclusively upon "friendly" trade. It felt that it was quite natural and reasonable for Japan to embark on a a programme of increased trade with Communist nations from "an independent standpoint," i.e. without yielding or paying heed to pressures from the United States.[11]

Negotiations for the second year LT trade began in Sep-

tember 1963 when a 25-member Japanese trade delegation[12] led
by Kaheita Okazaki, Chairman of All Nippon Airways, arrived
in Beijing on 16 September 1963. Before the mission left
Tokyo, Foreign Minister Ohira assured Okazaki (on 11
September 1963) that the Japanese Foreign Office would not
interfere with Party or Diet members joining the mission since
the nature of the mission was purely private and its objective
purely economic, the Government being involved only while
dealing with problems of foreign exchange control or export
financing. In the joint communique that Okazki signed with
Lu Hsu-chang on 23 September 1963, the two parties agreed
to expand trade in the second year in accordance with the
principles set forth in the memorandum on the good foundation
already laid. They maintained that the continuous expansion
of Sino-Japanese trade on the basis of equality and mutual
benefit not only conformed to the desire of the people of China
and Japan, but also strengthened the friendly relations between
the two countries.[13]

On 4 October 1963, one day before the opening of the
Japanese Industrial Exhibition in Beijing, an organization known
as the China-Japan Friendship Association with Kuo Mo-jo
as the Honorary President was set up under the auspices of
nineteen people's organizations, including the All-China Fede-
ration of Trade Unions, the National Women's Federation, the
All-China Youth Federation, the China Peace Committee, the
Chinese Committee for Afro-Asian Solidarity, and the Chinese
People's Association for Cultural Relations with Foreign
Countries.

The continuous development of friendly trade and LT trade,
which formed the "two wheels of a cart," led to a two-fold
increase in Sino-Japanese trade, from $137 million in 1963 to
$310.36 million in 1964.

On 19 April 1964 representatives of the office of Liao Cheng-
chih and the office of Tatsunosuke Takasaki exchanged three
documents in Beijing. One was an agreement on exchange of
representatives and establishment of liaison offices. Under this
agreement Liao Cheng-chih was to maintain an office in Tokyo,
with three representatives and a staff consisting of two members. Similarly, Tatsunosuke Takasaki was to maintain an
office in Beijing. These liaison offices were established in

February 1965. The second agreement related to exchange of correspondents. Each side was allowed to keep eight correspondents and was charged with responsibility for the security of the correspondents of the other side and with the obligation to provide them with facilities, including freedom of correspondence, for their reporting. The correspondents of both sides, the agreement stated, should abide by the rules governing foreign correspondents and enjoy the same privileges as given to other foreign correspondents. The third agreement was on trade based on the LT Trade Agreement.[14]

The "Yoshida Letter"

Taiwan strongly objected to the financing of the Kurashiki Rayon Company's sale of a vinylon plant (worth $20 million) on a five-year credit term in 1963 by the Export-Import Bank of Japan and the repatriation of Chou Hung-ching, a Communist Chinese defector, on 9 January 1964 to the People's Republic of China. The Ambassador of Nationalist China to Japan, Chang Li-sheng, said that the use of state bank funds to finance the transaction constituted a form of economic aid to China. Taipeh announced the resignation of its Ambassador to Japan and, on 31 December 1963, recalled *Charge d'Affaires* and four Councillors from Japan. On 11 January 1964, it suspended all new Government procurement in Japan, thereby creating a serious crisis in its relations with Japan.

In order to pacify the feelings of Taiwan, Prime Minister Ikeda on 21 January 1964 stated before a joint session of the Diet that Japan would adopt "realistic policies" in dealing with the People's Republic of China by engaging in trade relations on the basis of the principle of "separating politics from economics" and without prejudice to the friendly ties with Taiwan. This statement, however, did not prove adequate. Ikeda, therefore, sent Shigeru Yoshida, a former Premier and senior leader of the Liberal Democratic Party, to Taiwan in March 1964 to meet Jiang Jieshi (Chiang Kai-shek). Yoshida wrote a letter on 30 May 1964 to Chang Chun, Secretary-General of the Presidential office, assuring Taiwan that the Government of Japan would not allow Japanese exporters to use Export-Import Bank funds for the purpose of financing their sales to China. Taiwan was obviously satisfied by this so-called "Yoshida Letter" because on 18 July 1964, it lifted its ban on the purchase of Japanese goods.

The "Yoshida Letter" proved to be a major obstacle in the expansion of Sino-Japanese trade. In accordance with the "Yoshida Letter" the Japanese Government refused to extend credit for the sale of a vinylon plant (contracted for by the Dai Nippon Spinning Company in September 1964) and for a $3.7 million (freighter (contracted for by the Hitachi Shipubilding and Engineering Company on 16 November 1964). This prompted China to cancel already signed contracts for the export of Nichibo Company's vinylon plant (worth $26.5 million), freighters from Hitachi Shipbuilding and Engineering Company and fertilizer plants of Toyo Engineering Company. In fact, out of a total twenty-one orders for complete plants placed by China with non-Communist countries during 1964-65 only two went to Japan.[15]

The Chinese Press regarded the "Yoshida Letter" as casting a "dark shadow over Sino-Japanese trade" and a repudiation of the principle of "separating politics from economics", a principle said to be basic to the policy of the Japanese Government towards China. Sato was even accused of being a spokesman of the forces of militarism in Japan "which were thinking of staging a comeback and eventually seizing once again the Chinese territory of Taiwan."[16]

Influential Japanese businessmen and Diet members urged the Government of Japan and the ruling Liberal Democratic Party to disown the "Yoshida Letter" by declaring that it did not represent official policy. On 2 August 1965, Japanese Minister of International Trade and Industry Takeo Miki stated in a Diet Committee that Japan was not bound by the "Yoshida Letter". The following day, Prime Minister Sato told the House of Councillors that the "Yoshida Letter" was a private lettter and hence was not binding on the Government of Japan. Beijing demanded the retraction of the Letter. Japan, however, continued to bar the use of Export-Import Bank funds for financing trade with mainland China.[17] It was obviously difficult for Japan to casually discard Taiwan, which was a very important market for Japanese goods and had Japanese investments exceeding $100 million.

Non-governmental trade between China and Japan continued to rise inspite of the handicaps placed by the "Yoshida Letter". Thus, the volume of trade in 1965 stood at $470 million, which was 50 per cent higher than the 1964 level of $310 million. A strong lobby against the "Yoshida Letter" gradually emerged. Japanese firms began circumventing the "Yoshida Letter" by selling plant and equipment to British, French, and West German firms engaged in trade with China and a second vinylon plant was exported to China in 1965 without major repercussions.

After negotiations extending up to four months, Japan and China signed a contract in January 1966 for the supply of chemical fertilizers worth US $66 million—nearly 85 per cent of which was under the LT Agreement. This was the single largest contract to be signed between the two countries. With this contract, the LT Agreement was more or less completed with the value of the total trade reaching US $200 million, and import and export equalized as the Chinese had insisted while signing the LT Agreement for the fourth year.

During the Great Proletarian Cultural Revolution, Sino-Japanese trade could not make much headway. This was also partly due to the success of export drives of certain West European nations in China. As a result, Sino-Japanese trade decreased by about 10 per cent in 1967, compared with the previous year, dropping to $557 million. Beijing criticised the Sato regime for conniving at the attempts allegedly being made by certain Japanese Right-Wing organisations to sabotage and obstruct Sino-Japanese trade. When the relations between the Chinese Communist Party and the Japanese Communist Party (JCP) became severely strained late in 1966, China cut off all contact with the JCP-guided Japan-China Trade Promotion Association (JCTPA), which had been carrying on a large proportion of the friendship trade. Under pressure from China, Japanese firms transferred their allegiance from the JCTPA to the China-backed Japan International Trade Promotion Association (JITPA). As a result, the JCTPA was eventually dissolved. Over two hundred firms left the JCP-supported Japan-China Friendship Association also and joined the rival Japan-China Trade Association.

Although the yearly agreements under LT trade had a better record of implementation than the trade agreements in the fifties. yet they were not fully carried out. The percentage of fulfilment was 96.5 per cent for the first agreement, 77.8 per cent for the second agreement, 81.5 per cent for the third agreement, and 90.6 per cent for the fourth agreement. Political differences between China and Japan, the embargo, and Japan's refusal to finance Sino-Japanese trade with Export-Import Bank funds were among the main reasons for the failure to fulfil agreements.

The main Chinese exports to Japan were agricultural products (soyabean, rice, fruits, vegetabless), minerals (coal, pig iron, iron ore), and other raw materials. In return, China imported from Japan fertilizers, steel, machinery, textiles, chemicals, and other manufactured goods.

The LT trade had several shortcomings from China's point of view. Those firms designated by China as friendly trading firms were mostly financially weak, small and medium-scale enterprises. Moreover, since many major trading firms in Japan had formed "dummy" companies to engage in trade with China, most of the friendly trading turned out to be nothing more than a temporary transaction involving only a small amount of business. Besides, as demands for Japanese industrial plants, heavy machinery, fertilizers, and the like increased, such small-scale trade through the friendly trading firms made it impossible for China to carry out the planned transactions that it desired.[18]

Memorandum Trade 1968-1971

The LT Trade Agreement expired at the end of 1967 and thereafter trade relations between China and Japan were placed on an annual basis, under the Memorandum Trade (MT). The two sides renamed their respective offices as the Memorandum Trade Offices. At the time of the signing of annual trade agreements, China usually insisted on the insertion of political statements criticising the policy of the Sato government. The exchange of trade offices and the participation of important LDP leaders imparted an official colouring presumably pleasing to Beijing. Besides, permission to station journalists at these offices greatly facilitated the gathering and dissemination of information. Another very interesting feature was that the

Japanese Ministry of International Trade and Industry allocated government funds to the Japan Export Trade Organization (JETRO). These funds amounted to roughly $180,000 annually which covered all expenses, including personnel and maintenance of the Japanese MT trade offices.[19]

After protracted negotiations, a one-year agreement was signed on 6 March 1968 providing for trade to the tune of $100 million. The Japanese delegation led by Furui and Tagawa accepted China's three political principles. In the minutes of the talks signed in Beijing on 19 March 1968, they also expressed the view that "friendly contacts and trade relations between the peoples of China and Japan can grow only if tit-for-tat struggles are carried out against the . . . enemies headed by U.S. imperialism."[20] On his return to Japan, Furui urged Sato to put an end to what he called "anachronous separation of politics and economics" and to assume a truly positive posture in dealing with China politically as well as economically.[21]

By 1968, the "friendly firms" also began to feel the heat of Chinese disfavour, for several of their representatives in Beijing were arrested, at least one of them for espionage.[22]

In 1969 Japanese negotiators headed by Yoshimi Furui were able to secure another annual agreement on 4 April 1969 after they had agreed to the insertion of political statements. The communique issued after the talks fixed the responsibility for the deterioration in Sino-Japanese relations on the Sato Government; reaffirmed faith in the three political principles; reiterated that the principle of separating economics from politics was a great obstacle in the way of the development of relations between the two countries; agreed that the government of the People's Republic of China was the only legitimate Government representing the Chinese people and that Taiwan was an inseparable part of China; denounced the Peace Treaty between Japan and Taiwan as "hostile to the Chinese people" and "illegal", and denounced the US-Japanese Mutual Security Treaty as a menace not only to China but to all Asian peoples. Moreover, the Japanese delegation expressed "its understanding" of the Chinese position that the Sato Government was collaborating with "US imperialism in its policy of aggression in Asia" by prepetuating the US-Japanese Mutual Security Treaty which was an obstacle to improved relations between Japan and

China.[23]   There was an outcry in Japan when the Furui communique was made public. It was, however, shortlived. No disciplinary action was taken against Furui, a member of the Liberal Democratic Party and a leading advocate of *detente* in Sino-Japanese relations.   The Miki and Fujiyama factions within the ruling Liberal Democratic Party defended Furui by saying that he had signed the communique merely to save trade relations between Japan and China and that there was nothing improper in the means he had chosen.   The Japanese Premier might not have been happy about the Furui communique, but he stated in public that Furui was to be congratulated on his success in keeping the Memorandum Trade link intact.

The trade talks held in 1970 were concluded only after the Japanese side had agreed to sign statements critical of the Government of Japan.   The communique issued on 19 April 1970 sternly condemned the US-Japanese communique of 21 November 1969.   It alleged that the US-Japanese communique of November 1969 had carried US-Japanese military collusion to a new stage and had enlarged and reinforced the US-Japanese Security Treaty.   The Japanese delegation, headed by Furui, also accepted the Chinese contention that the Sato Government had been stepping up arms expansion by increasing its military budget and that "the revival of Japanese militarism" was a serious threat to the countries of Asia and further aggravated tension in the Far East.[24]   The trade agreement envisaged trade worth $70.4 million.

On 19 April 1970 Premier Zhou Enlai ennunciated four additional conditions—the "four principles of Sino-Japanese trade"—which were later reproduced in the communique issued at the conclusion of the trade talks in 1971.   These principles asserted that China would not trade with (i) factories and firms supporting Taiwan or South Korea; (ii) enterprises with large investments in Taiwan or South Korea; (iii) enterprises supplying arms and ammunition to US "imperialism for aggression" against Vietnam, Laos, and Cambodia; and (iv) US-Japanese joint enterprises or subsidiaries of US companies in Japan.[25]

The communique issued on 1 March 1971 condemned Japanese "reactionaries" for intensifying collusion with US imperialism in reviving Japanese militarism and joining US imperialism's aggression and expansion in Asia.   It criticized various aspects of Japan's foreign policy. It denounced a joint enterprise undertaken by Japan, South Korea, and Taiwan to exploit undersea oil deposits off their coasts and said that it was a "flagrant encroachment of China's sovereignty." It declared that Taiwan was an inseparable part of China. The communique described Japan's treaty with Taiwan as "illegal and null and void" and called for its abolition.[26]

Mitsui and Mitsubishi, the "hawks of big business" engaged in trading heavily with Taiwan and South Korea and thus little interested in the China trade, criticized the above-mentioned new trade conditions. (They joined the "friendly firms" in 1972.) Other industrial giants, however, were not prepared to do likewise. Indeed, one by one, they expressed their willingness to comply with them. Even Japan Airlines, a Government corporation, made it known early in 1971 that it would abide by Zhou's terms.[27]

The annual Memorandum Trade talks had become a ritual in which the Chinese authorities would make the Japanese sweat for a week or so on the political section of the communique before expeditiously agreeing to the economic content. The Japanese negotiators passed this off as justifiable duty, and publicily Sato bore these annual humiliations serenely.[28] Japanese negotiators had their fill of painful experiences, being caught in a sort of vice between the Chinese and Japanese Governments.

Memorandum Trade constituted 21.1 per cent of total Sino-Japanese trade in 1968. Thereafter it showed a downward trend. It declined to 9.1 per cent in 1971 (see Table 1 on page 77).

Fishery Co-operation

Fishery co-operation between China and Japan was also renewed in 1963, i.e. after five years. A delegation of the Japan-China Fishery Association, headed by Tsunejiro Hiratsuka, paid a friendly visit to China in January 1963 at the invitation of the Chinese People's Institute of Foreign Affairs. The delegation had "cordial talks" with Premier Zhou Enlai, Vice-Premier Chen Yi, and other Government leaders and specifically discussed fishing in the Yellow Sea and the East China Sea with

TABLE 1

Japan-China Trade and LT (MT) and Friendly
Trade, 1962-1971
(in thousand dollars)

Year	Total Volume of Foreign Trade (1)	LT (MT) Trade (2)	Friendly Trade (3)
1963	137,016	64,115 (46.7%)	72,901 (53.3%)
1964	310,489	128,427 (41.1%)	182,026 (58.6%)
1965	469,741	179,186 (38.1%)	290,555 (61.9%)
1966	621,387	205,228 (33.0%)	416,159 (67.0%)
1967	557,733	153,483 (27.5%)	404,250 (72.5%)
1968	549,623	115,920 (21.1%)	433,703 (78.9%)
1969	625,343	69,600 (11.7%)	555,743 (89.9%)
1970	822,696	70,000 (8.5%)	752,696 (91.5%)
1971	900,000	84,220 (9.1%)	815.780 (90.9%)

Note: (1) The total volume of foreign trade is based on the customs clearance basis.

(2) LT (1963-1967) and MT (1968-1970) trade are estimates based on the contract basis.

(3) Friendly trade: (1)—(2).

Source: Japan External Trade Organisation (JETRO), *How to Approach the China Market* (New York, 1972), 131.

the China Fishery Association and the Chinese People's Association for Cultural Relations with Foreign Countries. A memorandum was exchanged as a result of these talks.

An important event in Sino-Japanese economic relations was the signing of a non-official fishery agreement in Beijing on 9 November 1963 by the China Fishery Association and the Japan-China Fishery Association. The agreement was to be effective for two years from the date of signature. This agreement not only provided for the facilities needed by fishermen of the two countries in the Yellow Sea and the East China Sea for peaceful and safe operations and for protection of fishery resources but also set up procedures for avoiding disputes during operations of the fishing boats of the two sides. It also stipulated scientific and technical exehanges and intercourse of personnel between the fishery circles of China and Japan. Besides, it provided workers in the fishing industry with favourable conditions against sea emergencies. For these reasons, the new agreement was considered to be of "important significance to the growth of friendly cooperation between the fishery circles of China aad Japan and of Sino-Japanese friendship". It was stated to have been signed "at a time when Sino-Japanese friendship reached a new upsurge."[29]

A joint statement issued on 9 November 1963 on behalf of five Chinese and Japanese Organisations (namely, the two fishery associations mentioned above, the two friendship associations in the two countries, and an organization called the Chinese People's Association for Cultural Relations with Foreign Countries) expressed the belief that the fishery agreement "will contribute to deepening the friendship and fraternity between the Chinese and Japanese peoples, normalizing the friendly intercourse between the two countries and safeguarding peace in Asia and the world."

As compared to the April 1955 agreement, the November 1963 fishery agreement provided for an area of restricted catch for sea-bream and permitted many more Chinese fishing vessels to operate in the East China Sea and Yellow Sea. Japan agreed to open three ports (Nagasaki, Tamanoura, and Yemakawa) for Chinese fishing boats while China agreed to open two of its ports (Woosung and Lienyu-chiang) for Japanese fishermen.[30] On the expiry of the 1963 agreement, another two-year non-Governmental fishery agreement was signed on 17 December 1965.[31] The life of the 1965 agreement was twice prolonged, in 1967 and 1968, at the request of the Japanese. However, on 23 December 1969, in response to a Japanese request for a third extension, the Fishery Association of China consented to such an extension only for a period of six months.

This step was taken because the Chinese Fishery Association alleged that Japanese fishing boats had committed various violations of the agreement, e.g. extensively using nets with meshes smaller than those stipulated in the agreement in a deliberate attempt to ruin the fishing resources, and for encroaching continually upon China's fishing preserves and territorial waters. The Chinese Fishery Association in its cable to the Japan-China Fishery Association of Japan also condemned the "reactionary" forces among Japanese fishery circles for following the Sato Government's pro-US and anti-Chinese policy and for sabotaging the Sino-Japanese non-Governmental fishery agreement. It said that the Japanese side should, within six months, give a satisfactory explanation for all the charges, if it wanted a prolongation of the agreement beyond six months.[32]

Conclusion

Beijing's tough approach towards trade with Japan after 1958 was reflective of the radicalism in Chinese foreign policy and domestic economic policies, e.g. the Great Leap Forward. If China's intention was to defeat the Government headed by Nobusuke Kishi, its hopes remained unrealized. In fact, such a step probably harmed the Socialists and helped Kishi in getting re-elected. The growing Sino-Soviet rift, especially the wholesale departure of Soviet experts engaged in the execution of various projects in China and the declining trend in Sino-Soviet trade, led China to adopt a more concilatory attitude and to resume trade contacts with Japan.

There was no significant development in Sino-Japanese relations in the late sixties largely because of the Cultural Revolution and the controversial "Yoshida Letter" (abrogated in 1968). The Yoshida Letter underlined the continuing influence of Taiwan in Sino-Japanese trade. This was because trade between Japan and Taiwan rose steadly from $280 million in 1964 to $576 million in 1968, with a balance decidedly in favour of Japan. Japan also ranked third in foreign investment in Taiwan.

Japanese exports to China began to exceed imports in 1965 for the first time since 1950 largely because of an increase in Chinese demand for Japanese goods and lower freight rates (about one fourth) than those on the West Europe-China route. Japan's advantage over West European nations lies in its exports to China of deadweight and bulky cargos as well as perishable goods.[33] Japanese imports from China could not rise because of problems involving protection of domestic agriculture and price fluctuations.[34]

Trade between China and Japan continued to grow despite Beijing's seemingly hostile public attitude towards the Sato administration, particularly to his policies of normalizing relations with South Korea, his support for America's Vietnam policy, and his equivocal stand on the admission of China to the United Nations. Occasionally, however, the Chinese leaders. laid stress on the inseparability of politics and economics, and observed that a conducive political atmosphere and friendly relations are required for the development of Sino-Japanese trade.[35]

NOTES

[1] See *Peking Review*, 14 September 1960, 25-6.
[2] Statement of Zhou Enlai made to Kazuo Suzuki, Managing Director of the Japan-China Trade Promotion Association, 27 August 1960. *China Today*, 24 September 1980, 7-8.
[3] Dan Fenno Henderson and Tasuku Matsuo, "Trade with Japan," in Victor H. Li, ed., *Law and Politics in China's Foreign Trade* (London, 1977), 38.
[4] Japan External Trade Organization (JETRO), *How to Approach the China Market* (New York, 1972), 76.
[5] Ibid., 76-7.
[6] *Peking Review*, 18 October 1960, 11.
[7] Jetro, n. 4, 76 and 100.
[8] Ibid., 78-9.
[9] *Survey of China Mainland Press*, no. 2860, 15 November 1960, 39-40.
[10] *Peking Review*, 11 January 1963, 20.
[11] This was stated in a report (which had been under study for nine months) released by the Japan Economic Research Council on 17 September 1963. The report had also noted that the Chinese, like the Russians, had never failed to fulfil their contractual obligations till then. Besides, China had managed to tide over its foreign currency crisis.
[12] The Mission included four Diet members belonging to the Liberal Democratic Party, officials of JETRO (Japan External Trade Organization), and representatives of different industries such as a fertilizers, chemicals, farming tools and machinery, special steel, food and animal foodstuffs, and banking as well as of agriculture.
[13] *Survey of China Mainland Press*, no. 3069, 27 September 1963, 24. See also *Peking Review*, 27 September 1963, 4.
[14] *Xinhua News Agency*, 19 April 1964, as reproduced in *Survey of China Mainland Press*, no. 3205, 24 April 1964, 27-8.
[15] Colina MacDougall, "China's Foreign Trade," *Far Eastern Economic Review*, 27 January 1966, 124, Table V.
[16] See *Peking Review*, 19 February 1965, 31.
[17] See George P. Jan, "Japan's Trade with Communist China," *Asian Survey*, December 1969, 914.

18 JETRO, n. 4, 78.
19 Henderson and Matsuo, n. 3, 42-3.
20 See Jan, n. 17, 915.
21 Yung H. Park, "The Politics of Japan's China Decision," *Orbis*, Summer 1975, 563.
22 See Lawrence Olson, *Japan in Postwar Asia* (London, 1970), 128.
23 *Peking Review*, 11 April 1969, 38-9.
24 For the text of communique, see ibid., 24 April 1970, 31-3.
25 For the text of communique, see ibid., 12 March 1971, 24-5.
26 Ibid.
27 *Japan Times Weekly*, 27 February 1971.
28 Armin H. Meyer, *Assignment Tokyo: An Ambassidor's Journal* (New York, 1974) 126-7.
29 Foreign Broadcast Information Service, *Daily Report*, 24 December 1969, A 1-2.
30 See *Far Eastern Economic Review*, 28 November 1963.
31 For text of agreement see Luke T. Lee, *China and International Agreements: A Study of Compliance* (Durham, N.C., 1969) 204-7.
32 Foreign Broadcast Information Service, *Daily Report*, 24 December 1969, A1-2.
33 JETRO, n. 4, 95.
34 Ibid., 93.
35 *Survey of China Mainland Press*, no. 3514.

6. Normalization of Relations

By pursuing a hard line and assuming a tough posture in international affairs, Beijing had landed itself in a very difficult situation—encirclement by hostile Powers (almost a combination of India, Japan, the Soviet Union, and the United States), diplomatic isolation in the world, military confrontation with the USSR, a stagnant economy, and loss of diplomatic flexibility in the world. Hence, as soon as the dust settled down over the Cultural Revolution, the Chinese leaders, especially Zhou Enlai, sought to repair the damage. By playing down the demand that foreign Governments should accept Taiwan as an inseparable part of China,[1] they sought to expand China's trade relations further and gain diplomatic recognition from a large number of countries, especially from the Western Powers. By inviting President Nixon for a visit and thereby initiating a process of *rapprochement* with the United States, by gaining membership in the United Nations with a permanent seat in the Security Council, and by securing repudiation of Taiwan's claim to be represented in the world body,[2] China succeeded in ending its diplomatic isolation in the world, in breaking the chain of encirclement, in effectively countering the power and influence of the Soviet Union, in undermining Soviet ability to generate and exploit Sino-US hostility, in isolating Taiwan, and in recovering flexibility in international diplomacy.

China's decision to normalize relations with Japan was to a considerable extent motivated by the perception of the greater threat from the Soviet Union and the desire to forestall any possible Soviet-Japanese *entente*.[3] The overwhelming concern for the national survival and security led the Chinese to adopt a more flexible foreign policy and to think in terms of improving relations with the United States, Japan, and Western Europe. Moreover, it was felt that the normalization of Sino-Japanese relations would be a step forward in further strengthening China's position *vis-a-vis* Taiwan. It would ensure that the pretensions of the Nationalist Government as a rival claimant were undermined at every turn and to eliminate Japan as Taiwan's most powerful diplomatic prop after the United States. It would also enable Beijing to import Japanese plants and technology which would ensure faster economic development at home and open up the possibility of closing, with Japan's help, the technological gap which separated it from the two Super Powers. Thus realizing that the stakes were quite high, China did not insist on Japan fulfilling the conditions it had laid down earl'er for normalization of relations with Japan.

On the Japanese side, too, the compulsions—domestic, economic, and political—were no less strong for normalization of relations with Ch'na. Normalization was necessary to close the unhappy chapter in its history which was climaxed by the Second World War. With China's entry in the United Nations, Sino-US *detente*, and the recognition of the Mao regime by a growing number of countries, Tokyo realized that if it did not recognize the reality of the existence of China and continued its association with a regime that was not politically significant and had no standing in the international field, it would be making its own diplomatic position ridiculous. An initiative in regard to relations with China, besides being economically rewarding, would demonstrate Japanese independence in foreign policy and freedom from American influence. Normalization of relations with China would also tend to increase Japan's leverage with the Super Powers, particularly the Soviet Union, and enable it to play a political role in the world commensurate with its enormous economic power. Moreover, it was becoming increasingly difficult for any administration in Japan to stem the growing tide in favour of China within the country.

There was widespread feeling in Japan against the policy of opposition to the People's Republic of China. All the opposition parties more or less favoured the restoration of diplomatic relations with China. Although the majority of the ruling Liberal Democratic Party Dietmen had endorsed the Government's basic policy of *seikei bunri* (separation of political and economic relations) in the 1960s, a small minority had actively opposed that policy. In January 1965 the dissidents consisting largely of members of the Kono, Matsmura, Ono, Miki, and Fujiyama factions of the LDP, formed the Asian-African Study Group (*Ajia afurika mondai Kenkyukai*), which continuously pressed for greater diplomatic autonomy for Japan and for a speedy normalization of Sino-Japanese relations. There was another group, the Asian Problems Study Group (*Ajia mondai Kenkyukai*). This group, which was dominated by the Sato, Ishii, and Kishi-Fukuda factions, endorsed the essentially pro-Taipei orientation of the Government. It also doubted if Red China was a peace-loving nation, and said that the best policy for their country lay in maintaining close political and economic relations with the countries of the Free World.[4]

Soon the strength of the Asian-African Study Group rose from nineteen members to seventy-seven members. This was a clear indication that there was considerable dissatisfaction with the Government's China policy. The group kept up an intra-party debate on China during Sato's tenure and succeeded in 1968 in persuading the Government to abrogate the Yoshida Letter of 30 May 1964. Moreover, in collaboration with the Discussion Society for New Policy (*Shinseisaku danwaku*), a cross factional body of LDP headed by Munenori Akagi, it played a leading role in the adoption of a "Unified LDP View" on the China issue by the Investigating Committee of Foreign Affairs. This Unified View (25 May 1968), couched in rather moderate language, urged that efforts should be made to encourage Red China to play an active role in international affairs, and said that Japan should proclaim its willingness to co-exist with the People's Republic of China on the basis of the principles of mutual respect and non-interference in each other's domestic affairs.[5]

On 9 December 1970 the LDP critics of the Government's China policy went beyond the confines of their own party to join hands with the opposition parties (the Japan Socialist Party and the Komeito) to form the Dietmen's League for the

Normalization of Japanese-Chinese Relations (*Nitchu kokko kaifuku sokushin giinrenmei*) with Aiichiro Fujiyama as Chairman. Composed of a majority of Dietmen, its membership, consisting of 255 representatives and 124 councillors—95 from the LDP, 151 from the JSP, 71 from the Komeito, 37 from the DSP, 21 from JCP, and one independent Dietman, surpassed a simple majority of all Dietmen.[6] The League vigorously urged the the Government "to take such measures as may be necessary" to restore diplomatic relations with China. It also carried on various activities to promote a "national consensus" supporting speedy reognition of Beijing. Although limited in organizational effectiveness on account of its heterogeneous membership, it was fully united in its criticism of Sato's China stance and emerged as a powerful parliamentry challenger of the Government's policy of according precedence to Taiwan.[7]

Powerful faction chiefs within the LDP such as Nakasone, Takeo Miki, Fujiyama, and Masayoshi Ohira also became disenchanted with the Sato Government's pro-Taipeh orientation and openly called for normalization of Japan's relations with China. Nakasone had taken a prominent part in the making of the Government decision to rescind the Yoshida Letter in 1968.[8]

Takeo Miki, a former Chief of the Kaishinto (Progressive Party) faction and closely associated with Matsumura, had chidden Kishi as early as 1960 for pursuing a "backward-looking" policy towards Beijing. After his exit from the Sato Cabinet in 1968, his criticism of Sato became especially strident, and by January 1971 he expressed willingness to remove the "unnatural situation" between the two countries by making various contacts on the government level. In April 1971, prior to Nixon's China announcement, he told a business group in a speech that "Japan has more to gain from normalized Japanese-Chinese relations than from maintaining ties with Taiwan." Apart from growing criticism within the LDP and by opposition parties, increasing support among the Japanese people for improved Sino-Japanese relations was also evident.

After his election as Chairman of the non-partisan Dietmen's League in December 1970, Aiichiro Fujiyama emerged within the LDP as the strongest champion of a policy of normalization of Sino-Japanese relations. In July 1971 he was the prime

mover in the abortive attempt to secure a Diet resolution recognizing the Mao regime as China's sole legitimate Government.[9] From 17 September to 4 October 1971 he made a tour
of mainland China as the leader of the Japanse Dietmen's
League delegation. The joint statement of 2 October 1971
which the Japanese delegation signed with the delegation of
the China-Japan Friendship Association of China affirmed that
China and Japan should establish diplomatic relations "at the
earliest possible date" on the basis of the following four
principles: (1) The Government of the People's Republic of
China is the sole legal Government representing the Chinese
people. (2) The Taiwan Province is an inseparable part of
the territory of the People's Republic of China. (3) The so-
called "Japan-Chiang treaty" is illegal and invalid and should
be abrogated. (4) It is imperative to restore all the lawful rights
of the People's Republic of China in all the organs of the
United Nations, including the seat in the Security Council as
a permanent member, and expel the "representatives of the
Chiang Kai-shek clique" from the United Nations.[10]

By mid-1971 public support for normalization of relations
with China had become quite widespread. Even under the
Prime Ministership of Eisaku Sato (November 1964 to July
1972), Governmental action (or inaction) to normalize diplomatic relations with mainland China lagged considerably
behind Japanese public opinion. As a matter of fact, the
Japanese public itself sensed this gap between its expectations
and governmental actions.[11] Increasing pressure seems to have
been exerted within the LDP for stalling normalization of
relations with China. While the majority supported the policy
of caution in regard to Beijing, it became obvious that the
China issue would affect unity of the LDP and prove to be
decisive in the Sato succession struggle.

When the Government of Japan decided to co-sponsor a
resolution in the UN General Assembly in September 1971 in
favour of Taiwan's continued membership of the United
Nations, all the opposition parties in Japan combined to introduce a no-confidence motion in the Diet. To dramatize his
protest against the Government's anti-Beijing stance Fujiyama
led eleven other Liberal Democrats in a boycott of the voting
on the no-confidence motion.[12] China criticized the decision

as another reactionary feature of "a double accomplice of US imperialism."[13]

The announcement on 15 July 1971 of President Nixon's forthcoming visit to the People's Republic of China produced a pervasive shock in Japan. Armin H. Meyer, former US Ambassador to Japan from 1969 to 1972, feels that the announcement led to an "over-reaction" in Japan. To a certain extent it was an entirely normal emotional reflex. But, he adds, there were also vested interests who seized on the "Nixon shokku" to voice more shrilly their customary denunciations of the United States, the Japan-United States partnership, and the Sato Government. There may also have been a few Japanese officials who found the American President's surprise action "a convenient scapegoat for other troubles currently besetting Japan."[14] The Nixon move signalled an erosion of the US policy of diplomatic isolation and military containment against China which Japan had faithfully followed since the San Francisco Conference. Although it did not cause an immediate movement for Sino-Japanese diplomatic relations within the Government, it certainly added a new momentum to that movement in Japan.[15] Besides, Japanese firms reduced their investment in Taiwan after the summer of 1971.

President Nixon's initial moves in regard to China had a significant impact on the LDP critics of the Sato Government's China policy. These critics believed that there was a close link between Nixon's desire to wind up the domestically unpopular Vietnam War and his new-found enthusiasm for China. They, therefore, expected that an effective dialogue would soon be established between Beijing and Washington and that China had would gain entry into the United Nations sooner than they originally thought that it would. Furui and other leaders of the Asian-African Study Group were anxious that as an Asian country and as a close neighbour of China, Japan should establish diplomatic ties with China before the United States did.[16]

Thus, the small but assertive pro-Beijing group within the LDP assumed an increasingly offensive posture and put the pro-Taipeh members of the LDP on the defensive. The party itself moved progressively towards a position of accepting many of China's political terms for the establishment of Sino-Japanese diplomatic relations. The intra-party struggle within the LDP was not an exclusive party affair; for the business community too, did its best to influence the thinking of the party as a whole in favour of Beijing. A number of influential business leaders feared lest Tokyo's failure to accommodate Beijing's political stipulations for normalization of Sino-Japanese relations should result in the exclusion of Japan from the China market.[17] With a view to strengthening the hands of the pro-Beijing elements in Japan, China had indicated in 1968 that it would be prepared to reconsider cancelled contracts involving export of Japanese textile plants and ships if Tokyo would abrogate its policy on Government loans. For the same reason, it had departed somewhat from its original rigid stance on Taiwan in formulating the four principles that Zhou Enlai laid down on its behalf on the subject of Sino-Japanese trade. It had let it be known in 1971 that it was not averse to Japan's continuing its economic dealings with Taiwan even after the abrogation of the Tokyo-Taipeh Treaty, so long as such dealings did not involve massive Japanese investments in the island.[18] The business community in Japan finally succeeded in building up a consensus in favour of normalization of relations with China. Mitsui and Mitsubishi accepted Zhou's four principles. Kogoro Ueumura, Chairman of the *Keidanren*, also decided, in May 1972, to support Japanese recognition of Beijing.[19] There was, however, a strong sentiment among business leaders that normalization of Sino-Japanese relations must await the formation of a Government more congenial to Beijing.

Thus, apart from the four opposition parties, the leading members of the LDP and prominent men of the business and industrial world started demanding a settlement of the China problem by a normalization of relations with Beijing. China was quick to utilize the growing public feeling in Japan in its favour and tried to strengthen it further by inviting a number of delegations including those of businessmen who constituted the main prop of the LDP, and also threw generous hints about the possibility of a greater measure of flexibility in its attitude. For instance, it signed a joint statement with a delegation of the Komeito (Clean Government Party) which visited China from 16 June to 4 July 1971. This statement contained the following five principles relating to the termination of the state of war and restoration of diplomatic relations between the two countries:

(1) There is only one China, and the Government of the People's Republic of China is the sole legitimate Government representing the Chinese people.

(2) Taiwan is a Province of China and an inalienable part of Chinese territory.

(3) The Japan-Jiang (Chiang) Peace Treaty is illegal and must be abrogated.

(4) The United States must withdraw all its armed forces from Taiwan and the Taiwan Straits area.

(5) The legitimate rights of the People's Republic must be restored in all the organizations of the United Nations and the representatives of Taiwan expelled.[20]

In another statement issued at the end of a visit paid by a 19-member delegation of the non-partisan Japanese Dietmen's League for Promoting Restoration of Japan-China Diplomatic Relations on 2 October 1971, there was no mention of the fourth principle—viz. that the United States should withdraw all its armed forces from the Taiwan area.[21] Obviously, China had recognised that the fulfilment of that principle was beyond the competence and powers of the Government of Japan. However, a statement jointly issued by the Japan-China Friendship Association (Orthodox) and the China-Japan Friendship Association fourteen days later repeated all the five principles mentioned above.[22]

After China's entry into the United Nations in November 1971, the fifth principle noted above, no longer being valid, was removed from the list. Thus, the communique issued on the China-Japan Memorandum Trade Talks in Beijing on 21 December 1971 and the joint statement which the China-Japan Friendship Association of China signed with a visiting delegation of the Democratic Socialist Party of Japan on 13 April 1972 enumerated only three basic principles as prerequisites for the restoration of diplomatic relations between China and Japan.[23]

Tokyo had been watching with anxiety the expanding trade between China and the countries of Western Europe for some time past. Now, with the United States also in the field, it was hardly possible for Japan to resist the temptation of entering the China market It badly needed to correct the imbalance in its trade with the United States and strengthen its burgeoning economy. Moreover, it was inclined to adopt an independent posture in world affairs in view of the changes in the international environment and gain a greater measure of flexibility and manovevrability in its diplomatic posture and policies.

Sato had never been favourably inclined towards Beijing during his tenure as Prime Minister. In the face of mounting opposition to his China policy, however, he now began to think in terms of working out some compromise solution on the question of normalization of relations with China. Thus, in the early 1970s, the Sato Government was seen vaciliating between the pro-Taipeh tradition and a "forward-looking" posture towards China. Sato's departure from his usual position became progressively noticeable as the clamour grew within the LDP and the business community for a Sino-Japanese *detente*. In a speech made in 1970 the Premier stressed that he expected Beijing "to assume a cooperative and constructive" attitude towards other countries. He also stated that while "maintaining friendly relations with South Korea and Taiwan," his Government was planning to promote contacts and exchanges of personnel with China. He expressed the hope that his efforts would lead to "an improvement of friendly relations." For the first time he purposely called China "the Peking government" and made no reference to the traditional definitive Japanese policy of separating political from economic relations. He did not even rule out the possibility of contacts at the official level.[24]

In October 1971, i.e. after Nixon had announced that he was going to visit China, Sato acknowledged for the first time that Beijing was the legitimate Government of China. He also expressed the hope that the future status of Taiwan would be settled "through negotiations between the parties concerned" without any interference from other parties.[25] He later sent a message to Zhou Enlai, in the name of the LDP Secretary-General, Shigeru Hori, accepting two of China's preconditions for normalization of relations (viz. that Beijing should be recognized as the only legitimate Government of China and that Taiwan should similarly be regarded as but a Province of China) and agreeing to fulfil the third (viz. abrogation of the

Japan-Taiwan Treaty) in the course of negotiations for normalization. The letter also said that Hori wanted to visit Beijing for preliminary talks.[26] In the beginning of 1972, a China Section was set up in the Japanese Ministry of International Trade and Industry; the Memorandum Trade Office in Beijing was strengthened to a total of ten members; and technical assistance began to be extended to China on an *ad hoc* basis.

Beijing was not impressed by Sato's overtures partly because even after President Nixon had announced his intention to visit China Sato considered it most important "to maintain and promote friendly and amicable relations with the Republic of Korea and the Republic of China."[27] His Government continued to support Taipeh's claim to a UN seat by co-sponsoring a resolution in the UN General Assembly that sought to find room for both Taipeh and Beijing in the world body. The Chinese leaders, therefore, felt that they could place no faith in Sato's *bona fides*. Accordingly, they told Ryokichi Minobe, the Japanese Socialist Party Governor of Tokyo who carried Hori's letter to Beijing, that they did not trust Sato and the letter he had sent.[28] To other visiting members of the LDP and business leaders, they made it clear that they would not accept Sato as a negotiating partner in the process of normalization of relations, though any successor of Sato would be welcome in Beijing as long as he accepted the three basic political principles.[29] Wang Kuo-chuan, Vice-President of the China-Japan Friendship Association, who went to Japan in August 1971 to attend the funeral of Kenzo Matsumura, is said to have refused to meet Premier Sato. He, however, met Takeo Miki, then a likely contender for the Prime Ministership in the event of Sato's retirement. China's Japan strategy, thus, had a two-fold objective—to end the Sato regime and to normalize relations with Japan under a more favourable Premier.[30]

China on its part continued to be concerned about Soviet efforts "to expand and deepen its relations with Japan." Thus, in January 1972, when Soviet Foreign Minister Gromyko paid a visit to Japan, it saw in it a "criminal design to oppose socialist China in collusion with Japanese militarism." The Xinhua commentary accused the Soviet Union of trying its best "to sour the relations between Japan and the United

States" and of adopting an intransigent attitude on the question
of the Northern Territories for fear of touching off "a chain
reaction" as regards territories of other countries in Europe
and Asia which were then under Soviet occupation. It said
that the Soviet "revisionist social-imperialism" was further
intensifying "its counter-revolutionary collaboration with the
Japanese reactionaries" to oppose the people of the Asian
countries.[31]

The Chinese news media also criticized the 1972 Japanese
budget for its increased military expenditure. They said that
the increased spending on military hardware reflect an intensification of "armament build-up, war preparations, and
expansion abroad."[32] On 5 April 1972 a Chinese broadcast
criticized both Japan and the Soviet Union for their advocacy
that the Straits of Malacca should be internationalized. It
accused Japan and the Soviet Union of entering into a conspiracy aimed at "turning the Straits into their gateway for
external expansion and aggression."[33]

After Kakuei Tanaka replaced Sato as Japanese Premier
on 7 July 1972, the progress towards improved relations with
China was much accelerated. The process was hastened by
conciliatory gestures from both the Chinese and Japanese
sides. For instance, immediately after assuming office as Japan's
Prime Minister, Tanaka said the time was ripe for Japan to
normalize its relations with China and that he would expedite
the process of normalization of relations.[34] On 12 July 1972,
Foreign Minister Ohira, in an interview to the Nationalist
Chinese Ambassador, Peng Meng-chi, made it clear that when
Japan established diplomatic relations with People's Republic
of China, the peace treaty with the Taiwan regime would
automatically cease to be valid.[35] He, thus, gave evidence of
an understanding of China's three principles on the restoration
of Sino-Japanese diplomatic relations, as Zhou Enlai observed
in the speech he made at a banquet given in honour of Zentaro
Kosaka, leader of a visiting LDP delegation, on 18 September
1972.

The Japanese Government also took what Zhou called
"certain positive measures and steps."[36] For instance, it
quietly abolished the stipulations of the controversial Yoshida
Letter by approving the use of State funds (i.e. the grant of

loans from the Export-Import Bank of Japan) to finance the export of the second vinylon plant to be sold to China by the Kuraray Company of Japan since 1964.[37] Subsequently, the Bank of Tokyo reached agreement with Bank of China on the settlement of accounts in both Japanese yen and Chinese yuan— an important issue in Sino-Japanese trade, an issue that had been pending since the early 1960s.[38] Thus, the Bank of Japan agreed to the use of Chinese currency for contracts relating to fertilizer exports. The ban on the import of Chinese meat (cooked/boiled) was removed. The Metropolitan Government of Tokyo, with the concurrence of the Japanese Foreign Office, granted diplomatic status to the Memorandum Trade Office in Tokyo for tax purposes. The Japanese Ministry of Justice lifted the ban on the re-entry into Japan of such Chinese residents as had visited the mainland.[39]

Above all, Prime Minister Tanaka and members of his Cabinet made a series of statements and gestures intended to demonstrate their sincerity in seeking normalization of relations with China. At his first Press conference on 19 July 1972, Tanaka described the China problem as the biggest diplomatic question for Japan, referred to the long history of contacts between China and Japan, and expressed the opinion that it would be best for the two countries to normalize their relations. He pointed out that there was a sincere desire among the Japanese people for normalization of relations between the two States.[40] On 11 August 1972 Sun Ping-hua, leader of the Shanghai Dance Drama Troupe of China, and Hsiao Hsiang-chien, Chief Representative of the Tokyo Liaison office of the China-Japan Memorandum Trade Office of China conveyed to Foreign Minister Ohira an official message from Foreign Minister Chi Peng-fei that "Premier Zhou En-lai welcomes and invites Prime Minister Kakuei Tanaka to visit China."[41] Prime Minister Tanaka met these Chinese officials at the Imperial Hotel in Tokyo on the afternoon of 15 August 1972 and accepted Zhou's invitation with gratitude.

China also adopted a conciliatory posture towards Japan with a view to facilitating normalization of its relations with Japan. Chinese leaders realized that the occasion of the political transition from Sato to Tanaka presented the best opportunity for China to open direct communications with the

Japanese Government especially before Tanaka hardened his position on Taiwan.[42] In May 1972 Zhou Enlai made an important concession which helped to form the general framework for peace talks between the two countries. He was reported to have told the chairman of a visiting Komeito delegation that China was willing to waive its claim of war reparations (estimated at $50,000 million) against Japan; that the Japan-US Security Treaty and the Sato-Nixon communique of 21 November 1969 would not be regarded as obstacles in the way of normalization of relations between the two countries; and that China would not insist on a peace treaty with Japan. Indeed China proposed to conclude with Japan a treaty of peace and friendship which would have the effect of invalidating Japan's peace treaty with Taipeh.[43]

In short, China gave up its insistence upon a prior acceptance of the three principles for normalization of relations. In reply to the personal message that Tanaka had sent him through the Komeito delegation and which contained a pledge on Tanaka's part to work for normalization of Sino-Japanese relations, the Chinese Premier observed: "If, upon assuming the premiership, you are determined to wrestle with the normalization task, we shall refrain from doing anything that might embarrass you."[44] Thus, Zhou Enlai responded promptly and positively to Tanaka's appeal for normalization of relations.

Besides, China also strengthened the Memorandum Trade Office in Tokyo by sending Hsiao Hsiang-chien as Chief Representative. It also suspended its anti-Japanese propaganda and invited Tanaka to visit Beijing. Moreover, it dropped hint to convey that it would not insist on the severance of all Japanese connections—economic, cultural, commercial, etc.—with Taiwan. Furthermore, after the formation of the Tanaka cabinet in July 1972, not a single person of importance in the Chinese Government ever uttered a word about the three principles.[45]

Encouraged by Beijing's attitude Tanaka and Ohira addressed themselves to the task of devising a formula that would be satisfactory to both China and Japan. The compromise had to be couched in a language that would not ruffle overmuch the Right-wing pro-Taipeh group within the LDP. That is to say, the settlement was not to give the impression of a surrender to Beijing, for any such impression was sure to complicate matters with the Right-wing faction within the ruling party.

On 11 August 1972 Japanese Foreign Minister Masayoshi Ohira met Sun Ping-hua and Hsiao Hsiang-chien and conveyed to them the wish of Prime Minister Tanaka "to visit China for negotiations to realise the normalization of diplomatic relations between Japan and China." On the following day the Chinese Foreign Minister, Chi Peng-fei, announced that Premier Zhou Enlai had invited the Japanese Prime Minister, Kakuei Tanaka, to visit China "for negotiations and settlement of the question of normalization of diplomatic relations between China and Japan."[46] On 31 August 1972 a 13-member advance party arrived from Japan in Beijing on a five-day mission to make preparations for Tanaka's visit.

Meanwhile, Tanaka set up a 312-member Council for the Normalization of Japan-China Relations on 24 July 1972 with Zentaro Kosaka, Ex-Foreign Minister and a Member of the House of Representatives, as Chairman, in order to achieve a consensus within the ruling LDP. After much discussion, the Council passed on 8 September certain guidelines to help the Tanaka Cabinet in the negotiations regarding the establishment of diplomatic relations with China.[47] Kosaka later led a 23-member delegation to Beijing which was incidentally the first official delegation of the LDP ever to visit China. He had a "frank and full exchange of views with Premier Zhou Enlai and other Chinese leaders."[48]

Normalization

Prime Minister Kakuei Tanaka visited China from 25 to 30 September 1972. He signed a nine-Article joint statement with Zhou Enlai on 29 September 1972, which put an end to the abnormal state of relations between the two countries.

At the banquet given in honour of Premier Tanaka Zhou Enlai said:

Prime Minister Tanaka's visit to China opens a new page in the history of Sino-Japanese relations. Friendly contacts and cultural exchanges between our two peoples have forged a profound friendship; all this we should treasure. However, in the half-century after 1894, owing to the Japanese mllitarists' aggression against China, the Chinese people were made to endure tremendous disasters and the Japanese people, too, suffered a great deal from it. The past not forgotten is a guide for the future.[49]

Zhou felt that despite the different social systems of the two countries, there were bright prospects for Sino-Japanese relations.

Premier Tanaka replied:

We should not for ever linger in the dim blind alley of the past. In my opinion, it is important now for the leaders of Japan and China to confer in the interest of tomorrow... the two sides have their own basic positions and peculiar conditions. But despite the fact that some minor differences exist between the positions and views of the two sides, I believe it is possible for Japan and China to overcome their divergence of views and reach agreement in the spirit of seeking common ground on major questions and of mutual understanding and mutual accommodation.[50]

The Sino-Japanese joint statement stipulated that Japan recognized the People's Republic of China as the sole legal government of China. Beijing reaffirmed that Taiwan is "an inalienable part" of its territory and Japan "fully understands and respects" this stand in accordance with Article 8 of the Potsdam Declaration. Other countries like Canada, Italy, the Netherlands, etc. had only "taken note" of the Chinese position. The reference to Potsdam was a surprise development. Japan had not anticipated that it would come up but agreed to it in the joint statement when China insisted upon it. Japan thus agreed to the restoration of Taiwan to China in accordance with the Cairo Declaration of 1943, which is what Article 8 of the Potsdam Declaration stipulates. Japan's "understanding and respect" of Beijing's position on Taiwan was not an acceptance of it. It meant that it had morally bound itself not to play any active role in regard to the disposition of Formosa (including independent Taiwan) in a way other than as envisaged by China.[51] Japan gave this undertaking without prejudice to the right of the victorious Allies to dispose of Taiwan in any way they liked. All that Japan did was to give up openly asserting its security interest in Taiwan, as it had done in the Nixon-Sato communique of November 1969. It did not even rule out the possibility of its extending to the United States the usual military facilities on its territories, including the use of the Okinawa base.

Both sides agreed to establish diplomatic relations and to exchange ambassadors.

As regards the three principles that China had insisted upon at the time for the restoration of diplomatic relations, all that Japan now did was to express its "full understanding" of those principles—and that too in the preambular portions of the joint statement—without in any way indicating its "acceptance" of them formally. It was thus able to avoid any mention of its peace treaty with the Republic of China in the statement. Foreign Minister Ohira later asserted at a Press conference on 29 September 1972 that as a result of normalization of relations with Beijing that treaty had lost all practical meaning.[52] In other words it meant that unlike the Chinese, who held that the Tokyo-Taipeh treaty was illegal and null and void from its very inception, Ohira considered that treaty legal and valid up to 29 September 1972, i.e. the day on which normalization of relations between Tokyo and Beijing took place.

Ohira while addressing a meeting of the Research Institute of Japan said on 6 October 1972 that normalization was sought and achieved within the framework of the San Francisco Peace Treaty of September 1951. He added that Japan would have hesitated if China had forced Japan to make a choice between the San Francisco Peace Treaty system and normalization of Sino-Japanese relations.

While reference was made in the preamble of the joint statement to the termination of the state of war and the normalization of relations between China and Japan, Article 1 of the operative part of the statement merely stated that the "abnormal state of affairs" that had characterized their relations had ended as from 20 September 1972. This was a device designed to uphold the Chinese position as well as bear out the Japanese claim that the state of war was terminated in 1952 with the signing of a peace treaty with Jiang Jieshi (Chiang Kai-shek). Lest China's declaration renouncing "its demand

for war indemnities from Japan" in Article 5 of the joint
statement create any doubt about the state of war and make
people think that the issue of reparations had not been settled
by the treaty of 1952, Ohira clarified the Japanese position by
saying that what China had renounced was the "demand ' and
not the "right to demand" such indemnities or reparations.
Even then it closed the chapter of war indemnities or reparations when Prime Minister Tanaka expressed his grief about
his country having caused "great trouble" to the Chinese people
and promised on behalf of his people to enter upon a 'profound
self-examination.[53] The question of reparations was not allowed
to stand in the way of Sino-Japanese reconciliation, and Tanaka
was not compelled to tender an abject apology for the misdeeds of Japanese militarists.

Both sides agreed to establish peaceful and friendly relations on the basis of the five principles of peaceful co-existence
and to settle all disputes by peaceful means without resorting
to the use or threat of force, in accordance with the UN
Charter.

The joint statement contained the following provision
regarding "anti-hegomony":

> The normalization of relations between China and Japan
> is not directed against third countries. Neither of the two
> countries should seek hegemony in the Asia-Pacific region
> and each country is opposed to efforts by any other country
> or group of countries to establish such hegemony.

China and Japan also agreed to conclude a "treaty of peace
and friendship." They also resolved to hold negotiations
aimed at the conclusion of agreements on trade, navigation,
aviation, fishery, etc. in accordance with the needs and taking
into consideration the existing non-governmental agreements.

In order not to spoil the development of friendly relations
between the two Powers, the question of the Senkakus, or the
Diaoyutai as the Chinese call them, was not taken up seriously
and side-stepped.

In the wake of the Sino-US *rapprochement* the US-Japan
Security Treaty had lost much of its military significance for
China. Beijing, therefore, did not insist on the abrogation of
that treaty. In fact, it felt that in the changed context of the

Sino-US *rapprochement*, the US-Japanese Security Treaty would serve a useful purpose in that it might be used to counter the Soviet moves in the region and to restrain Japan from going nuclear or embarking upon an undue expansion of its Self-Defence Forces. The alliance, by guaranteeing Japan's security against any threat of a nuclear war and against any large-scale use of conventional weapons, had removed the need for Japan to develop its own nuclear weapons or expand its military forces beyond certain well-defined limits.

Zhou Enlai in December 1972 not only expressed his "under-standing" of Japan's right to self-defence but also identified the Soviet nuclear threat as the only cause of justification for the continued existence of the US-Japanese Security Treaty.[54] Foreign Minister Chi Peng-fei is reported to have expressed similar views.[55] Thus, given its preoccupation with the Soviet military threat, Beijing was quite willing to tolerate the US presence in Japan and the rearmament of Japan. Concern about Japanese militarism seems to have become a thing of the past.

The normalization of Sino-Japanese relations was a com-promise settlement which took into account the interests and susceptibilities of both sides. Tokyo agreed to snap diplomatic ties with Taipeh and repudiate its peace treaty with Taiwan as these two steps were recognized to be a prerequisite of and basic to the whole normalization process. However, that did not signify that Japan was willing to give up all its economic, cultural, and trade links with Taiwan.[56] In fact, to look after these interests, Japan established a "private" Liaison Office named *Koryo Kyokai* (Exchange Association) on 1 December 1972 with Horikoshi Teizo (Vice Chairman of *Keidanren*) as President. Japanese leaders apparently did not anticipate any conflict over Taiwan and the Taiwan Straits in the near future perhaps because they had received some sort of an informal assurance from Beijing about not disturbing the *status quo* there.

Political Relations, 1972-1978

The power equation in Northeast Asia underwent a fundamental change with the normalization of Sino-US and Sino-Japanese relations. The Soviet Union felt that the balance of power in the region, static for two decades, had shifted in favour of China, its main adversary. The normalization of Sino-American relations clearly upset the Soviet strategy of the "encirclement" of China, a strategy in which the United States was to have played a major role. Moscow also feared that the consolidation of Sino-Japanese relations coupled with the close economic, political, and military ties of Japan with the United States might even give birth to some kind of a coalition to contain the Soviet Union.[57]

The changes in the international environment in the early 1970s led the Soviet Union to accelerate the process of *detente* with the United States, to bring about a speedy reduction of tension in Europe by responding favourably to Willy Brandt's *Ostpolitik*, and to deepen economic relations with Japan and reduce political tensions between Japan and the Soviet Union. The Soviet Press reduced its criticism of Japan and the US-Japanese Security Treaty since it may hinder the improvement of relations between Japan and the Soviet Union and lead to further cementing the growing intimacy between China, Japan, and the United States.

The Japanese Government welcomed the normalization of relations with Communist China since it removed the basic political hurdle in the way of the expansion of Sino-Japanese economic relations. Besides, it did not adversely affect Japan's economic stake in Taiwan. Nevertheless, friendship with China was not to be preferred to antagonizing the Soviet Union by developing excessively close relations with China. Thus, in October 1972, Foreign Minister Ohira was sent to Moscow to allay Soviet misgivings about the Sino-Japanese *rapprochement*. The Soviet leaders were not satisfied with Ohira's explanation. Their displeasure was reflected in Ohira's failure to secure an appointment with Brezhnev.

The Zhou-Tanaka joint statement of September 1972 paved the way for the exchange of ambassadors between the two countries in March 1973. Next month they agreed to hold regular annual consultations at the Foreign Minister's level.[58] The statement envisaged the conclusion of four major agreements—a trade agreement, a civil aviation agreement, a shipping aggreement, and a fisheries agreement—and also the signing of a treaty of peace and friendship. All the four administrative agreements were signed by 15 August 1975.

There has been considerable improvement on the economic and cultural fronts since the establishment of diplomatic relations between the two countries. As many as 10,000 Japanese tourists and 5,000 businessmen visited China in 1973. Over 1,000 Chinese went to Japan during the first eight months after the establishment of diplomatic relations. There has been a rapid increase in the number of exchanges at the government level also. Special mention may be made here of the visit of a 55-member goodwill mission to Japan under the leadership of the Japanese-educated Liao Cheng-chih. This mission went to Japan in the spring of 1973 in pursuance of China's people-to-people diplomacy. Carefully chosen to represent different fields and walks of life, the members of the mission fanned out all over the country to establish contact with every important interest group in the style of a political campaign. The doings of the mission received massive media coverage. Liao himself figured prominently on the front-pages of the leading newspapers. He was pictured as wearing his old Waseda University school cap and singing the school song. "No Russian could top that.[59]

Normalization with Japan marked a fresh advance in China's quest for international responsibility and strengthened its international position by broadening its contacts with the outside world and improved its strategic position, particularly *vis-a-vis* the Soviet Union. China now felt more confident about thwarting any Soviet design to encircle or contain China and to counter Soviet influence more effectively than before.

The Sino-Japanese *rapprochement* was achieved by Japan's acknowledgement of three Chinese demands centring on the question of Taiwan: recognition of the People's Republic as the sole legal Government of China, acceptance of Taiwan as an inalienable part of the territory of the People's Republic, and abrogation of Japan's peace treaty with Taiwan. The Government of Japan accepted the first Chinese demand without reservation, expressed its "understanding and respect" for the principle underlying the second, and complied with the third by means of a Press statement.

An official trade agreement granting each other the most-favoured-nation treatment was signed in early January 1974. However, the civil aviation agreement signed on 20 April 1974 was the outcome of seventeen months of ardous negotiations.

During the negotiations which began in March 1973, Beijing's main demand was that Japan must stop treating Taiwan as a stat. The Chinese argued that Taiwan was only a province of China and that, therefore, the use of the name "China" by the China Air Lines (CAL) and its flying the "Chinese nationalist flag" were misleading. They also contended that to allow the CAL, Taiwan's flag-carrier, to use the same airport in Tokyo, the Haneda Airport, that the CAAC, the real Chinese flag carrier, had been allowed to use would inevitably create the impression that Japan recognized two Chinas. Pro-Taiwan Dietmen led by Takeo Fukuda, Minister of Finance since November 1973, countered this contention by saying that while the representatives of the People's Republic and Taiwan "co-existed" in Washington it was "absurd" that their airplanes could not bear to be parked side by side at Haneda.[60] All the same, despite strong protests from the Rightists at home, the Government of Japan concluded a civil aviation accord on Beijing's terms. It held that the flag and the emblem carried by the CAL were "private indentification marks" and that they did not imply any Japanese recognition of Taiwan as a "state".[61] It took this view because failure to conclude the aviation accord would have meant a devastating blow to the newly established relationship with China.[62]

Under the civil aviation agreement, Japan Air Lines (JAL) secured the right to fly to Beijing and Shanghai, and the Civil Aviation Administration of China (CAAC) gained the right to serve Tokyo and Osaka. From China, JAL could fly to London via New Delhi, or Bombay or Karachi; Tehran; Beirut; or Cairo, or Istanbul; Rome or another point in Europe; and Paris. The CAAC was authorized to serve the following points beyond Japan: Vancouver, Ottawa, or another point in Canada; one point in North America, excluding Canada; and four points in Latin America, including Mexico.[63] Hailing this agreement, a commentator of the *People's Daily* expressed the conviction that it would "powerfully push ahead friendly contacts between the Chinese and Japanese peoples and economic and cultural exchanges between the two countries."[64]

The Japanese Foreign Minister, Ohira, declared that while the air transport agreement between Japan and the People's Republic of China was "a governmental agreement," flights between Japan and Taiwan were "non-Governmental" regional air traffic. He stated that Japan did not recognize the emblem on the aircraft belonging the China Air Lines (CAL) of Taiwan "as a so-called national flag." Nor did it recognize "the China Air Lines as an air firm representing a state."[65]

Taiwan interpreted Foreign Minister Ohira's statement as casting a reflection on the national flag of the Republic of China. It, therefore, suspended all flights operated by JAL and CAL on the Japan-Taiwan air route. With thirty-seven weekly flights carrying over a thousand passengers per day on an average, the Japan-Taiwan air route was one of the most lucrative routes operated by JAL with an estimated sales total of $45 million in 1973. These flights between Japan and Taiwan were resumed only after a private agreement had been signed on 9 July 1975. Foreign Minister Miyazawa retracted somewhat from Ohira's statement when he observed on 1 July 1975 that for those countries which still recognized the Republic of China, the Taiwanese flag was certainly a national flag. This made Liao Cheng-chih, President of the China-Japan Friendship Association, accuse Miyazawa of following a policy of recognizing two Chinas in effect. However, the resumption of air services between Japan and Taiwan was not likely to affect Sino-Japanese relations in any significant way and China refrained from lodging an official protest with the Government of Japan and confined its outbursts to the people-to-people level.

A 12-Article shipping agreement was signed between China and Japan on 13 November 1974 in Tokyo. On 15 August 1975, after nearly two years of intermittent negotiations over fishing rights and territorial limits in the Yellow Sea and the East China Sea, the two countries signed a fishery agreement, the fourth and the last of the administrative agreements envisaged by the Sino-Japanese joint communiqe of September 1972.[66]

NOTES

1 See J.P. Jain, *China in World Politics* (New Delhi, 1976), 109-10.
2 Ibid., 213.
3 In the first half of 1972 there were certain unmistakable signs of growing cordiality between the USSR and Japan, Gromyko's visit to Japan that year signified resumption of consultations after a lapse of four years. Prospects of the Soviet plan to exploit the economic resources of Siberia on a large scale with Japanese help seemed bright. One also discerned a change in Tokyo's attitude towards the Soviet proposal of collective security for Asia.
4 *Asahi Shimbun*, 24 December 1962.
5 Yung H. Park, "The Politics of Japan's China Decision," *Orbis*, Summer 1975, 565.
6 Chae-Jin Lee, *Japan faces China: Poliical and Economic Relations in the Postwar Era* (London, 1976), 94.
7 Park, n, 5, 565. On 13 December 1970, under the sponsorship of the Komeito Party, the People's Council for the Normalization of Japan-China Relations was formed and ten days later a promoters conference was convened of an organization sponsored by the Japan Socialist Party and tentatively named the "People's Conference for Japan-China Friendship and Restored Diplomatic Relations." See Royama Michi, "Why should Japan Recognize China," *The Japan Interpreter* (Summer-Autumn 1972), 256.
8 For a discussion on the factional elements involved in the LDP's China policy, see Frank C. Langdon, "Japanese Liberal Democratic Factional Discord on China Policy," *Pacific Affairs*, Fall 1978, 403-15.
9 Park, n. 5, 566-7.
10 For text of joint statement, see *Peking Review*, 8 October 1971, 14-6.
11 For a review of public opinion data on Sino-Japanese relations from 1968, see George P. Jan, "Public Opinion's Growing Influence on Japan's China Policy," *Journalism Quarterly* (Spring 1971), 111-9; Kan Ori, "Japanese Public Opinion and Sino-Japanese Relations, 1969-1972," in Shumichi Takayanagi and Kimitada Miwa, ed., *Postwar Trends in Japan* (Tokyo, 1975), 55.
12 Park, n. 5, 566. For specific reasons given by the dissidents for their actions, see *Sande Mainichi*, 21 November 1971, 16-21.
13 *People's Daily*, 26 September 1971.
14 Armin H. Meyer, *Assignment Tokyo: An Ambassador's Journal* (New York, 1974), 137.
15 Lee, n. 6, 99.
16 See Park, n. 5, 565.
17 Ibid., 572.
18 *New York Times*, 28 November 1971.
19 *Asahi Shimbun*, 24 May 1972. More important than the opposition parties was the bourgeoning strength of the pro-Beijing pressures within the Liberal Democratic Party, particularly of the business community. Shigeo Nagano, Chairman of Nippon Steel Corporation, a giant con-

cern, accepted Zhou Enlai's four principles as early as August 1971.

20 *Peking Review*, 9 July 1971, 20-1. The joint statement held out the prospect of concluding a mutual non-aggression treaty between China and Japan on the basis of the Five Principles of Peaceful C-oexistence "depending on developments" after the establishment of diplomatic relations and the signing of the peace treaty. See *China Quarterly*, January-March 1974, 103.

21 See *Peking Review*, October 1971, 14-5.

22 Ibid., 22 October 1971, 16-7 and 23.

23 Ibid., 21 April 1972, 17-9.

24 *Asahi Shimbun*, 2 February 1970.

25 Richard Halloran, "Japanese to Seek Closer China Ties," *New York Times*, 20 October 1971.

26 *Jeji Menkan*, 1963, 45, cited in Park, n. 5, 582; also see *New York Times*, 21 November 1971.

27 Sato's speech to both Houses of the Diet shortly after the Nixon announcement of 15 July 1971. See "No New Approach on China Problem Revealed in Speech," *Japan Times*, 18 July 1971, 1 and 4.

28 *Asahi Shimbun*, 21 September 1972.

29 Kojo Nakamura, "Twice a Loser," *Far Eastern Economic Review*, 20 November 1971, 12. See also *Asahi Shimbun*, 21 November 1971 (Eve).

30 See Park, n. 5, 582.

31 Foreign Broadcast Information Service, *Daily Report*, 11 February 1972, 19-20.

32 Xinhua News Agency, 3 April 1972.

33 Ibid.

34 See *Asahi Shimbun*, 8 July 1972. For Zhou Enlai's reaction, see *Peking Review*, 14 July 1972.

35 See *Japan Times*, 17 July 1972.

36 See *Peking Review*, 22 September 1972, 3.

37 See *Japan Times*, 27 July 1972.

38 Ibid., 19 August 1972.

39 Ibid., 10 September 1972.

40 See Foreign Broadcast Information Service, *Daily Report*, 20 July 1971 A 6 and C1.

41 *Peking Review*, 18 August 1972, 3.

42 Lee, n. 6, 113.

43 See *Japan Times*, 29 August 1972.

44 *Asahi Shimbun* (evening), 22 September 1972. See also *Japan Times*, 29 August 1972.

45 Shinkichi Eto, "Japan and China: A New Stage," *Problems of Communism*, November-December 1972, 8.

46 *Peking Review*, 19 August 1972, 3.

47 These were (1) normalization of diplomatic relations on the basis of the UN Charter, the ten principles of the Bandung Conference and the five principles of peaceful co-existence; (2) respect by the two sides for each other's relations with other friendly countries; (3) mutual forbearance from using or threatening to use force against each other; (4) promotion

of equal economic and cultural relations among all nations ; and (5) co-operation for the peace and prosperity of Asia. The preface to this platform emphasized that the Japanese government "must" conduct negotiations with China in such a way that it can maintain its "hitherto existing relations" with the "Republic of China." Lee, n. 6, 116.

48 See banquet speeches by Kosaka and Zhou Enlai in Beijing on 18 September 1972. *Peking Review*, 22 September 1972, 3-4.

49 *Peking Review*, 29 September 1972, 7-8.

50 Ibid.

51 Commenting on the provision in the joint Statement that Japan "fully understands and respects" the Chinese stand and "adheres to its stand of complying with Article 8 of the Potsdam Proclamation," the *People's Daily* observed: "This once again affirmed the fact that Taiwan has been returned to China since World War II. This is a hammer blow to those who trumpet the fallacies of two China's or one China one Taiwan." *Peking Review* 6 October 1972.

52 *Peking Review*, 6 October 1972, 15.

53 Ibid , 29 September 1972, 8.

54 Zhou Enlai said this in a "casual talk" with Takeo Kimura, a senior LDP Dietman and a former Minister of Construction. Cited in Gene T. Hsiao, "Prospects for a New Sino-Japanese Relationship," *China Quarterly*, December 1974, 736-7.

55 Chi Peng-fei said: Japan might feel threatened by the USSR, just as China does. So in order to protect itself from the Soviet threat, it is quite natural that Japan should maintain the Japan-US Security Treaty until it has enough self-defence power." See *Mainichi*, 17 December 1973.

56 See Foreign Minister Ohira's statement in the Diet, October 1972. *Asahi Shimbun*, 28 October 1972.

57 R.K. Jain, *The USSR and Japan, 1945-1980* (New Delhi, 1981), 131.

58 *Japan Review* (New Delhi), April 1973, 18.

59 Robert A. Scalapino, "China and the Balance of Power," *Foreign Affairs*, January 1974, 374. See also G. Hudson, "Japanese Attitudes and Policies towards China in 1973," *China Quarterly*, October-December 1973, 700-7.

60 See *Japan Times*, 25 May and 26 May 1973. See also Hsiao, n. 54, 722-3.

61 See *Far Eastern Economic Review*, 25 February 1974, 5. See also *Japan Times*, 8 March 1974.

62 Hsiao, n. 54, 726.

63 See *Japan Review*, April 1974.

64 See *Peking Review*, 24 May 1974, 19.

65 Ibid, 26 April 1974, 28.

66 For details, see Chapter Nine on Economic Relations.

7. Peace and Friendship Treaty

The signing of the China-Japan Peace and Friendship Treaty on 12 August 1978 constitutes an important landmark in the relations between the two countries. It was the outcome of "an intermittent, tortuous, and delicate dialogue, until they found a compromise solution to their conflcting positions."[1]

Background

The Sino-Japanese joint communique of 29 September 1972 envisaged the holding of negotiations for the conclusion of a treaty of peace and friendship in order to consolidate and develop peaceful and friendly relations between the two countries. The successful conclusion of the inter-governmental agreements on trade (January 1974), aviation (April 1974), and navigation (November 1974) as envisaged in the 1972 joint communique created a propitious climate for negotiations to begin on the conclusion of a Sino-Japanese peace and friendship treaty.

Preliminary negotiations between China and Japan began in Tokyo on 14 November 1974 between the Vice Minister for Foreign Affairs, Fumihiko Togo, and his Chinese counterpart, Han Nianlong, when the latter was on a visit to Japan to sign an agreement on shipping. Subsequently, from 16 January 1975 to early May 1975 Togo and the Chinese Ambassador to Japan, Chen Chu, resumed negotiations in Tokyo. In early March Togo informed Chen Chu that Japan could not accept the "anti-hegemony" clause since Moscow could interpret it as directed against the Soviet Union. Togo also stressed the

Japanese viewpoint that the inclusion of a provision pertaining to a third country (or countries) ran counter to the very principle and practice of bilateral treaty-making.[2]

The Chinese responded by pointing out that the inclusion of the "anti-hegemony" principle should not create a problem because it was stipulated in both the Sino-Japanese joint communique and in the Sino-American joint communique of 28 February 1972 as well. The Japanese replied that there was a fundamental difference between a treaty and a joint communique, for the former prescribed legal rights and obligations, whereas the latter merely expressed policy intentions.[3]

The Chinese desire to give the peace treaty the trappings of an alliance specifically directed against the Soviet Union was reflective of a toughening of the Chinese attitude towards the Soviet Union since relations were normalized between China and Japan. This is evident from Vice Premier Deng Xiaoping's speech before the United Nations General Assembly on 10 April 1974 (wherein he enunciated his "three worlds" theory) and the incorporation of anti-hegemonism in the State Constitution of 17 January 1975. The Chinese Constitution declared that China would "oppose the imperialist policies of aggression and war and oppose the hegemonism of the super powers."

The Soviet Union had been worried over the inclusion of the "anti-hegemony" clause in the China-Japan peace treaty because of China's continued identification of the Soviet Union with hegemonism and its intense hostility towards the USSR. The Soviets strongly felt that a treaty signed on Chinese terms would mean Japanese endorsement of China's anti-Soviet policy in the Asia-Pacific region. A spate of articles appeared in the Soviet Press urging Japan not to submit to Chinese pressure regarding the anti-hegemony clause. Soviet leaders clearly indicated, both through diplomatic channels (their statement to the Government of Japan of 12 June 1975) and through a Tass statement of 18 June 1975, that if the Japanese should ever agree to the inclusion of an "anti-hegemony clause" in the proposed Sino-Japanese peace and friendship treaty, it would prove seriously "detrimental" to the cordial relations obtaining between Japan and the Soviet Union. Soviet objections succeeded in inducing the Japanese to be more cautious and conscious of the political consequences of the treaty. As a result, the Japanese began to take a more critical look at the hegemony clause since they did not wish to be drawn in the Sino-Soviet rivalry. The Japanese Premier stated in the Diet in June 1975 that Soviet opposition to the peace treaty was the product of misunderstanding and that the proposed treaty was not directed against the Soviet Union or any third country.

On 24 September 1975 Foreign Minister Miyazawa had discussions lasting about ten hours with Foreign Minister Chiao Kuan-hua at the United Nations Headquarters in New York. In his discussions the Japanese Foreign Minister disclosed the so-called "four Miyazawa principles", viz. that "anti-hegemony" should not be directed against any specific third nation, that it does not mean joint action by China and Japan, that the two countries are opposed to hegemony everywhere in the world, and that it should be in accordance with the spirit of the UN Charter. Miyazawa said his country was prepared to include an anti-hegemony clause provided it only dealt with general principles. An "anti-hegemony" clause would also not be acceptable if it could in any way be invoked to restrain specific acts such as Japan's trade activities or even against the United States, Japan's ally. The remarks of Chinese Deputy Prime Minister Chi Teng-kuei to a visiting Japanese delegation lent some weight to Japanese fears. While denying that the proposed clause was directed against any specific state, he asserted that the Soviet Union only opposed it because it was itself seeking hegemony. Chi Teng-kuei also warned that if Japan persisted in dragging its feet over the clause, it might come to be regarded as being guilty of the same offence. Thus, while China viewed the peace treaty with Japan primarily in the context of Sino-Soviet relations, Japan merely sought to stabilize its relations with China without getting involved in Sino-Soviet rivalry.

China did not accept the Miyazawa principles. As a result negotiations abruptly broke off. Japan was not prepared to submit to Chinese demands and accept either explicity or implicitly a strong anti-Soviet anti-hegemony clause.

During 1976 treaty negotiations could not be pursued with vigour because Premier Miki's Government was preoccupied with the "Lockhead payoff scandal". China was also confronted with an intense power struggle and unstable political conditions in the wake of the demise of Premier Zhou Enlai, Chu Teh, and Chairman Mao Zedong. The Chinese leadership could not altogether ignore the "Gang of Four". Besides, Soviet Foreign Minister Gromyko, during his visit to Japan in 1976, tried to dissuade the Japanese Government from succumbing to Chinese pressure to include an anti-hegemony clause in the proposed Sino-Japanese treaty. He also endeavoured to promote the idea of a preliminary friendship treaty between Japan and Soviet Union pending the conclusion of a peace treaty.

Two rounds of talks were held at the United Nations Headquarters between Foreign Minister Kosaka and Foreign Minister Chiao Kuan-hua in October 1976 and again in September 1977 between Foreign Minister Hatoyama and Foreign Minister Huang Hua. But no progress was made in the negotiations even though the political situation in both countries had stabilized by mid-1977. This was largely because Fukuda was keenly aware of the attitude of pro-Taiwan elements within the LDP who were opposed to an early conclusion of the treaty with China. Moreover, the Soviets had threatened that Japan would be barred from the Soviet Union's 200-mile exclusive fishery zone if Japan accepted the controversial "anti-hegemony" clause. It was felt that if Japan went ahead with its peace treaty talks with China it could jeopardize Soviet-Japanese fishery negotiations.[4] Meanwhile, business circles in Japan urged Fukuda to expeditiously sign the treaty with China so that economic relations between the two countries could be given a boost. On 30 March 1977 the Japan-China Association presented an appeal to Prime Minister Takeo Fukuda urging swift conclusion of the peace treaty.

In his policy speech to the Diet in January 1978, Premier Fukuda felt the time to be growing ripe for negotiations. Informal negotiations began in Beijing in February 1978 between Japanese Ambassador to China, Shoji Sato, and Vice Foreign Minister Han Nianlong. Talks dragged on for another two months before they were suspended in mid-April due to the Senkaku Islands dispute. Meanwhile, Chairman Hua Guofeng in his Report on the Work of the Government to the first session of the Fifth National People's Congress on 26 February 1978 called for an early conclusion of the treaty.[5]

The Soviet Union published the text of the Soviet-Japanese

good neighbourliness and co-operation draft treaty in *Izvestia* on 23 February 1978.[6] The Chinese criticized the draft treaty as an attempt to legalize Soviet occupation of the Northern Territories and "to edge out and replace U.S. influence." A commentary in *Peking Review* stated that the Soviet-proposed treaty not only sought to weaken the US-Japanese Security Treaty, but aimed at "disintegrating or replacing the Japanese-U.S. military alliance by a Soviet-Japanese military alliance so as to put Japan in the orbit of Soviet strategy for world domination." Moreover, it was pointed out that the Japanese Press considered the Soviet move to be intended to drag Japan into the Soviet-proposed Asian collective security system.[7] Tokyo did not welcome the Soviet draft treaty because of its adverse implications for Japan.

In March 1978 the Komeito and the Japan Socialist Party delegations visited China to promote the cause of Sino-Japanese friendship. However, just when it looked that things had begun to move, the Senkaku Islands incident occured on 12 April 1978.

The Senkaku incident temporarily weakened the pro-Treaty forces and strengthened the anti-Treaty ones in Japan.[8] In the wake of the incident anti-Treaty groups demanded that this issue be resolved as part of the treaty negotiations. The Chinese urged Japan not to make this a precondition to the conclusion of the treaty as it would tend to further complicate the negotiations. Prime Minister Fukuda and Foreign Minister Sonoda, therefore, confined themselves to expressing dissatisfaction with Chinese actions and statements. They continuously attempted to keep the Senkaku incident in perspective, thus also allaying Chinese suspicions that Fukuda was not genuinely interested in signing the treaty.[9]

Considerable controversy raged within the LDP regarding the peace treaty. The party was polarised between two opposing groups, viz. the pro-Beijing "doves" which were heavily represented in the Ohira and Tanaka factions, and the anti-Beijing "hawks" which deminated the Fukuda and Nakasone factions.[10] It took Fukuda nearly the whole of May to win sufficient consensus within the LDP to move forward. During their meeting on 29 May 1978 Foreign Minister Sonoda and his Chinese counterpart, Huang Hua, held discussions at

UN Headquarters in New York and the two governments subsequently agreed to resume working-level negotiations on 21 July 1978.

Eleven meetings were held from 21 July to 5 August 1978 in Beijing; but differences in the wording of the "anti-hegemony" clause prevented the signing of the treaty.[11] The issue was finally resolved when Foreign Minister Sonoda visited China on 8 August. The final draft was finalized on 11 August and the Sino-Japanese peace and friendship treaty signed the next day. The Standing Committee of the National People's Congress unanimously ratified it a few days later. On 18 October both Houses of the Japanese Diet approved it with an overwhelming vote. On 23 October 1978 the treaty came into force when the two countries exchanged the instruments of ratification in Tokyo.

Japanese Motives

Soviet susceptibilities and protests regarding the inclusion of an "anti-hegemony" clause in a peace treaty with China, the desire not to annoy the Soviets or to be seen as submitting tamely to Chinese demands had led Japan to adopt a somewhat cautious attitude. Prime Minister Fukuda, however, was finding it increasingly difficult to ignore mounting public support for the early conclusion of the treaty. Moreover, almost all the opposition parties also advocated that negotiations should be expedited. In such a situation and especially with a general election around the corner and LDP's presidential election scheduled for the end of 1978, Fukuda badly needed to score some successes in the international field in order to refurbish his own image and that of his Government at home and regain prestige within the Liberal Democratic Party. It was hoped that the treaty would tend to improve his position *vis-a-vis* his principal rival, viz. Masayoshi Ohira. To that end, Fukuda had started a consensus-building operation among ruling LDP members from the beginning of March 1978.

Economic motives were no less important. Increasing competition with and greater restriction on Japanese exports in Western Europe and the United States led Japan to protect the "China market" to the maximum extent possible. It was felt that the conclusion of the Sino-Japanese peace treaty would facilitate the implementation of the February 1978 long-term trade agreement. Pressure from the industrial magnates (in view of the recession at home in 1977-78) may also have been a contributory factor.

Japanese policy-makers may have reasoned that there was little likelihood of a change in the intransigent Soviet attitude towards the Northern Territories issue irrespective of whether or not Japan signed a peace treaty with China. They probably concluded that relations with the Soviet Union would not deteriorate further and that Moscow would eventually reconcile itself to a *fait accompli.*

Furthermore, the conclusion of the peace treaty with China would reflect Japan's independent posture in international politics since it was signed in the face of stiff Soviet warnings. It would also be testimony of Japanese determination not to succumb to Chinese pressures regarding the wording of "anti-hegemony" clause.

Tacit, if not express, US support also seems to have encouraged Japanese leaders to conclude the peace treaty with China. It was reported that at the Carter-Fukuda summit in May 1978 the US President had given his blessings to Japan in the matter. The emphasis of leading American officials on the long-term strategic nature of US-Chinese relations and "the identity of certain common basic interests" led Tokyo to conclude that its ally would welcome closer Sino-Japanese relations and favourably view the signing of the China-Japan peacet reaty.[12]

Chinese Motives

China pressed for and obtained the treaty presumably with a view to align Japan psychologically with China against the Soviet Union, and to commit Japan, with its remarkable technological capacity and foreign exchange surplus, to the modernization of China.[13] In order to broaden and deepen Japanese economic relations with China and prevent Japan from developing close economic ties with the Soviet Union, the Chinese found it expedient to enter into a $20 billion long-term trade agreement in February 1978. This agreement contributed in no small

measure to fostering a favourable climate in Japan for concluding the treaty with China.

China was increasingly concerned about growing Soviet
influence on its periphery, especially after its estrangement with
Vietnam and the coming into power of a pro-Soviet regime in
Afghanistan. Consequently, the Chinese considered it imperative to develop closer relations with Japan, the United States,
and the countries of Western Europe. A peace treaty with Japan
would improve China's politico-strategic position *vis-a-vis* the
Soviet Union in Northeast Asia. It would also be welcomed by
the United States, Japan's political and military ally. Moreover,
vis-a-vis the Third World, a peace treaty with Japan would be
evidence of China's peaceful intentions.[14]

An Examination of the Treaty

The Sino-Japanese treaty of peace and friendship consists of
a preamble and five brief articles.

The Preamble states that the Treaty has been concluded
"for the purpose of solidifying and developing the relations of
peace and friendship between the two countries" in the hope of
contributing to the peace and stability of Asia and the world.

Article One (like paragraph 6 of the 1972 joint communique)
stipulates that the two countries shall develop durable relations
of peace and friendship on the basis of the principles of mutual
respect for sovereignty and territorial integrity, mutual non-
interference in each other's internal affairs, equality and mutual
benefit and peaceful coexistence.

Article Two (like paragraph 7 of the 1972 joint communique) contains the anti-hegemony clause, which was declared
to be "an innovation in international treaties" by the *People's
Daily*.[15] It reads as follows:

> The contracting Parties declare that neither of them should
> seek hegemony in the Asia-Pacific region or in any other
> region and that each is opposed to efforts by any other
> country or group of countries to establish such hegemony.

The language of this clause is exactly the same as in the 1972
communique except that the treaty goes one step forward in
that it extends the area of application of this Article from the

"Asian-Pacific region" (as stipulated in the 1972 communique) to "any other region" as well.[16] Thus, on the one hand, this clause is a pledge of self-restraint on the part of the signatories not to themselves seek hegemony and, on the other hand, a statement of opposition to the efforts of others to seek hegemony anywhere.[17] Moreover, the treaty nowhere either defines or clarifies which acts can or cannot be considered hegemonistic. Each signatory can interpret hegemonism as it deems fit. For example, can one consider China's invasion of Vietnam as "hegemonistic"? If so, then it constitutes an infringement on the part of China of the provisions of the Sino-Japanese peace treaty. The Japanese were undoubtedly discomforted by China's punitive action against Vietnam, but there was little they could do in the matter.

Article Three provides that China and Japan shall endeavour to further develop economic and cultural relations with one another and to promote exchanges between the peoples of the two countries.

Article Four stipulates that the present treaty "shall not affect the position of either Contracting Party regarding its relations with third countries." Sonoda stated that this clause maintains the position of Japanese foreign policy based upon the US-Japanese relationship and the maintenance and development of friendly relations with all nations regardless of their social systems.[18]

Article Five provides that the treaty shall be ratified and shall enter into force on the date of the exchange of instruments of ratification which shall take place at Tokyo. It also provides that the treaty shall remain in force for ten years and thereafter shall continue to be in force until either Contracting Party, by giving one year's written notice to the other Contracting Party, terminates it at the end of initial ten years period or at any time thereafter.

Conclusions

In their public statements, the Japanese government leaders tended to assess the treaty's importance in historical, moralistic, and somewhat romantic ways.[19] Prime Minister Fukuda welcomed the Sino-Japanese peace treaty saying that it aimed at "placing Japan China relations which have so far developed on a more stable basis and promises their further extensive development."[20]

Japanese leaders also emphasized that the treaty did not constitute an anti-Soviet alliance and that Japan did not share China's anti-Soviet foreign policy. Thus Foreign Minister Sonoda stressed that Japan had "no intention of forming exclusive relationships with the People's Republic of China, either politically or economically."[21]

All Japanese political parties (except the Japanese Communist Party)—the LDP, the Japan Socialist Party, Komeito, the Japan Democratic Socialist Party, and the United Social Democratic Party—welcomed the signing of the peace treaty.[22] All Japanese political parties supported ratification of the treaty in the Diet just prior to the arrival of Chinese Vice Premier Deng Xiaoping in Japan.

The business community in general considered it as establishing a stable political environment between the two countries as the basis for the smooth expansion of bilateral economic exchanges. Shigeo Nagano, President of the Japan Chamber of Commerce and Industry, felt that the better atmosphere brought about by the formal establishment of friendly relations will benefit economic exchanges and economic co-operation. Toshiwo Doko, President of the Federation of Economic Organizations (*Keidanren*), felt that the Treaty revealed the determination of both countries to establish true friendship and prosperity for the future.[23]

The Japanese Press also favourably viewed the the Sino-Japanese peace and friendship treaty. The *Nihon Kezai Shimbun* considered the inclusion of the anti-hegemony clause as likely to have good effects on the security of Southeast Asia since China and Japan, would not seek hegemony. It was convinced that it did not imply either common action or a military alliance. On the contrary, it allowed both countries to pursue their respective independent diplomatic policies. The *Asahi Shimbun* considered the treaty as "a forward looking agreement which will direct the future courses of both countries." The *Youmiri Shimbun* said the treaty was significant since it serves as "a model for peaceful coexistence by countries which have different political systems from one another." The *Mainichi*

Shimbun also highlighted the beneficial effects of the treaty *vis-a-vis* Southeast Asian countries.[24]

The *People's Daily* editorial of 14 August 1978 regarded the treaty as "a political summation of relations between the two countries up till now, and a new starting point for the development of good-neighbourly and friendly relations between the two countries.[25] The influence of the treaty in the Asian-Pacific region would be "lasting and positive" and would be conducive to preserving peace and security." The *Peking Review* said the treaty established "a firm political basis" for developing and consolidating their good-neighbourly relation and for strengthening and promoting friendship between their peoples.[26] It was expected to "open new and broader prospects" for furthering the friendly exchanges and co-operation between China and Japan.[27] The Soviet Union was said to have adopted "a ludicrous attitude of hostility" ever since the treaty negotiations began. The development of friendly relations between China and Japan and the signing of treaty was stated to have put "a thorn in the flesh of the Soviet Union."[28]

The Chinese are very clear about the nature of the Sino-Japanese treaty. Soviet hegemonism, Chinese leaders assert, is the basic cause of international insecurity and instability in the world and "anti-hegemonism" is described as "the nucleus of the China-Japan Treaty of Peace and Friendship."[29] Vice Premier Deng Xiaoping asserted on 25 October 1978 that both China and Japan face the real threat of hegemonism. A new world war can be put off if "the people of all countries heighten their vigilance, strengthen their unity, get prepared and upset the strategic plans of the hegemonists".[30] Deng's visit to Tokyo to attend the ratification ceremony of the treaty was described as having "aided the growth of the international united front against hegemony and dealt a heavy blow at Soviet social-imperialism's attempt to drive a wedge between China and Japan and isolate China."[31] The Sino-Japanese peace treaty may be considered as symbolic of China's political and psychological victory against the Soviet Union since it was the first international legal document in which the principle of anti-hegemonism was prominently asserted despite vigorous Soviet protest.[32]

The initial reaction of the Soviet Union to the conclusion

of the Sino-Japanese peace treaty was one of keeping Tokyo off balance, warning that it would resort to unspecified actions to protect its interests in the event of Japan's going ahead and cementing its ties with China and that Japan would be responsible for all the consequences of such actions. Moscow was not convinced by statements of Japanese leaders that the treaty was not directed against the Soviet Union. "Only concrete steps, not words will show whether Tokyo is farsighted enough so as not to allow itself to become involved in Peking's dangerous policy."[33]

The Kremlin indicated its displeasure by recalling its Ambassador in Tokyo (though it maintained that the Ambassador had left for consultations). It also refused to renew the visas of the Japanese officials, engaged in negotiations for a possible agreement on joint fishing ventures in the 200-mile exclusive Soviet economic zone. It put off a visit by Foreign Minister N. Firyubin to Japan scheduled for August end. It allowed hard-hitting articles to appear in the Soviet Press. All this was probably intended to influence public opinion and perhaps prevent the ratification of the treaty. However, after the treaty was ratified by the Diet and came into force, the Soviet Union adopted a somewhat milder attitude. It also desisted from taking any precipitate retaliatory measures. This was partly because it did not wish to drive Japan any closer to China and the United States and partly because it had not given up hope of continuing mutually beneficial economic and trade relations with Japan, particularly the involvement of Japanese technological skill and capital in in the exploitation of Siberia's vast natural resources.

Moscow felt that the Sino-Japanese peace treaty had tended to improve China's geo-strategic position in Northeast Asia and undermine that of the Soviet Union. One researcher, therefore, feels that a Soviet countermove—its treaty with Vietnam and the backing of Hanoi's intervention in Kampuchea—became necessary in order to wrest the geo-strategic initiative from the emerging Sino-Japanese-US "axis."[34] The US-Japanese Mutual Security Treaty coupled with the Sino-Japanese peace treaty and the normalization of Sino-US relations in December 1978 gave rise to Soviet fears that a so-called "US-China-Japan axis" had emerged. Chinese statements that "anti-hegemonism" was the essence of the Sino-Japanese peace treaty and speeches by US leaders that the United States and China had "parallel strategic interests" and "shared concerns" lent credence to Soviet fears.

The United States, Japan's political and military ally, approved of the Sino-Japanese treaty because it served American foreign policy objectives of fostering China's anti-Soviet stance. It also reflected the common positions of China and the United States in safeguarding their interests against Soviet advances in Asia. Washington welcomed the treaty by saying that it contributed to "stability and security" in East Asia [35] At the same time, the treaty may be somewhat unwelcome because if may lead to an even greater expansion of Sino-Japanese trade and thereby adversely affect American trade prospects in China.

Southeast Asian nations, on the other hand, were apprehensive of the Sino-Japanese peace treaty and felt that it signified some kind of ganging together. They felt that this might have adverse implications for them.

The Sino-Japanese treaty can be said to have had several positive results from the Japanese point of view. Firstly, it can said to have improved the political climate between China and Japan. It is, therefore, likely to have a wholesome effect in accelerating trade and economic co-operation between the two countries.

Secondly, Vice Premier Deng Xiaoping promised Foreign Minister Sonoda that the incident in which Chinese boats began operating around the Senkaku Islands would not be repeated.[36] However, the treaty by no means resolves the issue. But both sides seem to have realized that economic relations should not suffer on account of it.

Thirdly, that Japanese were able to confirm from Chinese leaders that China would take necessary steps to terminate the Sino-Soviet Treaty of Friendship, Alliance, and Mutual Assistance (1950) in April 1979.

The Sino-Japanese peace treaty has not fostered political instability in Northeast Asia. It is not a military alliance.[37] However, it does apparently reflect some kind of a political understanding between China and Japan *vis-a-vis* the Soviet Union.

NOTES

1. Chae-Jin Lee, "The Making of the Sino-Japanese Peace and Friendship Treaty," *Pacific Affairs*, Fall 1979, 420.

2. Hong N. Kim, "The Fukuda Government and the Politics of the Sino-Japanese Peace Treaty," *Asian Survey*, March 1979, 299.

3. Tadashi Shibauchi, "Haken Mondai to Tsuna hiki, sareru Nihon," *Chou Koron*, July 1975, 159. Cited in ibid., 299.

4. *Japan Economic Journal*, 11 April 1978.

5. Foreign Language Press, *Documents of the first session of the Fifth National People's Congress of the People's Republic of China* (Peking, 1978), 110.

6. *Tass*, 23 February 1978 and *Pravda*, 24 February 1978, as translated in *Soviet Review* (New Delhi), 16 March 1978, 46-8. For an analysis of the Soviet draft treaty, see R.K. Jain, *The USSR and Japan, 1945-1980* (New Delhi, 1981), 154-7.

7. *Peking Review*, 17 March 1978, 44-5.

8. Daniel Tretiak, "The Sino-Japanese Treaty of 1978: The Senkaku Incident Prelude," *Asian Survey*, December 1978, 1245.

9. Ibid., 1243.

10. See Lee, n. 1, 428-30.

11. For details see *Look Japan*, 10 October 1978; Lee, n. 1, 433-7.

12. In his farewell dinner speech on 22 May 1978 in Beijing, Zbigniew Brezezinski, Assistant to the US President for National Security Affairs, stated:

> "Our commitment to friendship with China is based on shared concerns and is derived from a long-term strategic view: we recognize and share China's resolve to resist the efforts of any nation which seeks to establish global or regional hegemony."

    A week later in an interview to the *New York Times* he said that the US-China relationship is based on "certain congruence of fundamental issues and it reflects a mutual understanding that these interests are enduring." *Facts on File*, 2 June 1978, 399. See also Brezezinski's NBC "Meet the Press" interview, 28 May 1978 in *Department of State Bulletin*, no. 2016, July 1978, 27.

13. T.B. Millar, "Triumph of Pragmatism: China's Links with the West," *International Affairs* (London), April 1979.

14. Ibid.

15. *Peking Review*, 18 August 1978.

16. The 1972 joint communique reads as follows:

> "The normalisation of relations between China and Japan is not directed against third countries. Neither of the two countries should seek hegemony in the Asia-Pacific region and each country is opposed to efforts by any other country or group of countries to establish such hegemony."

17. See statement by Deng Xiaoping, 25 October 1978. *Peking Review*, 3 November 1978, 14.

18. *Japan Review* (New Delhi), August 1978, 8-9.

19. Lee, n. 1, 440.

[20] *Japan Review*, August 1978, 7.

[21] Interview of Foreign Minister Sunao Sonoda to *Look Japan*. *Look Japan*, 10 October 1978, 2. Also see Yosuke Nakae (Director-General of the Asian Affairs Bureau, Japanese Ministry of Foreign Affairs), "Significance of the Japan-China Treaty of Peace and Friendship," Ibid., 3.

[22] For their reactions, see ibid., 13.

[23] Ibid., 11.

[24] Reproduced in ibid.

[25] *Peking Review*, 18 August 1978; also statement by Foreign Minister Huang Hua at the banquet given by Foreign Minister Sonoda, 12 August 1978, *News from China* (New Delhi), 14 August 1978, 7.

[26] *Peking Review*, 20 October 1978, 19. Also see statement by Foreign Minister Huang Hua, 12 August 1978.

[27] *News from China*, 27 October 1978, 5.

[28] *Peking Review*, 18 August 1978, 10.

[29] Ibid., 3 November 1978, 15.

[30] Ibid., 11.

[31] Report by Liao Cheng-chih, Vice-Chairman of the NPC Standing Committee, to the Standing Committee on Deng's visit to Japan. See *News from China* (New Delhi), 7 November 1978, 3.

[32] Lee, n. 1, 438.

[33] S. Levchenko, "The Teng Visit," *New Times* (Moscow), no. 45, November 1978, 13.

[34] Avigdor Haselkorn, "Impact of Sino-Japanese Treaty on the Soviet Security Strategy," *Asian Survey*, June 1978, 572.

[35] *Japan Times*, 12 August 1978.

[36] See statement by Foreign Minister Sonoda, 12 August 1978. *News from China*, 14 August 1978, 9.

[37] The Sino-Japanese peace treaty unlike Article 9 of the Indo-Soviet Treaty of Peace, Friendship and Co-operation, does not even stipulate "immediate mutual consultations" in the event of an attack upon either Contracting Party. For the text of the Indo-Soviet treaty, see R.K. Jain, *Soviet-South Asian Relations, 1947-1978: vol 1, India* (New Delhi, 1979), 113-6.

8. The Senkaku Islands Dispute

One of the problems bedevilling Sino-Japanese relations is the problem of the Senkaku Islands or the Dioayutai as the Chinese call them. The Senkakus are a group of eight, small, uninhabited islands, located 118 miles north-east of Taiwan, whose combined area is about 4.2 square miles. The sovereignty over these islands is a matter of dispute between China, Japan, South Korea, and Taiwan.

The Senkakus first came into public notice in 1968 when the Economic Commission for Asia and the Far East (ECAFE) conducted a seismic survey of the East China Sea and the Yellow Sea in October and November 1968. The report of the survey (published in May 1969) revealed the existence of rich oil deposits in the Yellow Sea and the continental shelf between Japan and Taiwan. This was confirmed by a Japanese survey undertaken in June-July 1969.

Shortly thereafter Taiwan asserted its claim to the Senkaku Islands by passing a statute controlling the exploration and drilling for oil and gas in Chinese territorial waters and continental shelf. The Executive Yuan established four zones for undersea oil prospecting in a 69,000 square mile area in the Taiwan Straits and in the sea north of Taiwan, including the Senkaku Islands area. The Nationalist China Petroleum Corporation, a state-owned company, signed agreements with several oil companies to jointly develop these four zones.[1] In order to strengthen its legal position, Taipei also ratified the 1958 Geneva Convention on the Continental Shelf (with reservations to Article 6). The Japanese also asserted their claims. Thus, on 10 September 1970, Foreign Minister Aichi asserted in the

the Diet Foreign Relations Committee that the Senkakus were without any doubt, Japanese territory.[2] This statement succeeded in its objective of dissuading foreign oil companies from going ahead with their plans to prospect for oil under contracts from Taiwan.

In an effort to reconcile differences, Japan, South Korea, and Taiwan formed a "Liaison Committee" on 12 November 1970 to jointly explore and exploit the undersea oil resources around the Senkakus. Beijing criticized the formation of the Committee. The intention of the committee, a Chinese commentary stated, was to temporarily "shelve" or "freeze" the title of China and North Korea to the islands and the undersea resources and make them surrender their sovereignty and let "Japanese militarism ravage and occupy the islands and resources at will."[3]

In view of its efforts to normalize relations with China, the United States advised American companies in mid-1971 against participation in sea areas whose ownership was under dispute. In June 1971 under the Okinawa Reversion Agreement the United States returned the Senkakus to Japan. In its statement of 30 December 1971 the Chinese Foreign Ministry declared the agreement "utterly illegal."[4] The territorial dispute over the Senkakus also led to heated exchanges between the Chinese and Japanese representatives in the United Nations Committee on the Peaceful Uses of the Seabed and the Ocean Floor Beyond the Limits of National Jurisdiction in March 1972. An Chih-yuan, the representative of China, asserted:

> The Japanese government's wild attempt to occupy China's territory of Tiaoyu and other islands and plunder the seabed resources in the vicinity of these islands is a glaring act of aggression, to which we of course cannot remain indifferent [5]

The Senkaku Islands issue was not seriously taken up during Tanaka's visit to China in September 1972 apparently because neither side considered it advisable to retard the process of the normalization of Sino-Japanese relations.

The Japanese Position[6]

The Japanese Government asserts that the Senkakus were first discovered by a Japanese national, Tatsushi Koga, in 1884 and were formally incorporated (by the Japanese Cabinet decision of 14 January 1895) into Japanese territory shortly before the signing of the Treaty of Shimonoseki. Tokyo argues that they were not included in Taiwan and the Pescadores, which were ceded by China under the terms of the Shimonoseki Treaty (1895). Further, the Japanese argue that the Senkaku Islands were not included in the territory relinquished by Japan under Article 2 of the San Francisco Peace Treaty. They were placed under US administration as a part of the Nansei Islands, in accordance with Article 3 of the San Francisco Peace Treaty, and are included in the areas the administrative rights over which reverted to Japan under the Okinawa Reversion Agreement and form part of the Okinawa Prefecture.

The Japanese Government challenges the historical, geographical, or geological bases of the Chinese argument. Tokyo asserts that Beijing has not advanced any objection to the inclusion of these US administrative areas under Article 3 of the San Francisco Peace Treaty. The arguments of Japanese scholars on the subject revolved around the effort to prove

(1) that the disputed islands were *terra nullius* in 1859 and
(2) that Japan has since maintained an "effective occupation" of the islands.[7]

The judicial drawback in the Japanese argument, Mendl points out, is that the reference to Article 8 of the Potsdam Declaration in the Sino-Japanese joint communique of 29 September 1972 implied Japanese admission of a territorial dispute because the Senkakus had never been specially mentioned among the "minor islands" or in the definition of the Ryukyus in the Treaty of San Francisco.[8]

The Chinese Position

The Chinese case rests on the claim that the islands were mentioned in documents of the Ming dynasty in the early sixteenth century. The Senkakus have been China's territory since "ancient times". This is "a historical fact no one can change."[9] The Senkakus were part of Taiwan province when it was formed in 1887. China refuses to recognize the cession of these islands under the unequal Shimonoseki treaty. And since

Taiwan was returned to China by the Cairo and Potsdam Declarations, the Statement of Surrender, and the Peace Treaties, the Senkakus also reverted to Beijing. The Chinese have invoked both the law of territorial acquisition and the concept of the continental shelf.[10]

That the Chinese were willing and able to assert their claims over what they considered their own territory was evident from their military occupation of the Paracel Islands in the South China Sea in January 1974. The Paracel Islands are important for China because of their strategic value in observing Soviet naval movements and also becauase of the mineral and marine resources around them. However, since the South China Sea area between the Paracel Islands and the Spratly Islands (which are under the occupation of Vietnam) was a primary route for the tanker trade between Japan and the Middle East, China's forcible occupation of the Paracel Islands became a matter of concern in Japanese Government circles.

Japan-South Korea Agreement

On 30 January 1974 Japan and South Korea signed an agreement to jointly explore an area totalling approximately 82,000 sq. km. south of Cheju island. The ultimate recoverable reserves of this area are estimated at about 112 million kilolitres of petroleum and about 260 million cubic metres of natural gas. Japan is expected to secure about 5 million kilolitres of oil annually over a period of twelve years, i.e. a total of 60 million kilolitres, if the oil reserves are fully recovered.[11]

The Chinese Ministry of Foreign Affairs issued a statement on 4 February 1974 declaring the marking off of a so-called Japan-South Korea "joint development zone" on the East China Sea continental shelf as "an infringement of Chinese sovereignty." It asserted that the signatories to the Agreement would be responsible for all the consequences therefrom should they arbitrarily carry out development activities in the area. This statement cited the natural prolongation principle in support of China's right to a voice in delimiting the continental shelf and suggested that the question of how to divide the continental shelf should be decided by China and the other countries concerned through consultations.[12] This seemed to indicate Chinese willingness to come to some kind of a compromise settlement.

South Korea ratified the agreement in July 1974 and urged Japan to do the same at an early date. The Japanese, however, proceded with much caution partly because of intense in-fighting among the various factions of the LDP[13] and party because of the desire to refrain from any steps that might retard the growth of Sino-Japanese trade. (Trade between China and Japan had increased three-fold from $1.1 billion in 1972 to $3.3 billion in 1974.)

China reiterated its views on several other occasions. On 27 May 1977 Chinese Vice Minister of Foreign Affairs Ho Ying told the Japanese Ambassador to China, Heishiro Ogawa, that it was regrettable that the Japanese Government had ignored the Chinese position and submitted the agreement to the Diet for ratification. Ho Yong felt that Japan was trying to present China with a *fait accompli*. He warned that the ratification of the agreement would prove harmful to the development of Sino-Japanese relations and that the Japanese Government must bear full responsibility for all the consquences arising therefrom.[14] The Chinese Ministry of Foreign Affairs also lodged a serious protest with the Japanese Government. China reiterated its stand and asserted that the Japan-South Korea agreement was a violation of the principle that the continental shelf is the natural extension of the continental territory.[15]

The Senkaku Incident, April 1978

On 12 April 1978 about 100 Chinese fishing boats armed with machine guns approached the Senkaku Islands and waved placards claiming that the islands belonged to China. The Japanese coast guard ordered them to leave the area, but refrained from challenging them militarily. Japan immediately protested. It asked Beijing to promptly withdraw the boats and investigate the incident. Two days later, the Chinese Embassy brushed aside Japan's protest on the ground that the islands belonged to China. However, the next day Vice Premier Geng Biao said the incident was accidental and was neither intentional nor deliberate.[16] He also urged the Japanese Government not to let the Senkaku issue complicate the on-going negotiations for the conclusion of a peace treaty. The incident, however, tended to strengthen the hands of the anti-Treaty forces.[17]

The Chinese Vice Premier lodged a strong protest with the Japanese Ambassador in Beijing on 10 May 1978 against the passing of the "special measures act for the implementation of the Japan-South Korea agreement on the joint development of the continental shelf" by the Japanese House of Representatives and its submission to the House of Councillors for its deliberation.[18]

The special bill for implementing the Japan-South Korea continental shelf agreement was passed in the Diet on 14 June 1978, i.e. after four years since it was first introduced in the Diet.[19] Eight days later the two countries exchanged instruments of ratification. On this occasion, the Chinese Foreign Ministry issued another statement. It asserted on 26 June 1978 that China could not tolerate this "obdurate act of infringement on China's sovereignty." It reiterated that this agreement was entirely illegal and null and void and that should any country or private person undertake development activities in the so-called "joint development zone", it or he must bear full responsibility for all the consequences arising therefrom.[20]

In an attempt to establish Japanese sovereignty over the disputed islands, the Okinawa Development Agency had constructed a heliport in one of the disputed group of islands in May 1979 and sent a team of scientists to "study marine conditions" around the islands in 1979. The Chinese delivered a protest.[21] Japanese Foreign Minister Sonoda reiterated the Japanese claim, but considered it diplomatically unwise for Japan to take any concrete steps to demonstrate its sovereignty over the disputed territory. He felt that the islands should be left as they are for the sake of Japan's national interest in general as well as for Japan-China friendship. The survey team sent by the Okinawa Development Agency left the islands on 7 June 1979 after completing their task and leaving some meteorological observation equipment on Utsuri Island.

In March 1979 Japan and South Korea reached an agreement on prospecting, exploitation, and management of the "joint development zone". Nippon Oil Exploration Co., a

subsidiary of the Nippon Oil Co., agreed to serve as operator
for exploration in six out of the seven sections. It was stipulated that the cost would be equally split between the two
countries. After successful exploration, both sides would
equally share the oil and natural gas.[22] Drilling and test exploration work started a year later in May 1980. In a statement
of 7 May 1980, China reiterated its position.[23] The next day
Renmin Ribao published an article challenging the Japanese
argument that the "joint development zone" does not extend
beyond the "midline" of the East China Sea. It stated that the
Japanese position was untenable because the "mid-line" referred to by Japan had been defined unilaterally and was not a
recognized principle under international law for demarcating
the waters between littoral states. On the contrary, it added,
international law required that such demarcation, including
temporary measures prior to reaching a formal agreement,
must be made through consultation and agreement between the
parties concerned.[24]

The Nippon Oil Exploration Co. had reportedly failed in
its first exploration attempt.[25] It was also reported that towards
the end of November 1980 China had expressed its willingness to develop seabed reasorces in the East China Sea with
Japan by putting aside complicated territorial problems, including the ownership of the Senkaku Islands.[26]

Conclusions

The Senkaku Islands dispute is largely the by-product of a
struggle for the resources of the continental shelf at a time of
depleting resources the world over.

All Japanese political parties support the official viewpoint
on the Senkakus. However, in contrast with the vexing issue of
the Northern Territories, the dispute over the Senkaku Islands
has not generated the same degree of heat and passion as the
dispute between Japan and the Soviet Union has done. This is
largely becaue of the absence of any great emotional attechment
to the Senkakus in Japan. Moreover, it is China which is the
aggrieved party in case of these islands. The Japanese feel a
direct, immediate danger to their security by the stationing of
troops and the construction of military bases by the Soviet

Union on the Northern Territories, a few miles from their country. This fear is accentuated all the more given the traditional distrust and suspicion of the Soviets. Given its considerable economic stake in China, the business community in Japan prefers to go along with the Government's present politico-strategic tilt towards China. It apparently urges the Japanese Government to keep the issue in proper perspective. It is also quite possible that Japanese companies may have received some kind of an assurance from China before they decided to proceed with drilling and exploration work. It does not, however, follow that the Senkaku Islands issue is of no significance whatsoever in Japan's domestic politics. The Right, in fact, had endeavoured to exploit the issue in order to complicate negotiations for the conclusion of the Sino-Japanese peace treaty and succeeded in delaying its signature, especially in the aftermath of the Senkaku Incident of April 1978.

Japan may perhaps prefer trilateral, especially American, co-operation in the development of oil around the Senkakus in the hope that such participation may ensure the security of investment. The United States Government, however, does not apparently wish to get mixed up with this problem. Thus, the US Department of State and the Senate do not consider the reversion of Okinawa to Japan as in any way affecting the determination of the sovereignty over the disputed islands which must be settled between China and Japan. Both China and Japan have advanced sophisticated legal arguments to support their case. Beijing will continue to insist on the natural prolongation principle and link its claim to the Senkakus with the argument that they are an integral part of Taiwan. Japan, on the other hand, prefers a settlement on the basis of the median line. Legal issues relating to the law of the sea are also involved and these are still the subject of the on-going discussions.

China's present leadership has decided to shelve the Senkaku Islands issue for the time being for several valid reasons. Firstly, Japanese possession of the Senkakus does not pose any adverse military or strategic implications for China. Secondly, the extent of oil and gas reserves is yet uncertain and a better picture would emerge only after the conclusion of drilling work.

And this would certainly take some time. Chinese policy-makers may reason that in this situation the advantages are as yet uncertain and not much would be gained by exacerbating the issue. On the contrary, harsh tactics or military action would seriously impair the prospects of procuring Japanese credits, plants, and technology which is considered vital for China's Four Modernization programme. Thus, Vice Premier Deng Xiaoping stated at a Tokyo Press conference in October 1978:

> It is true that two sides maintain different views on this question . . . It doesn't matter if this question is shelved for some time, say, ten years. Our generation is not wise enough to find common language on this question. Our next generation will certainly be wiser. They will surely find a solution acceptable to all.[27]

China feels that it has nothing to lose by letting foreign exploration activities proceed around the Senkakus because it can use the findings for its own oil programme. It would for the present be satisfied with recognition of its legal rights and permit the Japanese to gain material benefit in return for some arrangement involving transfer of technology and payment of royalties.[28]

Looking to the future, domestic politics in China and Japan can make it increasingly difficult to arrive at a compromise on the territorial issue. Indeed the dispute over the Senkaku Islands may well prove to be a flash-point in their bilatral relations. However, it seems that both China and Japan are likely to proceed with a flexible attitude. They would neither wish to exacerabate things nor resort to force and escalate the issue into military confrontation lest it have adverse consequences on Sino-Japanese economic and political relations.

NOTES

1 Victor H. Li, "China and Off-shore Oil : The Tiao-yu Tai Dispute," *Stanford Journal of International Studies* (Spring 1975), 146.

2 *The Okinawa* (Tokyo), 122-3. Cited in Tao Cheng, "The Sino-Japanese Dispute over the Tiao-yu-Tai (Senkaku) Islands and the Law of Territorial Acquisiton," *Virginia Journal of International Law* (Winter 1974), 245.

3 *Peking Review*, 11 December 1970, 15-6, *People's Daily*, 29 December

1970.

4 *Peking Review*, 7 January 1972, 12.

5 Ibid., 17 March 1972, 10-1.

6 See Japan, Ministry of Foreign Affairs, *Senkaku Islands and the Territorial Issue* (Tokyo, n. d.). The Japanese Foreign Ministry issued a statement on 8 March 1972 entitled "The Foreign Ministry's view concerning the Rights to the Ownership over the Senkaku Islands." US Embassy (Tokyo), Daily Summary of Japanese Press, 8 March 1972 15-6. Cited in Cheng, n. 2, 244-5.

7 See Cheng, n. 2, 245-7.

8 Wolf Mendl, *Issues in Japan's China Policy* (London, 1978), 89.

9 *Peking Review*, 1 January 1971, 22.

10 Cheng, n. 2, 222.

11 *Japan Economic Journal*, 20 June 1978; *Asahi Evening News*, 13 September 1978, 13.

12 *Peking Review*, 8 February 1974, 3.

13 For details see Selig S. Harrison, *China, Oil, and Conflict Ahead ?* (New York, 1977), 139-41.

14 *Peking Review*, 3 June 1977, 7, also Chinese Embassy in India, *News from China* (New Delhi), 1 June 1977, 4-5.

15 *Peking Review*, 17 June 1977, 16-7; *News from China*, 15 June 1977, 5-6.

16 *Asahi Shimbun*, 15 April 1978.

17 Daniel Tretiak, "Sino-Japanese Treaty of 1978: The Senkaku Incident Prelude," *Asian Survey*, December 1968.

18 *Peking Review*, 19 May 1978, 4-5.

19 *Japan Economic Journal*, 20 June 1978.

20 *Peking Review*, 26 June 1978, 25.

21 *Beijing Review*, 8 June 1979.

22 *Japan Economic Journal*, 15 July 1980.

23 *Beijing Review*, 19 May 1980, 6-7.

24 Ibid., 7.

25 *Japan Economic Journal*, 15 July 1980.

26 *Japan Times*, 23 November 1980.

27 *Peking Review*, 3 November 1978, 16.

28 Mendl, n. 8, 108- 9.

9. Economic Relations, 1972-1980

The normalization of relations gave a fillip to Sino-Japanese trade and led to a brisk exchange of economic and trade delegations. The Japan-China Association on Economy and Trade with Yoshihiro Inayama as Chairman was established on 27 November 1972. Trade increased almost two-fold from $1.1 billion in 1972 to $2.015 billion in 1973. This exceeded the total volume of Soviet-Japanese trade by about $500 million. Bilateral trade registered a further increase in 1974, totalling $3.293 billion, an increase of 63.4 per cent over the figure for 1973. It was also the first time that Sino-Japanese trade exceeded Japan's trade with Taiwan ($2.953 billion). The complementary nature of the economies of China and Japan, the extension of Japanese Export-Import Bank credits, and increased Chinese imports of Japanese manufactured goods and plants were among the major factors which led to the rapid increase in trade between the two countries.

China and Japan signed a trade agreement in January 1974 whereby they granted the most-favoured-nation treatment in tariff and customs clearance to each other. The agreement provided for the settlement of trade account in Japanese yen, Chinese yuan, or other convertible currencies recognized by both the countries; for facilities for exchange of industrial technology etc. for the promotion of trade; and for the use of commercial arbitration machinery. The agreement was to be valid for three years and to be automatically renewed thereafter unless either party decided to terminate it.

Shipping Agreement, November 1974

A 12-Article shipping agreement was signed between China and Japan on 13 November 1974 in Tokyo. This agreement, initially valid for three years, provided for guarantees in respect of revenue remittances of shipping enterprises, confirmation of the cargo transport right, approval of certificates of nationality of ships, and co-operation in rescue operations in the event of accidents at sea. It also granted the most-favoured-nation (MFN) treatment for ships of each country calling at the port of the other country. It said that there would be further mutual consultations at the governmental level to solve other questions such as mutual exemption of taxes on shipping, shipping tariffs, and loading shares of the ships of the two countries.[1] In so far as the agreement guaranteed free remittances of profits, it represented a concession by China to the Japanese side because the Japanese earned much more on this route than the Chinese did. In August 1976, Chang Kung-chen, Director General of the Ocean Shipping Bureau of the Chinese Transport Ministry visited Japan to attend the first China-Japan government consultation on shipping held at the Japanese Foreign Ministry to review the shipping agreement between the two countries. As a result of Chang's visit, Japan and China signed an agreement in Tokyo on 25 August 1976 on the establishment of a private-level shipping representative office in each other's country.

Fishery Agreement, August 1975

After nearly two years of intermittent negotiations over fishing rights and territorial limits in the Yellow Sea and the East China Sea, the Fishery Agreement between the two countries was signed on 15 August 1975. Earlier, in June 1974, the private-level fishery agreement, which was due to expire on 22 June 1974, had been extended for another year. The eight-Article fishery accord of August 1975 provided for a number of measures for the preservation and effective utilization of fishery resources. It also placed certain restrictions on the operations of trawling vessels, enumerated the steps to be taken by both sides to provide guidance to and exercise surveillance over fishery operations, and spelt out the ways in which breaches of the accord are to be dealt with. It also provided for rescue operations in the event of accidents at sea and specified the ports that might be used at shelters in emergencies by each other's fishing vessels.[2] It declared a zone of some 100 to 150 miles from the Chinese coast out of bounds for Japanese trawlers and said that, in certain specific areas outside this zone, only fishing trawlers of up to 600 HP capacity would be permitted to fish.

As regards the Gulf of Bohai and the areas around Shanghai, which the Chinese had declared "security zones," the Japanese side gave its virtual recognition to the alert military zone. In an appendix to the agreement, China declared that no Japanese fishing boat would be allowed into the zone without specific permission since the area was considered vital to China's defence and security. The Japanese rejected this demand as unacceptable, but promised not to operate in this area in order to "preserve China's fishery resources." Thus Japan acknowledged the substance of the Chinese demands though it rejected the form in which they had been presented. In so far as the fishery agreement was effective only in the area north of the 27°N latitude, it avoided the ticklish question of Taiwan and the sea areas around it.

Foreign Minister Miyazawa considered the fishery agreement to be reflective of the steady progress of friendly relations between the two countries. Ambassador Chen Chu of China stated that the signing of the fishery agreement would help consolidate and develop the traditional friendship between the two peoples, particularly between the fishery circles of the two countries, and would have "a positive effect" on the development of good-neighbourly and friendly relations between the two countries.[3]

The year 1976 witnessed a fall in trade of about 20 per cent to $3.03 billion from $3.789 billion in 1975. Thus for the first time since 1967 exports decreased and the drop for imports and two-way trade was the first fall in eight years. This was primarily due to Chinese efforts to adhere to its import-export adjustment measures to hold down imports and to boost exports following the deterioration of its trade balance from

1974. Beijing also apparently tried to rectify its adverse trade
balance with Japan. The influence of the "Gang of Four" as
well as natural disasters such as earthquakes, cold and dry
weather, etc. were contributory factors. Besides, the competi-
tiveness of Japanese products in some areas, e.g. chemicals,
had declined.[4]

Sino-Japanese trade increased in 1977 due to the elimination of the adverse influence of the Gang of Four, China's
reappraisal of the active role that foreign trade played in furthering its modernization, brisker Chinese demand for Japanese
products, and the substantial improvement in China's external
trade balance into a surplus. Japan's imports steadily increased,
primarily due to increased crude imports.[5]

China-Japan Long-Term Trade Agreement, 16 February 1978

Understanding had been reached in March 1977 to conclude a
China-Japan Long-Term Trade Agreement when a *Keidanren*
delegation led by President Toshiwo Doko visited China and
conferred with Chinese Foreign Trade Minister Li Chang.
On 14 October a Promotional Committee for the Japan-China
Long-Term Trade Agreement with Yoshihiro Inayama as
Chairman was set up in Tokyo. This Promotional Committee
consisted of a co-ordination committee, and four specialized
sub-committees, viz. export, petroleum, coking coal, and
finance and settlement. Meanwhile, during the visit of
Vice Minister of Foreign Trade Liu Hsi-wen in September
1977 the broad framework of the agreement was agreed upon.
Liu said that China would also establish a promotional committee for facilitating the early conclusion of the agreement.
The Japanese Government also began studying possibilities of
how to meet Chinese requests for low interest and long repay-
ment period credits.

Negotiations for the conclusion of the agreement were held
from 26 to 30 November 1977 when Yoshihiro Inayama, Chairman of the Japan-China Association on Economy and Trade,
visited China.

The main cause for the delay in the formulation of the
proposed draft of the agreement was the lack of agreement
over Chinese crude exports to Japan. In March 1977

Toshiwo Doko had proposed the import volume from China after five years to 50 million tons a year for petroleum and 5 million tons a year for coal. This was subsequently scaled down to 11.3 million tons in the draft adopted by the Japanese Promotional Committeee on 22 November primarily because of the recession in Japanese iron and steel industries, the improvement in oil supply, and the properties of Chinese crude.

Earlier, on 15 November Vice Premier Gu Mu told a visiting Japanese delegation led by Hideyuki Aizawa that China was capable of exporting nearly 15 million tons in five years. In the negotiations held towards the end of November the Chinese side confirmed this figure and Inayama proposed a figure of 15 million tons. Progress was also evident in the case of export of industrial plants. However, the two sides failed to reach agreement on the supplies of ordinary coal and metal-lurgical coal. On 31 January 1978 the Committee for the Promotion of the Japan-China Long-Term Trade Agreement was renamed the Japan-China Long-Term Trade Consultation Committee. A delegation led by Inayama left for China on 14 February to sort out the remaining issues. Two days later, the China-Japan Long-Term Trade Agreement was signed.

The agreement consists of a preamble and twelve articles. The preamble defines the agreement as "a general agreement" between the Japan-China Long-Term Trade Consultation Committees set up in both countries. It is based on the joint communique of 1972 and the trade agreement of 1974. It envisages the development of economic and trade relations between the two countries over "a long period of time and in a stable manner" with the backing of the respective governments of the two countries. The agreeement is valid for eight years and stipulates the export of $10 billion by each signatory to the other during this period (Article 1). During the first five years (1978-82) Japan will export technology and plants worth $7-8 billion and $2-3 billion worth of construction materials and machinery. During 1978-82 China will export 47.1 million tons of crude oil, 5.15-5.3 million tons of coking coal and 3.3-3.9 million tons of steam coal.[6] The export quantities of coal and crude for 1983 and the subsequent years will be worked out in 1981 and shall increase year after year (Article 2). The two sides agreed in principle that Japanese exports of technology, industrial plants, construction materials, machinery, and equipment shall be on a deferred payment basis (Article 3). Transactions based on the agreement shall be conducted in accordance with individual contracts on the basis of reasonable international prices and international trade practices (Article 4). Article 5 envisages the promotion of technological co-operation and expansion of economic exchanges between the two countries. The representatives of the two sides shall hold meetings every year, alternatively in Tokyo and Beijing to discuss the implementation of and the problems relating to the agreement (Article 9).

The China-Japan Long-Term Trade Agreement is a private agreement; but because it has the support of the two countries it may be considered a quasi-governmental agreement. It is a comprehensive arrangement addressed to large-scale deals. A considerable level of trade transactions, which are going on outside the purview of the arrangement, are expected to continue unchanged as long as China has adequate foreign exchange funds.[7] It was felt that this agreement would prove a boon to the depression-ridden Japanese industry, especially chemicals and steel products, and assist Japanese efforts to diversify sources of energy supplies.[8]

The Long-Term Trade Agreement was formally revised when Chinese Vice Minister of Foreign Trade Liu Hsi-wen and Yoshihiro Inayama, Chairman of the Japan-China Long-Term Trade Agreement Committee, signed and exchanged memoranda in Tokyo on 29 March 1979. The validity of the agreement was extended by another five years to 1990 and its value raised to $60 billion. It was also agreed that all of the contracts on import of technology and plants which the Technology Import Corporation of China concluded in and after 1979 would be considered as transactions coming under the trade agreement.[9]

Sino-Japanese trade totalled $5,079 million in 1978, an increase of 46 per cent over the previous year: Japanese exports to China amounted to $3,049 million, up 57 per cent from the previous year, and imports from China stood at $2,030 million, an increase of 31 per cent. Thus, for the first time in the history of Japan-China trade, the imbalance exceeded $1 billion.[10]

Long-Term Financing

In early 1979 a major issue surfaced in Sino-Japanese economic relations, viz. the question of long-term financing of Japanese exports to China. The problem had arisen because Chinese imports of complete plants, machinery, and construction materials had risen much faster than anticipated in the February 1978 agreement. The traditional arrangement of executing export orders by supplier credits also proved to be inadequate given the considerable value and huge inflow of Chinese orders. Another contributory factor had been slower purchases of Chinese oil and coal by Japan.

After some deliberation the Japanese Government opted for a deferred payment formula for exports of plants to China by extending yen loans from the Export-Import Bank of Japan. It also favoured the extension of low-interest loans for China's oil and coal development projects, which would enable China to solve its difficulties in financing trade to a certain extent.[11]

In October 1978 China rejected the offer of a $1 billion loan denominated in yen by the Export-Import Bank of Japan. Beijing indicated its preference for a loan denominated in dollars because it felt that the appreciation of the yen would make yen loans harder to repay.

Meanwhile, criticism of the Japanese Government's inaction mounted at home. Thus, Yoshiro Inayama, President of the Japan-China Association on Economy and Trade and Board Chairman of Nippon Steel Corporation, criticized the Japanese Government's indecisiveness in resolving the issue of financing Chinese imports from Japan.[12] In response to such criticism, the Minister for International Trade and Industry, Masumi Esaki, proposed that half of the necessary funds for deferred payment imports by China should be provided in yen from the Export-Import Bank of Japan and the other half in the form of syndicated loans denominated in dollars from Japanese commercial banks.[13] Japanese trading companies, plant manufacturers, and commercial banks were reportedly concerned about this decision primarily because it did not explain how risks of foreign exchange losses involved in dollar loans would be shared.

Negotiations for a solution to the problem of long-term

financing for Japanese exports to China began in March 1979 when a Bank of China delegation led by the International Development Manager, Niu Hsuan-chi, visited Tokyo. Broad understanding was soon reached on the amount of both long-term and short-term loans etc., but there was basic disagreement on two problems, viz. the rate of interest that China should pay and whether the loans should be denominated in yen or US dollars. While Japanese bankers sought a margin of 0.625 per cent over the Eurodollar average rate of around 11 per cent, China strongly felt that it was being asked to pay too much interest. The Japanese, however, maintained that the rate of interest they offered was the second lowest rate a consortium of Japanese banks had provided to foreign countries. Moreover, the Chinese were reluctant to accept the Japanese proposal that loans be denominated in yen because they felt that China's financial burden would increase if the yen's exchange value further appreciated.

The first breakthrough came on 15 May 1979 when the Export-Import Bank of Japan and the Bank of China signed a "Memoranda Concerning Basic Matters of a Loan for the Development of Oil and Coal Resources". The agreement provided China with yen-denominated credits to the order of 420 billion yen or US $2 billion at an annual interest rate of 6.25 per cent. These loans were meant for the development of China's coal and oil reserves, with development of the Gulf of Bohai a priority item. The agreement provided for varying periods of repayment depending on the individual project, fifteen years in the longest case, five in the shortest.[14]

Three days later, a consortium of 22 Japanese commercial banks reached an agreement with the visiting Bank of China delegation to provide a medium and long-term loan of US $2 billion in dollar-denominated funds for a period of four and a half years with an interest rate of London Interbank Offered Rate (LIBOR) (i.e. about 11 per cent) plus 0.5 per cent annually. It was also agreed that a group of 31 banks, including all the 22 large commercial banks as well as smaller regional banks, would provide a short-term loan of $6 billion for a period of six months at an interest rate of LIBOR plus 0.25 per cent. Both these loans are tied loans. They shall be used to finance the projects contracted in accordance with the

Japan-China Long-Term Trade Agreement of February 1978.
Formal agreements were signed by the Bank of China and the
representatives of the Japanese banks on 16 August 1979. It
was also agreed that except for the Baoshan Integrated Steel-
works to be exported on a deferred payment basis, all other
contracts would be retained in their original terms.

The United States and West European countries strongly
criticized Japan's "bargain basement" interest rate on official
Exim Bank funds for China. They asserted that Japan's objective in offering more favourable terms than would have been
possible reflected a concerted Japanese desire to monopolise
the China market. They pointed out that the annual 6.25 per
cent rate of interest was well below the export financing guideline
established under the Organisation for Economic Co-operation
and Development (OECD) for loans by Member States to
developing nations, viz. minimum 7.25 per cent for credit up to
five years and minimum 7.5 per cent for longer maturities.[15]
The Japanese responded by saying that its loan was not meant
to finance exports, but rather to help China develop its oil and
other natural resources. This argument thus enabled Tokyo to
circumvent guidelines on interest rates by the OECD. Japan's
competitors in the China market also demanded that the funds
should have been untied so as to permit China to purchase
goods from any part of the world, not necessarily Japan.

The Japanese Government obviously changed its attitude
because more and more Japanese businessmen apprehended
that unless they came up with more favourable terms the
Chinese authorities might arbitrarily cancel Japanese contracts
and turn to competing Western suppliers. It was also the result
of increasing domestic criticism of the Government and
pressure on Japanese private banks to extend commercial
loans. The Chinese felt that at 6.25 per cent rate of interest
the Eximbank loans were attractively cheap. They may have
also realized that the Japanese were willing to bend further
than almost anyone else in softening loan terms and that they
had probably been pushed as far as they could go.[16]

It was hoped that the inflow of Japanese commercial credit
would go a long way to support the 1978 trade agreement.
Many Japanese exporters hoped that it would enable the
Chinese to revive some of the industrial projects for which an

estimated US $2.6 billion of sophisticated Japanese technology and machinery had been contracted for.

"Readjustment" of the Chinese Economy

In the wake of numerous problems encountered in its ambitious modernization drive, China initiated a process of readjusting and restructuring its national economy in order to put it on "a course of planned, proportionate and high-speed development."[17] Readjustment aims at a balanced, multisectoral development strategy.[18] Its key aims, according to Yao Yilin, Vice Premier and Head of the State Planning Committee, are diminishing the scope of basic construction projects, correcting the fiscal deficit, stabilizing prices, improving the balance between farming, light industry and heavy industry, and economization of energy.[19] In mid-February 1979, therefore, China decided to postpone the execution of contracts worth 560 billion yen concluded with Japan after 16 December 1978 for the import of plants.[20] By 10 March 1979 the import contracts shelved by the Chinese reached $2.7 billion.[21] It may be recalled that in 1978 China had concluded import contracts worth $7 billion with foreign countries; including $3.7 billion (about 740 billion yen) with Japan. The Chinese decision to postpone the implementation of contracts caused much worry in Japan. The China fever in Japanese industry had suddenly cooled.

The reasons behind the Chinese decision to suspend the contracts included the following. The amount of Chinese plant purchases had swelled too much in proportion to its foreign exchange reserves. The outbreak of the border conflict with Vietnam also increased China's financial difficulties. The tempo, Vice Premier Li Xiannian remarked on March 1979, had slowed down because the other side is "asking for higher price and we [the Chinese] want a lower price."[22] It was pointed out that China's programme of capital construction was very much overextended. Consquently, realistic adjustments were being made in accordance with a sober-minded estimation so as to realize a balanced growth of its national economy.[23]

Foreign Minister Sonoda felt that the Chinese decision to "readjust" its economy occured because China and Japan had been somewhat "too hasty and impatient to promote trade and economic cooperation, sometimes even without drawing up a blueprint."[24]

In September 1979 the Japanese Embassy in Beijing reached a verbal agreement with the Chinese Foreign Ministry and the Ministry for External Trade on the establishment of permanent resident trade offices in the two countries provided that such offices and their staffs would not enjoy any diplomatic privileges or immunities, but would be granted one year special visas.[25] Japan, thus, became the first country to be allowed to formally establish permanent trade offices in Beijing.

Sino-Japanese trade in 1979 increased to $6.652 billion, up 31 per cent from $5.079 billion in 1978. Japanese exports to China amounted to $3.698 billion, up 21.3 per cent and imports stood at $2.954 billion up 45.5 per cent.

In April 1980 Tokyo extended the preferential tariff system to Chinese exports to Japan.[26] China had first requested that Japan extend the Generalized Scheme of Preferences (GSP) to Chinese imports during a meeting of the Mixed Committee on Japan-China Trade held on 28-29 November 1978.[27] Prime Minister Masayoshi Ohira conveyed his acceptance of the Chinese proposal in December 1979. This system will permit an increase in China's sales to Japan, especially textile products. It will thereby help in correcting the trade imbalance presently in favour of Japan and in turn stimulate further industrialization and economic development in China. Moreover, many Western nations had already extended GSP facility to China in 1979.[28]

Nothing tangible was apparently achieved in the December 1980 meeting of the ministers of the two countries, but its chief merit was that "a channel of commuication was laid out through candid exchange of opinions regarding each other's economic policies and implementation."[29]

Sino-Japanese trade in 1980 registered a 41.3 per cent increase over 1979 to $9.407 billion. Japanese exports to China were $5.078 billion, up 37.2 per cent and imports from China stood at $4.323 billion, up 46.3 per cent. Imports' growth was sharper because of price increases in crude oil, which accounted for 45 per cent of the total imports.[30]

Foreign exchange difficulties nd over-ambitious targets led

China to either postpone or cancel a sizable number of projects, many of them involving Japanese companies. Thus towards the end of January and early February 1981 the Chinese National Technical Import Corporation notified Japanese companies of its decision to cancel contracts or suspend projects, involving about 300 billion yen worth of industrial plants. These included the Baoshan Steel Mill (estimated to cost 400 billion yen and regarded as the symbol of the two countries' economic co-operation), and 15 petrochemical plants. In many cases, about half of the products for the contracted projects had been manufactured and shipped while others were waiting for loading at port.[31]

The Japanese Government and businessmen became extremely concerned about the cancellation of these contracts. Tokyo sent Saburo Okita, Representative of the Japanese Government on External Economic Affairs, to China in February 1981 to discuss ways and means in solving the problems arising out of cancellation. The Chinese leaders explained that the programmes had proved beyond China's economic means and cited three major difficulties, viz. the failure to rapidly increase oil production, existence of a large government deficit and decelerating inflation.[32] Vice Premier Deng Xiaoping sought to allay Japanese apprehensions by stating on 11 February 1981 that

we will assume appropriate economic responsibility through consultation and in accordance with conventional practice in the world.[33]

The next day Deng suggested that the cancelled projects could be continued if government or private loans could be extended or set up as joint ventures.[34]

The Japanese accorded top priority to the solution of problems arising from the cancellation of projects. MITI officials reportedly said that China's failure to pay compensation would lead Japanese manufacturers and exporters to claim payment from the government-run export insurance. In that eventuality China would be classed as a "bankrupt country". As a result it would no longer be possible to provide export insurance to future deals with China. This would seriously hamper exprots and the extension of credit to China.[35]

It was reported that China had failed to utilize any of $8 billion credit extended by Japanese commercial banks to the Bank of China primarily because of slow progress in the implementation of projects and China's policy of economic readjustment.[36]

Development Projects

During his visit to Japan in September 1979, Vice Premier Gu Mu made a formal request for Japanese assistance for the following eight projects estimated to cost $5.54 billion: (1) construction of Shijiusuo port; (2) construction of railways between Yanzhou and Shijiusuo; (3) construction of Long Tan hydroelectric power plant; (4) expansion of railways between Beijing and Qinhuangao; (5) expansion of railways between Heng Yang and Guangzhou; (6) expansion of Qinhuangdao port; (7) construction of Wu Qiang Xi hydroelectric power plant; and (8) construction of Shuikou hydroelectric power plant. In response to this request, a Government delegation led by Shinichi Yanai, Director-General of the Economic Co-operation Bureau of the Japanese Foreign Ministry, visited China from 1 to 9 October 1979 to exchange views with Chinese officials and conduct an on-the spot survey. The Japanese delegation expressed Japan's difficulties in providing such substantial assistance and suggested that materials that could be domestically procured should be excluded from the assistance contents as local costs. Two hydroelectric power projects, viz. the Long Tan and the Shuikuo projects were, therefore, dropped from the list, bringing the amount to $3.15 billion. Japan agreed to extend a loan of 370 billion yen or $1.5 billion within three to six years, by 1985. This constituted the foreign exchange component of the six projects.

During his visit to China in December 1979, Prime Minister Ohira pledged a loan of 50 billion yen.[37] A formal agreement providing for a Japanese loan for 50 billion yen or about $200 million to China in fiscal 1979 was signed in Beijing on 30 April 1980 between the Foreign Investment Commission of China and the Overseas Economic Co-operation-

Fund of Japan.[38]

The details of the six projects (See Table 4) are as follows:

Shijiusuo Port

This port is located near some of the largest coal deposits in China (including those at Yanzhou in Shandong province and at Gujiao in Shanxi). The first phase of this project involves the construction of a berth to accommodate 100,000-ton-class vessels, another to handle 25,000-ton-class vessels, and auxiliary facilities for handling coal. Upon completion, the port would be capable of loading 15 million tons of coal annually after 1985. Phase two of the port expansion involves the construction of another berth for 100,000-ton-class vessels and its auxiliary facilities in order to facilitate the annual import of five million tons of iron ore for processing by the Baotou, Taiyuan, and three other steel foundaries. A sum of 7.085 billion yen has been allocated to this project out of the loan of 50 billion yen.[39]

Yanzhou-Shijiusuo Railway Project

This project seeks to build a single, 300-kilometre-long non-electrified railway line from the Yanzhou coal mines to Shijiusuo port. It would also be used to transport Gujiao coal for export. A sum of 10.1 billion yen has been allocated for this project for fiscal 1979.[40]

Qinhuangdao Port Project

It is planned to expand port loading facilities at this port by the construction of two 50,000-ton-class berths and related facilities so as to expand coal-loading capacity to approximately 20 million tons a year upon its completion in 1984. A total of 4.915 billion yen has been earmarked for this project out of the loan of 50 billion yen.[41]

Beijing-Qinhuangdao Railway Project

This project aims at the construction of a 300-kilometre double-track electrified line between Beijing and Qinhuangdao to primarily transport coal produced at the Datong and other mines in Shanxi province. The first phase of work will consist of the construction of new double line between Qinhuangdao and Langwopu. In the second phase the single line between Shuangqiao and Langwopu will be converted into a double line. The electrification of the rail link between Beijing and Shanhaiguan and expansion of electrification in the Beijing terminal region are the tasks reserved for phase three. A sum of 2.5 billion yen has been allocated for this project.[42]

Guangzhou-Hengyang Railway Project

This project envisages the construction of a new railway line running paralled to the Hengyang-Guangzhou line and its electrification. It also envisages the construction and electrification of the 14.3-kilometre-long Dayao Tunnel which will connect Pingshi and Yaochang. Funds for the initial year have been set at 11.4 billion yen to cover preparatory work and the first phase of tunneling.[43]

Wuqiangxi Hydroelectric Power Station Project

This is a hydroelectric power station on the lower reaches of the Yuanshui river in Hunan province with an installed capacity of 1 5 million kilowatts and capable of generating 7.1 billion kilowatt-hours annually. This project will also serve the purposes of flood control, irrigation and navigation in western Hunan. A 104-meter-high, 785-metre-long dam is proposed to be constructed. This dam will be equipped with five 300 to 350 megawatt generators.[44] The whole project is estimated to cost 1.8 billion yuan (about 288 billion yen). Preliminary work was scheduled to begin in April 1980 and full-fledged construction work a year later. It is expected that the first generator with a 350,000-kilowatt capacity will go into operation in December 1986. By December 1988, all five generators are expected to become operational. Negotiations to work out details are in progress.[45]

Of the six projects, Japan is extending assistance to the expansion of two ports, and three railway lines which will facilitate the expansion of the export of Chinese natural resources, especially coal, to Japan from the mid-eighties onwards. The emphasis on coal export is obvious for several reasons. For one thing, increased coal exports would be basic to further increases in Chinese imports of Japanese plants and technology. Moreover, from Japan's own perspective the development of necessary infrastructure in China for increasing the quantity for export would enable Japan to enter into long-term arrangements for the import of coal from China which would be helpful in enabling Tokyo to realize its plans for substituting energy consumption and placing greater reliance on coal rather than petroleum. Another possible reason may be that while Chinese crude exports are likely to decline and may be less than the quantity envisaged in the 1978 Long-Term Agreement, the prospects for increased coal exports are brigher. In fact, the Japanese have been urging the Chinese to export larger volumes of coal. The Chinese have also responded favourably to these requests. Thus, Japanese financial assistance is closely related to its own needs and requirements. A basic motive is to lay the foundation for the further expansion of Sino-Japanese trade in the eighties on the basis of increased Chinese coal exports.

The commitment of 50 billion yen to develop the above-mentioned six projects aroused some concern among other recipients of Japanese aid. The Association for Southeast Asian Nations (ASEAN) feared that this would tend to reduce their share of Japanese aid. The Soviet Union and Vietnam considered the aid as basically strengthening the Chinese economy and thereby indirectly adding to its military potential. In order to allay such fears Tokyo explained that its economic co-operation with China would not be at the expense of their commitment to other developing countries or for military-related projects.[46]

During the Sino-Japanese ministerial consultative meeting held in early December 1980 notes were exchanged for the extension of a second loan of 56 billion yen during fiscal 1980 by the Japanese Overseas Economic Co-operation Fund for the six projects underway. This brought the total OECF loan to China to a total of 106 billion yen. The loan will have an annual rate of interest of 3 per cent to be paid over 30 years with a grace period of ten years. It was, however, reported that actual construction and material purchase was being delayed and that these projects were three months behind schedule. OECF was expected to send experts in the near future to confirm their status.[47]

China-Japan Friendship Hospital

In October 1979 China requested Japanese financial assistance for the construction of a new 1,000-bed hospital in Beijing.[48] Notes on a Japanese grant to China for the construction of this hospital were exchanged in Beijing on 26 January 1981.

Major Trends of the 1970s

The significant aspects of Sino-Japanese trade in the 1970s may be described as follows:

Firstly, Sino-Japanese trade has generally continued to expand in the seventies. Since the normalization of relations in 1972, trade between the two countries has increased by almost nine times in 1980. It was only during 1976 that trade declined by about 20 per cent.

Secondly, raw materials (including textile materials, metal materials, soyabeans, etc.) and mineral fuels (viz. coal, crude, and petoleum products) accounted for nearly 55 per cent of total Chinese exports to Japan in 1979 (about $1.6 billion), as against about 20 per cent in 1972. Of this mineral fuels constituted $1.27 billion. Thus the basic relationship between the two countries continues to be of a Japan importing raw materials from and exporting manufactured goods to China.

Thirdly, Chinese crude oil sales have rapidly become the principal commodity in Japanese imports from China. Thus, as against a mere 3.4 per cent in 1973, crude oil accounted for 34 per cent of total Japanese imports from China in 1979.

Fourthly, chemical goods, metals and articles thereof, and machinery and equipment have constituted the major Japanese export items to China. The percentage share of chemicals and chemical goods has generally declined over the years: from 20.6 per cent in 1972, they constituted 13 per cent in 1979. Metals and metal articles have, however, maintained their leading position. They comprised 52 per cent of total Japanese exports to China in 1972 and about 47.5 per cent in 1979.

Fifthly, the passing of a law on joint ventures undertaken by Chinese and foreign enterprises in July 1979 has led many Japanese companies to show active interest in entering into such deals with China.[49] The *Keidanren* established an Adhoc Committee on Joint Ventures in December 1979 to serve as an intermediary between the interested Japanese enterpris[ ] Chinese organizations.[50] Sino-Japanese joint venture[ ] possibly increase in the future.

Conclusions

China seeks to develop closer economic relations with Japan for both economic and political reasons. Economically, Japan is a convenient and near source of plant imports, advanced technology, and credits on favourable terms, which would facilitate the speedier realization of China's Four Modernizations. Politically, Beijing considers economic collaboration with Japan as an instrument to dissuade Japan from entering into too close a political and/or economic relationship with the Soviet Union. Economic inducements have been offered and used to reduce Japanese enthusiasm for co-operation in the development of Siberian resources. Thus, China offered to export crude oil to Japan in the wake of the on-going Soviet-Japanese negotiations on the Tyumen oil project. An increase in Sino-Japanese trade may also be viewed as facilitating the further cementing of political relations between the two countries. For example, the conclusion of the Long-Term Trade Agreement in February 1978 created a more congenial environment for the conclusion of the Sino-Japanese peace and friendship treaty in August 1978.

Economic relations with China, Professor Reischauer points out, seem even more important to most Japanese than those with the Soviet Union. The prewar expansionists had created the strong impression that China was "Japan's most natural and largest trading partner—its economic promised land."[51]

Japan is eager to deepen its economic ties with China in order to diversify its export markets and its sources of raw materials as well as reduce the degree of economic dependence upon the United States. The attraction for the China market has grown over the years as Japan confronted keener competition from and protectionism in the United States and Western Europe. Moreover, China, given its present stage of development, is viewed as having a greater market growth potential than the Soviet Union. Japan's trade with China has been more substantial than with the Soviet Union. In 1979, for example, Soviet-Japanese trade was about $4.4 billion whereas Sino-Japanese trade stood at $6.65 billion, i.e. about 50 per cent more. Furthermore, a energy-hungry Japan, looks upon China as a potential source of raw materials, especially oil.

Prospects

Geographical contiguity, cultural affinity, and the mutually complementary nature of the economies of China and Japan have facilitated a substantial growth in Sino-Japanese trade in the post-war era, especially in the seventies. Looking to the future, one may say that China would strive to diversify its trade partners partly to secure better terms and improve its bargaining position, partly for political reasons, and partly because it would not prefer to become unduly dependent upon the ups and downs in Japan's economy. It is likely that the scramble for the China market between Japan, the United States, and the West European nations would further intensify. Many Japanese businessmen fear that the normalization of Sino-US relations in 1979 could pose a serious challenge to Japanese exports to China in the eighties.

The complementary nature of the economies of the two countries, however, does not necessarily guarantee that Japan would be willing to import increasing quantities of agricultural products from China. In fact, Japanese agricultural protectionism has so far excluded a great deal of Chinese export goods. The same protectionism occurs in the Japanese fishing industry as well.

Intense economic competition between China and Japan in Asian markets, especially Southeast Asia, is a distinct possibility as China seeks more and more outlets for exports. The problem could be accentuated further if Japan endeavours to boost exports in Southeast Asia in the face of the problems its exports are already encountering in the United States and Western Europe.

The more serious issue in Asian minds is how close the Sino-Japanese partnership will be and this in turn, is viewed in relation to the growth of Western protectionism and the evolving global power equation among Moscow, Beijing, Washington, and Tokyo.[52] To the Soviets, closer Sino-Japanese economic relations is a cause of growing concern. China is accused by Moscow of trying to inhibit Soviet-Japanese trade and emphasizing the unreliability of the Soviet Union as a trading partner. Many Southeast Asian countries are apprehensive of the possible consequences of the normalization of Sino-US and Sino-Japanese relations and the increase in Soviet influence in Southeast Asia, especially Indochina. Close and continuously expanding Sino-Japanese economic relations and the realization of the considerable potential of the Chinese market by Japanese businessmen led the Association of Southeast Asian Nations (ASEAN) to feel that it might be neglected economically by Japan. It also added to the fear of political domination of the region by China and Japan. It is feared that the combination of Japan's industrial might and China's labour and raw materials increases the dangers of these two neighbouring northern major powers dominating smaller countries in a "Greater East Asia Co-prosperity Sphere" which would largely serve Chinese and Japanese interests.[53] Southeast Asian nations also apprehend that the extension of substantial loans by the Overseas Economic Co-operation Fund of Japan to China would tend to drastically reduce the amount of loans that would be available to them.[54] Thus, Southeast Asian countries feel that their industrialisation may not materialise and the region will forever remain a supplier of raw materials to both Japan as well as China.[55]

A major restriction on Sino-Japanese trade has been the COCOM list. With greater political understanding having been reached between China and the Western countries including Japan and the existence of shared perceptions *vis-a-vis* the Soviet Union, it is likely that the latter would make joint efforts to gradually ease COCOM restrictions in the future. Since the fall of 1975, Japan together with several European countries joined hands to decontrol 50 of the 167 items still restricted by COCOM.

In the past Japan's trade with the People's Republic of China failed to grow to the extent many Japanese had hoped for primarily because of Japan's recognition of and close relations with Taiwan and the resultant political tension in its dealings with China. In the wake of the normalization of relations between China and Japan, Tokyo had severed diplomatic relations with Taiwan and embassies have been withdrawn by the two countries from each other's capitals. Nevertheless, Japan's trade with and investment in Taiwan continues to be significant. However, this is not likely to adversely affect Sino-Japanese relations. Recognition of the mounting Soviet threat and the need to accelerate economic development of the country with the help of the Western countries has led China to take into account Japanese and American susceptibilities in regard to Taiwan and assure them that it favours a non-military, peaceful solution of the problem. Beijing has declared that if and when Taiwan is restored to the People's Republic, it would respect the *status quo* on Taiwan and its present system and adopt fair and reasonable policies and measures so as not to change the way of life of the people of Taiwan or affect the economic interests of foreign countries in Taiwan.

The extension of long-term credits on competitive terms, the granting of a "preferential tariff" arrangement to China, etc. has apparently laid the foundation of expanded economic relations between China and Japan in the eighties and beyond. China's reluctance to meet its commitments regarding the supply of crude oil, its policy of economic "readjustment" and the cancellation or postponement of many projects in which Japanese companies were involved has undoubtedly created new difficulties. The present policy of "readjustment" of the economy appears to be merely a temporary phase which may continue till 1983 and possibly a few years more. An increase in Chinese crude exports to Japan may not be immediately possible; but the development of new fields, especially in the Bohai Gulf, may enable an increase in exports in the near future. Increased exports of coal may somewhat compensate for declining or stagnant export of crude oil. The complementary nature of the economies of China and Japan and the continuing need of the present leadership under Deng Xiaoping to import Western plants and technology to realize the Four Modernizations would probably ensure the growth of Sino-Japanese relations in the future as well. Another important determinant in the economic relations between the two countries would be the nature of China's internal politics. An unstable domestic situation may have adverse consequences on China's foreign trade and lead to changes or modifications in the present economic policies and priorities of China.

The China market has been traditionally important for Japanese businessmen and would continue to be important in the near and distant future as well. However, it is doubtful whether it would offer Japan unlimited opportunities for expansion of trade.

NOTES

1 *Japan Times*, 3 and 14 November 1974.
2 Ibid., 16 August 1975.
3 See ibid., 6 and 16 August 1975. See also Xinhua News Agency, 16 August 1975.
4 Jetro, *China Newsletter* (Tokyo), April 1977, 18.
5 Ibid., April 1978, 9-10.
6 For details, see Chapter Eleven on Sino-Japanese energy co-operation.
7 Keidanren, *Keidanren Review on Japanese Economy* (Tokyo), February 1978, 6.
8 *Oriental Economist*, March 1978, 2.
9 *Japan Times*, 30 March 1979.
10 The considerable expansion of Sino-Japanese trade was primarily due to the depreciation of the dollar. The growth rates were much lower in yen. Thus, two-way trade totalled 1,058,300 million yen, an increase of 13 per cent over the previous year. Japanese exports to and imports from China amounted to 633,000 million yen and 425,200 million yen respectively, up 22 per cent and 2 per cent over the previous year. Japan, Ministry of Foreign Affairs, Asia Affairs Bureau, China Division, "Relations between Japan and the People's Republic of China," (mimeographed), December 1979, 5.
11 *Japan Times*, 3 January 1979.
12 Ibid., 16 March 1979.
13 Ibid., 17 March 1979.
14 *China Trade Report* (Hong Kong), July 1979, 10.
15 Ibid., March 1979, 12.
16 Ibid., July 1979, 10-1.
17 Statement by Premier Hua Guofeng at a meeting arranged by six Jpan-China Friendship Organizations to welcome him, 29 May 1980. *Beijing Review*, 9 June 1980, 10.
18 *People's Daily*, 24 February 1979; *Japan Times*, 5 March 1979.
19 *Japan Economic Journal*, 16 December 1980.
20 *Japan Times*, 2 March 1979; also *Japan Economic Journal* 6, 13 and 27 March 1979.
21 *Asahi Shimbun* 19 March 1979.
22 *Japan Times*, 2 March 1979.
23 Statement by Vice Chairman Deng Yingchao at a press conference at the National Press Club, Tokyo, 11 April 1979. Beijing *Review*, 20

154 *China and Japan*

April 1979, 13.

[24] *Japan Times*, 2 March 1979.

[25] At that time, representatives of Japanese trading firms in Beijing numbered about 300 for approximately 70 companies. On the other hand, China now had 20 persons associated with its five corporations including the Machinery Export-Import Corporation, staying in Japan. *Japan Economic Journal*, 25 September 1979.

[26] *Japan Economic Journal*, 5 December 1978.

[27] For detalis See Jetro, *China Newletter*, June 1980, 21-2.

[28] Japanese cotton fabric and apparl manufecturers are already feeling the adverse impact of Chinese textiles and sundries. It was felt that the extension of preferential tariifs to China would tend have a detrimental impact on the Southeast Asians now benefitting from the tariffs. *Japan Economic Journal*, 15 May and 21 August 1979.

[29] Ibid., editorial, 16 December 1980.

[30] Ibid., 24 February 1981.

[31] Ibid., 10 February 1981; *Japan Times*, 31 January 1981.

[32] *Japan Times*, editorial, 18 February 1981.

[33] Xinhua News Agency, 12 February 1981, 15. Vice Premier Gu Mu reiterated these views. See *Japan Economic Journal*, 17 February 1981.

[34] Xinhua News Agency, 13 February 1981, 4; also see *Japan Economic Journal*, 17 February 1981.

[35] *Japan Economic Journal*, 10 February 1981.

[36] Ibid., 24 February 1981.

[37] Chinese Embassy in India, *News from China* (New Delhi), 11 December 1981, 6; *Beijing Review*, 14 December 1979, 3-4.

[38] *Beijing Review*, 26 May 1980, 8.

[39] Jetro, *China Newsletter*, August 1980, 18.

[40] Ibid., 19.

[41] Ibid., 20; *Japan Economic Journal*, 13 January 1981.

[42] *China Newsletter*, August 1980, 19.

[43] Ibid.

[44] Ibid., 20.

[45] *Japan Economic Journal*, 8 April 1980.

[46] *Times of India* (New Delhi), 26 December 1979.

[47] *Japan Economic Journal*, 24 February 1981.

[48] *Japan Times*, 10 October 1979.

[49] For details of Sino-Japanese joint ventures currently under negotiation, see *China Newsletter*, March 1980, 16-9.

[50] Keidanren, *Keidanren Review on Japanese Economy*, February 1981, 11-2.

[51] Edwin O. Reischauer, *The Japanese* (Cambridge, Mass., 1977), 360.

[52] Selig S. Harrison, *The Widening Gulf: Asian Nationalism and American Policy* (New York, 1978), 348-9.

[53] Statement by Philippine Foreign Minister Carlos P. Romulo at a television interview in Manila, 1 January 1979. *Japan Times*, 5 January 1979.

[54] Ibid., 3 January 1979.

[55] Romulo, n. 53.

Table 2

Chinese Exports to Japan, 1975-1979
(in thousand dollars)

	1975		1976		1977		1978		1979	
	Value	%	*Value*	%	*Value*	%	*Value*	%	*Value*	%
Foodstuffs	202,038	13.2	247,471	18.05	252,416	16.32	361,525	17.81	432,087	14.62
Raw Materials[1]	248,286	16.2	249,187	18.18	281,014	18.16	371,914	18 32	550,398	18.63
Mineral Fuels	763,609	49 9	591,469	43.14	684,518	44.24	818,718	40.33	1,188,771	40.23
Manufactured Products[2]	306,353	20 0	276,167	20.14	319,962	20 68	467,887	23.05	770,747	26 09
Others	10,790	.7	6,621	.5	9,389	.6	10,248	.5	12,832	.43
Total	1,531,076	100.0	1,370,915	100.0	1,547,344	100 0	2,030,292	100.0	2,954,781	100.0

[1] includes textile maerials, metal materials, and others.

[2] includes chemicals, machinery and equipment and other products.

Source: Jetro, *White Paper on International Trade, 1977*, 227; *1978*, 244-5; *1979*, 189-90 and 288-9.

Table 3

Chinese Imports from Japan, 1975-1979
(in thousand dollars)

	1975		1976		1977		1978		1979	
	Value	%	Value	%	Value	%	Value	%	Value	%
Light Industrial Products	185,627	8.2	184,140	11.1	239,607	12.4	271,000	8.9	306,711	8.3
Textiles	122,694	5.4	161,926	9.7	198,240	10.2	197,613	6.5	164,339	4.4
Heavy & Chemical Industrial Products	2,038,856	90.3	1,446,401	88.1	1,665,956	85.9	2,745,359	90.0	3,332,179	90.1
Chemicals	452,795	20.0	205,021	12.3	342,952	17.7	419,597	13.8	459,614	12.4
Metals	890,171	39.4	866,694	52.1	1,105,660	57.0	1,688,842	55.4	1,747,972	47.3
Machinery and Equipment	695,890	30.8	392,685	23.6	217,344	11.2	636,921	20.9	1,124,593	30.4
Others	34,094	1.5	13,241	.8	33,080	1.7	32,389	1.1	59,780	1.6
Total	**2,258,577**	**100**	**1,662,568**	**100**	**1,938,643**	**100**	**3,048,748**	**100**	**3,698,670**	**100**

Source: Jetro, *White Paper on International Trade*, 1977, 227; 1978, 2 44; 1979, 189; 1980, 288-9.

Table 4

Japanese-aided Projects in China

Name of Project	Outline	Foreign fund (million dollars)	Period of Completion (years)	Remarks
Ports (2)				
1. Shijiusuo Port Shandong Province	For coal shipping one 100,000t class berth two 50,000t class berths For iron ore shipping one 100,000t class berth	18.1	4	to expand coal-loading capacity to 15 mn tons and that of ore to 5mn tons
2. Qinhuangdao Port	Two 50,000t class berths	10.4	5	to expand coal-loading capacity to approximately 20 mn tons
Hydrodectric Power Station (1)				
1. Wuqiangxi station, Hunan Province	1.5 mn kw.	53.0	6	equipped with five 300 to 350 nw generating stations dam—104 metre high, 785 metre long expected to generate 7.1 mn kw hours annually

Name of Project	Outline	Foreign fund (million dollars)	Period of Completion (years)	Remarks
Railways (3)				
1. Yanzhou-Shijui port railway	300 km. diesel train, single-track railway	10.3	5	to transport Gujiao and Yanzhou coal to the coast
2. Beijing-Qinhuangdao port railway	300 km. double-track electric railway line	37.5	5	to transport coal produced from the Datong and other mines in Shanxi Province
3. Guangzhou-Hengyang	a new railway line parallel to the Hengyang Guangzhou line and its electrification	10.8	5	
	the construction and electrification of the 14.3 km. Dayao tunnel to connect Pingshi and Yaochang			

Source: Beijing Review, 21 January 1980, 8; Jetro, *China Newsletter,* August 1980, 18-20; *Look Japan,* 10 June 1980, 17.

10. Co-operation in Energy

Japan is an economic giant, but its Achilles Heel is its excessive dependence on supplies of overseas raw materials and energy resources. It must import 88 per cent of all its primary energy needs, of which oil accounts for 73 per cent. It must import almost all its requirements of oil. The 1973 oil crisis highlighted Japan's vulnerability in this respect. It adopted an energy policy whose major elements were the diversification of oil supply sources, the expansion of oil storage facilities, the development of alternative energy sources, and the promotion of energy-saving measures at home. Japan, like other nations, considered China an important source of oil and coal supplies. The 1970s have generally witnessed a gradual increase in Chinese exports of energy resources so much so that they have assumed considerable importance in Sino-Japanese economic relations.

Chinese Motives

Chinese motives in seeking foreign, especially Japanese, fiinancial and technological participation in the development of its energy resources are very much similar to those of the Soviet Union. Foreign collaboration would result in a more efficient, less time-consuming, and less costly development of its energy resources than would be possible on its own. Increased production would enable China to meet the increasing energy requirements of its fast expanding economy as well as leave more surplus for export. Moreover, exports of energy resources, especially oil, have become an extremely important source of earning foreign exchange to pay for imports of machinery and plants, vital for the realization of the Four Modernizations. They would also ease Beijing's balance of payments position. The constantly rising price of crude is an added incentive. A major motive behind increased Chinese exports of energy resources to Japan has been to dampen Japanese enthusiasm for participation in the development of Siberian resources and slow down the pace of Soviet-Japanese economic co-operation.

Japanese Motives

Japan is interested in securing long-term supplies of Chinese oil and coal in order to diversify its sources of supply and reduce the strategic vulnerability inherent in a one-sided dependence on the Middle East. About 75 per cent of Japan's oil imports come from the Persian Gulf through the narrow Hormuz Strait. Thus, if oil exports from the Persian Gulf area stop, Japan will lose almost 70 per cent of its primary energy supply, quite enough to throw Japan's economy into chaos. Any possible dangers in the transportation of crude over long routes could also be avoided if oil suppliers were located near Japan. Japan has, therefore, been attracted by the potential of both China and the Soviet Union. It was felt by some that the China option may also improve Japan's ability to bargain for lower prices with producer nations and the oil majors, apart from increased leverage in negotiations with the Soviet Union on various Siberian projects. Besides, geographical proximity reduces transportation costs and this contributes to Japan's attraction for Chinese coal and crude. More importantly, oil is regarded as an important factor in ensuring the expansion of Sino-Japanese trade. It is felt that the greater the volume of oil exports, the greater would be China's ability to purchase Japanese goods and plants.

Crude Oil

Japan today is the largest importer of Chinese crude oil. The Chinese offer to supply crude oil to Japan in 1973, came in the wake of on-going Soviet Japanese discussions regarding the Tyumen oil project. China viewed Soviet overtures to Japan with serious concern. Thus, during his month long tour of Japan in the spring of 1973, Liao Cheng-chih, President of the China-Japan Friendship Association, advised the Japanese to minimize the military significance of the project. Otherwise, he said, China would be forced to take "appropriate measures". He also pointed out that given the strategic nature of the project it could also be used, when completed, against Japanese interests.[1] Japanese enthusiasm had apparently waned given the financial risks and the uncertainty involved in dealing with the Soviets. At any rate the Chinese offer seems to have led to a hardening of the Japanese position. The Japanese became reluctant to participate, especially after the Soviets proposed the construction of a second railroad, which was likely to have an adverse effect on the Chinese military position *vis-a-vis* the Soviet Union. The Japanese eventually decided to shelve the project.

Meanwhile, a channel for importing Chinese crude was created with the establishment of International Oil Trading Co.[2] (hereinafter called International Oil) on 8 March 1973 with a capitalization of 82.3 million yen. Next month, China signed an agreement with International Oil for the export of one million tons of Daqing (Taching) crude in 1973.

A second channel, viz. the Importers of Chinese Petroleum Conference (hereinafter called Importers Conference) was established on 10 July 1974 for facilitating the import of Chinese crude. The Conference was headed by Ryutaro Hasegawa, President and Chairman of Asia Oil, and included in its membership a number of oil firms and trading companies.[3]

Japanese imports of Chinese crude have been on an annual contract basis. After fixing the annual volume, Japanese importers negotiated the actual quantity and price every three months. The terms of settlement for shipments made in 1973 and 1974 were quotation and payment in renminbi yuan. Japanese importers paid between $3.80 a barrel and $4.59 a barrel for the deliveries made in 1973. However, with the sudden rise in international oil prices in 1973, China charged $14.80 a barrel in the first deal made in January 1974. This brought about the "incomprehensible situation" in which China's crude was priced 37 per cent higher than Indonesia's Minas crude[4] which is of relatively the same quality. Subsequently, Beijing

lowered the price to $12.85 a barrel for July-Sepember and
$12.80 for October-December 1974,[5] because Japan threatened
to reduce oil imports and increase purchases of Minas crude.

In October 1974 Japanese importers agreed to import 4.5
million tons of Chinese oil in 1974—3 million tons by International Oil and 1.5 million tons by the Importers Conference.
Subsquently, however, oil refineries and domestic distributors
asked both International Oil and the Importers Conference to
cancel some of the imports they had recently contracted and
not carry over into 1975 what could not be imported in 1974.
Japanese companies expressed their inability to take delivery
of the contracted volume citing the lack of storage facilities
and declining domestic demand especially by power companies
which burned Chinese crude as reasons. It was also feared that
the higher Chinese price ($11.80 per barrel compared to $11.60
per barrel of comparable Minas crude) could possibly complicate negotiations with Indonesia. Consequently, the volume of
Chinese crude exports to Japan in 1974 was reduced to 4 million tons (against the originally stipulated 4.9 million tons) and
the volume for 1975 was fixed at 8 million tons.

Japanese importers of Chinese crude were also unhappy
about the practice of quotation and payment in renminbi yuan
because given the artificially low dollar-yuan rate fixed by
Beijing, payment in yuan raised the price of Chinese crude by
as much as one dollar over Minas crude. In response to such
requests, China agreed to follow the international practice of
quotation and payment in US dollars for shipments made from
1975 onwards.[6]

The two Japanese private importers decided to reduce imports of Chinese crude to 6 million tons (3.9 million tons
for International Oil and 2.1 million tons for the Importers
Conference) from the 8.1 million tons (5.7 million tons
for International Oil and 2.4 million tons for the Conference) contracted for during fiscal 1976.[7] Declining demand of
oil consuming industries amid the overall business recession,
global petroleum oversupply, and the problems encountered in
refining Daqing crude were among the reasons cited. Chinese
dissatisfaction with this reduction was reflected in a tightening
of their purse for steel imports. The Japanese Ministry of
International Trade (MITI) urged the retention of the 8.1

million ton target in view of the importance of oil in ensuring the smooth development of Sino-Japanese trade. It considered it undesirable to cut oil imports especially when a government and private economic delegation led by Yoshihiro Inayama, Chairman of the Japan-China Association on Economy and Trade, was in China in January 1976 to discuss the possibilities of the conclusion of a long-term crude accord. Japanese importers subsequently agreed to import an additional 700,000 tons—300,000 tons for International Oil and 400,000 tons for the Importers Conference—(in addition to the 6.1 million tons) against the Chinese demand for 2 million tons. Chinese crude exports increased to 6.53 million tons in 1977.

The Japanese Natural Resources and Energy Agency, meanwhile, had reached the conclusion that an expansion of imports of Chinese crude would be possible only if some arrangements were made for tackling the problems encountered in refining Daqing crude. It, therefore, decided in 1975 to offer subsidies to refiners to help them instal the needed cracking equipment.[8] However, these incentives did not have the desired result. Consequently, the Japanese Government decided to take a "national project" approach to questions of constructing the cracking facilities and developing needed know-how for processing Daqing heavy crude oil.[9] It decided to build a large 500,000 b/d residual oil cracking facility at a cost of 300,000 million yen by 1982 to prepare for processing Chinese crude deliveries over the next five years. Oil refiners criticized the plan, stating that costly processing of expensive Chinese crude was commercially impractical. New equipment installations, they felt, would lead to greater excess capacity. It was even argued that the project could lead the Government to intervene in the oil industry.

The FOB price of Chinese crude oil between January 1975 and December 1976 fluctuated around 50 cents per barrel lower than that of Minas crude. However, in the first half of 1977 the gap between the two prices narrowed to 40 cents—to $13.15 per barrel (as against $13.55 per barrel of Minas crude). The price of Chinese crude oil was raised by five cents for the shipment made in the beginning of the second half of 1977, to $13.20 per barrel.[10]

Given the substantial share of Chinese ships in the trans-

port of freight volume the C&F price became an important
issue in price negotiations. Japanese importers had to pay
higher freight charges because of the inability of Chinese ports
and harbours to accommodate big tankers and because China
imposed a uniform freight charge notwithstanding the conditions of the unloading ports in Japan. However, in July 1976
China adopted a freight rate based on the distance from the
port of unloading. This reduced the ocean freight charge of
Chinese crude to Japan aboard Chinese flag vessels by about 20
cents per barrel to around $12.65 per barrel. This price reduc-
tion was facllitated by the improvement of loading facilities
at Darien by the construction of a berth capable of loading
50,000 DWT tankers.[11]

Crude Supplies under the Long-Term Trade Agreement
On his return from a trip to China in November 1975 Japanese
Minister for International Trade and Industry, Toshiro
Komoto, told a press conference that the prospects for importing Chinese crude on a long-term basis were bright because
Beijing had shown flexible terms as to both quantity and price.[12]
The desire to conclude a long-term crude agreement was reiterated by Yoshihiro Inayama, head of the Japan-China Association on Economy and Trade, during his visit to China in
January 1976. Basic understanding on the conclusion of a
long-term agreement on Chinese supplies of coal and oil was
reportedly reached with Chinese authorities in March 1977 by
the *Keidanren* delegation led by President Toshiwo Doko. In
his discussions with Chinese Foreign Trade Minister Li Qiang,
Doko had experessed Japan's willingness to import 50 million
tons of Chinese crude five years after the conclusion of the
agreement. This was subsquently scaled down to 11.3 million
tons in the Japanese draft agreement of 22 November 1977.
However, at the plenary session held four days later, Yoshihiro
Inayama in his discussions with the Chinese Vice Minister of
Foreign Trade, Liu Xiwen, proposed 6.8 million tons for 1978
and 15 million tons for 1982. The Chinese had apparently
assured their Japanese counterparts that they would be willing
to meet the enhanced export quantity because they intended to
export crude from the Shengli oil field and from several other
new fields. Moreover, the Chinese urged Japan to import more

heavy quality oil because this was increasingly becoming the prevalent oil of the world. Inayama eventually proposed a quantity of 15 million tons beginning 1982, when the Chinese confirmed their wiliingness to supply this quantity. On his return back home he justified the proposal on the ground that the proposal of 11.3 million tons was inadequate to guarantee the expansion of long-term trade, including the export of plants to China, and emphasized the need to secure Chinese crude oil in order to cope with the energy shortage.[13] The Japanese petroleum industry, however, strongly resisted this proposal primarily because of the problems encountered in refining Daqing crude. "Political considerations" seemed to have eventually prevailed and Japan agreed to accept the additional quantity of 3.7 million tons.

The February 1978 Long-Term Agreement stipulates that China shall export a total of 47.1 million tons of crude oil during the first five years (1978-1982). The year-wise breakdown is as follows:

Table 5

Chinese Export of Crude to Japan under the Long-Term Trade Agreement
(in million tons)

1978	1979	1980	1981	1982
7	7.6	8	9.5	15

The export quantities of Chinese crude for 1983 and the ensuing years are to be worked out in 1981. Article Three of the agreement stipulated that they should be larger than imports during 1982 and should increase year by year. The figures of Chinese crude exports to Japan from 1973 to 1980 are given in Table 6.

China and Japan

Table 6

Chinese Crude Oil Exports to Japan, 1973 to Jan-Sep 1980

Year	Quantity	Value (mn)	% in total exports to Japan
1973	1 mn t	32.6	3.3
1974	3.99 mn t	410	3.14
1975	8.14 mn t	740	48.3
1976	6.12 mn t	568	41.4
1977	6.63 mn t	655	42.3
1978	8,724 kkl	758	37.3
1979	8,506 kkl	1,006	34
Jan-Sep 1980	6,435 kkl	1,361	44.3

Note: [1] Figures for 1977 are the contracted volume (including 680,000 tons of crude oil not yet received in 1976).

[2] Figures for 1976 include 30,000 tons contracted for but shipped in 1975.

[3] kkl=thousand kilolitres. A kilolitre of petroleum weighs approximately one tonne.

Source: Jetro, *China Newsletter*, January 1978, 9; Jetro, *White Paper on International Trade*, *1976*, 252; *1977*, 130-1; *1978*, 142; *1979*, 105; *1980*, 129-30; *China Newsletter*, December 1980, 31.

Chinese crude oil exports to Japan in 1979 decreased slightly from the previous year. However, there was a 39.4 per cent growth in value in 1979 because of price hikes.

In January 1980 Chinese Minister for Foreign Trade Li Qiang admitted that it might be difficult for China to supply the targeted 8 million tons of crude oil for 1980 and 9.5 million tons for 1981 apparently because of an anticipated decline in oil output in future. On 11 September 1980 Vice Foreign Trade Minister Liu Xiwen told Toshiwo Doko that China would supply 8.3 million tons of crude oil to Japan each in 1981 and 1982, substantially lower than 9.5 million tons for 1981 and 15 million tons for 1982 stipulated in the 1978 Long-term Trade Agreement.[14] Japanese businessmen were considerably disturbed by China's failure to abide by its commitment to sell oil to Japan in the stipulated quantities because it would lead to a shrinkage in China's ability to buy from Japan.

At the first conference of Sino-Japanese government leaders

in December 1980 Japanese leaders expressed the hope that 30 per cent of Japan's total crude import by 1990 would come from China and neighbouring countries, as against the present 4 per cent.[15] Vice Premier Gu Mu indicated to Japanese leaders on 3 December that Chinese crude output was likely to decline. Consequently, it would be difficult to increase crude exports to Japan in the near future. He, however, stated that the export of coal could be guaranteed.

In mid-February 1981 price negotiations were reportedly bogged down. The Chinese sought to raise the price of Daqing crude by $3.825 to $37.80 per barrel, retroactive to January 1. International Oil and the Importers Conference, on the other hand, wanted the price to be lowered to $35.80 per barrel (i.e. to the same level as the price for comparable Minas crude).[16] The Chinese suggested supplying the same quantity as in 1979, i.e. 7.6 million tons.[17] Vice Premier Gu Mu informed Saburo Okita, Japanese Government Representative for External Economic Affairs, during the latter's visit to China in February 1981, that the Chinese output of crude was expected to decline to 80-90 million tons in 1985 from the slightly more than 100 million tons in 1980. It is, therefore, doubtful if China would be in a position to increase crude exports to Japan.

Bohai Bay Development Project

Negotiations for Sino-Japanese co-operation in the development of oil resources in the Gulf of Bohai began in June 1978 between the Japan National Oil Corporation (JNOC) (a semi-government non-profit oil development agency representing various Japanese commercial interests) and the National Oil and Gas Exploration and Development Corporation of China (a subsidiary of the Petroleum Company of China). A 14-member Chinese oil mission led by Li Jingxin, Deputy General Manager of the Chinese Oil and Natural Gas Exploration and Development Corporation, visited Japan for discussions. The Japanese proceeded cautiously. They initially sought to put up only a relatively small portion of the finances required and proposed a risk-sharing formula based on US participation.

In February 1979 Japan offered to provide China a credit of 400 billion yen (US $1 83 billion)—40 billion yen for exploration and development and 360 billion yen for production. China was to use the credit to purchase necessary equipment from Japan and repay the loan in the form of crude oil. Beijing agreed to repay the credit in cash if no oil field was discovered in Bohai. The JNOC announced that Japan was to receive two million tons of crude oil annually in the event of successful oil discovery. Japan was expected to take care of everything from surveying oil fields to building production facilities.[18] It was agreed that China would remain the leader of the project and would own all facilities. The two sides, however, failed to reach agreement on whether the credit should be denominated in yen or dollars.

Negotiations were conducted five times since June 1978. However, an agreement on the general principles of the project was reached only towards the end of 1979. A contract was signed on 18 October 1979 providing for geophysical survey by JNOC in about 14,000 square kilometres out of the area covering about 25,000 square kilometres in the southern and western parts of Bohai Bay.[19] The total reserves of oil in Bohai Bay are estimated at about 110 million kilolitres. Discussions were also held on co-operation for exploration and development after the completion of geophysical survey, but final accord was not reached.

Eventually on 6 December 1979 an agreement was signed in Beijing between Akira Masuzawa, Executive Director of JNOC, and Li Jingxin, Deputy General Manager of the China National Oil and Gas Exploration Corporation. The agreement provided for exploration in an area of about 25,000 square kilometres in the southern and western parts of Bohai Bay.[20] The agreement envisaged Japanese investment of $210 million for the initial exploration work.[21]

Formal agreement on joint development of the Cheng Bei oil field in western Bohai Bay was signed in February 1980.

Two new Japanese Oil development companies were established in April 1980 to promote exploration in Bohai Gulf, viz. the Japan-China Oil Development Corporation and the Chengbei Oil Development Corporation. These two companies were set up by 47 Japanese firms, including oil development, steel, and power companies. These two companies are expected to start with a combined capital of 11 billion yen. This is to be eventually increased to 44.05 billion yen. The JNOC will own 60 per cent of the total capital and private enterprises 40 per cent.[22] Of the 61.6 billion yen exploration fund, 44.05 billion yen will be appropriated by the combined capital, and the remaining 17.55 billion yen by the Japan National Oil Corporation.[23]

In continuation of the basic agreement reached in December 1979, a contract for the development of oilfields in the western and southern parts of the Bohai Gulf was signed towads the end of May 1980 between the China Petroleum Corporation on the one hand and the Japan-China Oil Development Corporation and Chengbei Oil Development Corporation on the other. The agreement evisages that the work of surveying and prospecting would take five years. This can be extended by another twyears. The production period is set at 15 years. The two countries agreed to sink 48 wells in the southern and western sections of the Gulf over a four and a half year period, with $210 million exploration costs paid by Japan.[24] China will share 51 per cent of all exploration costs and Japan the remaining 49 per cent. Japan is expected to pay about $700 million for the project. The agreement also stipulates that Japan will assume full responsiblity for production operations. China will take 57.5 per cent of all the oil produced and Japan 42.5 per cent.

The Japanese companies were expected to start geophysical surveys on the areas in question towards the end of July 1980. If prospecting and exploration proceeds on schedule, the Chengbei oil field)already prospected by China) is expected to start commercial production in the fall of 1982 and the oilfields in the southern and western parts of the Bohai Gulf in 1985.[25]

It was reported in December 1980 that the by Japan-China Oil Development Corporation had started test drilling an oil well in the Gulf of Bohai and plans to drill six wells in 1981 in order to obtain a picture of the oil potential of Bohai Gulf.[26]

Inland Oilfields
China has asked the Japan National Oil Corporation (JNOC) for help in the exploration and development of four major

inland oil fields. These are located in Talim Basin in Xianjiang Uygur Autonomous Region[27] (estimated reserves: 5 billion barrels), Chaidamu Basin in Qinghai Province (5.3 billion barrels), and Sichuan Basin in Sichuan Province (3.1 billion barrels), and Huabei Basin in Hebei and Henan Provinces (6.8 billion barrels). MITI and JNOC feel that the exploration and development of the oil field in the Huabei basin, located near the Bohai Gulf, could be carried out alongwith the bilateral joint oil development projects in the southern and western sections of the Gulf agreed upon in December 1979. Discussions are now in progress for the allocation of funds.[28]

Conclusions

Chinese exports of crude to Japan have so far been entirely of Daqing (Taching) crude, which has low sulpher content which is good for lowering the sulphur content in oil products. However, Daqing crude is a low gravity (i.e. heavy quality) crude oil with yield rates for gasoline and naptha being smaller than those for Middle East crude. As a result about 30 to 40 per cent of the oil imported from China is burned directly by electric power, iron and steel, and other industries while the rest is mixed with higher oils for refining

In crude oil negotiations with Japan, China is reportedly guided by the following principles: (1) respect for the decisions of the Oil Petroleum Exporting Countries (OPEC); (2) reference to international crude oil prices, including Indonesia (3) careful consideration of the quality and special characteristics of Chinese crude; (4) careful consideration of the special relationship between China and Japan; and (5) respect for the past and present ties between the two countries and would carefully take into account the future development of these ties. In actual price negotiations, however, China used price of Minas crude as the yardstick.[29]

The share of Chinese crude in Japan's crude oil imports was 0.5 per cent in 1973, 1.6 per cent in 1974, and 3.5 per cent in 1975. It declined to 2.6 per cent in 1976 because of a 24 per cent decline in imports.[30] Chinese crude now accounts for about 3 per cent of total Japanese imports of crude.

Crude oil has rapidly become the principal commodity in Chinese exports to Japan. The share of crude oil in Chinese total exports to Japan increased from 3.3 per cent in 1973 to 31.4 per cent in 1974 and 48.3 per cent in 1975. It declined to 41.4 per cent in 1976. It rose to 42.3 per cent in 1977, but declined again to 37.3 per cent in 1978 and 34 per cent in 1979. During January to September 1980, the share of crude in total Chinese exports to Japan China was 44.3 per cent. In fact, crude exports have enabled China to rectify the unfavourable balance in its trade withJapan. This explains why China has utilized the Japanese loans for energy projects smoothly whereas utilization of loans for other projects has lagged behind. Thus China has used $2C0 million for ccal-related projects and $495 million for crude oil development at Shengli field out of the total Export-Import Bank of Japan credit of $2 billion for the development of energy resources.[31]

China exports more crude oil to Japan than the Soviet Union. However, Moscow still exports more petroleum products to Japan than Beijing (see Table 7).

Table 7

*Chinese and Soviet Exports of Petroleum Products to
Japan, 1975-1979*
(in million dollars)

Year	China	Soviet Union
1975	5.7[1]	59.5
1976	7.89[1]	81.9
1977	23.35	70.4
1978	23.35	68.7
1979	113.3	153.6

[1] Figures for export of petroleum coke.

Source: Jetro, *White Paper on International Trade, 1977,* 130-1, 228; *1978,* 142, 246; *1979,* 105, 190; *1980,* 129-30, 291.

Optimistic projections about crude production seem to have been largely responsible for ambitious economic targets set out at the first session of the fifth National People's Congress in February-March 1978. However, the anticipated oil bonanza has failed to materialize. In fact, production is expected to fall below 90 million tons by the mid-eighties from the 106 million tons in 1979 and 1980 primarily because of the 10 to 20 per cent annual increase in oil production during the seventies. Declining production means that much less will be available for export. The resultant decline in foreign exchange earnings would thus necessitate reduced imports of Japanese industrial plants and manufactured goods and the concellation or postponement of contracts already concluded.

Given the vital significance of petroleum as a source of foreign exchange earnings, China is most likely to provide substantial funds to the petroleum industry in order to ensure the infusion of foreign capital and technology. Beijing can be expected to adopt a mult ifaceted energy policy, including, *inter alia*, the development of alternate sources like coal and hydropower and attempts to reduce domestic consumption of crude. Concerted efforts will have to be made to reduce many wasteful energy consuming practices prevalent in China. Petroleum now supplies a little over 20 per cent of China's energy needs and oil consumption has been increasing at an average rate of about 15 per cent annually.[32] Renewed efforts will have to be made to develop new fields whose development has lagged behind. They would, of course, take a few years to develop. Besides, the combined effect of the lag time between imported technology and production for export would hinder the immediate export of crude. It is also possible that China may not prefer the rapid depletion of this valuable and non-renewable resource.

Chinese oil exports to Japan in future would depend on the overall state of the world petroleum market, the pricing policies of OPEC, the production of crude and domestic consumption of petroleum in China, the speed and extent to which China is able to expand its pipeline, tanker, and port loading facilities. Geographical proximity of the two countries and the complementarity of their interests in resource development, and their crucial role in bilateral trade, is likely to ensure keen Japanese interest in Chinese energy projects.

Coal

Soaring oil prices, the desire to lower the dependence on petroleum as well as diversify and disperse sources of energy supplies, and the levelling off of demestic coal production has led

Japan to gradually step up its imports of foreign coal in the seventies. The People's Republic of China (whose coal production at present is over 600 million tons) is now increasingly looked upon as a major source of supply of coal.

Japanese manufacturers are well conversant with many varieties of Chinese coal. After the Sino-Japanese War in 1904-5 the Fushun and Penchi collieries in Liaoning Province became Japanese enterprises, and a part of the output of these collieries was shipped to Japan. In 1915, the Japanese "inherited" the German coal-mining enterprises in Shandong Province. By 1940 most of the coal-producing areas of the country which accounted for about 90 per cent of the national output, were under Japanese control. The share of Chinese coals in total Japanese imports (by value) was almost 90 per cent in 1940 and close to 98 per cent in 1943.[33]

Japan imported 100,000 tons of Chinese metallurgical coal in 1963 and 153,000 tons in 1964. This rose to 500,000 tons in 1965; 686,000 tons in 1966; and 920,000 tons in 1967.[34] The varieties of coal imported included Kailuan coal, Zhongxing coal, Fengfeng coal, and Zaozhan coal. The average prices paid by the Japanese for coking coals imported from China were US $13.10 in 1965, US $13.32 in 1966, and US $13.27 in 1967 (per ton, c i.f. by China).[35] In 1969, however, the import of coking coal was discontinued because of problems regarding the quality of import coal, the gap between guaranteed quality and the one actually delivered, and the political uncertainty caused by the Cultural Revolution.

Anthracite (hard coal), however, continued to be imported. Chinese export of anthracite coal increased from 116,000 tons in 1965 to 191,000 tons in 1967 and 202,000 tons in 1969. They stood at 227,000 tons in 1970 and rose to 344,000 tons in 1971. They constituted 9.96 per cent, 13.3 per cent, 15.53 per cent, 16.16 per cent, and 21.74 per cent in 1965, 1967, 1969, 1970, and 1971 respectively of total Japanese imports of anthracite coal. The average price paid by Japan (c.i.f. China) was $16.66 in 1965, $16.89 in 1967, $18.05, in 1969, $19.56 in 1970, and $23.60 in 1971.[36]

In the early seventies the Japanese steel industry unsuccessfully tried on several occasions to secure Chinese coking coal. It was during the Canton Fair in 1974 that Beijing reportedly expressed its willingness to sell Tatung coking coal to Japan.[37] Meanwhile, in the wake of the 1973 oil crisis Tokyo had resumed import of coal. Japan began to import ordinary coal, used mainly for thermal power generation, from China in 1974, confining them to Zhumpei and Tatung coal.

The organ for the export of coal on the Chinese side is the China National Metal and Mineral Export and Import Corporation. On the Japanese side the major importers are the Electric Power Development Co. (EPDC), the Tohoku Electric Power Co., the Chugoku Electric Power Co., the Overseas Metallurgical Coal Development Co. Taiheiyo Kohatsu, and Hokkaido Tanko. These six companies imported the following quantities of Zhumpei and Tatung coal: 105,700 tons in 1974; 120,500 tons in 1975; and 109,000 tons in 1976.[38] The largest consumer was clearly the EPDC accounting for 73 per cent of total imports in 1975 and about 92 per cent in 1976. From 1976 onwards, this company began to negotiate directly with the Chinese side in Beijing. After signing the contract it consigned the work of conductingt he import to various trading companies. Other consumers purchased coal at China's trade fairs.

In November 1975, the EPDC proposed to Chinese officials at the Kwangchow Trade Fair that it wished to receive 1.5 to 2 million tons of steam coal from China in July 1980 when the No. 1 power unit having a 500,000 kw capacity would start operation at its Matsushima Station, Nagasaki Prefecture and an additional 1.5 million tons in July 1982 when the No. 2 unit would begin operation there.[39]

EPDC originally planned to buy Chinese coal in exchange for supplying its technology on operation of hydropower or coal-burning thermal power stations. But the Chinese did not accept this suggestion. Therefore a cash payment basis was agreed upon. The EPDC purchased 100,000 tons of Huaipei and Tatung coal in 1976 for trial use at its Takasago power station in Hyogo prefecture.[40] The test use proved satisfactory.

The figures for Chinese coal exports to Japan from 1975 to January/September 1980 are given in Table 8.

Article Two of the Sino-Japanese Long-Term Trade Agreement signed on 16 February 1978 stipulated the purchase of large quantities of Chinese coal (see Table 9).

Table 8

Chinese Exports of Coal to Japan, 1975 to Jan-Sep 1980

| | Anthracite | | Coking Coal | | Steaming Coal | | Total Coal Exports | | |
	Qty (thousand tons)	Value mn $	Qty (thousand tons)	Value mn $	Qty (thousand tons)	Value mn $	Qty (thousand tons)	Value mn $	% of total Chinese Exports
1975	333 (32.46)	13.42 (30.9)	..	..	120.5	..	456 (.73)	17.5	1.14
1976	200 (18.66)	7.99 (16.6)	16.61 (.03)	.661	105.4	..	322 (.53)	12.0	0.88
1977	295 (19.81)	12.68 (17.08)	6.0 (.01)	.266	190 (21.6)	6.95 (23.30)	491 (.81)	19.9 (.56)	1.29
1978	329 (31.27)	16.6 (27.96)	272.4 (.54)	13.6	170 (16.60)	6.60 (17.04)	772.2 (1.48)	36.8 (1.20)	1.81
1979	402 (39.11)	21.6 (33.87)	749.3 (1.33)	38.0	256 (18.2)	9.56 (16.66)	1,407.1 (2.4)	69.1 (1.95)	2.3
Jan to Sep 1980	336.2	21.9	769.6	42.3			1,486.5	83	2.7

Note: 1 Coking coal as defined here is coal primarily used for iron and steel production and household fuel.

2 Steaming coal is primarily used for thermal power generation.

3 Figures in brackets below the quantity columns denote percentage of total Japanese imports of coal.

⁴ Figures in brackets below the columns denote percentage share of the value of total 'Japanese imports of coal.

Source: Jetro, *White Paper on International Trade (Summary), 1977,* 227; *1978,* 245; *1979,* 105; *1980,* 129-30. Jetro, *China Newsletter,* April 1978, 21; June 1980, 27; December 1980, 31.

Table 9

Chinese Coal Exports to Japan Under the Long-Term Trade Agreement
(in thousand tons)

Year	Steaming Coal	Coking Coal
1978	150 to 200 (150)	150 to 300 (300)
1979	150 to 200 (220 to 240)	500 (711)
1980	500 to 600 (600)	1,000,
1981	1,000 to 1,200	1,500
1982	1,500 to 1,700	2,000

Note: Figures in brackets are actual amounts contracted.

Source: Jetro, *China Newsletter*, June 1980, 26.

Thus in the first five years of the agreement China will export 5.15-5.3 million tons of coking coal and 3.3-3.9 million tons of steam coal. The export quantities for 1983 and subsequent years are to be determined in 1981. Japan seems to have met Chinese wishes in the matter by agreeing to "increase year after year" its imports of Chinese coal and crude. It seems that political considerations ultimately prevailed despite the reluctance of Japanese industry to accept such large quantities. It was felt that increased imports of coal, like those of crude, were necessary if Sino-Japanese trade was to continuously expand.

In March 1980 Japanese steam and electric power firms reached agreement with China on the purchase of 600,000 tons of steaming coal for fiscal 1980. The Chinese proposed a price of more than $40 per ton, far higher than the previous year's estimated price of about $31 (c.i.f.), citing the recent spiraling prices of steaming coal the world over. This was nearly $10 more t han the price of coal produced in Japan.[41] Next month, Minister of International Trade and Industry Yoshitake Sasaki expressed Japan's willingness to purchase 10 million tons of coal annually in 1985. The Chinese agreed to consider the Japanese request. Japanese imports of Chinese coal during January-September 1980 was 1,486,500 tons.

In January 1981 the Japanese Cabinet approved the Supply Target of Alternative Energy Sources to meet half of Japan's energy needs in fiscal 1990. The coal supply target for fiscal 1990 was fixed at 163.5 million tons and accounts for 35.4 per cent of all alternative sources—69 million tons of steam coal and 94.5 million tons of coking coal.[42]

A Japanese coal mission was scheduled to visit China in March 1981 to ascertain the possibility of supply of 10 million tons of coking and steaming coal to Japan in 1985. It was also expected to seek a confirmation whether the Chinese can meet a request for an additional 500,000 to 1 million tons of steaming coal in 1981 and 1982.[43]

Japanese imports of coal are likely to increase significantly in the eighties in keeping with the Japanese Government's decision to expand thermal power capacity. However, it is essential for China to improve its domestic transportation and loading ports, stabilize its coal price, and increase the number of its export coal varieties.

Joint Development of Coal Mines

China made a request for Japanese assistance in the development of its coal resources during the visit of a Japanese coal technology and friendship delegation in June 1978.[44] In response to this request the Japan Coal Association (JCA) sent an official delegation next month. Subsequently five Japanese coal companies, viz. Mitsui Mining, Mitsubishi Coal Mining, Sumitomo Coal Mining, Taiheiyo Coal Mining, and Matsushima Coal Mining, indicated their interest in participating in the development of two coalfields—one at Gujiao (Shanxi Province) and the other at Yanzhou (Shandong Province). They indicated their willingness to provide the technology and services needed to raise production to approximately 20 million tons annually in return for a portion of that production. An investigatory and survey coal delegation led by JCA President, Shingo Ariyoshi, visited China in late September-October 1978.[45] The delegation undertook a survey of not only Gujiao and Yanzhou but also coal mines in Hebei, Henan, and Liaoning Provinces. The delegation exchanged letters of intent on joint development of the Gujiao and Yanzhou mines with the China National Mining Technology and Equipment Corporation.[46] The settlement formula agreed upon included production sharing. Commencement of coal output in these two regions, estimated at four million tons each, was planned for 1983.[47]

Negotiations were temporarily suspended in the beginning of 1979 by the Chinese primarily due to the "readjustment" policy. Negotiations were resumed in April 1979 when a JCA delegation consisting of the five Japanese coal companies visited China. During the discussions, the Chinese side said that it did not wish Japanese co-operation in the development of the above-mentioned two mines because the coal produced there would be used to generate electric power within the country. Coal, thus, would not be available for export. Instead China proposed that Japan participate in developing the seven new regions. In May the Japanese companies mutually agreed that Mitsui, Matsushima, and Taiheiyo would develop the Baodian and Jining mines in Yanzhou, and Mitsubishi would develop the Tunlan mines in Gujiao. Coal production was scheduled to begin in 1982, with payment being made in the form of coal.[48] This proposal was presented to China in October when a JCA delegation visited China. In response, the Chinese made a concrete porposal seeking Japanese participation in four coal mines. In December 1979 eight more coal mines were added at the request of Ministry of Coal Industry (see Table 10) These mines are to be developed with a loan from the Export-Import Bank of Japan.

During his visit to China in April 1980 Minister of International Trade and Industry Sasaki reached agreement with Vice Premier Yu Qiuli that Japan would extend a $90 million loan in fiscal 1980 for development of three coal mines, viz. the Baodian and Jiangzhuang mines in Shandong Province and the Xiqu mine in Shanxi Province.[49] This loan was within the framework of the Exim Bank loan of $2 billion extended to China earlier.

A joint government industry fact-finding mission visited China in June-July 1980 to probe coal qualities and transportation availability at seven mines, viz. Datong, Taiyuan, Yanzhou, Gujiao (site of three mines), and Kailuan. The seven mines were estimated to be capable of an annual production of 14-15 millon tons in all. China wanted the Exim Bank to arrange for a loan distribution for the other mines to fill the year's quota of $200 million. The Japanese delegation concluded that China could export five million metric tons of steam and coking coal each annually starting 1985.[50]

Table 10

Joint Coal Development Projects Proposed by China

	Annual output (1,000 tons)	Type of coal	Construction period	Estimated reserves (million tons)
Financed by Exim Bank loan				
Yanzhou region, Shandong Province				
Baodian	2,000	Steam	1977-1984	570
Jiangzhuang	1,500	Steam, feitan	1979-1984	300
Huainan region, Anhui Province				
Panji	3,000	Steam	1976-1985	600
Kailuan region, Hebei Province				
Qianjiaying	1,500	Feitan	1977-1985	520
Gujiao region, Shanxi Province				
Xiqu	3,000	Feitan, coking	1977-1984	570
Malan	4,000	Feitan, coking	1981-1986	1,050
Zhenchengdi	1,500	Feitan, coking	1981-1984	380
Heilongjiang Province				
Yiminhe	3,000	Brown (used domestically)	1981-1985	1,280
Production-sharing formula				
Yanzhou region, Shanxi Province				
Jining No. 2	4,000	Steam	undetermined	undetermined
Gujiao region, Shanxi Province				
Tunlan	4,000	Coking	undetermined	undetermined
Joint venture formula				
(Gujiao region, Shanxi Province)				
Guishigou	3,000	Coking	undetermined	undetermined
Nei Mongol (Inner Mongolia) Autonomous Region				
Jungar	10,000 to 20,000	Steam	to 1990	30,000

Source: Jetro, China Newsletter, June 1980, 27.   Feitan is a high calorie Chinese coal.

It was reported that Mitsui Mining Co. had reached basic agreement with Chinese authorities to jointly develop coal at Datong, Shanxi Province. China envisages raising the mine's output to around four million tons a year at a total estimated cost of 20-30 billion yen. Beijing planned to supply Mitsui with 1.2-1.3 million tons of coal annually for 10 years.[51] The Japanese company reportedly prefers the establishment of a consortium to handle project planning and management, technology licensing. Details are yet to be worked out regarding coal export volumes, development schedule, etc.[52]

Conclusions

China is undoubtedly eager to export a large volume of coal to Japan and has sought Japanese financial assistance to develop its coal mines and related infrastructure. Coal exports are likely to assume greater importance as declining oil output will restrict China's ability to increase oil exports. For instance, the lag in China's oil supplies to Japan in 1979 was compensated to a certain extent by near doubling of Japan's imports of China's anthracite, coking, and steam coal over the preceding year to a total of 1.4 million tons.

While China has taken the lead as a supplier of oil, the Soviet Union supplies more coal (See Table 11). Soviet coal

Table 11

Chinese and Soviet Exports of Coal to Japan, 1975-1979
(in thousand tons)

	Chinese Exports		Soviet Exports	
	Qty.	Value (*mn* $)	Qty.	Value (*mn* $)
1975	456	17.5	3,195	164
1976	322	12.0	3,290	175
1977	491	19.9	3,141	165.6
1978	772.2	36.8	2,483	133.3
1979	1,407.1	69.1	2,343	124

Source : Jetro, *White Paper on International Trade*, *1977*, 130-1, 228; *1978*, 142, 246; *1979*, 105, 190; *1980*, 129-30, 291.

exports to Japan went up by six times, from 542,000 tons in 1960 to 3,224,000 tons in 1976.[53] Japan's decision to import coal from China has led to a short-term reduction in the volume of Japanese imports from the Soviet Union. This was partly because of the Sino-Japanese Long-Term Trade Agreement (February 1978) providing for Chinese coking coal and steam coal supplies. Thus, during negotiations for fixing the quantity of imports for 1978, the Japanese sought a 30 per cent reduction in the cotracted volume because of the recession in major steel companies. Eventually the Soviets agreed to export two million tons of coal in 1978, which represented a 20 per cent decrease over the previous year. From the long-term point of view, however, it is doubtful whether Chinese coal exports to Japan would have a significant impact given the Japanese commitment to develop South Yakutia coking coal project. Japan has so far provided a total of $540 million in bank credits for the development of the South Yakutia coal project in return for 104 million tons of coking coal, including 84 million tons from the South Yakutian fields (starting 1983) and 20 million tons from the Kuznetsk coal basin (starting 1979). In fact, of all the Siberian projects, the South Yakutia coal project seems to have been the most successful one.

Japan's import of coal is likely to increase from an estimated 22 million tons in 1985 to 53.5 million tons in 1990, and 80.5 million tons in 1995.[54] Tokyo estimates that 40 per cent of its imports of coal in 1990 will be supplied by Australia, with China and North America accounting for 30 per cent each.[55] Consequently, the Japanese are eager to participate in the development of coal mines in other countries in order to stabilize the price and volume of coal from a long-term point of view and enable Japan to diversify its sources of supply.

Japanese imports of Chinese coal in the eighties would depend on the progress in the construction of new coal-fired thermal power plants in Japan and China's coal output. China must also improve its domestic transport systems, develop adequate shipping and port loading facilities and other infrastructural aspects as they relate to coal exports.

NOTES

1 Gene T. Hsiao, "Prospects for a Sino-Japanese Relationship," *China Quarterly*, December 1974, 744-5.

2 It consists of Idemitsu Kosan, Maruzen Oil, Daikyo Oil, Kyodo Oil, Mitsubishi Oil, and Kyushu Oil. It includes nine electric power companies, viz. Hokkaido Electric Power Co., Tohoku Electric Power Co., Tokyo Electric Power Co., Chubu Electric Power Co., Kansai Electric Power Co., Hokuriku Electric Power Co., Shikoku Electric Power Co., Chugoku Electric Power Co., and Kyushu Electric Power Co. It also includes six iron and steel makers, viz. Nippon Steel Corp., Kawasaki Steel Corp., Nippon Kokan, Sumitomo Metal Industries, Kobe Steel, and Shin Nippon Seiko.

3 It consists of seventeen oil companies, viz. Asia Oil, Kyokuto Oil, Koa Oil, Showa Oil, Showa Yokkaichi Oil, Seibu Oil, General Sekiyu, Taiyo Oil, Toa Oil, Toa Kogyo, Nenryo Toho Oil Tohoku Oil, Nansei Oil, Nippon Oil Refining, Nippon Oil, Nihankai Oil, and Fuji Oil. Seibu Oil has *de facto* withdrawn from the Importers Conference following its import of Chinese crude in June 1975. Toa Nenryo Kogyo and Nippon Oil Refining joined the Conference in January 1976 and Nansei Oil joined the Conference in February 1976. The Importers Conference also includes eight trading companies. viz. C. Itoh and Co., Sangyo Boeki, Sumitomo Shoji, Toko Bussan, Nissho Iwai, Mitsui and Co., Mitsubishi Corp., and Wako Koeki.

4 Because contracts for crude were made in reminbi yuan, China did not have to worry about depreciation if the value of the US dollar fell. However, according to the international practice of making quotation in US dollars, the actual price of Daqing crude was higher than Minas crude. Thus in 1978 the contract price was $3.93 per barrel but the actual price was $4.552. In the first half of 1974, when the contract price was $14.80 per barrel, the actual price was $15.642 Jetro, *China Newsletter*, January 1975, 10-1.

5 Ibid., 10.

6 Ibid.

7 Ibid.

8 Idemitsu Kosan's proposal in 1975 to instal residual oil cracking and dewaxing equipment at its Hyogo plant to be used exclusively in refining Chinese crude was eventually shelved after two years.

9 Keidanren, *Keidanren Review on Japanese Economy*, February 1978, 6.

10 Jetro, *China Newsletter*, January 1978, 13.

11 *Japan Economic Journal*, 13 July 1976.

12 Ibid., 25 November 1975.

13 *China Newsletter* January 1978, 7.

14 *Japan Economic Journal*, 16 September 1980.

15 *Beijing Review*, 15 December 1980, 10.

16 *Japan Economic Journal*, 3 March 1981.

17 Ibid., 24 February 1981.

18 Ibid., 20 February 1979.

[19] Ibid., 23 October 1979.

[20] *News from China*, 11 December 1979, 6-7; *Beijing Review*, 14 December 1979, 3.

[21] *Japan Economic Journal*, 11 December 1979.

[22] Oil development companies are expected to put up 27 per cent of the private capitalization, oil refiners 9 per cent, power utilities 2.4 per cent, and steelmakers 1.6 per cent.

[23] *Japan Economic Journal*, 11 December 1979.

[24] Ibid., 16 December 1980.

[25] Ibid., 3 June 1980.

[26] Ibid., 16 December 1980.

[27] The Chinese proposed co-operation in the development of this area in September 1978 when Minister of International Trade and Industry Komoto visited China. *China Newsletter*, December 1978, 21.

[28] *Japan Eonomic Journal* 29 April 1978.

[29] *China Newsletter*, January 1978, 10.

[30] Ibid., June 1978, 12; *Japan Economic Journal*, 6 April 1976 and 22 February 1977.

[31] *Japan Economic Journal*, 24 February 1981.

[32] S.H. Chou, "Industrial Modernization in China," *Current History*, September 1979, 64.

[33] A.B. Ikonnikov, "China's Coal Export Potential," *Australian Outlook*, August 1973, 181.

[34] *China Newsletter*, June 1978, 18.

[35] Ikonnikov, n. 33, 186.

[36] Ibid., 181.

[37] *Japan Economic Journal*, 15 July 1975.

[38] *China Newsletter*, January 1978, 16.

[39] *Japan Economic Journal*, 25 November 1975, 1 February, 1 March and 1 April 1977.

[40] Ibid., 1 February 1977.

[41] Ibid., 1 April 1980.

[42] Japan, Ministery of Foreign Affairs, *Information Bulletin* (Tokyo), 15 January 1981, 6 and 7.

[43] *Japan Economic Journal*, 7 February 1981.

[44] Ibid., 13 June 1978.

[45] Ibid., 3 October 1978.

[46] *China Newsletter*, June 1980, 27.

[47] Ibid.

[48] Ibid., 28.

[49] *Japan Economic Journal*, 6 May 1980.

[50] Ibid., 22 July 1980.

[51] Ibid., 1 April 1980.

[52] Ibid., 9 September 1980.

[53] V. Andrayev, "The Capitalist Coal Market," *Foreign Trade USSR*, vol. 7, 1977, 29.

[54] *Japan Economic Journal*, 1 April 1980.

[55] Ibid.

11. Political Developments, 1979-1980

The signing of the Peace and Friendship Treaty in August 1978 created a favourable climate for developing closer economic and political relations between China and Japan. Contacts in the military field were also established between the two countries. While a number of high-level Japanese defence personnel had gone to China in 1977.[1] Col Atsushi Shima, Chief of Intelligence Division, was the first serving officer of the Japanese Self-Defence Forces to visit China in March 1978. The first-ever Chinese military delegation led by Chang Tsai-chien, a Deputy Chief of General Staff, arrived in Tokyo in September 1978. The Chinese delegation reportedly expressed the desire to import Japanese defence technology.[2] Foreign Minister Sunao Sonoda, however, clarified that Japan could help China's general modernization efforts, but not in the military sphere.[3]

During the 1970s China continued to support Japanese claims and aspirations for the return of the Northern Territories from the Soviet Union. Beijing encouraged various Japanese organizations and activists seeking their return and cultivated them through visits and contacts. China's objective in so doing had been to sour Soviet-Japanese relations and perhaps to strengthen its own claim to Taiwan.

China asserts that the Soviet occupation of the Kuriles is "a constant military threat to Japan"[4] and is reflective of Soviet "expansionism"[5] and Soviet "hegemonic ambition".[6] In fact, Zhou Enlai remarked that one of the criteria for determining Soviet sincerity in seeking relaxation of world tensions would be its readiness to return the Northern Territories to Japan.[7]

Japan is no doubt grateful for China's sympathy but it fears that vociferous Chinese support on the issue is likely to stiffen the Soviet attitude and complicate the process of finding a solution for the problem. It disapproves of the linkage of this issue with "anti-hegemonism". Japan prefers to negotiate with the Soviets on a strictly bilateral basis. Thus, Beijing's support is considered to be "more embarassing than helpful" and tantamount to an "interference" in its internal affairs. The Soviet Union has accused China of being a "sower" of discord between two neighbours.[8]

China criticized the Soviet military build up in the Northern Territories, which began in June 1978 and gained momentum in January 1979. The *Beijing Review* asserted that the Soviet intention in reinforcing its military installations on the Northern Territories was to achieve a *fait accompli* through the military occupation so that Japan might eventually permit or acquiesce in the merger of the Northern Territories in the Soviet Union. China warned that Moscow's aim was to place Japan under its own influence and interfere with its foreign policy.[9] The Soviet military buildup was said to be "a dagger pointed at Japan's throat" because the Hokkaido coast was now within range of Soviet guns developed on Kunashiri. A landing on Hokkaido, the Chinese commentary added, could be staged within twenty minutes.[10]

China has denounced in strong terms the Soviet proposal for collective security in Asia. China views the Soviet proposal as an offshoot of the Brezhnev Doctrine, which was used to justify the Soviet intervention in Czechoslovakia in August 1968 in the name of the collective security interests of the "Socialist Commonwealth" of nations and the "stability and inviolability" of the postwar frontiers in Eastern Europe.[11] China is convinced that the primary motive behind the Soviet proposal is to contain China by means of a Soviet-sponsored *cordon sanitaire* around China and to secure a simultaneous increase in Soviet influence in Asia. The *modus operandi* is to forge a series of bilateral friendship treaties on the pattern of friendship and co-operation treaties with India (August 1971), Vietnam (November 1978), and Afghanistan (December 1978).[12]

Consequently Beijing cannot view with equanimity any Japanese endorsement of, or support for, the Soviet proposal for a collective security system in Asia.

Japan has so far cold-shouldered the proposal not only because of its implications for the security of China, but also because of the clear possibility of its affecting its own national interests. For one thing, any affirmation by it of the territorial *status quo*, which this scheme advocates, would entail a renunciation by it of its claim to the Northern Territories. Moreover, the proposed dissolution of military alliances and bases would deny Japan the wherewithal needed to preserve its security. It is also important for Japan to pay due heed to Chinese susceptibilities in the matter. Since China regards the proposal essentially as anti-Chinese in character, Japan is reluctant to endorse it.[13]

A trilateral relationship between China, Japan, and the United States seemed to be emerging with the signing of the China-Japan peace and friendship treaty and the formalisation of the establishment of diplomatic relations between Beijing and Washington on 1 January 1979. Vice Premier Deng Xiaoping emphasized the importance of this relationship during his three-day unofficial visit to Japan on his way back from the United States in February 1979. A *Pravda* commentary of February 1979 by Igor Latyshev felt that Deng had tried to encourage Japanese leaders to play a more active role in Beijing's plan for the formation of an anti-Soviet united front.

Several high-level Chinese delegations visited Japan in 1979. In April 1979 the first-ever NPC delegation led by Madame Deng Yingchao, Vice Chairman of the Standing Committee of the National People's Congress, visited Japan. She sought to assure the Japanese people that China would endeavour to settle the Taiwan question by peaceful means and that the *status quo* on Taiwan and its present system would be respected and that the economic interests of foreign countries in Taiwan would not be adversely affected. She also said that the normalization of Sino-US relations would not adversely affect Sino-Japanese economic relations. She felt that there were broad prospects for the expansion of economic co-operation between the two countries despite the fact that difficulties of one kind or another cropped up at times.[14]

A 600-strong Chinese friendship delegation on board the ship, *Ming Hua*, led by Liao Cheng-chih, Vice Chairman of the NPC Standing Committee and the President of China-Japan Friendship Association, arrived in Japan on 9 May 1979 for a month long tour. The deputy leader of this mission was Chinese Vice Defence Minister Su Yu. He was the highest ranking Chinese military leader to visit Japan since 1949.

In September Vice Premier Gu Mu requested Japanese credits for the development of several projects in China. Emphasizing the importance of close Sino-Japanese ties, he stated:

An economically developed and technologically advanced Japan and a gradually prospering and modernized China working in close co-operation with other friendly countries in the Asia-Pacific region would in a very large measure ensure stability in the East.[15]

Ohira's Visit to China

Prime Minister Masayoshi Ohira visited China from 5 to 9 December 1979. At the banquet given in honour of the visiting Japanese Premier, Prime Minister Hua Guofeng stated that though China and Japan decided their own policy independently, there was "a common language between us [China and Japan] on many international issues."[16] The joint press communique issued on 7 December expressed satisfaction with the progress of Sino-Japanese relations since the normalization of relations in 1972. The two sides agreed to hold annual meetings between high-level Foreign Ministry officials alternatively in their respective capitals. It was also agreed to start negotiations in 1980 for concluding an agreement on co-operation in the field of science and technology. A cultural agreement was also signed during the visit. Ohira conveyed Japan's decision to extend the preferential tariff system to China in April 1980.[17] He also expressd the intention of providing a loan of up to 50 billion yen for fiscal 1979.

The developments in Afghanistan were used by Beijing to draw Japan closer to China as it felt deeply concerned about the Soviet intervention in Afghanistan (December 1979). The

Afghan events were said to have exposed Kremlin's *detente* "fraud" and proved that it was only "a smokescreen to cover up its aggression and expansion."[18] The Soviet intervention in Afghanistan, Xinhua News Agency asserted, had "awakened the Japanese people like a hurricane from their fond dream of peace."[19] It cited a commentary pubished in *Sankei Shimbun* (18 January 1980) stating that the ostensible Soviet objective was "to vietnamize and then afghanize Japan through a treaty of good neighbourhood and cooperation between the U.S.S.R. and Japan."[20] *Beijing Review* criticized Soviet attempts to exert pressure on Japan to withdraw the steps[21] it had taken in the wake of the Afghan crisis.[22] Moscow, it asserted, sought to take advantage of its geographical position and military strength to force Japan to withdraw its measures of disapproval so that Western unity against Soviet invasion of Afghanistan would be disrupted. China advised Tokyo to improve its defence capabilities in the circumstances.[23] While Japan has been critical of Soviet intervention in Afghanistan and even took some economic measures against the Soviet Union, it adopted a cautious approach and refused to identify itself with the anti-Soviet stance of Chinese policy as it did not want to hurt the prospects of long-term economic co-operation with that country.[24]

During his visit to China in January 1980, Foreign Minister Saburo Okita, reiterated Japan's intention not to co-operate with China in military areas and said that the Sino-Japanese relationship was not "an exclusive relationship" but a relationship of co-operation with other advanced industrial countries.[25] The two neighbours decided to establish Consulates at Sapporo and Guangzho (Canton). The first bilateral annual consultations between the two countries at the Vice Foreign Minister level were held in March 1980 when Vice Minister Han Nianlong visited Japan. Vice Premier Yu Qiuli paid a two-week visit to Japan next month.[26]

Premier Hua Guofeng's Visit, May 1980

Premier Hua Guofeng was the first Chinese Head of Government to visit Japan in the 2,000 years of the history of Sino-Japanese relations. During the visit, he reiterated Chinese views regarding Soviet hegemonistic designs. In a statement at a Press conference on 29 May he stated that so long as South Korea did not launch a war, there would be no such thing as a "southward advance." The seven-page communique issued on 29 May 1980 expressed the determination of the two countries to make sustained efforts for the preservation and securing of peace and stability in the Asia-Pacific region as well as in other parts of the world. The two countries resolved to further develop and deepen their relationship on the basis of deepening mutual understanding and mutual trust through promoting mutual exchanges. Ohira was careful not to identify himself with the outright anti-Soviet stance of China. The fact that no specific reference was made in the joint communique to Afghanistan, Iran, Korea, and Kampuchea reflected the divergent viewpoints held by the two sides. The two leaders also agreed that bilateral co-operation in the development of natural resources and energy, especially petroleum and coal, should be further expanded on a long-term and stable basis. The two leaders agreed to hold meetings on the level of the Japanese Cabinet and Chinese State Council alternately in the capitals of the two countries to facilitate wide-ranging consultations on bilateral matters. It was decided to hold the first meeting in Beijing in autumn. Besides, it was agreed to start the negotiations for a treaty on the preservation of migratory birds.[27] A two-year agreement on scientific and technical co-operation was signed on 28 May.

Zenko Suzuki was elected Prime Minister of Japan in the general elections held in Japan on 22 June 1980 after the demise of Premier Masayoshi Ohira. Prime Minister Hua Guofeng visited Japan for three days (8-10) in July to attend Ohira's funeral. During this visit he met President Jimmy Carter of the United States who had also come to Tokyo to attend the funeral of Ohira. The two leaders had a wide-ranging exchange of views on the current international situation and on issues of mutual concern. It was stated that among the issues discussed were recent developments threatening the peace and tranquility of Southwest Asia and Indo-China.[28] The holding of the Sino-US summit on Japanese soil and Carter's statement on the need for co-operation between China, Japan, and the United States to counter the Soviet military threat seemed to confirm

Soviet fears about the "Beijing-Washigton-Tokyo" axis. Beijing also apparently favourably viewed one of the first decisions of the new Japanese Government to increase defence expenditures from the financial year beginning April 1981.

First Ministerial Conference, December 1980

The first Ministerial level conference since the nomalization of Sino-Japanese relations in 1972 was held in Beijing from 3 to 5 December 1980. Representing China at the conference were Vice Premiers Gu Mu, Yao Yilin and Huang Hua, and nine ministers and government officials of ministeral level, including Minister of Foreign Trade Li Qiang. Representing Japan were Minister of Foreign Affairs Masayoshi Ito and five other ministers and members of the ruling party.

Following the Conference, the two countries exchanged notes in which Japan pledged to extend 55 billion yen in Yen credits to China in fiscal 1980, as the second annual instalment of Japanese assistance for six development projects. A joint press statement issued at the end of the discussions referred to the smooth development of bilateral relations since 1972 and expressed the resolve of the two countries to create lasting peaceful and co-operative relations through increased exchanges. China and Japan agreed to further promote co-operation in developing oil, coal, and other energy resources. They further agreed to start negotiations for the conclusion of a taxation convention and investment guarantee agreement. During the discussions the Japanese side expressed the hope that China would eventually become Japan's long-term and stable energy supplier. China promised to do its best in this regard.[29] Foreign Minister Huang Hua underlined the common strategic interests of China and Japan and emphasized that the two countries shared converging views on a number of international issues.[30]

During the conference, Chinese leaders informed the Japanese delegation that the three-year economic adjustment in China's plans for modernization which had been launched in 1979 would not be concluded in 1981 and that the review might continue till 1983. The Japanese side emphasized the considerable inconvenience Japan had been put to as a result of successive Chinese decisions to drop major projects in which

Japanese firms were participating. Commenting on the consultations, the *Japan Times* editorially observed that the discussions were more useful in the sense of improving communication rather than in terms of immediate results achieved.[31]

Conclusion

The Sino-Soviet conflict during the sixties and the developing
US-Soviet *detente* had made it possible and desirable for the
Soviet Union to get closer to Japan despite unresolved political
differences between the two countries, especially the thorny
territorial issue. Japan reciprocated Soviet efforts in order to
forge closer economic relations with the Soviet Union and
acquire a foothold in the Soviet market. However, the
normalization of Sino-Japanese relations in the autumn of
1972 brought about a qualitative change in East Asian politics
and led to keener Sino-Soviet competition for Japanese
support. The seventies reflected the considerable strategic and
political importance of Japan in the foreign policy priorities
of the two Communist giants.

In these circumstances, Japan adopted a policy of equidistance in the early seventies. Prime Minister Takeo Miki
felt that it was possible for Japan to construct friendly triangular relations among Japan, China, and the United States.
He felt that Japan could seek a path of friendship that did not
favour one over the other. He even expressed the possibility
of Tokyo being able to play the role of a middleman in
adjusting relations between China and the Soviet Union.[32] Equidistance, in fact, enabled Japan not to offend either Communist neighbour and derive maximum advantages from the two
Communist Powers. However, a tilt in favour of China became
eventually apparent in 1978, a tilt which was partly encouraged
by the United States but which arose chiefly owing to the
frustration felt over the territorial question and mounting
domestic pressure for accelerating and broadening Japan's
economic relations with China. These developments lent
credence to Soviet fears that a triangular Sino-Japanese-US
relationship or "axis" had come into being.

China's political and economic courtship of Japan in the
seventies is primarily designed to enlist Japan's support in

countering the Soviet threat and to wean Japan away from too close an economic or political relationship with Moscow. It also seeks to benefit by technological and economic co-operation with Japan.

The seventies show that the Chinese fear of a US-inspired encirclement of the Mainland has been replaced by encirclement backed by the Soviet Union and Vietnam, Afghanistan and India. The expanding Soviet influence, particularly in Asia, made China, the United States, and Japan conscious of the possibilities of seeking and working for a new political equilibrium in the Far East to counter Soviet ambitions by developing closer ties with one another. The need to check and balance the Soviet Union also explains why China now supports the US-Japanese Security Treaty, favours continued military preparedness and increased military expenditure on the part of Japan and continued American presence in Asia and elsewhere. The perception of a greater Soviet treat to its security also led Japan to modify its policy of equidistance and to forge closer political relations with China by signing the Sino-Japanesepeace treaty in August 1978.

China's response to the perception of mounting Soviet threat has, *inter alia* been to further cement its ties with Pakistan and explore possibilities of improved relations with India. It is in the overall framework of Soviet threat perception that Japan in Northeast Asia, the West Europeans and the EEC in Europe, and the United States regionally and globally have become extremely important in Chinese foreign policy calculations for economic as well as political and strategic reasons.

NOTES

[1] Professor Hsiao Iwashima, an eminent Japanese military historian and strategist, visited China in April 1977 (and again in March 1980); Hideo Miyoshi, former Chief of Staff of the Self-Defence Forces, in June; followed by Osamu Kaihara, former National Defence Council's Secretary General. A delegation of former Self-Defence Force generals led by Kenjoro Mitsuoka visited China in September 1977 and a delegation of the Japanese Military Academy in November 1977.

[2] *Times of India* (New Delhi), 11 September 1978.

[3] Ibid., 14 October 1978.

4 *Peking Review*, 30 June 1978, 27. Also see, for example, Premier Hua Guofeng's report to the First Session of the Fifth National People's Congress, 26 February 1978. *Peking Review*, 10 March 1978, 39.

5 See ibid., 8 September 1972, 8 December 1972, 2 February 1973 and 16 March 1973.

6 *Beijing Review*, 2 January 1979, 36-7.

7 See Zhou's report to the Tenth Party Congress, 24 August 1973. *Peking Review*, 7 September 1973, 17 and 23.

8 See R.K. Jain, *The USSR and Japan, 1945-1980* (New Delhi, 1981), 59-60.

9 *Beijing Review*, 12 October 1979.

10 Ibid., 16 February 1979, 26 and 21 September 1979, 27.

14 See L.I. Brezhnev's speech to the Fifth Congress of the Polish United Workers Party. *Pravda* and *Izvestia*, 13 November 1968, as translated in the *Current Digest of the Soviet Press*, 4 December 1968, 3-4.

12 Jain, n. 8, 147.

13 Ibid.

14 Statement at a press conference in Tokyo, 11 April 1979. *News from China*, 14 April 1979, 4.

15 *Beijing Review*, 14 September 1979, 4.

16 *News from China*, 11 December 1979, 4.

17 See *Beijing Review*, 14 December 1979, 3-4.

18 Ibid., 25 February 1980, 9.

19 Xinhua News Agency, 2 February 1980, 7-8.

20 Ibid., 19 January 1980; *Beijing Review*, 8 September 1980, 12-3.

21 These included temporary freezing of contacts with Soviet officials, suspension of new loans, restrictions on export of sophisticated technology to the Soviet Union, etc.

22 *Beijing Review*, 8 September 1980, 14.

23 See *News from China*, 1 April 1980, 2-3; *Beijing Review*, 31 March 1980, 10.

24 For a discussion of the Japanese attitude towards the Soviet intervention in Afghanistan, see Jain, n. 8, 163-5.

25 Speech in the Diet, 25 January 1980. *Information Bulletin* (Tokyo), 15 February 1980, 5.

26 *News from China*, 8 April 1980, 2.

27 *Beijing Review*, 9 June 1980, 8-9; Japan, Embassy in India, News from Japan, Press Release No. 17, 31 May 1980.

28 *News from China*, 12 July 1980, 2.

29 Ibid., 9 December 1980, 4.

30 Ibid.

31 *Japan Times*, 10 December 1980.

32 Takeo Miki, "Future Japanese Diplomacy," *Japan Quarterly*, January-March 1973, 20 and 22.

12. Outlook for the Future

Northeast Asia is an area of considerable strategic importance to China. The political, economic, and security interests of China, Japan, the Soviet Union, and the United States converge in the region. A clear understanding of the intricacies of this quadrangular relationship is essential for understanding the dynamics of Sino-Japanese relations.

Chinese Perspective

The Soviet Union is China's Adversary No.1, and Chinese leaders feel that Soviet foreign policy aims at the encirclement and containment of China. The strategic climate around the Chinese periphery at the turn of the eighties appears to have turned inclement on account of cordial Indo-Soviet relations, the Soviet treaty with Vietnam, and Soviet intervention in Afghanistan. China has sought to neutralize the adverse consequences of Soviet policy by normalizing its relations with Japan and the United States. Simultaneously, it has redoubled its efforts to forge closer ties with the countries of Western, as well as Eastern, Europe. Japan, being situated in a close, strategically vital region, is of considerable importance to China. Chinese leaders are particularly anxious to arrest the development of close economic and diplomatic ties between Japan and the Soviet Union lest such ties should lead eventually to a renewed attempt to contain China. This nightmarish possibility apparently continues to haunt Chinese policy-makers.

China's over-riding foreign policy objective since the early

1970s seems to have been the containment (or counter-containment) of the Soviet Union, including prevention of the growth of Soviet influence in Asia, as it considers "social imperialism" to be a greater mence than "US imperialism".[1] Its economic and political courtship of Japan is aimed to achieve this end. It seeks to dissuade Japan from siding with the USSR in political matters and from collaborating too closely in economic matters, especially in ways that may improve the Soviet military and strategic position in the region. Moreover, unlike in the past, it now finds the American military presence in Asia desirable. It has also started appreciating the usefulness of the US-Japanese Security Treaty and the close political and defence ties obtaining between Japan and the United States.

China realizes that unlike the Soviet Union, it does not have any major political or security problem with Japan. Such cultural ties as obtain between China and the Soviet Union certainly cannot match those obtaining between China and Japan. The Chinese motives in emphasizing repeatedly that the Soviet Union should return the Northern Territories, in characterizing the bait of economic co-operation being dangled by the Soviet Union before Japan as a wedge driven between the United States and Japan and between China and Japan,[2] in seeking to expose the pressure tactics used by the Soviet Union during the fishery negotiations, and in drawing attention to the repeated violations of Japanese airspace and territorial waters by Soviet planes and warships respectively and the sinister implications of such violations is obviously to sour Soviet-Japanese relations, impede their further development, and draw Japan closer to itself as against the USSR. It wants to capitalize on the increasing perception in Japan that the Soviet Union poses a greater threat to Japan's security than any other country and prepare the ground for increasingly close political and military relations between Japan and itself. Ideally, it would like to see Japan persuaded that its present refusal openly to take sides in the Sino-Soviet dispute is against its long-term interests and that the danger of the Soviets attempting to "exercise hegemony" over Northeast Asia is real and imminent.[3] Though it supports and encourages a conventional rearmament of Japan at an accelerated pace, it may not (like the Soviet Union and the United States) welcome Japan's going nuclear. The Soviet Union naturally enough accuses China of encouraging Japan's rearmament with an anti-Soviet bias.

Apart from politico-security interests, China has certain economic interests as well. It recognizes that Japan's influence in world affairs and the regional status that Japan enjoys by virtue of its economic activities are already large and can only grow larger.[4] Not only is Japan a very close neighbour and an extremly important source of advanced technology and manufactured goods, but it is also the largest market for Chinese exports. China's aim in cultivating Japanese political, economic, and labour interests is to create a strong consensus in Japan in favour of expanded trade relations with China and at the same time to restrict Japan's trade relations with the Soviet Union. Besides, close ties with the Japanese businessmen carrying on trade with China and the expansion of Sino-Japanese "material interdependency".[5] improves China's ability to influence Japanese domestic politics. In order to discourage Japan from undertaking any long-term involvment in the various Siberian projects and retard the growth of Soviet-Japanese trade China stepped up its crude deliveries to Tokyo. In fact, its leaders have emphasized time and again that they look to Japan for scientific, technological, and financial assistance in their plans to modernize.

So long as China regards the Soviet Union as its main enemy, it would woo Japan and be willing to make concessions so that it may improve its own position *vis-a-vis* the Soviet Union in Northeast Asia. A pro-Soviet and anti-Chinese regime across the Sea of Japan is certainly not in China's interest. China now refrains from taking a hard line towards Japan for fear of pushing it closer to the USSR or encouraging militaristic and nuclearization tendencies in the Japanese people. It has kept up its efforts to influence key interest groups in Japan and to exploit the geographical proximity and the cultural, linguistic, and religious affinities between China and Japan. It has also sought to play upon the deeply felt sense of guilt among the Japanese people over their acts of aggression in China during the Second World War and their desire to atone for their misdeeds. It uses these factors to reinforce the negative image of the USSR in the Japanse people. The China factor in Japanese domestic politics is, therefore, going to be an important one in the foreseeable future.

Japanese Perspective

Given its geographical situation and its military inadequacy
to maintain its own security, Japan truly has no viable alternative to the US-Japanese security alliance. Although its
relations with the United States are not all smooth and there
are significant differences between them over bilateral economic
issues, it must maintain its ties with the United States as it
finds that those ties enhance its abiliy to manoeuvre between
China and the Soviet Union. In the 1980s, too, it is likely to
pursue an increasingly autonomous foreign policy without
qualitatively weekening its core relationship with the United
States.

Japan is also going to assume increasing responsibility for
its defence against any possible conventional attack by stren-
thening its defence capability so as to be able in some measure
to prolong holding time and to enable the United States to
render more effective mediation, military or diplomatic. The
pressures from the United States, its own perception of a
growing threat from the Soviet Union, the nudging it gets from
political, business, and bureaucratic elements at home, (for
their own reasons), and the increasing public acceptance and
awareness of the need for a credible defence capability have
led the Japanese Government to go in for increased defence
capabilities.

Japan considers it desirable to maintain cordial relations
with China for political and, more importantly, economic
reasons. Friendly relations with China give it greater diplomatic independence and perhaps also enable it to ensure a
certain degree of restraint in the Soviet foreign policy behaviour towards it. It does not, therefore, regard China's nuclear
power any more as a source of instability and as a threat.[6] On
the contrary it accepts the assurance given to it by China that
its nuclear arsenal is purely defensive in nature. Obviously it is
anxious like China not to vitiate the cordiality now obtaining
in Sino Japanese relations by focussing on the political
problems.

Japan is caught between the rival pulls and pressures of the

two Communist giants, China and the Soviet Union. Its
objective of achieving a balance in its relations with its two
Communist neighbours has undoubtedly proved to be extremely
difficult since it cannot afford to antagonize either of them.
Both China and the USSR court Japan for their own reasons,
each wants to use Japan against the other. Each sees some
elements of Japan's relations with the other as harmful to
itself. Neither wants Japan to align itself with the other lest
it should disturb the regional balance of power.

Sino-Soviet relations are going to be an important determinant of Sino-Japanese relations. The acute concern of the
Soviet Union about the threat it perceives from China, its
Adversary No. 1, and vice versa, together with the political,
territorial, and ideological problems in their relations, is not
likely to disappear soon. War between the two Communist
giants does not seem likely in the near future. The demise of
Chairman Mao Zedong and the rise of a new leadership to
power have not introduced any fundamental change in China's
policy towards the Soviet Union although both sides kept have
their options open. One cannot, of course, altogether rule out
the possibility of an improvement in Sino-Soviet relations. The
prospects of a *rapprochement* between China and the Soviet
Union are not quite bright at the moment.

Sino-Soviet differences no doubt offer opportunities to Japan
to play off one against the other but they also create for it a
number of problems. Any *rapprochement* in Sino-Soviet relations would not only lead Japan to lean more on the United
States but also make it imperative for it to rearm. Japan on its
part favours the continuance of the *status quo* in Sino-Soviet
relations, especially the detemined but nonbelligerent competition between the two Communist giants. The likely pattern of
relations between China and the Soviet Union would be one of
"controlled conflict and limited accommodation."[7] The Sino-
Soviet competition for the friendship of Japan would continue.
And as long as it does, Japan need not fear that there would
be any excessive pressure by either Communist power. On the
whole it is likely to keep out of the quarrels between the two
Communist giants. It would continue its policy of trying to
separate economics from politics with an emphasis on participation in China's drive to modernize with a view to increasing

and expanding economic relations. In view of the superior military strength of the Soviet Union and the economic potentialities of Siberia, it would keep the Soviet option open. It would not seek to antagonize the Soviet Union, for it wants to maintain a flexible and independent approach in international affairs and keep up its leverage *vis-a-vis* China.

US and Soviet Perceptions

The attitude of the United States is also of significance for Sino-Japanese relations. The United States, as George F. Kennan has pointed out, has a vital interest in ensuring that the immense industrial potential of the Japanese archipelago does not, through any relationship of dependence or undue influence, become associated with the vast manpower of mainland China or the formidable military potential of the Soviet Union. In the context of the hostility between China and the Soviet Union, it prefers China and Japan to come closer so that it may be able to play off one Communist country against the other to greater purpose and obtain better terms from both. American leaders have repeatedly asserted that closer US-Chinese relations would contribute to stability in the Far East and enable the United States to derive "a genuine strategic benefit." They have also stated that "in some parts of the world we [China and the United States] may have complementary interests."[9] Thus, Cyrus Vance, former US Secretary of State, asserted :

> The United States derives important benefits from its evolving ties with China. Strategically, Sino-American friendship improves our position in the Pacific, reinforces stabilty in potential trouble spots such as Korea, and constitutes an important factor in the global equilibrium.[10]

However, US policy-makers may not favourably view any significant strengthening of the economic relations between China and Japan.

The Soviets believe that the new China-Japan-US trilateral combine is essentially the handiwork of China and United States and that the aim is to marry Japan's technology to China's manpower and resources of raw material so as to contain the increasingly menacing Soviet "threat." They regard the recent normalization of relations between China and the United States and the economic and military refurbishment of Ch'na as constituting attempts to turn China into "an instrument of pressure on the world of socialism."[11] Their response has partly been to warn the Americans that any encouragement of China's military ambitions is incompatible with the consolidation of *detente*. Inwardly, the Japanese may share the American perception of the strategy of building up China as a strategic counterweight to Soviet power. Outwardly, however, they maintain a different stance. Prime Minister Masayoshi Ohira discounted fears that China, Japan, and United States intend to create a kind of tripartite bloc in Northeast Asia. He asserted in February 1980: "Any notion of forming a bloc or an alliance of these three parties would not be well advised or wise."[12] The Soviets, however, would continue to watch the development of Sino-Japanese relations and the Sino-US *rapprochment* with misgivings and suspicion.[13]

Problems and Prospects

The *Korean Peninsula* and Taiwan are two unresolved issues. Both are of vital concern to China and Japan. Japan's substantial economic stake in South Korea would continue to underline its concern for Korean security. A Communist Korea would no doubt pose complex political, economic, and security problems for Japan. The prepetuation of the *status quo*, i.e. the division of Korea, suits Japan very well. However, in the event of hostilities breaking out in the Korean Peninsula, Japan is unlikely to intervene militarily by itself to safeguard its interests or to maintain peace. It is certainly safer and more convenient for it to rely on the United States. It would continue to be an interested, but essentially powerless, bystander. It feels that China, the United States, and the Soviet Union would neutralize one another's moves in the Korean Peninsula.[14]

Moreover, Japan considers the presence of American troops in South Korea essential for stability in the peninsula. The American presence in South Korea would also restrain the North Koreans from attempting any forcible unification of the two Koreas. President Carter's initial policy of withdrawal of troops from South Korea unnerved the Japanese, who feared that it signalled a gradual American disengagement from the region. Carter's subsequent decision to freeze the withdrawal of troops till 1981 and to continue the old policy of strengthening South Korea's capabilities by means of arms aid and loans must have reassured the Japanese to a certain extent. A substantial withdrawal of US troops from South Korea would significantly erode the credibility of the American guarantee to Japan.

China too would not like or welcome any aggravation of the situation in the Korean Peninsula. Nor is it likely to encourage any military adventurism on the part of Kim Il Sung lest it should lead to accelerated rearmament on the part of Japan and even spur Japan on to acquire nuclear weapons. Assuring the Japanese peoples, Premier Hua Guofeng, during his visit to Tokyo in May 1980, asserted: "So long as the South Korean authorities do not launch a war to divert the people's attention, there will be no such thing as a 'southward advance'."[15] Thus, Beijing was impressing the need for restraint on its North Korean ally.

Despite the ingenuous compromise effected in the joint communique of September 1972 over the status of *Taiwan*, it remains a potential cause of conflict. In fact, many members of the Liberal Democratic Party are still strongly persuaded that the independence of Taiwan should be safeguarded. For the time being, China is likely to refrain from resorting to military force to occupy Taiwan for fear of causing serious complications in its relations with Japan and the United States, which together account for over two thirds of Taiwan's total trade. Besides, it needs the co-operation and assistance of Japan, the United States, and the West European nations for both economic and political reasons in its confrontation with the Soviet Union. In December 1979 China and the United States announced the establishment of full diplomatic relations, as also US withdrawal of recognition from Taiwan, abrogation of the associated 1954 Defence Treaty, withdrawal of US troops from Taiwan, but retention of an option to continue to sell offensive weapons to Taipeh. On the contrary, China, as Vice-Chairman Deng Yingchao declared on 11 April 1979, is desirous of settling the matter by peaceful means. She added:

We have repeatedly stated that in settling the question of China's reunification, the status quo on Taiwan and its present system will be respected and that fair and reasonable policies will be adopted so as not to cause any loss to the people on Taiwan, or change their way of life, or affect the economic interests of foreign countries in Taiwan.[16]

Nevertheless, Japanese businessmen realize that China would eventually excercise control over Taiwan. They are, therefore, wary of making new investments in Taiwan. Japan's policy towards Taiwan, as Wolf Mendl points out, would be determined by the importance attached to its stake in Taiwan's economy, by considerations of national security in so far as they affect the sea routes which pass by the island, and by the interplay of domestic politics and national emotions. In any event, it is most likely that Japan would, in the light of its widespred interests, seek to adjust to changes in Taiwan and its status rather than take an active part in determining its future.[17]

The dispute over the *Senkaku Islands* may well prove to be a flash-point between China and Japan. Chinese leaders have discreetly decided to shelve the issue for the time being since they do not wish to place the process of deepening of Sino-Japanese relations in jeopardy.

In spite of cultural affinity with China, geographical proximity, the complementary nature of the economies of the two countries, and widespread popular sentiment, both among the people at large and in influential business and political circles, in favour of improved relations with China an *entente cordiale* between China and Japan does not seem likely. As Professor Scalapino rightly points out, the "respective stages of development, political systems and patterns of foreign affiliation—thus the basic goals and instruments of foreign policy—are not sufficiently compatible. Competition will be as prominent as co-ooeration."[18]

A formal alliance is not likely to yield any advantage that Japan cannot enjoy otherwise. Besides, if Sino-Japanese co-operation should acquire depth, especially in the political and military spheres, it would only accentuate Soviet animosity.

Japan may also become inextricably involved in the Sino-Soviet confrontation with all its implications. It is difficult to see how Japan's security can be safeguarded by an alliance with China. On the contrary, such an alliance would make conflict with the Soviet Union more, rather than less, likely. Thus, while the "tilt" towards China is likely to continue, it might be rendered less sharp if the Soviet Union decides to accommodate Japanese sentiment on the Northern Territories issue.

While a certain degree of economic competition in Southeast Asia cannot be ruled out, it is not likely that China and Japan would invitably become rivals on the international scene, especially in Asia. Given its strong anti-Soviet orientation, its determination to counter the Soviet political and military threat and its need to procure technology and credits from Japan, China cannot easily think of antagonizing Japan. On the other hand, Japan's vulnerability to nuclear attack makes it imperative for Japan to avoid hostile relations with any of the three Great Powers, viz. China, the Soviet Union, and the United States.

Japan's policy towards East Asia in the 1908s would most probably focus on economic interests. It is not likely to develop close or cordial relations with the Soviet Union because of its political distrust of the Soviet Union, its increasing perception of the Soviet threat to its security, and the continuing irritants in the form of the unresolved Northern Territories issue and the pressures over the question of fisheries. It would continue to deepen and broaden its relations, espeically economic ties, with China and base its foreign policy towards the two Communist giants on the US-Japanese security alliance. In fact, the main focus in the coming decade would rest on the level, the financing, and the pace of Sino-Japanese economic relations. Japan is likely to pursue an increasingly autonomous foreign policy without qualitatively weakening its core relationship with the United States. It would seek to maintain a dynamic balance between the two Communist giants. Political and strategic interests—such as the retention of US military presence, the continuance of the US-Japanese alliance, the deepening of of Sino-American *detente*, the ensuring of stability in Northeast Asia, etc.—between China and Japan are likely to be reinforced by economic ties. Nevertheless Japan would keep the

Soviet option open.

The future course of Sino-Japanese relations would depend on the intensity of competition and confrontation between the two Super Powers and the two Communist giants and the nature of, and changes in Sino-Japanese, Sino-US, and US-Japanese relations.

NOTES

1 Xinhua News Agency; 8 July 1974.
2 For a recent commentary see "Socialist-Imperialist Strategy in Asia," *Beijing Review*, 19 January 1979, 14.
3 Stephen FitzGerald, *China and the World* (Canberra, 1978), 81.
4 Ibid., 80.
5 Chae-Jin Lee, *Japan Faces China : Political and Economic Relations in the Postwar Era* (London, 1976), 194.
6 See statement of Japanese Government, 18 June 1974. *Japan Review* (New Delhi), June 1974.
7 Parris H. Chang. "China's Forign Policy Strategy: Washington or Moscow 'Connection ?" *Pacific Community*, April 1976, 422.
8 George F. Kennan, "After the Cold War : American Foreign Policy in the 1970s," *Foreign Affairs*, October 1972.
9 Statement by Zbigniew Brezezinski, Assisstant to US President for National Security Affairs, at a National Town meeting in Washington, D.C., *Span* (New Delhi: International Communication Agency), August 1980, 48.
10 Cyrus Vance, "American Foreign Policy for the Pacific Nations," *International Secvrity*, Winter 1980-81, 6.
11 See *Tass*, 20 October 1978.
12 *Time*, 25 February 1980, 31.
13 See R.K. Jain, *The USSR and Japan, 1945-1980* (New Delhi, 1981), 172.
14 "Defense of Japan," White Paper released by the Japanese Defence Agency on 24 July 1979, as reproduced in *Strategic Digest* (New Delhi), October 1979, 643.
15 Statement at a press conference at the Japan National Press Centre, 29 May 1980. *Beijing Review*, 9 June 1980, 12.
16 Statement by Vice Chairman Deng Yingchao at the Japan National Press Club in Tokyo, 11 April 1979. Ibid., 20 April 1979, 12.
17 Mendl, *Issues in Japan's China Policy* (London, 1978), 110-1.
18 Robert A. Scalapino, "China and the Balance of Power," *Foreign Affairs*, July 1974, 375.

Documents

Documents

1. Zhou Enlai's statement on the San Francisco Peace Treaty, 18 September 1951 (Extract)

1. The separate peace treaty with Japan which was concluded under U.S. Government's coercion and without the participation of the People's Republic of China at the San Francisco Conference is not only not an over-all peace treaty but is in no way a genuine treaty. It is only a treaty for reviving Japanese militarism, a treaty of hostility towards China and the Soviet Union, a menace to Asia and a preparation for a new war of aggression. A few hours after the conclusion of the so-called peace treaty, the U.S. Government concluded a U.S.-Japan Bilateral Security Pact with the Yoshida Government of Japan which aims at clearing the road for the rearmament of Japan and turning it completely into an American military base. This Pact is unmistakable evidence that the U.S. Government is preparing for another war of aggression in Asia and the Far East on an even bigger scale. The Central People's Government of the People's Republic of China considers that the San Francisco Peace Treaty with Japan and the U.S.-Japan Bilateral Security Pact made under U.S. Government's coercion constitute a serious threat to the security of the People's Republic of China and of many other countries of Asia. . . .

2. Zhou Enlai's statement on the US-Japanese "peace treaty," 5 May 1952 (Extracts)

2. This separate peace treaty with Japan which has been manufactured by the U.S. government alone is by no means a treaty to restore sovereignty and independence to Japan or to change her status as an occupied country. On the contrary, it is a treaty for war and enslavement by which Japan is turned completely into a U.S. military base and dependency. . . .

With the coming into effect of this illegal peace treaty, the so-called "U.S.-Japanese Security Pact," and "Administrative Agreement" also came into force on April 28. The "treaty," "pact" and "agreement" are deeds of betrayal of the Japanese nation and are American contraptions for enabling overall military, economic and political domination to be imposed upon Japan. They are the means whereby, under the rule of the U.S. occupationists and their loyal lackeys, the Yoshida government, Japan becomes a U.S. military beachhead in the Far East. . . .

The whole economy of Japan becomes an appendage to the economy of U.S.A. and is compelled to serve this latter's war preparations. . . .

By the operation of these illegal treaties, Japan is dragged by the U.S. into a position of open antagonism to China, the Soviet Union and the other Asian states concerned, thus encompassing the isolation of Japan in Asia. . . .

The Central People's Government of the People's Republic of China considers it necessary to repeat the following statement. We insist that all occupation troops should be withdrawn from Japan; the illegal separate "peace treaty" with Japan which the U.S. has announced as coming into effect can in to way be recognised; we are firmly opposed to the Yoshida-Chiang Kai-shek "peace treaty" which is an open insult and act of hostility to the Chinese people. The announcement and conclusion of these illegal "treaties" demonstrate that the U.S. reactionaries and their lackeys have taken another step in their scheme of creating a new war in the Far East. The Chinese people are deeply convinced that if China, the Soviet Union and all other peace-loving states in Asia as well as their peoples, including the Japanese people, unite closely togther to take the cause of preserving peace into their own hands, the U.S. war schemes in the Far East can undoubtedly be checked and the peace and security of the Far East and the rest of the world safeguarded.

3. Zhou Enlai's conversation with Prof. Ikuo Oyama, Chairman of the Japanese National Peace Committee, 28 September 1953 (Extracts)

We stand for the restoration of normal relations with all countries of the world and in particular, with Japan. If, however, the Japanese Government continues to act as the tool of the United States in aggression against China and other countries in the Far East, continues to pursue a hostile policy towards the People's Republic of China and the Chinese people, and continues to maintain so-called diplomatic relations with the remnant Chiang Kai-shek gang, Japan would day by day become a factor of unrest in the Pacific, thereby creating obstacles to the possibility of her concluding a peace treaty with New China and establishing normal diplomatic relations. . . .

We welcome the Japanese people's delegation coming to visit China; simultaneously, our people are also willing to send delegations to visit Japan. But the American imperialists and the Japanese reactionaries are obstructing the development of friendly relations between the Chinese and Japanese people. The Japanese government which is openly carrying out the US government's "embargo," is trying its best to block the development of trade and cultural exchange between China and Japan. Therefore to surmount this obstruction requires the common efforts of the two peoples.

The trade relations between China and Japan must be built upon the basis of equality and mutual benefit. Some Japanese people hold that "there will be no prospects for Sino-Japanese trade with China's industrialisation." It must be pointed out that this is completely incorrect. For, only by China's industrialisation, will the past imperialism-semi-colony economic relations of so-called "industrialised Japan and raw material China" be completely changed. Only thus can trade relations be established between the two countries on a basis of genuine equality and mutual benefit, and of supplying each other's needs. As China is being industrialised step by step, her production and needs will become more and more expanded and the more she will need to develop international trade relations. Japan is China's close neighbour. Good prospects exist for development of Sino-Japanese trade and economic exchange on the basis of peaceful co-existence. . . .

In order to defend peace and security of the Pacific, it is necessary to prevent the danger of new wars being increased by reason of Japan's transformation into a US military base and remilitarisation.

We consider that an independent, democratic, peaceful and free Japan should have her own defence power. Yet, it is very unfortunate that Japan is now occupied by US military forces dominated by the US and is proceeding with rearmament and reviving Japan's militarism in compliance with the aims of the US aggressors. This threatens the peace and security of the Pacific and requires our careful attention. . . .

The Chinese people clearly understand the agony of the Japanese people under the occupation of foreign forces, and this agony is unprecedented in Japan's history. The Chinese people hope that the Japanese can achieve a new life and independence for their country and that China and Japan can really achieve coexistence and co-prosperity on the basis of living in peace with each other.

4. *People's Daily* commentary on the signing of US-Japan "Mutual Defence Assistance Agreement," 13 March 1954 (Extracts)

The signing in Tokyo on March 8th between the US and the reactionary Yoshida government of the "US-Japan Mutual Defence Assistance Agreement" and related agreements—a new yoke imposed on the Japanese people by the American imperialists—is obviously directed at stepping up the rearming of Japan and making use of Japan as a tool for US aggression against Far Eastern and other Asian countries. It is another step in the enslavement of the Japanese people by US and Japanese reactionaries. It will not only bring disastrous consequences to the Japanese people but will once again place the Far East and the rest of Asia under the menace of Japanese militarism. It, therefore, meets with the firm opposition of the Japanese people and the people of all other Asian countries as well as peaceloving people throughout the world.

The rearming of the Japan and the use of Japanese people as cannon fodder is only part of the US policy of aggression. . . .

To carry out the US-enforced policy of rearmament, the Yoshida government has not only signed this calamitous "Mutual Defence Assistance Agreement" but has also prepared a "national defence forces organisation bill" and a "national defence board organisation bill" in a coordinated effort to revive Japanese militarism. . . .

With the cessation of hostilities in Korea, tension in Asia has been somewhat relaxed. The increased US efforts to rearm Japan are obviously designed to maintain and create a tense situation in Asia in order to menace the peace and security of all countries in the area. . . .

5. Joint Declaration of the Governments of China and the Soviet Union, 12 October 1954

As provided for in the Potsdam Declaration, after the conclusion of the Second World War, Japan should have received complete national independence, established its own democratic institutions, and developed its own independent and peaceful economy and national culture.

However, the United States of America, as the chief occupying power in Japan which had been charged with the main responsibility for implementing the Potsdam decisions crudely violated these decisions, trampled on the interests of the Japanese people and imposed upon Japan the San Francisco "peace treaty" and other agreements which run counter to the above-mentioned agreement between the Major Powers.

Nine years after the end of the war, Japan has still not received independence and remains in the position of a semi-colonial country. Its territory is covered with numerous American military bases, which have been set up for purposes having nothing in common with the task of maintaining peace and securing the peaceful and independent development of Japan. The industry and finances of Japan are made dependent on American war contracts, Japan suffers restrictions in its foreign trade. All this has ruinous effects on its economy, and particularly on the peaceful branches of its industry.

All this cannot but injure the national self-respect of the Japanese people, create an atmosphere of uncertainty among the Japanese, and fetter the varied abilities of the Japanese people.

The present situation of Japan has evoked a legitimate apprehension among the peoples of countries in Asia and the Far East that Japan may be used to carry out schemes of aggression which run counter both to the interests of the Japanese people and to the task of maintaining peace in the Far East.

The peoples of the People's Republic of China and the Soviet Union express their deep sympathy for Japan and the

Japanese people who have been placed in a difficult position as a result of the conclusion of the above-mentioned "treaty" and agreements which are dictated by foreign interests. They believe that the Japanese people will find adequate strength in themselves to take the course of freeing themselves from dependence on foreign power, the course of achieving the rebirth of their motherland and establishing normal relations and economic cooperation and cultural ties on a broad scale with other countries, first and foremost with their neighbours.

The policy of the Government of the People's Republic of China and the Government of the Soviet Union in their relations with Japan is based on the principle of the peaceful coexistence of states with different social systems and on the conviction that this conforms with the vital interests of all peoples. They stand for the development on mutually beneficial terms, of broad trade relations and the establishment of close cultural ties with Japan.

They also express their readiness to take steps to normalise their relations with Japan and declare that Japan will meet with the full support of the People's Republic of China and the Soviet Union in its efforts to establish political and economic relations with the People's Republic of China and the USSR as well as in all measures Japan undertakes to secure the conditions for its peaceful and independent development.

6. Xinhua report on Sino-Japanese Non-Official Agreement on Fishery in the Yellow Sea and the East China Sea, 15 April 1955 (Extracts)

Working on the principle of equality and mutual benefit and the reasonable use of the fishing grounds, with avoidance of fishing disputes, the people's delegations divided the fishing grounds in the Yellow Sea and East China Sea into six fishing areas and agreed on the number of fishing boats of both sides according to the fishing seasons. Understanding had been reached through memoranda exchanged by the delegations concerning those fishing grounds in which competitions may occur. The agreement also stipulates regulations that both sides should observe during fishing. . . .

The area covered by the agreement does not include the

patrolled areas near the Pohai Bay, the military areas under the Chousan Islands in which navigation is forbidden and the military operation areas south of 29 degrees North Latitude which are concerned with the liberation of Taiwan. Nor does the agreement include the "area forbidden to motor trawler fishing" established by the Chinese Government for the protection of fishery resources. The establishment of the "area forbidden to motor trawler fishing" is in the interest of the fishing population not only of China but also of Japan. The two sides have achieved understanding through exchange of letters that Japanese fishing motor boats will not fish in this area.

The agreement provides for fishing vessels of both sides to anchor in each other's harbours in case of emergency and for the rescue of fishing vessels of either side in distress and also for the exchange of data obtained through investigation and research into fishing resources and the exchange of technique. These provisions express the spirit of friendly co-operation and mutual assistance between the fishing circles of China and Japan. They create conditions favourable to growth of fishing in China and Japan.

This agreement between the people's fishery organisations of the two countries being provisional in character and limited, the China Fishery Association and the Japan-China Fishery Association of Japan have indicated their willingness in the agreement to try and urge their respective governments to enter into fishery negotiations promptly at a governmental level.

7. Zhou Enlai's speech at the Second Session of the First National People's Congress, 30 July 1955 (Extract)

Ten years have passed since the conclusion of the World War II, and yet even now the state of war between China and Japan has not ended. A joint declaration was made by China and the Soviet Union in October 1954 concerning their relations with Japan and since then, many further steps have been taken by the Chinese Government to promote the normalization of Sino-Japanese relations. But response from the Japanese Government is not entirely in the same direction. With the support and assistance of the Chinese Government, the Red

Cross Society of China, together with the Red Cross Society of Japan, the Japan-China Friendship Association and Japan Peace Liaison Council, has already settled satisfactorily the question of the return to their own country of Japanese nationals in China. But the whereabouts of the large number of Chinese who were taken to Japan by force during the war still remains unknown, and the Chinese nationals in Japan are prevented from having intercourse and contacts with their motherland. The Chinese Government holds that artificial barriers should be removed so as to increase trade between China and Japan. But up to now, trade between the two countries is still subjected to unwarranted restrictions. The Chinese Government hopes that this abnormal state of affairs will be remedied. It should be pointed out that in the past year, intercourse between the Chinese and the Japanese people has become more frequent, and, through friendly negotiations between the people's organizations of the two countries, positive results have also been achieved in regard to fishery and trade. This is a cause for gratification.

8. Zhou Enlai's interview with a Japanese press delegation, 17 August 1955 (Extracts)

The Chinese people's attitude towards the San Francisco treaty does not hinder the promotion of normal relations between China and Japan up to the conclusion of a peace treaty between the People's Republic of China and Japan.

3. *Question*: Is the "Japan-China peace treaty" between Japan and Chiang Kai-shek the basic obstacle to the normalization of Sino-Japanese relations?

Answer: The Japanese Government did not sign a peace treaty with the Government of the People's Republic of China which the Chinese people have chosen for themselves, but signed a so-called peace treaty with the Chiang Kai-shek clique which the Chinese people repudiated. The Chinese people cannot but feel indignant over this. Now, there are still some people who do not want a real change of this situation, but attempt to follow the plotting for the so-called "two Chinas." This is also what the Chinese people firmly oppose. Therefore, all sincere efforts towards the the normalization of Sino-Japanese relations should lead to the abolition of the Japan-Chiang peace treaty.

Even though there exists the Japan-Chiang peace treaty, the Chinese Government has still taken a series of steps to promote the normalization of Sino-Japanese relationships. It is regrettable that the Japanese Government has so far not made corresponding efforts. If the Japanese Government has similar sincerity, it is possible to find the road to normalize Sino-Japanese relations. . . .

Direct contacts between the government leaders of various countries are helpful to the furtherance of mutual understanding. But, in view of the present Sino-Japanese relations the time is perhaps not yet ripe for the leading members of the governments of China and Japan to exchange visits.

9. **Joint communique by Peng Zhen, Secretary-General of the Standing Committee of the Chinese National People's Congress, and Eikichi Kanbayashiyama, Leader of the Japanese Diet Mission to China, 17 October 1955 (Extract)**

As a result of the exchange of views, the two sides agreed on the following questions :

"One. China and Japan should make positive efforts for the achievement of normalization of diplomatic relations between the two countries.

"Two. In respect of trade relations, more and more goods and material from Japan for China have been under embargo owing to stipulations of the COCOM in Paris. This situation must be changed and efforts must be made to have them swiftly abolished.

"Three. Convert the commodity exhibitions in the capitals of China and Japan into permanent organizations to handle liaison affairs relating to trade between the two sides. The two countries should mutually accord due protection to the personnel sent by the other side.

"Four. The cultural exchange between the two countries is helpful to the promotion of peace and friendship between China and Japan. Hereafter the two countries should strive for its further promotion.

"Five. Both China and Japan should actively look after their nationals residing in each other's country enabling them to travel freely to and from their home country.

"Six. China and Japan have in the past sent back to each other the remains of the dead. Hereafter the two sides should continue to send back the remains of the dead to their home country as speedily as possible.

"Seven. The Chinese side declares that the disposition of war criminals is a matter of China's sovereign rights and that she will publicly announce the final disposition of the war criminals in the near future.

The Chinese and Japanese sides affirm the above-mentioned views, with which they are in agreement, and agree to issue a communique expressing willingness to do their utmost for their realization.

10. **Zhou Enlai's Political Report to the Second Session of the Second National Committee of the Chinese People's Political Consultative Conference, 30 January 1956 (Extract)**

Ten years have elapsed since the end of the war. But Japan still remains under US occupation, manacled by various enslaving unequal treaties and agreements. US military bases and installations are all over Japan. The US embargo policy is hampering Japan's normal trade with other countries, making its economic plight even more difficult. The Japanese nation, always independent in the past, is now being interfered with and controlled by the United States in all respects. This situation is becoming more and more intolerable to the Japanese people. Recently in Japan there has been a tremendous growth in the movement to throw off foreign control. The people and far-sighted statesmen of Japan have come out more and more for an independent policy and against going along with and being subservient to the US aggressive circles. They oppose foreign military bases and demand a ban on atomic and hydrogen weapons. They stand for the extension of ties with other countries of the world, first of all the normalization of Sino-Japanese and Soviet-Japanese relations. The Chinese people deeply sympathize with the Japanese people in their difficult situation, and fully support their desire for independence. We have developed political, economic and cultural ties with the Japanese people. We have consistently made efforts to facilitate the normalization of Sino-Japanese relations in accordance with the principle of peaceful co-existence. On August 17 and November 4, 1955, the Chinese Government twice proposed to the Japanese Government that consultations be conducted between the two Governments on promoting the normalization of Sino-Japanese relations. We regret that no reply has yet been forthcoming from the Japanese Government. The promotion of the normalization of Sino-Japanese relations is an urgent demand of both peoples, and the Chinese Government proposes once again that consultations be held between the two Governments on this question. We hope that Japan will be able to pursue an independent foreign policy, and would welcome Japan back to the big family of Asian countries, living in peace and friendly co-operation with the countries of Asia and the world.

11. Zhou Enlai's address to the Third Session of the First National People's Congress, 28 June 1956 (Extract)

The Chinese Government has more than once proposed to the Japanese Government that talks be conducted by the two governments on the question of promoting the normalization of Sino-Japanese relations. Recently, the Japanese Government has adopted a comparatively more positive attitude in promoting Sino-Japanese trade but, as a whole, it has not yet responded to China's initiative with concrete action. Although the state of war between China and Japan has not yet been terminated, yet, taking into consideration the growth of friendly relations between the Chinese and Japanese peoples and Japan's present position, the Chinese Government has now taken the initiative to deal—in accordance with the policy of leniency and treating each according to its merits—with the cases of the Japanese who committed crimes during the war and had long been held in custody for their cases to be examined. Prosecution of the great majority of them has been waived and they are being repatriated in groups. A few Japanese guilty of serious crimes were given lenient sentences and it was decided that if they showed good conduct while serving their sentences, they could be released before the completion of their terms. The way the Chinese Government dealt with these Japanese who committed crimes during the war is fully in line with what we had indicated to our Japanese friends who came to visit China. The Chinese Government is making these unremitting efforts because we have correctly assessed the strong desire of the Chinese and Japanese peoples for peaceful co-existence and friendly contact with each other and for early restoration of normal relations between the two countries.

In the past several years, the number of Chinese and Japanese peoples making visits to each other's country has grown steadily and the scope of contacts has widened. In 1955, the number of Japanese friends who visited China amounted to more than 800, the greatest number from any country. In spite of various difficulties, the number of Chinese representing different popular organizations who visited Japan by invitation has also increased, amounting in 1955 alone to about 100. What is particularly worth noting is that Chinese and Japanese peoples' organizations have settled certain matters of common interest through direct contact and negotiation. Since 1952, a total of 15 agreements and joint communiques have been signed by people's organizations of China and Japan. These concern trade, fisheries, residents in each other's country and the question of friendly co-operation in many fields; and the implementation of these documents has been encouraging. These frequent and fruitful contacts between the peoples of China and Japan are warmly welcomed and supported by the Chinese Government; and they cannot but have an increasingly marked influence on the Japanese Government.

12. Joint statement by Chang Hsi-jo, President of the Chinese People's Institute of Foreign Affairs, and Inejiro Asanuma, Head of the Goodwill Mission of the Japanese Socialist Party, 22 April 1957 (Extract)

During the meeting views were exchanged frankly on the following questions:

1—Basic principles concerning the restoration of diplomatic relations between China and Japan; 2—Questions concerning Asia and international questions which are of common interests; 3—Economic cooperation between Japan and China; 4—Further promotion of trade; 5—Cooperation in fisheries;

6—Technical exchange; 7—Cultural exchange; 8—Cooperation in meteorological and postal services; 9—Mutual visits of nationals of the two countries and the return of the remains of deceased to their respective countries.

The meetings were conducted throughout in a friendly and sincere atmosphere. The meeting achieved many concrete results and played a very important part in enhancing goodwill and friendship between the two countries. On both sides it was completely agreed to state the following points:

A. On the Restoration of Diplomatic Relations between China and Japan:

1. In view of the geographical and historical relations between the two countries and the present situation, the two sides fully agree that the time has come for the Governments of Japan and the People's Republic of China to restore diplmatic relations as soon as possible, formally and completely; that the establishment of long-term and positive cooperation between China and Japan is the basis of the friendly settlement of various outstanding issues.

The goodwill mission of the Japanese Scialist Party explained the basic policy of the Japanese Socialist Party to be nonrecognition of the existence of two Chinas. Taiwan is China's internal question. It is hoped that the tense international situation around Taiwan can be settled peacefully and the right of representation of the U.N. Organization should belong to the People's Republic of China. The Chinese Government welcomed these viewpoints.

2. It is necessary to overcome various difficulties and obstacles so as to increase mutual visits of nationals between the two countries and also economic, technical, and cultural exchange. Certain existing agreements between the people's organizations of the two countries, together with matters on which agreement might be reached, should be developed into agreement between the two governments at the earliest possible date.

13. Zhou Enlai's interview with Japanese correspondents, 25 July 1957 (Extracts)

The fact that normal relations have not yet been restored

between China and Japan, and, what is more, in international law a state of war still exists between the two countries, has not hampered friendly intercourse and the signing of non-official agreements between the peoples of the two countries. In this way starting from the frequent non-official visits and agreements, relations can be advanced considerably between the two countries, finally leaving only the questions of the diplomatic announcement of the ending of the state of war and the resumption of normal relations. . . .

It may be said that this approach of ours sets a new example in the annals of international relations. It is with such a feeling of pleasure and hope that we are carrying on our people's diplomacy. We regard this people's diplomacy as an important integral part of our diplomacy as a whole. He hoped our Japanese friends will take the same view.

Premier Chou En-lai said that this view of his has evoked a favourable response among many Japanese friends. As to the Japanese Government, some concrete analysis is necessary. Ex-Premier Yoshida was hostile to China. So a desire for friendship on his part was out of the question. But his successors Hatoyama and Ishibashi had the desire. As to Premier Nobusuke Kishi, though he should have gone further in manifesting this desire, in fact he has fallen back from the stand taken by his predecessors, Hatoyama and Ishibashi. . . .

There are many facts proving that we are willing to co-exist peacefully with all other Asian nations. Time and again we have said that after normal relations have been restored between them, China and Japan can sign a treaty of friendship and non-aggression. In talks with the delegation of the Japanese Socialist Party, both Chairman Mao Tse-tung and Premier Chou pointed out that as soon as Japan abrogates the Japan-U.S. Security Treaty and the United States removes its military bases from Japan and withdraws its armed forces to enable Japan to gain full independence, the provisions of the Sino-Soviet Treaty of Friendship, Mutual Assistance and Alliance aimed at guarding against the revival of Japanese militarism and its being used by others may be revised.

We have said all this before, but the Japanese Government has failed to act on the basis of these facts. On the contrary in disregard of the facts, Kishi made slanderous statements

about China while he was in the United States. We consider
this highly regrettable.

We cannot but wonder whether Premier Nobusuke Kishi has
not set out deliberately to seek trouble with China, to alienate
other Asian countries from China, and to curry favour with
the United States by vilifying China so as to procure U.S.
aid for rearming Japan and reviving militarism. We hope that
Japan will be able to free itself from the control of the United
States and soon restore normal relations with China. Premier
Kishi's way of doing things is contrary to our hopes. Nevertheless, we are always confident that the Japanese people desire
friendly relations with China.

14. Zhou Enlai's report to the Fifth Session of the First National People's Congress, 7 February 1958 (Extracts)

During the past half year, the present Japanese Government
adopted an unfriendly attitude towards New China in many
ways and a fourth non-official Sino-Japanese trade agreement
failed to be signed owing to the unreasonable restrictions and
insulting regulations which the Japanese Government tried to
impose on the Chinese side. Nevertheless, contacts and trade
relations between the Chinese and Japanese peoples still developed to a great extent, showing the common desire of our two
peoples for peace and friendship. During this period, the number of Japanese friends visiting China was again greater than
that from any other Asian or African country, and China also
sent many important delegations to visit Japan. The Chinese people are thankful to the Japanese people and organizations who
received and helped the various Chinese delegations so well. The
Chinese people are glad to see the opening in Canton of the
Exhibition of Japanese Commodities and wish it success. . . .

The movement of the Japanese people for the restoration
of Japan-China diplomatic relations has become an increasingly
powerful force that is not to be ignored in Japanese political
life. However, Japanese Prime Minister Nobusuke Kishi attempted to make use of this for ulterior purposes. On November
12, 1957 he stated before the Foreign Affairs Committee
of the Japanese House of Councillors that the tension in the
Taiwan Straits "is the result of the Nationalist and Commu-

nists claiming sovereignty over mainland China, and until their contentions are adjusted, there can be no allaying of tension." This is not only an attempt to shield the United States in occupying Taiwan, but also to justify the United States plot of creating "two Chinas." This attempt has long been seen through by the Japanese people. For example, the Goodwill Delegation of the Japanese Social-Democratic Party, the Delegation of the Japanese National Council for the Restoration of Japan-China Diplomatic Relations and the Delegation of the Japan-China Friendship Association, which visited China in succession during 1957, all expressed a warm desire to promote normalization of relations between China and Japan, were of the opinion that the liberation of Taiwan is China's domestic affair and opposed the creation of "two Chinas." This shows that it is impossible to hoodwink the Japanese people by confusing right with wrong through false arguments about "two Chinas," nor is it possible to make the Japanese people's widespread movement for the restoration of Japan-China diplomatic relations serve the plot of creating "two Chinas."

15. Statement by Chinese Foreign Minister Chen Yi on Sino-Japanese relations, 9 May 1958 (Extract)

The Chinese people. . . are willing to live with the Japanese people on a friendly basis and have always worked for the promotion of Sino-Japanese friendship. As a result, the economic and cultural ties and friendly contacts between the two countries have developed greatly within the past few years thanks to the continuous efforts made by the people of both countries, despite the fact that the Japanese Government was subservient to the will of the United States and that the state of war between China and Japan has not been terminated. More than forty agreements concluded between people's organizations and semi-official bodies of the two countries played a notable part in promoting friendly relations between the two peoples. The Chinese Government has consistently given active support to friendly contacts between the Chinese and Japanese peoples and these agreements. Our attitude was welcomed by the Japanese people. But the Kishi government, in contrast, has always adopted a hostile and ill-intentioned attitude towards our country, and has mistaken China's goodwill as a sign of weakness. Kishi, on the one hand, has expressed the intention of expanding Sino-Japanese trade in order to derive economic gains from China; but on the other hand, he crudely sabotaged the Sino-Japanese trade agreement, allowed thugs to insult the Chinese national flag in Nagasaki, and personally took the lead in repeatedly making slanderous statements against China. This outrageous attitude of Kishi's thoroughly exposes his true imperialist colours. . . .

16. Chen Yi's statement on the revision of the US-Japanese Security Treaty, 19 November 1958 (Extracts)

The Kishi Government of Japan is now negotiating with the United States Government for the revision of the Japanese-US "Security Treaty". Surely with no good intentions, the United States is anxious to get Japan involved and turn it into a tool for US aggression in Asia. The Kishi government of Japan on its part, is willing to enter into the service of the United States and tie Japan more tightly to the American war chariot so as to pursue its policy of continued hostility to China and of expansion in the direction of Southeast Asia. . .

The revisions which the United States and Kishi are planning to make in the Japanese-US "Security Treaty,". . . are diametrically opposed to the aspirations of the Japanese people. Taking advantage of the Japanese people's desire for independence and sovereignty, the US is trying in a fraudulent way to modify this treaty into one which is even more unequal for Japan. According to information already disclosed, this time the United States may make certain nominal concessions in exchange for even greater Japanese sacrifices in the US interest. The plan of the United States is obvious. The first step is to make Japan assume the obligation of defending US military bases under the name of mutual defence. The second step is to extend the mutual defence area to the West Pacific. The third step is to involve Japan in a nuclear war when the occasion arises, and make it pull the chestnuts out of the fire for the United States. In this way, the Americans can turn Japan into their permanent military base; they can stay on in Japan and lord it over the Japanese, ordering them to do this and that and depriving Japan of its independent position for ever. . . .

17. Paper by Yi Li-yu, Member of Editorial Board, *World Culture* (*Shihtze Chishih*) **at a joint conference of the Editorial Boards of** *International Affairs* **(Moscow, and** *World Culture*, **January 1959 (Extract)**

Japan fell under U.S. occupation following the Second World War. Her people demand independence, peace and neutrality, a demand which the country's ruling classes to a certain extent must reckon with. Japan, however, is a highly developed capitalist country, and her monopolies have their own ambitious imperialist aims. With U.S. assistance, they are gathering their forces again to attempt to secure a dominant position in Asia. As a result, a bitter struggle between two opposing tendencies has been raging in post-war Japan, the outcome of which will determine Japan's future development.

Because of their concern for peace and their desire to promote friendly relations between China and Japan, the Chinese people hope that Japan, having learnt the lesson of her defeat in the Second World War, will jettison U.S. control and pursue an independent policy. This would provide propitious conditions for peace. The Chinese people have repeatedly demonstrated their solidarity with the Japanese people, and actively supported their struggle for peace and independence, for friendship and the establishment of diplomatic relations with People's China. Guided by this policy, China has indicated her readiness to restore normal relations with Japan on the basis of peaceful co-existence.

Despite the fact that the state of war between China and Japan has still not been legally terminated, China's attitude is to let bygones be bygones, and she has taken a series of measures to develop friendly relations between the peoples of the two countries. Thus, China, for example, has repatriated about 30,000 Japanese, emigrants who desired to return to their homeland, magnanimously settled the cases of more than 1,000 Japanese war criminals, and has warmly received large numbers of visiting public figures who represent different strata of Japanese society. Moreover, as a result of understandings reached between Chinese and Japanese organizations, questions of trade, fishing and cultural exchange and other matters of mutual interest to the two countries have been settled to mutual satisfaction.

China's generosity and fair-mindedness was greeted with warm approval by wide sections of the Japanese public, including certain members of the ruling circles. But the Japanese monopolists mistook the goodwill of the Chinese people for a sign of weakness, and her desire to trade with Japan on the basis of equality and friendship as an indication of her inability to build socialism without Japan.

With the accession to power of the Kishi Government, it became particularly clear that Japanese monopolists were willingly trailing behind the United States. They began to revive Japanese militarism, reaching out for the Chinese territory of Taiwan. and nourishing expansionist aspirations in South-East Asia. The Kishi Government openly committed a whole series of acts hostile to China. During the past year, the Japanese Prime Minister has repeatedly come out against China and declared his support for the U.S. position regarding "two Chinas." Kishi has tried to bring about the rupture of trade between Japan and China and incited hooligans to commit outrages against the flag of People's China. By plotting provocations against People's China and other countries of the Far East, he has attempted to tie Japan more closely to the U.S. war chariot under the pretext of revising the Mutual Security Pact between Japan and the United States.

The Kishi Government's hostile policy towards People's China has already led to a deterioration in the relations between the two countries.

18. **Joint statement by Chang Hsi-jo, President of the Chinese People's Institute of Foreign Affairs, and Inejiro Asanuma, General Secretary of the Japanese Socialist Party containing three political principles, 17 March 1959 (Extracts)**

Owing to the Kishi government's policy of hostility towards China, relations between the two countries have greatly worsened, to the point of deadlock. This is entirely against the will of the peoples of the two countries.

The Chinese side holds that to break this deadlock the

following three principles must be put into effect and appropriate steps taken by the Kishi government: firstly, it must cease carrying out a hostile policy towards China; secondly, it must not take part in the "two Chinas" scheme; and thirdly, it must not obstruct the restoration of normal relations between China and Japan. If this is not done, it will also be impossible to resume Sino-Japanese trade.

The Japanese Socialist Party . . . not only fully agree with the above three principles put forward by the Chinese side, but unequivocally advocates non-recognition of "two Chinas"; holds that the liberation of Taiwan is China's internal affair; advocates recognition of the representation of the People's Republic of China in the United Nations Organization; and maintains that, to bring about the formal restoration of diplomatic relations between China and Japan, the "Japan-Chiang Kai-shek peace treaty" must first of all be abolished and a peace treaty signed with the People's Republic of China. The Chinese side welcomes these views of the Japanese Socialist Party.

The Chinese side further points out that the political and economic questions between the two countries cannot be separated. These questions of economics and politics must be negotiated and settled simultaneously. At the present moment, the political question must be given priority. The Japanese Socialist Party Delegation agrees with this. . .

After Japan puts an end to the Japan-U.S. "security" system, achieves complete independence and concludes mutual non-aggression agreements with China and the Soviet Union, then, it can be expected that the military clauses concerning Japan in the Sino-Soviet Treaty of Friendship, Alliance and Mutual Assistance directed against Japanese militarism will naturally become null and void. Following the conclusion of a collective security treaty between the Asian and Pacific countries, first of all between China, Japan, the Soviet Union and the United States, the neutrality of Japan will be further guaranteed. Both sides have reached a unanimity of views in these matters.

The Japanese Socialist Party Delegation stresses that although diplomatic relations between Japan and China have not yet been resumed and contacts between the two countries have been almost completely disrupted since spring last year, nevertheless to foster the friendship between the peoples of the two countries and people's diplomacy, friendly contacts and cultural interchanges should be promoted as practical circumstances permit. The Chinese side has concurred in this and agreed to invite friendly Japanese cultural, art, academic, technological, peasants' and workers' delegations to visit China.

19. Zhou Enlai's Report on the Work of the Government to the First Session of the Second National People's Congress, 18 April 1959 (Extract)

In the East, the US imperialists have persisted in reviving Japanese militarism. The Japanese monopoly capitalist group on its part is counting on the support of the United States to realise its lurking imperialist ambitions. Recently, the Kishi Government has again stepped up preparations for revising the the Japan-US "Security Treaty," entered into new military plots with the United States, and attempted to equip the Japanese armed forces with atomic weapons. The poses a serious threat to the security of the Asian countries, and that of our country in particular. The Chinese people have always supported the Japanese people's just demand to shake off US control, follow a policy of peace and neutrality, and turn Japan into an independent, peace-loving and democratic country. To promote normalisation of Sino-Japanese relations, the Chinese Government, forgiving past misdeeds has treated with leniency the overwhelming majority of the Japanese war criminals in the Japanese war of aggression against China and given active assistance in the repatriation of Japanese nationals from China and the development of trade and friendly contacts between the the two peoples. It was with such support of our Government that the fourth non-official Sino-Japanese Trade Agreement was signed on March 5, 1958 after clearing away many obstacles. The Kishi Government, however, refused to grant the proper assurances, thus making it impossible to implement the agreement. In May 1958, there occurred in Nagasaki the incident in which the Chinese national flag was insulted with the connivance of the Kishi Government. In October 1958, after our People's Liberation Army started shelling Quemoy, Kishi himself openly slandered our country as an "aggressor" and clamoured that the Chinese people should not be allowed to liberate Taiwan. In this way, Sino-Japanese relations have been almost completely broken off. This reactionary policy of the Kishi Government aroused great indignation among the Japanese people. Although the Kishi Government cannot but profess willingness to resume Sino-Japanese trade in the face of the pressure of the Japanese people, in actual fact it has continued to follow the United States in its hostility to China and plotting to create "two Chinas," and has continued to obstruct normalisation of Sino-Japanese relations, thus preventing upto now the realisation of the Chinese and Japanese peoples' desire to improve relations and resume trade between the two countries. The Chinese people's interests accord with those of the Japanese people. The Chinese people cannot sit idly by while Japanese militarism is being revived, nor can they tolerate the continued hostile policy of the Kishi Government towards China. The Chinese people welcome the great efforts made by the Japanese people to advance friendly relations between the two peoples. We regard as being entirely correct the series of proposals for improving Sino-Japanese relations and resuming diplomatic relations between China and Japan which were put forward recently by the delegation of the Japanese Communist Party and that of the Japanese Socialist Party during their successive visits to China. We are confident that the Japanese people will ultimately break down all obstacles and develop peaceful and friendly relations with the Chinese people.

20. Communique on talks between Zhou Enlai and Tanzan Ishibashi, former Japanese Prime Minister and a Leading Member of the ruling Liberal Democratic Party, 20 September 1959 (Summary)

The two parties held that the Chinese and Japanese peoples should work together to make their contributions to Far Eastern and world peace. To this end, the two peoples should make efforts to promote mutual friendship, strengthen mutual trust, improve the existing relations between China and Japan and work together for an early restoration of normal relations between the two countries on the basis of the five principles of mutual respect for sovereignty and territorial integrity, mutual non-aggression, non-interference in each other's internal affairs, equality and mutual benefit and peaceful coexistence, and the ten principles of the Bandung Conference.

Premier Chou En-lai pointed out that for this purpose Japan must free itself from foreign intervention, do away with its hostile policy towards China and not take part in the plot of creating "two Chinas." Mr Ishibashi indicated that far-sighted Japanese had not tolerated in the past and would not in the furture tolerate such ideas and actions.

Mr. Ishibashi held that China and Japan should work for exchanges and development in the political, economic and cultural spheres in accordance with actual conditions. Premier Chou En-lai agreed to this and pointed out that the growth of political and economic relations between China and Japan were necessarily linked together and could not be separated. Mr. Ishibashi expressed agreement to this.

Mr. Ishibashi indicated that in connection with the above-stated circumstances, there were things in Japan's present situation and international relations which gave rise to dissatis-faction and the maximum effort should be made to bring about an early change and, step by step, expedite its realization. Premier Chou En-lai welcomed this view. He pointed out that China would like to see the Japanese people fulfil the above-mentioned aspirations at an early date that the Chinese people would give energetic support to efforts by the Japanese people to attain this goal and that they sincerely sympathized with the desire of the Japanese people for independence, freedom, democracy, peace and neutrality.

21. Zhou Enlai's speech at the farewell banquet given in honour of Kenzo Matsumura, Adviser to the ruling Japanese Liberal Democratic Party, 11 November 1959 (Extracts)

We both believe that the Chinese and Japanese peoples should work together for mutual peace and friendship on the basis of the five principles of peaceful co-existence and the ten principles of the Bandung Conference. On this basis, the two countries which have different social systems, should be able to respect each other and establish good-neighbour rela-tions. I think this represents not only the essence of our talks but also the common aspirations of the Chinese and Japanese peoples. . . .

Mutual exchanges between the two peoples, especially of responsible and influential persons, can promote mutual understanding. In the course of the growth of friendly relations between the peoples of the two countries and following the improvement of relations between the two countries, it will be possible to restore interrupted Sino-Japanese trade relations. This will also lead to a further development of cultural exchanges between the two countries. We should promote the development of such relations. This is a political matter. Some people want to separate politics from economics. This is ridiculous. Our reception of Mr. Matsumura on his visit to China is itself a poiltical event, because basically human relations are always political. We are doing this with the aim of improving relations between China and Japan. I am convinced this expresses the desire of peoples of the two countries and this desire to improve relations between the two countries can be gradually realized.

22. Chinese Foreign Ministry's statement on the conclusion of the US-Japan military alliance, 15 January 1960 (Extracts)

In disregard of the firm opposition of the Japanese people and the repeated warnings of the Chinese people and the other peace-loving peoples of the world, Japanese Prime Minister Nobusuke Kishi has decided to go to the United States on January 16 for concluding with the U.S. Government at Washington on the 19th a Japan-U.S. treaty of military alliance under the pretext of revising the Japan-U.S. Security Treaty. This is an extremely serious step taken by the Japanese reactionaries and the US imperialists in collusion for the preparation of new aggression and war and menacing Asian and world peace.

The Chinese people have always been concerned about the Japanese people's struggle for independence, democracy, peace and neutrality and against the revival of Japanese militarism. Since Nobusuke Kishi came to power, the Chinese Government has moreover continually pointed out the danger couched in the active revival of Japanese militarism and outward expansion by the Japanese reactionaries with the support of the US imperialists. Now, the Chinese Government cannot but point out solemnly that this danger has become a real one and that the conclusion of the Japan-US treaty of military alliance signifies the revival of Japanese militarism and Japan's openly joining the US aggressive military bloc. This cannot but rouse the serious vigilance of the peoples of Asian countries.

Thanks to the joint efforts of the socialist camp headed by the Soviet Union and other peace-loving countries and people, there is a certain relaxation in the present international situation. The US ruling group has also professed peace and repeatedly made gestures as if willing to ease the international tension. However, at this very juncture, the United States is going to conclude a treaty of military alliance with Japan. This proves once again that the aims of the United States are aggression and war, while its pronouncements for relaxation and peace are but a camouflage for its war preparations.

23. Zhou Enlai's speech at the Second Session of the Second National People's Congress, 10 April 1960 (Extract)

The Chinese people have always been friendly towards the Japanese people. We offer our profound sympathy and support to the Japanese people in their heroic struggle for an independent, democratic, peaceful and neutral Japan. The Chinese Government and people resolutely oppose the Kishi Government's policy of hostility to China and of reviving Japanese militarism. The treaty of military alliance the Kishi Government signed with the United States runs counter to the interest of the peoples of Japan and United States. In the long run, this is a treaty of disaster for the Japanese people. This treaty not only treatens the security of China and the Soviet Union, but, first of all, poses a direct threat to the security of the peoples of the Southeast Asian countries. So long as the Kishi Government does not abandon its policy of hostility to China, there can be no possibility of improving Sino-Japanese relations. The responsibility for the the present abnormal situation in Sino-Japanese relations rests entirely with the Kishi Government.

24. Statement of Zhou Enlai made to Kazuo Suzuki, Managing Director of the Japan-China Trade Promotion Association enunciating three trade principles, 27 August 1960 (Extracts)

In the past, China and Japan made mutual agreements between private organisations, thinking that such agreements would serve to develop Sino-Japanese trade. During the period of the Nobusuke Kishi government, this method proved unworkable. Nobusuke Kishi would not recognise, would not guarantee the implementation of private agreements and furthermore, torpedoed it by his policy of hostility to China. We could not tolerate this behaviour and had to suspend Sino-Japanese trade interflow for two and a half years.

If according to the wishes of the Chinese and Japanese people, Sino-Japanese trade could be gradually resumed, this would be a good thing for the people of both countries. However, we still have to wait a while and see what the attitude of the new Japanese Government really is.

Now we put forward three principles, namely, one, government agreement; two, private contracts; three, special consideration in individual cases.

First of all, all agreements from now on must be concluded between the governments on both sides and only so are they guaranteed, because before with the private agreements the Japanese Government did not want to guarantee them. And as regards a government agreement it can only be signed in conditions when the relations of the governments of the two countries are developing in a friendly direction and, in fact, when normal relations are established; otherwise, it cannot be signed.

As regards the relations between the two governments, Comrade Liu Ning-yi made it very clear when he was in Tokyo that we still maintain the three political principles we stated formerly. The three principles stated formerly do not place a heavy demand on the Japanese Government; they are very fair. . .

The new Japanese Government, both Prime Minister Ikeda and Foreign Minister Kosaka, have recently made some statements which are not good. We still have to wait and see. I was Foreign Minister in 1957 and Vice-Premier Chen Yi be-

came Foreign Minister in 1958. Both of us condemned the
Nobusuke Kishi government's policy towards China, all entirely
on the basis of the numerous hostile activities of the Nobusuke
Kishi government to China. Therefore, we now have to wait
and see with regard to the Ikeda government.

In view of all this, we draw the conclusion that any agreement between the two countries must be concluded by the
governments; there is no guarantee for private agreements.
This applies to trade, fishery, postal service, navigation, etc.

Then, is it impossible to do business between the two
countries in the absence of agreements? No, business can be
done and private contracts can be concluded whenever conditions are mature. For instance, a certain Japanese enterprise
and a certain Chinese company may negotiate and sign
contracts and make a deal for a fixed term, if they want to be
friendly to each other and proceed from the requirements of
both parties. If the contract is fulfilled well, if both parties are on
good terms and if the political environment of the two countries
turns for the better, the short-term contracts may be converted
into relatively long-term ones. This is thinking of the future.

Further there is special consideration in specific cases, which
has been going on for two years. It is correct for the General
Council of Trade Unions of Japan and the All China Federation
of Trade Unions to mediate in the interests of labouring people
when the medium and small enterprises of Japan have special
difficulties. Special consideration for this kind of trade may
be continued in the future and the volume may even be
expanded a bit in accordance with the needs. This has already
been explained by Comrade Liu Ning-yi in Tokyo.

Your Japan-China Trade Promotion Association, in accordance with the three principles for Sino-Japanese trade mentioned
above, may recommend such business which you hold to be
friendly, possible and beneficial to both sides. You may contact
the Council for the Promotion of International Trade of our
country. They know this principle. The All China Federation
of Trade Unions also knows this principle of special consideration in specific cases, and you may also talk with them. After
Mr. Suzuki returns, you may talk it over with friends belonging
to firms connected with the Japan-China Trade Promotion
Association.

25. Joint statement by Chang Hsi-jo, President of the Chinese People's Institute of Foreign Affairs, and Mosaburo Suzuki, Adviser to the Japanese Socialist Party, 13 January 1962 (Extracts)

The Japanese Socialist Party Delegation holds that the conclusion of a collective security treaty among the countries of the Asian and Pacific region, particularly between China, Japan, the Soviet Union and the United States would be a guarantee for Japan's neutrality and for peace in Asia and the rest of the world. The Chinese side supports this view. Both sides also unanimously agreed that before the conclusion of such a collective security treaty, provided Japan abrogates the Japan-US "Security Treaty" and Japan-Chiang Kai-shek clique treaty, eliminates all foreign military bases and brings about the normalisation of Sino-Japanese relations, a bilateral treaty of friendship and mutual non-aggression between China and Japan may then be concluded as a first step. This is an effective way of achieving collective security. The Chinese side makes it clear that with the conclusion of a Sino-Japanese treaty of friendship and mutual non-aggression, the provisions of the Sino-Soviet Treaty of Friendship, Alliance and Mutual Assistance for the prevention of the resurgence of Japanese militarism will automatically become null and void. . . .

The Japanese Socialist Party Delegation notes that the normalization of Sino-Japanese relations is at present obstructed by the policy of hostility towards China pursued by US imperialism and its follower, the Ikeda government. The Japanese Socialist Party Delegation emphatically points out that at the 16th UN General Assembly, the Ikeda government. toeing the US line, was one of these countries which submitted the "important matter" resolution, actively obstructed the restoration to the People's Republic of China of its legitimate rights in the UN, and pushed ahead the "two Chinas" plot. The Japanese Socialist Party Delegation expresses its opposition to the policy of hostility towards China, declares its basic stand that there is only one China and will fight for Sino-Japanese friendship and restoration of normal relations between the two countries. The Chinese side expresses its endorsement and gratitude for this.

Both sides indicate that they will strive continuously to develop friendly trade between the peoples of the two countries and to promote the achievement of a trade agreement between governments on the basis of the three political principles on trade.

Both sides unanimously agree that to expand cultural contacts and the exchange of visits between the peoples of China and Japan, who have had close ties historically, geographically and culturally, will be conducive to the promotion of friendly relations between them

26. Memorandum on Sino-Japanese Trade signed by Liao Cheng-chih and Tatsunosuke Takasaki, 9 November 1962

Mr. Liao Cheng-chih and Mr. Tatsunosuke Takasaki, in accordance with the tenor of the talks held between Premier Chou En-lai and Mr. Kenzo Matsumura in September 1962 concerning the expansion of Sino-Japanese trade and for the further development of non-governmental trade between the two countries on the basis of equality and mutual benefit and by gradual and cumulative methods, exchanged the following memorandum:

(1) The two sides agree to develop long-term, comprehensive trade by exchange of goods, with 1963-1967 as the first five-year period for the trade arrangements, during which the average annual total of import and export transactions shall reach about 36 million pounds sterling.

(2) The major goods to be exported by the two sides are as follows:

Goods to be exported by the Chinese side: Coal, iron ore, soyabeans, maize, miscellaneous beans, salt, tin and other commodities;

Goods to be exported by the Japanese side: Rolled steel (including special rolled steel), chemical fertilizer, insecticides, agricultural machinery and farm implements, whole-set equipment and other commodities.

(3) Transactions based on this memorandum will be concluded through separate contracts to be signed between the parties concerned with each transaction on the Japanese side and the China National Foreign Trade Corporation (importers

and exporters.)

(4) Transactions based on this memorandum will be guaranteed by letters of credit or letter of gurantee, and the
accounts will be settled, in pounds sterling or any other currency
agreed by both sides.

(5) The two sides agreed that the methods of deferment of
payments for certain commodities, and payment by instalments
for whole-set equipment to be exported by Japan to China will
be discussed and decided by the two sides on other occasions.

(6) The two sides will endeavour to promote the technical
exchange and technical cooperation necessary for the implementation of this memorandum.

(7) Inspection of commodities, arbitration and the other
questions necessary for the implementation of this memorandum
will be discussed and decided by the two sides on other
occasions.

(8) This memorandum and the agreements and contracts
concluded in accordance with this memorandum shall not be
annulled unless by agreement of the parties concerned on the
two sides.

(9) This memorandum and the agreements concluded in
accordance with this memorandum can be revised and readjusted
after consultation between the two sides.

(10) This memorandum will be effective from the date of its
signature and will remain valid until the 31st day of December
1967. It can extended by mutual agreement.

27. Vice-Premier Chen Yi's interview with Japanese journalist Hirosi Hasimoto, 20 June 1964 (Extracts)

At present, relations between China and Japan are being
gradually improved by "accumulation." However the present
state of Sino-Japanese relations still falls far short of the two
people's strong desire for restoring diplomatic relations.

Normalizing relations between the two countries includes
normalization of both political and economic relations. Therefore, in gradually improving relations in the form of "accumulation," it is, as a matter of course, necessary to improve
simultaneously both political and economic relations. Moreover,
the development of political and economic relations influence

and promote each other. The Chinese Government has always held that in relations between China and Japan, politics and economics are inseparable. In plain words what the so-called "separation of politics and economics" implies is, politically, to continue to adhere to the attitude of non-recognition of China and economically, to develop Sino-Japanese trade on a limited scale. Obviously, this is not in full accord with the demand for promoting the normalization of relations between our two countries, in the interests of their own peoples, to pursue an independent foreign policy and gradually do away with outside obstacles. Recently some influential Japanese papers and periodicals have explicitly pointed out that the guiding principles for the normalization of Sino-Japanese relations should be the Five Principles of Peaceful Coexistence. I believe this view is reasonable and realistic. . . .

The Chinese people suffered great losses during Japanese militarists' war of aggression against China. The Chinese people have the right to ask for reparations. Although the war has been over for nearly 20 years, China and Japan have not even concluded a peace treaty, there is no basis for the discussion of the question. In dealing with Sino-Japanese relations, the Chinese Government and people have always looked forward, instead of looking backward. What the Chinese and Japanese Government must do at present is first of all to make joint efforts to solve the question of how to help bring about the normalization of relations. If the Japanese Government respects the wishes of the Japanese people it must show its sincerity and be prepared to solve step by step the major question of normalizing diplomatic relations between China and Japan; once diplomatic relations are restored, it will be easy to settle other specific questions through friendly consultation.

28. Zhou Enlai's Report on the Work of the Government to the First Session of the Third National People's Congress, 21-22 December 1964 (Extract)

The Japanese people's momentous mass struggle against U.S. imperialism and domestic reactionaries has dealt a powerful blow to the U.S. imperialist policies of aggression and war in Asia. The Chinese people staunchly support the Japanese people in their patriotic and democratic struggle. . . .

There has been some expansion of economic and cultural exchange between China and Japan in recent years, but the extremely unfriendly attitude of the Sato government towards China and its tailing after the United States in the "two Chinas" plot have created difficulties in the relations between the two countries. These actions taken by the Sato government go against the will of the masses of the Japanese people and are detrimental to Sino-Japanese friendship.

29. Japanese Prime Minister Eisaku Sato's policy speech before the Diet, 25 January 1965 (Extract)

It needs expatiation that the problem of China holds very great importance in present-day international politics. Especially for our country which has a close relationship with China both historically and geographically, this problem is one of great importance with a variety of implications. I believe, therefore, that our country should deal with this problem prudently and from its own independent viewpoint, without making unnecessary haste to reach a conclusion.

At the present stage our country intends to promote economic and cultural interchange with Communist China and on the basic principle of separation of political matters and economic matters, while maintaining the friendly relations with Republic of China with which Japan has regular diplomatic relations.

30. Chen Yi's press conference for Chinese and foreign correspondents, 29 September 1965 (Extract)

If the present Japanese Government stops tailing after the United States, pursues an independent policy and renounces its anti-Chinese policy, possibilities will increase for the normalization of Sino-Japanese relations. At present the Sato cabinet is politically following the US anti-Chinese policy, while economically it wants to reap gains from Sino-Japanese trade. Such a policy is self-contradictory and cannot help normalize Sino-Japanese relations. It is up to Japan to remove this obstacle. Out of consideration for the traditional friendship between the great nation and peoples of China and Japan, the Chinese Government is willing to carry on trade between the two countries on the present level, but it is impossible to expand it.

The Japanese nation is full of promise, and the Japanese people love peace. They demand the liquidation of US imperialist control and the dismantling of US bases in Japan. We have deep sympathy with their demands.

31. Chen Yi's interview with the Beijing correspondent of the Japanese paper, *Akahata*, 30 December 1965 (Extracts)

The forcible passage of the "Japan-ROK Treaty" by the Sato cabinet is a grave step taken by US imperialism in its scheme to enlarge its war of aggression in Asia; it is also a grave step taken by the Japanese reactionaries to accelerate the revival of militarism and the organization of a Northeast-Asia military alliance, a step which marks their determination to take an open part in US wars of aggression. The spearhead of aggression of the "Japan-ROK Treaty" is directed against Korea, and likewise against China and other Asian countries. . . .

Ever since it entered office, the Sato government has been following US imperialism and working hard to undermine the positive results accumulated over the years in Sino-Japanese relations. No improvement in Sino-Japanese relations is possible unless the Sato government changes its policy of tailing after US imperialism, reviving Japanese militarism and being hostile to China.

32. Address by Premier Sato in New York, November 1967 (Extract)

It is also important, in view of the close Japan-U.S. relationship, for the American people to understand my country's view of China which is related to the situation in Vietnam. Since this past summer, I have visited ten Asian countries, where I could observe how China is attempting in various ways to influence nations on its periphery. I noted also among the Southeast Asian nations subtle but resentful sentiments against the pressures of "this giant of the North." It is due to such sentiments that these nations understand and appreciate the sacrifices the United States is making now in Vietnam. The Japanese people also find it truly regrettable that China should try to influence, in a dogmatic and selfish way, the domestic and external policies of its neighbouring nations and that it should take the road of exploiting nuclear weaponry in defiance of the strong desire of the peoples of the world for nuclear disarmament.

At the same time, most Japanese have strong, good-neigh-bourly feelings toward the Chinese people. We do not want to see the the germination and imbedding of lasting hostile feelings between Japan and China, which are separated only by a narrow body of water.

With this thought in mind, it is indeed meaningful for my country to maintain contacts with the Mainland China through the exchange of goods, people and newspapermen on a non-governmental basis. These contacts are useful, and they leave the door open for the government of Mainland China to return, some day, to the international community on reasonable terms In this sense, I am pleased that the leaders of the United States have recently clarified their long-range policy toward China. For example, President Johnson pointed out, in his address to the American Alumni Council last year, that "a peaceful Mainland China is central to a peaceful Asia." He went on to say that "China must be encouraged toward understanding of the outside world and toward policies of peaceful cooperation."

I admire the courage and wisdom of American leaders in stating these farsighted goals with respect to Communist China even while they are dealing firmly with communist infiltration in Vietnam.

Japan and the United States consult regularly and closely on the question of China, as well as on other important inter-national problems of interest to both countries. There is no doubt that these friendly consultations have been most helpful in solving various issues between Japan and the United States, in political, economic and trade policies in the fields of aviation and fisheries, and even in the field of security.

33. Minutes of talks between representatives of China-Japan Friendship Association and Japan-China Friendship Association (Orthodox), 10 April 1968 (Extract)

The two sides unanimously reiterate that US imperialism is the common enemy of the Chinese and Japanese peoples and of the people of Asia and the whole world. During their talks last November, Johnson and Sato hatched the criminal plot of "maintaining" the US-Japan "security treaty"; this shows that the US-Japanese reactionaries are determined to be hostile to the people of China, Japan and the other Asian countries. Therefore, smashing the US-Japan "security treaty" is a militant task for the Chinese and Japanese peoples, and an urgent task for developing the China-Japan friendship movement at present. The Sato government has obstinately followed the US imperialist policies of aggression and war, and frantically revived Japanese militarism in an attempt to tie the Japanese people to the US war chariot. Facts have proved that the Sato government is the biggest accomplice of US imperialism in Asia. Actively serving US imperialism and the Japanese reactionaries, Soviet modern revisionism and the Miyamoto revisionist clique in the Japanese Communist Party have degenerated into faithful running dogs of the US-Japanese reactionaries. Both sides unanimously hold that the Japanese people's opposition to the four enemies, headed by US imperialism, conforms to the interests of the people of Japan, China, Asia and the whole world. In order to isolate to the maximum the chief enemy, US imperialism, and deal it the heaviest blow it is imperative to unite all anti-US forces that can be united and form the broadest united front which does not include the enemy. The China-Japan friendship movement is an inseparable component part of this united front against US imperialism.

34. "Counter-Revolutionary" collusion between Soviet revisionist renegades and Japanese reactionaries," Article by *People's Daily* commentator, 20 December 1968 (Extracts)

The Soviet revisionist renegade clique and Japanese reactionaries have been engaging in intense counter-revolutionary conspiratorial activities in recent years. Their relations have developed from economic "co-operation" to political and military collusion. The Soviet revisionists and Japanese reactionaries are now hatching a "peace treaty" under the signboard of "good neighbourliness and friendship" in order to speed up the formation of a "Moscow-Tokyo axis" and rig up a counter revolutionary alliance against China.

The counter-revlutionary collusion between the Soviet revisionists and Japanese reactionaries is in fact an extension of Soviet-U.S. collaboration. Everybody knows that to push its policies of aggression and war in Asia, U.S. imperialism has been actively reviving the Japanese militarist forces in an attempt to make Japan serve as a hatchetman in wars of aggression in Asia and as a base in the ring of encirclement against China. Proceeding from its counter-revolutionary needs, the Soviet revisionist renegade clique has also energetically fostered and collaborated with Japanese militarism. Singing the same tune as U.S. imperialism, the Soviet revisionists have praised Japanese militarism as a "stabilizing force in Asia." Both U.S. imperialism and Soviet revisionism want to enlist Japanese militarism into service, with the criminal objective of opposing socialist China and jointly suppressing the revolutionary movements in the Asian countries.

The Soviet revisionists and Japanese reactionaries have become more and more open in their military collaboration. The Soviet revisionist renegades have not only blatantly connived at and encouraged a military alliance between the United States and Japan; they have also taken further steps to ally themselves with the U.S. and Japanese reactionaries to encircle China militarily . . . .

To collude with Japanese militarism in jointly opposing China, this clique does not hesitate to sell out the country's national sovereignty and natural resources and the interests of the Soviet people to the Japanese monpolists. By throwing all Siberia, ground, sea and air space, wide open, it has made it possible for Japanese monopoly capital to exploit and plunder the Soviet people. Ironclad facts have proved that the Soviet revisionists are both social-imperialists and out-and-out traitors.

35. Communique on talks between Chinese and Japanese representatives of Memorandum Trade Offices, 4 April 1969 (Extracts)

The Chinese side points out: US imperialism and the Sato

government of Japan which tails after it have stubbornly pursued a policy of hostility towards China and have placed obstacles in the relations between China and Japan, including the relations between us.

The Japanese side frankly admits that the causes for the worsening of the relations between Japan and China lie with the Japanese Government. In view of its anxiety about the present situation and from the angle of serious self-examination, the Japanese side expresses its determination to make positive efforts to remove these obstacles and promote the normal development of relations between Japan and China. . . .

The Chinese side strongly denounces the Sato government for stepping up its efforts to follow US imperialism, for participating in the conspiracy to create "two Chinas" and for barefacedly adopting a policy of hostility towards China. The Chinese side reiterates that to liberate Taiwan is China's internal affair and that the Chinese people will definitely liberate Taiwan. The so-called "peace treaty" concluded by the Japanese Government with the Chiang Kai-shek gang, which has long been rejected by the Chinese people, is hostile to the Chinese people and is illegal and is resolutely opposed by the Chinese people. The Japanese side agrees with the just stand of the Chinese side. . . .

Both sides reached agreement on memorandum trade matters for 1969.

36. Joint communique by US President Richard M. Nixon and Premier Sato, 21 November 1969 (Extracts)

The President and the Prime Minister exchanged frank views on the current international situation, with particular attention to developments in the Far East. The President, while emphasizing that the countries in the area were expected to make their own efforts for the stability of the area, gave assurance that the United States would continue to contribute to the maintenance of international peace and security in the Far East by honouring its defence treaty obligations in the area. The Prime Minister, appreciating the determination of the United States, stressed that it was important for the peace and security of the Far East that the United States should be in a position to carry out fully its obligations referred to by the President. He further expressed his recognition that, in the light of the present situation, the presence of United States forces in the Far East constituted a mainstay for the stability of the area.

The President and the Prime Minister specifically noted the continuing tension over the Korean peninsula. The Prime Minister deeply appreciated the peace-keeping efforts of the United Nations in the area and stated that the security of the Republic of Korea was essential to Japan's own security. The President and the Prime Minister shared the hope that Communist China would adopt a more cooperative and constructive attitude in its external relations. The President referred to the treaty obligations of his country to the Republic of China which the United States would uphold. The Prime Minister said that the maintenance of peace and security in the Taiwan area was also a most important factor for the security of Japan.

In light of the current situation and the prospects in the Far East, the President and the Prime Minister agreed that they highly valued the role played by the Treaty of Mutual Cooperation and Security in maintaining the peace and security of the Far East including Japan, and they affirmed the intention of the two governments firmly to maintain the treaty on the basis of mutual trust and common evaluation of the international situation. They further agreed that the two governments should maintain close contact with each other on matters affecting the peace and security of the Far East including Japan, and on the implementation of the Treaty of Mutual Cooperation and Security. . . .

37. Premier Sato's address before the National Press Club, Washington, D.C., 21 November 1969 (Extracts)

In particular, if an armed attack against the Republic of Korea were to occur, the security of Japan would be seriously affected. Therefore, should an occasion arise for United States forces in such an eventuality to use facilities and areas within Japan as bases for military combat operations to meet the armed attack, the policy of the Government of Japan towards prior consultations would be to decide its position positively and promptly on the basis of the foregoing recognition.

The maintenance of peace in the Taiwan area is also an important factor for our own security. I believe in this regard that the determination of the United States to uphold her treaty commitments to the Republic of China should be fully appreciated, However, should unfortunately a situation ever occur in which such treaty commitments would actually have to be invoked against an armed attack from the outside, it would be a threat to the peace and security of the Far East including Japan. Therefore, in view of our national interest, we would deal with the situation on the basis of the foregoing recognition, in connection with the fulfilment by the United States of its defence obligations. However, I am glad to say, such a situation cannot be foreseen today. . . .

It could also be said that the 1970s will be a decade when the various major countries other than the United States and the Soviet Union should assume greater responsibilities. We have a profound concern over the future of Communist China which is at present devoting great efforts to the development of nuclear arms, and the relationship that the United States and the Soviet Union will have, respectively, with Communist China. Having the United States, the Soviet Union and Communist China as our neighbours, Japan strongly hopes that in the 1970's Communist China will live in peace with the United States and the Soviet Union, in the same way as the efforts for maintaining peace between the United States and the Soviet Union have developed. It is to be hoped also that Communist China will revise the rigid posture that it has been taking, and participate in international society as a country that will carry out its responsibilties in a constructive manner in the cause of international peace. For this purpose, I consider that both the United States and Japan should always keep their doors open towards Communist China.

38. Communique on China-Japan Memorandum Trade Office talks, 19 April 1970 (Extracts)

Both sides once again confirm that three political principles and the principles that politics and economy are insepab'e

are the principles that must be adhered to in the relations
between China and Japan, and are the political basis of the
relations between the two sides. Both sides express the determination to continue to make positive efforts to observe the
above-mentioned principles and to uphold this political basis.

Both sides sternly condemn the Japan-US joint communique
issued on November 21, 1969.

The Chinese side solemnly points out that the Japan-US
joint communique has turned the aggressive Japan-US "security
treaty" into a new US-Japan military alliance which covers
a wider range and poses even greater menace, directing its
spearhead as it does against the people of China, Korea and
the three countries of Indo-China, as well as against the people
of other countries in Asia. The Japanese reactionaries have
become the principal accomplice of US imperialism in pushing
the so-called new Asia policy of having Asians fight Asians, and
have become a shock force in opposing the people of different
Asian countries. The so-called return of Okinawa, advertised in
the Japan-US joint communique, is an out-and-out fraud. Under
the pretext of the "return of Okinawa," Eisaku Sato has no
qualms to sell out Japan's national interests and state sovereignty and to promise to tie the whole of Japan on to the US war
chariot, thereby Okinawanizing Japan proper and making it a
military base for US imperialist aggression against Asia. In the
Japan-US joint communique, Eisaku Sato brazenly asserted
that Taiwan was a "most important factor for the security of
Japan," that Korea was "essential to Japan's own security" and
that Japan was to play a "role" in bringing about "stability" in
the Indo-China area. The purpose of the US and Japanese reactionaries in stepping up military collusion is obvious, that is to
perpetuate the forcible occupation of China's sacred territory
Taiwan Province and prevent the Chinese people from liberating Taiwan; to perpetuate the forcible occupation of south
Korea, obstruct the reunification of Korea and even invade
anew the Democratic People's Republic of Korea; and to keep
Viet Nam divided for ever, prevent the Vietnamese people
from liberating the south, defending the north and then reuni-
fying the country, and to this end, go to the length of expanding the war of aggression against Indo-China. Unquestion-
ably, all this serves to reveal the aggressive ambitions of

Japanese militarism.

The Japanese side expresses understanding of the stand of the Chinese side and holds that the Japan-US joint communique has pushed the Japan-US military collusion to a new stage, further enlarging and escalating the Japan-US "security treaty." The clause providing for the so-called return of Okinawa in the Japan-US joint communique is deceptive . . . .

Both sides are unanimous in solemnly pointing out that in the past year the Sato government redoubled its efforts to follow US imperialism and stubbornly pursued a policy of hostility towards China, thus placing new, grave obstacles in the relations between China and Japan. The present situation of worsened relations between China and Japan is entirely created by the Sato government. The Japanese side further states that from now on it will resolutely oppose the Sato government's policy of hostility towards China, and make new and effective efforts to clear away all the obstacles the Sato government has placed in the way of relations between China and Japan and to promote the normalization of China-Japan relations . . . .

The two sides have reached agreement on matters concerning the 1970 memorandum trade.

39. Joint statement by China-Japan Friendship Association and visiting delegation of the Japanese Socialist Party, 1 November 1970 (Extract)

Both sides point out: The movement for Japan-China friendship and restoration of diplomatic relations between Japan and China is a component of the Japanese people's struggle against US imperialism and the revival of Japanese militarism by the US and Japanese reactionaries. The Delegation of the Japanese Socialist Party expresses willingness to make efforts to unite on a broad scale with all the forces in Japan that are truly for Japan-China friendship and the restoration of diplomatic relations between Japan and China, and determination to strengthen this movement, and at the same time raises the following four principles for carrying out the movement:

1. Unite with the anti-imperialist forces of the people of

Asian countries to oppose US imperialism and the revival of Japanese militarism and strive for the nullification of the Japan-US "security treaty";

2. Fight against all policies of hostility towards China, adhere to the stand of one China and demand the nullification of "Japan-Chiang Kai-shek treaty," and in accordance with the Five Principles of Peaceful Coexistence and the three political principles, struggle for the restoration of diplomatic relations between Japan and China;

3. In adherence to the stand of true friendship between Japan and China and that politics and economics are inseparable, develop exchanges in trade, culture, friendly relations and other fields between the people of Japan and China;

4. Rally on a broad scale forces in Japan which genuinely desire friendship between Japan and China and the restoration of diplomatic relations between Japan and China and organize a united front.

The Chinese side expresses its appreciation of the above-mentioned stand of the Delegation of the Japanese Socialist Party and reaffirms that the Chinese side will, as always, warmly support all efforts beneficial to opposing the US-Japanese reactionaries and their followers, to the development of friendship between China and Japan and the restoration of diplomatic relations between China and Japan, and to the promotion of the unity and alliance of forces genuinely and earnestly for friendship berween China and Japan.

40. Japanese Foreign Minister Kiichi Aichi's speech before the Diet, 22 January 1971 (Extract)

The problem of China is the major problem of the 1970s, both for our country and for the world at large. At the same time, it should be noted that this China problem is an unusually difficult and complicated one.

The Government is fully aware that both the Republic of China and the People's Republic of China take the position of "One China." We believe that this is the type of problem which should be solved by peaceful talks, avoiding at all costs the use of force, between the parties concerned. The Government of Japan will, for its part, respect whatever result that may emerge from such talks.

The Government has maintained friendly relations with the Republic of China, but also believes it desirable to improve its relations with mainland China under the principles of mutual respect for each other's position and non-interference in domestic affairs, and, to this end, wishes to have a dialogue with the People's Republic of China. I believe that it will become possible to understand each other's position even better if inter-governmental contacts were to materialize besides the private civilian interchanges between Japan and China.

At the debate on the question of Chinese representation at the United Nations' 25th General Assembly last fall, the Albanian draft resolution recognizing the representative of the People's Republic of China as the sole legal representative of China and calling for the expulsion of the Republic of China from the United Nations for the first time obtained more supporting votes than votes against. The Government intends to devote careful study to the future handling of this problem after detailed analysis of the international situation which led to such a result and while carefully scrutinizing the trend of the international situation in this matter.

41. Communique on China-Japan Memorandum Trade Office talks, 1 March 1971 (Extract)

The two sides unanimously condemn the Japanese reactionaries for intensifying collusion with US imperialism in reviving Japanese militarism and joining US imperialism's aggression and expansion in Asia. Actively following the line of the Japan-US joint communique, the Sato government has in the past year gone further in turning Japan into a base of US imperialist aggression against Asia. The Sato government has not only propagandized militarism in a big way, but has "automatically extended" the Japan-US "security treaty," put forward the "draft outline of the fourth national defence build-up programme" and the "national defence white paper," and stepped up armament expansion. Furthermore, it has worked in co-ordination with the US policy of aggression against Asia and helped US imperialism expand its war of aggression

against Viet Nam, Laos and Cambodia. All this shows that
the revival of Japanese militarism is already a reality. The
Japanese side states that it is determined to make still
greater efforts to denounce and smash the revival of Japanese
militarism . . . .

The Chinese side strongly condemns the Japanese reactionaries for their intensified collusion with the Chiang Kai-
shek and Pak Jung Hi puppet cliques in rigging up a new
military alliance in Northeast Asia and for directing the spearhead of their aggression against China and the Democratic
People's Republic of Korea. The newly established Japan-
Chiang-Pak "liaison committee" has gone so far as to decide
on the "joint exploitation" of the resources of the shallow seas
adjacent to China's coasts. This is a flagrant encroachment on
China's sovereignty. The Chinese people absolutely will not
tolerate this. The Japanese side states that it understands this
solemn stand of the Chinese side. . . .

Both sides reiterate and affirm once again that the three
political principles and the principle that politics and economics
are inseparable must be adhered to in the relations between
China and Japan, and they are the political basis of the relations between our two sides. To promote Sino-Japanese trade
on this basis, the Chinese side puts forward four conditions in
its trade with Japan, namely: The Chinese side will not have
trade exchanges with factories, firms and enterprises belonging
to any of the following categories:

First, factories and firms helping the Chiang Kai-shek gang
stage a come-back to the mainland or helping the Pak Jung Hi
clique intrude into the Democratic People's Republic of Korea;

Second, factories and firms with large investments in
Taiwan or south Korea;

Third, enterprises supplying arms and ammunition to US
imperialism for aggression against Viet Nam or Laos or
Cambodia; and

Fourth, US-Japan joint enterprises or subsidiaries of US
companies in Japan.

The Japanese side agrees to the stand of the Chinese side. . . .

Both sides maintain that promoting friendship between the
two peoples and normal relations between the two countries
conforms to the common desire of the Chinese and Japanese

peoples and is in the interests of safeguarding peace in Asia and the world.

The two sides reached agreement on 1971 memorandum trade matters, etc.

42. Joint statement of China-Japan Friendship Association and the visiting delegation of Komeito of Japan, 2 July 1971 (Extract)

The two sides fully exchanged views on China-Japan relations, the current situation and other questions of common concern, in the spirit of consultation on an equal footing and of seeking common ground while reserving differences.

The Delegation of the Komeito of Japan states: (1) There is only one China, and the Government of the People's Republic of China is the sole legitimate government representing the Chinese people; firm opposition to the scheme of creating "two Chinas" or "one China, one Taiwan." (2) Taiwan is a province of China and an inalienable part of Chinese territory. The question of Taiwan is China's internal affair; firm opposition to the assertion that "the sovereignty over Taiwan is unsettled." (3) The "Japan-Chiang treaty" is illegal and must be abrogated. (4) The occupation of Taiwan and the Taiwan Straits area by the United States is an act of aggression; the United States must withdraw all its armed forces from Taiwan and the Taiwan Straits area. (5) To the People's Republic of China must be restored her legitimate rights in all organizations of the United Nations and its legitimate right to the status of permanent member of the Security Council of the United Nations and the "representatives" of the Chiang Kai-shek clique must be expelled from the United Nations; firm opposition to all schemes obstructing the restoration of the above-mentioned legitimate rights to China.

The Chinese side holds that the 5-point position of the Komeito conforms to the desire and interests of the people of China and Japan, and expresses appreciation and support for it; it also holds that in the event of the Japanese Government's accepting the above-mentioned points and taking practical steps to this end, the state of war between China and Japan can be ended, diplomatic relations restored and a peace treaty concluded: and then depending on developments, a mutual non-aggression treaty between China and Japan can be concluded on the basis of the Five Principles of Peaceful Coexistence, mutual respect for sovereignty and territorial integrity, mutual non-aggression, non-interference in each other's internal affairs, equality and mutual benefit, and peaceful coexistence

43. Joint statement of China-Japan Friendship Association of China and visiting delegation of the Japanese Dietmen's League for Promoting Restoration of Japan-China Diplomatic Relations, 2 October 1971 (Extract)

The two sides unanimously affirm that the basic principles for the restoration of Japan-China diplomatic relations are:

1. There is only one China, that is People's Republic of China. The Government of the People's Republic of China is the sole legal government representing the Chinese people. "Two Chinas," "one China, one Taiwan," "One China, two governments" and other such absurdities must be firmly opposed.

2. Taiwan Province is an inalienable part of the territory of the People's Republic of China. The assertion that "the title to Taiwan remains to be settled" and the scheme of creating "an independent Taiwan" hatched by the US and Japanese reactionaries" must be strongly opposed. The Taiwan question is China's internal affair and brooks no interference by any foreign country.

3. The so-called "Japan-Chiang treaty" was signed after the founding of the People's Republic of China and therefore is illegal and invalid and should be abrogated.

4. It is imperative to restore all the lawful rights of the People's Republic of China in all the organs of the United Nations, including the seat in the Security Council as a permanent member. and expel the "representatives" of the Chiang Kai-shek clique from the United Nations.

The Japanese side expresses the view that the "Dietmen's League for Japan-China Relations" is a supra-party organization of Diet members aimed at restoring diplomatic relations between Japan and China.

44. Joint statement of China-Japan Friendship Association of China and visiting delegation of Japan-China Friendship Association (Orthodox), 16 October 1971 (Extract)

Both sides strongly condemn U.S. imperialism and the reactionary Sato government for their policy of hostility towards China, resolutely oppose "two Chinas," "one China, one Taiwan," "one China, two governments," "the status of Taiwan remaining to be determined" and other such absurdities and resolutely oppose the scheme hatched by the US and Japanese reactionaries to create an indepedent Taiwan.

The two sides unanimously reaffirm that the Government of the People's Republic of China is the sole legal government representing the Chinese people; Taiwan Province is an inalienable part of Chinese territory; the liberation of Taiwan is China's internal affair and brooks no interference by any foreign country; the illegal Japan-Chiang treaty must be abrogated; the United States must withdraw all its armed forces and military installations from Taiwan and the area of the Taiwan Straits; and it is imperative to restore to China all its legitimate rights in all the organs of the United Nations and resolutely expel the "representatives" of the Chiang Kai-shek clique from the United Nations.

45. Communique on talks between representatives of the Chinese and Japanese Memorandum Trade Offices, 21 December 1971 (Extract)

During the talks the two sides hold the identical view that the rapid development of the international situation has further proved the complete correctness of the communiques on the talks issued by the two sides in recent years. The political principles concerning China-Japan relations and the viewpoints on the revival of Japanese militarism, the fraud of ' reversion of Okinawa" designed by the US and Japanese reactionaries, the Japan-US military collusion and other questions as expounded in the previous communiques have won ever wider support. A new high tide is rising in Japan to promote Japan-China friendship and restore the diplomatic relations between Japan and China.

46. Xinhua commentary on Soviet Foreign Minister Gromyko's visit to Japan, 3 February 1972 (Extracts)

Nominally, Gromyko's visit to Japan was to resume the Soviet-Japanese "regular consultations at Ministerial level" but actually it was an important step taken by Soviet revisionist social-imperialism to step up its collusion with the Japanese reactionaries to oppose the people of China and other Asian countries and to contend with US imperialism for spheres of influence in Asia. This act has aroused the vigilance and attention of the people of the Asian countries. . . .

The Japanese press disclosed that during his stay in Japan Gromyko showed "extraordinary interests" in Japan's policy towards China and had deep-going discussions on the China question" with the Japanese side. . . .

After conspiring against China with Sato, Fukuda and their ilk, Gromyko clamoured that the Soviet Union and China "used to be very friendly but relations have worsened. This should be blamed on China." With this clumsy trick of "a thief crying 'stop thief,' " Gromyko tried to cover up his criminal design to oppose socialist China in collusion with Japanese militarism.

Japan has long been the main object of contention between US imperialism and Soviet revisionism in Asia. Gromyko's visit to Japan, which took place after the talks between the heads of the US and Japanese governments in San Clemente not long ago, has its ulterior motives.

When Soviet revisionism saw that the US-Japanese talks did not solve the increasingly acute contradictions in economy, trade and other fields between the United States and Japan, Gromyko scurried to Japan to woo it at this juncture, so as to expand the positions of Soviet revisionism in Asia. Since the latter half of last year, when the contradictions between Japan and the United States were sharpened as a result of the "new economic policy" announced by the US Government, Soviet revisionist journals have made a great fuss about it and tried their best to sour the relations between Japan and the United States. . . .

One of the questions for which Gromyko had shown great concern during his visit in Japan is that of "Soviet-

Japanese economic cooperation" and "economic cooperation guaranteed by the (Japanese) Government" in exploiting the Soviet Tyumen oil field. . . .

The Soviet Union is in urgent need to promote economic cooperation with Japan because it wants to get out of the economic difficulties at home and solve the problem of scanty resources and backward technique and because it wants to further attract Japan economically and restrain Japanese-US relations by seizing the opportunity when the contradictions between Japan and the United States in economy and trade have sharpened and when Japan is eager to find abroad a way out for her trade.

47. Joint statement of China-Japan Friendship Association of China and visiting delegation of Democratic Socialist Party of Japan, 13 April 1972 (Extract)

The Democratic Socialist Party, for its part, stated: In order that the two countries may end the state of war, conclude a peace treaty and restore diplomatic relations at an early date, it is necessary, first of all, to acknowledge the following basic principles:

1. There is only one China in the world and that is the People's Republic of China. The Government of the People's Republic of China is the sole legal government representing the Chinese people. Such absurdities as "two Chinas," "one China, one Taiwan" and "one China, two governments" should be firmly opposed.

2. Taiwan is an integral part of the territory of the People's Republic of China, and has already been returned to China. The Taiwan question is purely China's internal affair which brooks no interference by any foreign country. Advocacy of "the status of Taiwan remains to be determined" and the plot to engineer an "independent Taiwan" should be firmly opposed.

3. The "Japan-Chiang treaty" is illegal and invalid, and must be abrogated.

Both sides maintained that the above-mentioned principles are the prerequisites to the restoration of diplomatic relations between China and Japan and must be firmly implemented.

The Chinese side sternly condemn the Sato government for

continuing its policy of hostility towards China and obstructing
the restoration of diplomatic relations between China and Japan
in disregard of the strong desire of the Japanese people and in
defiance of the general trend of the world. Under domestic and
foreign pressure, the Sato government recently made gestures in
a vain attempt to deceive public opinion. But it still advocates
the fallacy "the status of Taiwan remains to be determined,"
and is taking part in the conspiratorial activities that aim at
creating an "independent Taiwan." This fully exposes the
Japanese reactionaries' ambitious designs on Taiwan and their
obdurate hostility to the Chinese people.

48. Zhou Enlai's speech at a banquet given in honour of Japanese Premier Kakuei Tanaka, 25 September 1972 (Extract)

Prime Minister Tanaka's visit to China opens a new page
in the history of Sino-Japanese relations. Friendly contacts
and cultural exchanges between our two peoples have forged a
profound friendship; all this we should treasure. However, in
the half-century after 1894, owing to the Japanese militarists'
aggression against China, the Chinese people were made to
endure tremendous disasters and the Japanese people, too, suffered a great deal from it. The past not forgotten is a guide for
the future. We should firmly bear the experience and the lesson
in mind. Following Chairman Mao Tse-tung's teachings, the
Chinese people make a strict distinction between the very few
militarists and the broad masses of the Japanese people. Therefore, since the founding of the People's Republic of China,
although the state of war between the two countries has not
been declared terminated, friendly contacts and trade relations
between the Chinese and Japanese peoples have continuously
developed instead of being interrupted. In the past few years, the
number of Japanese friends visiting China each year exceeded
the number of friends from other countries and the volume
of China's trade with Japan based on equality and mutual
benefit surpassed that with other countries. This has created
favourable conditions for the normalisation of Sino-Japanese
relations.

At present, tremendous changes are taking place in the world

situation, After assuming office, Prime Minister Tanaka resolutely put forward a new policy towards China, stated that the
normalization of relations with the People's Republic of China
would be expedited and expressed full understanding of China's
three principles for the restoration of diplomatic relations and
has to this end, taken practical steps. Proceeding from its consistent stand, the Chinese Government has made positive response. There is already a good basis for the normalization of
relations between the two countries. It is the common desire
of the Chinese and Japanese peoples to promote Sino-Japanese
friendship and restore diplomatic relations between China and
Japan. Now is the time for us to accomplish this historic task.

Your Excellency Mr Prime Minister, before you left for
China, you had said that agreement can be reached in the
negotiations between the two countries and that agreement
must be reached. I am deeply convinced that, through the
efforts of our two sides, conducting full consultations and seeking common ground on major points while reserving differences
on minor points, the normalization of Sino-Japanese relations
can certainly be realized.

The social systems of China and Japan are different. However, this should not be an obstacle to our two countries living
together as equals and in friendship. The restoration of diplomatic relations between China and Japan and the establishment
of friendly and good-neighbourly relations on the basis of the
Five Principles of Peaceful Co-existence will open up broad
prospects for the further development of friendly contacts between our two peoples and the expansion of economic and cultural
exchanges between our two countries. Sino-Japanese friendship
is not exclusive; it will contribute to the relaxation of tension in
Asia and the safeguarding of world peace.

49. Premier Tanaka's speech at the banquet, 25 September 1972

I flew non-stop from Tokyo to Peking on this trip. It makes
me once again deeply aware that Japan and China are close
neighbours with only a strip of water in between. The two
countries are not only so close to each other geographically, but
have a history of 2,000 years of rich and varied ties.

However, it is regretful that for several decades in the past the relations between Japan and China had unfortunate experiences. During that time our country caused great trouble to the Chinese people for which I once again make profound self-examination. After World War II the relations between Japan and China remained in an abnormal and unnatural state. We cannot but frankly admit this historical fact.

But we should not for ever linger in the dim blind alley of the past. In my opinion, it is important now for the leaders of Japan and China to confer in the interest of tomorrow. That is to say, to conduct frank and sincere talks for the common goal of peace and prosperity in Asia and in the world as a whole. It is precisely for that goal that I have come here. We hope that we can establish friendly and good-neighbourly relations with great China and its people and that the two countries will on the one hand respect each other's relations with its friendly countries and on the other make contributions to peace and prosperity in Asia and in the world at large.

It goes without saying that Japan and China have different political convictions and social systems. Yet, I think, in spite of all this, it is possible for Japan and China to establish good-neighbourly and friendly relations and, on the basis of equality and mutual benefit, strengthen contacts, respect each other's stand and carry out co-operation.

The normalization of relations is absolutely necessary to the establishment of good-neighbourly and friendly relations between Japan and China on a solid basis. Of course, the two sides have their own basic positions and peculiar conditions. But despite the fact that some minor differences exist between the positions and views of the two sides, I believe it is possible for Japan and China to overcome their divergence of views and reach agreement in the spirit of seeking common ground on major questions and of mutual understanding and mutual accommodation. I am willing to accomplish this important task and take a new step forward along the road of long-standing Japan-China friendship.

50. Joint statement of the Governments of China and Japan, 29 September 1972

At the invitation of Premier Chou En-lai of the State Council of the People's Republic of China, Prime Minister Kakuei Tanaka of Japan visited the People's Republic of China from September 25 to 30, 1972. Accompanying Prime Minister Kakuei Tanaka were Foreign Minister Masayoshi Ohira, Chief Cabinet Secretary Susumu Nikaido and other government officials.

Chairman Mao Tse-tung met Prime Minister Kakuei Tanaka on September 27. The two sides had an earnest and friendly conversation.

Premier Chou En-lai and Foreign Minister Chi Peng-fei had an earnest and frank exchange of views with Prime Minister Kakuei Tanaka and Foreign Minister Masayoshi Ohira, all along in a friendly atmosphere, on various matters between the two countries and other matters of interest to both sides, with the normalization of relations between China and Japan as the focal point, and the two sides agreed to issue the following joint statement of the two Governments:

China and Japan are neighbouring countries separated only by a strip of water, and there was a long history of traditional friendship between them. The two peoples ardently wish to end the abnormal state of affairs that has hitherto existed between the two countries. The termination of the state of war and the normalization of relations between China and Japan—the realization of such wishes of the two peoples will open a new page in the annals of relations between the two countries.

The Japanese side is keenly aware of Japan's responsibility for causing enormous damages in the past to the Chinese people through war and deeply reproaches itself. The Japanese side reaffirms its position that in seeking to realise the normalisation of relations between Japan and China, it proceeds from the stand of fully understanding the three principles for the restoration of diplomatic relations put forward by the Government of the People's Republic of China. The Chinese side expresses its welcome for this.

Although the social systems of China and Japan are different, the two countries should and can establish peaceful and friendly relations. The normalization of relations and the development of good neighbourly and friendly relations between the two countries are in the interests of the two peoples, and will also contribute to the relaxation of tension in Asia and the safeguarding of world peace.

(1) The abnormal state of affairs which has hitherto existed between the People's Republic of China and Japan is declared terminated on the date of publication of this statement.

(2) The Government of Japan recognises the Government of the People's Republic of China as the sole legal government of China.

(3) The Government of the People's Republic of China reaffirms that Taiwan is an inalienable part of the territory of the People's Republic of China. The Government of Japan fully understands and respects this stand of the Government of China and adheres to its stand of complying with Article 8 of the Potsdam Proclamation.

(4) The Government of the People's Republic of China and the Government of Japan have decided upon the establishment of diplomatic relations as from September 29, 1972. The two Governments have decided to adopt all necessary measures for the establishment and the performance of functions of embassies in each other's capitals in accordance with international law and practice and exchange ambassadors as speedily as possible.

(5) The Government of the People's Republic of China declares that in the interest of the friendship between the peoples of China and Japan, it renounces its demand for war indemnities from Japan.

(6) The Government of the People's Republic of China and Government of Japan agree to establish durable relations of peace and friendship between the two countries on the basis of the principles of mutual respect for sovereignty and territorial integrity, mutual non-aggression, non-interference in each other's internal affairs, equality and mutual benefit and peaceful coexistence.

In keeping with the foregoing principles and the principles of the United Nations Charter, the Governments of the two countries affirm that in their mutual relations, all disputes shall be settled by peaceful means without resorting to the use or threat of force.

(7) The normalisation of relations between China and Japan is not directed against third countries. Neither of the two countries should seek hegemony in the Asia-Pacific region and each country is opposed to efforts by any other country or group of countries to establish such hegemony.

(8) To consolidate and develop the peaceful and friendly relations between the two countries, the Government of the People's Republic of China and the Government of Japan agreed to hold negotiations aimed at the conclusion of a treaty of peace and friendship.

(9) In order to further develop the relations between the two countries and broaden the exchange of visits, the Government of the People's Republic of China and the Government of Japan agree to hold negotiations aimed at the conclusion of agreements on trade, navigation, aviation, fishery, etc., in accordance with the needs and taking into consideration the existing non-governmental agreements.

51. Japanese Foreign Minister Ohira's Press conference in Beijing, 29 September 1972 (Extract)

The basic understanding and attitudes of the Japanese and Chinese sides towards the normalization of relations are made clear in the foreword of the joint statement. We believe that the termination of the abnormal state of affairs which had unfortunately long existed between Japan and China and the establishment of relations of peace and friendship between the two countries will be an important contribution to the relaxation of tension in Asia and the safeguarding of the world peace.

As is stated in Article 1, the abnormal state of affairs between Japan and China is declared terminated today. The concrete expression of this is the establishment of diplomatic relations between the two countries as from today. About this point, please refer to Article 4.

Next, about the indispensable prerequisite for the normalization of relations between Japan and China—recognition of the Government of the People's Republic of China, the view of the Japanese Government has been expressed in Article 2.

In addition, the stand of the Japanese Government on the Taiwan question has been stated in Article 3. The Cairo Declaration stipulates that Taiwan be restored to China and Japan has accepted the Potsdam Proclamation that succeeded the above-mentioned declaration. The proclamation stipulates in Article 8 that "the terms of the Cairo Declaration shall be carried out." Therefore, it is only natural for the Japanese Government

to adhere to its stand of complying with the Potsdam Proclamation.

Considering the outcome of the unfortunate war between
Japan and China in the past and the great losses the Chinese
people suffered, we should give frank and appropriate appraisal
of the renouncing by the People's Republic of China of its
demand for war indeminities as expressed in Article 5.

Normalization of relations is indeed of important significance, but even more important is that Japan and China with
different social systems respect each other's stand and have
established durable relations of peace and friendship between
them. The principles that such relations between Japan and
China should adhere to are included in Article 6, and the
reference in Article 8 to the conclusion of a treaty of peace
and friendship also reflects the forward-looking attitude of both
Governments.

The Japanese Government holds that as a result of the
normalization of Japan-China relations, the Japan-China
peace treatv [the Japan-Chiang treaty—Ed] has lost the meaning of its existence and is declared to be terminated, although
this question is not mentioned in the joint statement.

52. Statement by the Spokesman of the Foreign Ministry of China on Japan-South Korea agreement concerning joint development of the continental shelf, 4 February 1974

On January 30, 1974 the Japanese Government and the
south Korean authorities signed in Seoul a so-called agreement
concerning the joint development of the continental shelf. In
the agreement they unilaterally mark off a large area of the
continental shelf in the East China Sea as a so-called Japan-
south Korea "Joint Development Zone," in which petroleum
and natural gas will be exploited by their joint investment.

In this regard, the spokesman of the Ministry of Foreign
Affairs of the People's Republic of China is authorized to state
as follows: The Chinese Government holds that, according to
the principle that the continental shelf is the natural extension
of the continent it stands to reason that the question of how to
divide the continental shelf in the East China Sea should be
decided by China and the other countries concerned through

consultations. But now the Japanese Government and the south Korean authorities have marked off a so-called Japan-south Korea "Joint Development Zone" on the continental shelf in the East China Sea behind China's back. This act is an infringement on China's sovereignty, which the Chinese Government absolutely cannot accept. If the Japanese Government and the south Korean authorities arbitrarily carry out development activities in this area, they must bear full responsibility for all the consequences arising therefrom.

53. Statement by Foreign Minister Masayoshi Ohira on the signing of China-Japan Air Transport Agreement, 20 April 1974 (Extracts)

I hold that the opening of the air route between Japan and China according to the Japan-China air transport agreement is of no small international significance as it will establish another huge major route in the world aviation network.

Both the form and contents (of the Japan-China air transport agreement) are not different in substance from the aviation agreements Japan has signed with other countries.

It is well known, that together with the signing of this agreement, there is the handling of the problem of the Japan-Taiwan air route. The Japanese Government holds that it is important that the maintenance of the Japan-Taiwan air route should in no way be in contradiction with the new relations between Japan and China. . . .

With regard to the aviation relationship between Japan and Taiwan . . . the exchange of letters on aviation business which existed in the past has become null and void as a result of the normalization of diplomatic relations between Japan and China on September 29, 1972. The Japanese Government's policy is to maintain it through non-governmental agreement.

On this question the Japanese Government makes clear the following points as views which were expressed to the Government of the People's Republic of China.

The air transport agreement between Japan and the People's Republic of China is a governmental agreement and flights between Japan and Taiwan are non-governmental regional air traffic. On the basis of the joint statement of the

two governments, the Japanese Government since its publication
has not recognized the emblem on the Taiwan aircraft as a so-
called national flag, nor has it recognized the China Airlines
(Taiwan) as an air firm representing a state.

54. *Peking Review* **article on Moscow's stick-and-carrot tactics
towards Japan, 29 August 1975**

In their scramble for hegemony with US imperialism in Asia
and the Pacific, the Soviet social-imperialists adopt hard and
soft tactics, alternating military threats with economic blandish-
ments, in an attempt to bring Japan into the Soviet sphere of
influence.

While Brezhnev and company talk glibly about "Japan-
Soviet friendship" and "Japan-Soviet goodneighbourliness,"
which is pleasing to the ear, they make no mention of returning to Japan the Soviet-occupied territories. One reason is that
military bases established in Japan's northern territories are
important strongholds in Soviet contention for hegemony with
the United States and a dagger aimed at Japan.

The Japanese press has disclosed that many military installations have been set up on these islands. Soviet warships an-
chored in the Hitokappu Gulf and Soviet military aircraft taking
off from Tofutsu and Tennei Airports can reach Japan proper
in a matter of minutes. The Soviet social-imperialists need only
to make a slight move in order to land in Hokkaido.

Soviet warships frequently ply the waters of the Soya,
Tsugaru and Tsushima Straits and Soviet military aircraft con-
stantly patrol around Japan, posing a threat to the US Pacific
Fleet and directly menacing Japan's security.

According to the Japanese press, three to four hundred
Soviet warships have in recent years passed through the Soya,
Tsugaru and Tsushima Straits to cruise into the Pacific annually. The number is on the increase this year. Moreover, 11
formations of Soviet military planes flew near Japanese air
space between late June and early July. To guard against intru-
sions into Japanese air space by Soviet military planes, Japanese
planes have to make "urgent flights," sometimes as many as
over 20 sorties a day. The Japanese press apprehensively com-
mented, "The Japanese air space from Hokkaido to Okinawa

has been converted into a stage for Soviet reconnaissance planes to show their strength," and "the whole of Japan is put under the shadows of Soviet naval and air force might."

Japan, which is short of raw materials, has to bring in imports of major industrial materials including petroleum and send its exports overseas through the Pacific and the Indian Ocean. With the rivalry between the two superpowers growing in intensity Moscow has in recent years multiplied the number of Soviet warships in the Pacific and naval detachments in the Indian Ocean. *Asahi Shimbun* reported that Soviet naval vessels operating in the Indian Ocean have increased greatly in number and ship days. Moreover, the Soviet Union has set up "permanent buoys" as submarine bases at many places in the ocean.

The Soviet social-imperialists have tried to coerce and cajole Japan into taking part in an "Asian collective security system." The calculations of these men in the Kremlin are that once Japan come into the "system," it will submit to the Soviet Union and give up its northern territories. And once Japan bites the hook of this so-called "Asian security system," the Soviet Union will get the upper hand in its rivalry with the United States in Asia. Former Japanese Vice-Foreign Minister Shinsaku Hogen pointed out on July 26 that the Soviet Union would intensify its offensive against Japan and propose again the setting up of an "Asian security system" following the "European security conference" with the aim of maintaining the status quo of the northern territories.

Then there is the so-called "new plan for developing Siberia" recently dished up by the Soviet Union to lure Japan. This is a new Soviet trick following its failure to inveigle Japan into taking part in exploiting the Tyumen Oil field in Siberia.

An official of the Japanese Foreign Ministry pointed out: The so-called plan is a "stick-and-carrot" tactics peculiar to the Kremlin. Through such "economic co-operation" the Soviet Union is trying to perpetuate the bonds of Japan-Soviet relations to such a degree that eventually Japan will be shackled with the "Asian collective security system." This explains why the Soviet Union is so eager, even to the point of being obsessive, to force Japan to develop Siberia. An influential personage in Japan's economic circles warned that Japan should not put its neck into the noose.

55. *People's Daily* **commentary on the just struggle of the Japanese people for the return of the Northern Territories, 8 May 1977 (Extracts)**

The heated dispute during the Japanese-Soviet fishery talks focused on demarcation of waters off Japan's four northern islands, which in fact is a question of Japan's territorial sovereignty. It is known to all that the northern islands are territories inherent to Japan. Their reversion is the common desire of the Japanese nation for which the Japanese people have been waging an unremitting struggle. . . .

The Soviet Union occupies Japan's northern territories because of the need of its counter-revolutionary strategy for world hegemony. . . . It is turning many islands, including Japan's four northern islands, into an important part of its network of Pacific military bases. This is why the Soviet Union has been firmly holding on to Japan's northern territories.

Soviet truculence has taught the Japanese people by negative example to see clearly the reactionary nature of Soviet social-imperialism. They have come to understand more and more distinctly that Soviet hegemonism jeopardizes the national interest and security of Japan with increasing gravity. From its behaviour, they saw how this superpower threw its weight around and bullied others to the extent of unscrupulously trampling underfoot the principles of international law and showing no respect for international faith. Its professed "true neighbourly relations between the Soviet Union and Japan" and "friendship and cooperation" are sheer lies. The Japanese people are taking action to combat the hegemonic acts of this superpower. People of various circles have urged the government to stand up firmly to the Soviet diplomacy of intimidation and never to give up permanent rights for the sake of immediate interests. In Japan, both the ruling and opposition parties are unanimous in opposing superpower hegemonism. A broader and deeper struggle for the return of the northern territories and against Soviet hegemonism is sure to rise tempestuously.

56. **Statement of the Chinese Foreign Ministry on the ratification of the Japan South Korea Agreement on the joint development of the continental shelf by the Japanese Diet, 13 June 1977 (Extracts)**

According to the principle that the continental shelf is the natural extension of the continental territory, the People's Republic of China has inviolable sovereignty over the East China Sea continental shelf. Recently the Japanese Government, in disregard of the firm opposition of the Chinese Government, forced through by extension of the Diet session and consequent "automatic approval" the so-called Japan-south Korea "agreement on joint development of the continental shelf" which unilaterally marks off a "joint development zone" on the East China Sea continental shelf. The Chinese Government seriously protests this action on the part of the Japanese Government which flagrantly infringes on China's sovereignty. . . .

Recently, during the Diet discussion of the "agreement" submitted by the Japanese Government, the Chinese Government again solemnly pointed out to the Japanese Government that the "agreement" infringed on China's sovereignty and that if the Japanese Government ignored the position of the Chinese Government and insisted on having the Diet ratify it at the current session, this would be harmful to the development of Sino-Japanese relations. The Chinese Government firmly objected to this and expressed the hope that the Japanese side would set store by Sino-Japanese friendly relations and give serious consideration to the position of the Chinese Government. Yet, now the Japanese Government, ignoring the Chinese Government's repeatedly stated position and disregarding China's sovereignty and the interests of the development of Sino-Japanese relations, willfully put the "agreement" into effect and deliberately took this act infringing on China's sovereignty. The Chinese Government deems it necessary to point out again that the Japanese Government must bear full responsibility for all the consequences arising therefrom.

The Ministry of Foreign Affairs of the People's Republic of China is authorized to state as follows: The East China Sea continental shelf is the natural extension of the Chinese continental territory. The People's Republic of China has inviolable sovereignty over the East China Sea continental shelf. It stands to reason that the question of how to divide those parts of the East China Sea continental shelf which involve other countries should be decided by China and the countries through consultations. The so-called Japan-south Korea "agreement on joint development of the continental shelf" signed by the Japanese Government, with the south Korean authorities unilaterally behind China's back is entirely illegal and null and void. Without the consent of the Chinese Government, no country or private person may undertake development activities on the East China Sea continental shelf. Whoever does so must bear full responsibility for all the consequences arising therefrom.

57. "Chairman Mao's Theory of the Differentiation of the Three Worlds is a Major Contribution to Marxism-Leninism," article by Editorial Department of *People's Daily*, 1 November 1977 (Extract)

In the Far East, Japan is also faced with a serious threat. The massive Soviet military build-up in the Far East aimed at China as it is, is directed primarily against the United States and Japan. The Soviet Union has forcibly occupied Japan's northern territorial seas, and it is posing a growing threat to Japan and intensifying its infiltration of the latter. This has aroused strong indignation and resistance on the part of all Japanese patriotic forces.

58. China-Japan Long-Term Trade Agreement, 16 February 1978

In accordance with the spirit of the Joint Statement issued by and the Trade Agreement reached between the governments of both Japan and China the Japan-China Long-Term Trade Consultation Committee of Japan and the China-Japan Long-Term Trade Consultation Committee of China have consulted in a friendly manner in order to develop economic and trade relations between the two countries over a long period of time and in a stable manner, and with the backing of the respective governments, conclude, as a part of the trade between Japan and China, a long-term trade agreement wherein technology and industrial plants, as well as construction materials, machinery and equipment will be exported from

Japan to China, while crude oil and coal will be exported from China to Japan, as follows:

Article 1. The term of validity for this Agreement shall be eight years from 1978 to 1985. The total value of exports by both parties during the term of validity for this Agreement shall be about U.S. $10 billion respectively.

Article 2. The value of technology and industrial plants to be exported from Japan to China from the first year (1978) of this Agreement to the fifth year (1982) thereof shall be about U.S. $7-8 billion and that of construction materials, machinery and equipment, about U.S. $2-3 billion.

Both parties agree that the contract value to be agreed upon each year constitutes the final value.

Commodities and quantities thereof to be exported from China to Japan from the first year (1978) of this Agreement to the fifth year (1982) thereof are as follows:

Year	Unit	Crude Oil	Coking Coal	Ordinary Coal
1978	10,000 tons	700	15—30	15—20
1979	10,000 tons	760	50	15—20
1980	10,000 tons	800	100	50—60
1981	10,000 tons	950	150	100—120
1982	10,000 tons	1,500	200	150 170

Both parties agree to consult each other on and finalize in 1981 commodities and quantities thereof to be exported from China to Japan from the sixth year (1983) of this Agreement to the eighth year (1985) thereof. Quantities of crude oil and coal to be exported from China to Japan in the last three years of this Agreement shall increase year after year based on the quantities for the fifth year of this Agreement.

Article 3. Both parties agree in principle that technology and industrial plants, as well as construction materials, machinery and equipment shall be exported from Japan to China on a deferred payment formula,

Article 4. Transactions based on this Agreement shall be conducted in accordance with individual contracts to be concluded between the Japanese parties concerned and the Export & Import Corporations concerned, of China.

Both parties agree that transactions shall be conducted on the basis of reasonable international prices and international trade practices.

Article 5. Both parties agree to extend technological cooperation to each other in necessary fields of scientific technology for the purpose of implementing this Agreement and expanding economic exchanges between Japan and China.

Article 6. Both parties agree to designate one authorized foreign exchange bank respectively and to place it in charge of the statistical compilation necessary in order to grasp the progress of settlements of transactions based on this Agreement.

The banks designated are the Bank of Tokyo for Japan and the Bank of China for China.

Both banks shall take necessary measures for compiling statistics and shall consult with each other on these measures.

Article 7. Written contracts for transactions, letters of credit, bills of exchange and letters of guarantee based on this Agreement shall carry the following designations LT-1 for the first year, LT-2 for the second year, and so forth.

Article 8. Both parties shall respectively establish a secretariat, which handles liaison and relevant business matters in order to implement this Agreement.

The Japanese side shall establish in Tokyo the Secretariat of the Japan-China Long-Term Trade Consultation Committee of Japan and the Chinese side shall establish in Peking the Secretariat of the China-Japan Long-Term Trade Consultation Committee of China.

Article 9. Both parties agree that their respective representatives shall hold a conference alternatively in Tokyo and Peking each year in order to deliberate on the implementation of and problems related to this Agreement.

Article 10. This Agreement shall not be annuled unless by mutual consent.

Contracts concluded based on this Agreement shall not be annuled unless by mutual consent of both parties concerned.

Article 11. This Agreement shall be valid on and after the date of signing until December 31, 1985.

This Agreement may be modified by mutual consent upon consultation.

Article 12. This Agreement was signed on the 16th day of February, 1978, in Peking. The written Agreement has been made out in duplicate in Japanese and Chinese, and both parties shall retain one copy each.

59. Hua Guofeng's Report on the Work of the Government to the First Session of the Fifth National People's Congress, 26 February 1978 (Extract)

China and Japan are close neighbours separated only by a strip of water, and the friendship between their two peoples goes back to ancient times. Since the normalization of relations, contacts and exchanges have been growing in many fields and a long-term trade agreement was recently signed. It is in the fundamental interests of the people of China and Japan to conclude at an early date a treaty of peace and friendship based on the joint statement of the two governments. We firmly support the Japanese people in their just struggle to recover their four northern islands. The people of China and Japan should live in friendship for countless generations.

60. "Motive behind the Draft Soviet-Japan Good Neighbourliness and Co-operation Treaty," *Peking Review* commentary, 17 March 1978 (Extracts)

The Kremlin unilaterally and suddenly made public in *Izvestia* on February 23 the draft of the "Soviet-Japan good neighbourliness and co-operation treaty" without consulting Japan. Such an act of power politics is indeed a rare occurrence in the annals of international relations. It reflects Soviet impetuosity in its contention with the United States over Japan.

The draft treaty was aimed in the first place at legalizing Soviet occupation of Japan's northern territories. The text makes no mention of the pending territorial issue between the two countries in a vain attempt to fix by treaty the proposition that "the territorial issue has been solved" between the Soviet Union and Japan—a proposition which the Kremlin has been obstinately pursuing for many years. . . .

Proceeding from its policy of aggression and expansion as well as its strategic need in its contention with the United States for hegemony, the Soviet Union has kept a firm grip on Japan's northern territories. Strategically the four northern islands are very important. In World War II, Japan attacked Pearl Harbour, a U.S. naval and air base in the Pacific, from its stronghold in the Kitokappu Gulf of Etorofu Island. Today, the Soviet Union has not only turned the Kitokappu Gulf into a naval base but has established military bases and installations on all the four islands for providing protection to vessels of the Soviet Pacific Fleet passing through the Soya and Tsugaru Straits into the Pacific. According to the Japanese press, in the Sea of Okhotsk the Kremlin has set up military bases for submarine-launched long-range guided missiles with multiple warheads. Japan's four northern islands and all of the Chishima Islands form a natural screen for this sea area. . . .

In trying to impose such a treaty on Japan, the Soviet Union does not limit itself to occupying these Japanese islands. The contents of the draft treaty reveal that Moscow contemplates bringing the whole of Japan under its control. Suffice it to compare a few articles of the "Japanese-U.S. treaty of mutual cooperation and security" (1960) and the Soviet-proposed treaty:

Article 6 of the Japanese-U.S. "security" treaty stipulates that "the United States of America is granted the use by its land, air and naval forces of facilities and areas in Japan"; while article 3 of the Soviet-proposed treaty states that "the Union of Soviet Socialist Republics and Japan undertake not to allow the use of their territories for any actions, which could prejudice the security of the other party." These two articles are obviously conflicting. If the Soviet-proposed treaty is signed it will undermine the Japanese-U.S. "security" treaty.

Another instance is that the Japanese-U.S. "security" treaty provides for the forming of a military alliance between the two countries. Article 4 stipulates that "the parties will consult together from time to time regarding the implementation of this treaty and at the request of either party, whenever the security of Japan or international peace and security in the Far East is threatened," while article 5 of the Soviet-proposed treaty says that "should a situation arise, which in the opinion of both sides is dangerous for maintaining peace. or if peace is violated, the two sides shall immediately contact each other with the aim of exchanging views on the question of what can be done for improving the situation." It is not difficult to see that in proposing such a treaty the Soviet Union aims not only at weakening the Japanese-U.S. ''security'' treaty but at disintegrating or replacing the Japanese-U.S. military alliance by a Soviet-Japanese military alliance so as to put Japan in the orbit of Soviet strategy for world domination.

Article 12 of the draft "Soviet-Japan good neighbourliness and co-operation treaty" provides that the Soviet Union and Japan "do not claim and do not recognize anyone's claims to any special rights or advantages in world affairs, including claims to domination in Asia and in the area of the Far East." It is quite clear that in the world today only the United States is in a position to contend with the Soviet Union for "special rights" and "advantages" in world affairs including claims to so-called "domination" in Asia and in the area of the Far East. While only revealing its dishonesty in disowning its "claims," the Soviet Union is in reality refusing to recognize the "special rights" and "advantages" of and "domination" by the United States. Moscow is trying to utilize this stipulation to edge out and replace U.S. influence. The Japanese press noted that this is intended to drag Japan into the Soviet-proposed "Asian security system."

The Soviet scheme to perpetuate the occupation of Japan's four northern islands and to replace the Japan-U.S. military alliance has torn to shreds the veil of "good neighbourliness and co-operation." Having obtained certain hardwon improvements in its relations with the United States, Japan will not allow itself to be ordered about by the Soviet Union through the "Soviet-Japan good-neighbourliness and co-operation treaty." The fact that the Soviet-proposed draft treaty met with strong opposition from both the ruling and opposition parties as soon as it was trotted out reflects the true feelings of the Japanese people.

61. Chinese Foreign Ministry statement protesting against exchange of instruments of ratification of Japan-South Korea agreement on joint development of the continental shelf, 26 June 1978 (Extract)

The unilateral marking off of a so-called Japan-ROK "joint development zone" on the continental shelf in the East China Sea by the Japanese Government and the south Korean authorities through signing behind China's back the "Japan-ROK Agreement on Joint Development of the Continental Shelf" is an infringement on China's sovereignty to which China will never agree. The Chinese Government has also repeatedly expressed its hope that the Japanese Government would set store by the friendly relations between China and Japan and not act arbitrarily and do such harmful things to the development of the relations between the two countries. The Japanese Government has now, in utter disregard of the solemn position repeatedly stated by the Chinese Government, exchanged with the south Korean authorities instruments of ratification of the so-called "Japan-ROK Agreement on Joint Development of the Continental Shelf." This obdurate act of infringement on China's sovereignty is what the Chinese Government cannot tolerate. In this connection, the Chinese Government solemnly reiterates that the so-called "Japan-ROK Agreement on Joint Development of the Continental Shelf" is entirely illegal and null and void and that should any country or private person undertake development activities in the so-called "joint development zone" marked off by the "agreement," it or he must bear full responsibility for all the consequences arising therefrom.

62. Treaty of Peace and Friendship between the People's Republic of China and Japan, 12 August 1978

The People's Republic of China and Japan,
    Recalling with satisfaction that since the Government of the People's Republic of China and the Government of Japan issued a Joint Statement in Peking on September 29, 1972, the friendly relations between the two Governments and the peoples of the

two countries have developed greatly on a new basis,

Confirming that the above-mentioned Joint Statement constitutes the basis of the relations of peace and friendship bet-
two countries and that the principles enunciated in the Joint
Statement should be strictly observed,

Confirming that the principles of the Charter of the United
Nations should be fully respected,

Hoping to contribute to peace and stability in Asia and in
the world,

For the purpose of solidifying and developing the relations
of peace and friendship between the two countries,

Have resolved to conclude a Treaty of Peace and Friendship
and for that purpose have appointed as their Plenipotentiaries:

The People's Republic of China: Huang Hua, Minister of
Foreign Affairs

Japan: Sunao Sonoda, Minister for Foreign Affairs

Who, having communicated to each other their full powers,
found to be in good and due form, have agreed as follows:

Article I

1. The Contracting Parties shall develop durable relation of
peace and friendship between the two countries on the basis of
the principles of mutual respect for sovereignty and territorial
integrity, mutual non-aggression, non-interference in each
other's internal affairs, equality and mutual benefit and peaceful
coexistence.

2. In keeping with the foregoing principles and the principles of the United Nations Charter, the Contracting Parties
affirm that in their mutual relations, all disputes shall be settled
by peaceful means without resorting to the use or threat of
force.

Article II

The Contracting Parties declare that neither of them should
seek hegemony in the Asia-Pacific region or in any other region
and that each is opposed to efforts by any other country or
group of countries to establish such hegemony.

Article III

The Contracting Parties shall, in a goodneighbourly and
friendly spirit and in conformity with the principles of equality
and mutual benefit and non-interference in each other's internal
affairs, endeavour to further develop economic and cultural

relations between the two countries and to promote exchanges between the peoples of the two countries.

Article IV

The present Treaty shall not affect the position of either Contracting Party regarding its relations with third countries.

Article V

1. The present Treaty shall be ratified and shall enter into force on the date of the exchange of instruments of ratification which shall take place at Tokyo. The present Treaty shall remain in force for ten years and thereafter shall continue to be in force until terminated in accordance with the provisions of Paragraph 2 of this Article.

2. Either Contracting Party may, by giving one year's written notice to the other Contracting Party, terminate the present Treaty at the end of the initial ten-year period or at any time thereafter.

In witness whereof the respective Plenipotentiaries have signed the present Treaty and have affixed thereto their seals.

Done in duplicate in the Chinese and Japanese languages, both texts being equally authentic, at Peking this twelfth day of August 1978.

63. Chinese Foreign Minister Huang Hua's statement on the signing of the China-Japan Treaty of Peace and Friendship, 12 August 1978 (Extracts)

The conclusion of the China-Japan Peace and Friendship Treaty is a political summing-up of relations between China and Japan, and demonstrates that the good neighbourly relations between the two countries have achieved a new starting point. It is of important and practical significance and of far-reaching historical importance. The conclusion of the treaty will further consolidate and develop peaceful and friendly relations between the two countries. This not only conforms to the common aspirations and fundamental interests of the two peoples, but will also help to improve the situation in the Asia-Pacific region and to defend world peace. We are confident that the treaty will be supported not only by the peoples of China and Japan but will also be welcomed by all the Asian people and by other countries throughout the world who are bullied and undermined by hegemony. . . .

Though China and Japan have different social systems, we express our belief that so long as both sides abide by the various principles of the treaty, the peaceful and friendly relations of cooperation between China and Japan will certainly expand and develop. The peoples of China and Japan will surely live in friendship for generations to come.

64. Japanese Foreign Minister Sonao Sonoda's statement after the signing of the Japan-China Peace Treaty, 12 August 1978 (Extracts)

Article 2, like paragraph 7 of the Japan-China Joint Communique, provides that neither Japan nor China should seek hegemony and that each is opposed to efforts by any other country or group of countries to establish such hegemony. This article goes one step beyond paragraph 7 of the Joint Communique in that the area of application is not restricted to 'the Asia-Pacific Region' having especially close relations with Japan and China but is broadened to 'any other region' as well. The treaty's statement is that each is opposed to efforts by any other country or group of countries to establish hegemony, and this is clearly not directed against any specific country. . . .

Article 4 stipulates that the treaty shall not affect the position of either contracting party regarding its relations with third countries. This provision is the logical converse of the treaty's having as its purpose in the preamble solidifying and developing the relations of peace and friendship between the two countries. For Japan, this means that the basic position of Japanese foreign policy based upon the Japan-U.S. relationship and seeking to maintain and develop friendly relations with all nations regardless of their social systems will be secured for posterity by this article. . . .

Concerning the treaty of friendship, alliance and mutual assistance between the Union of Soviet Socialist Republics and the People's Republic of China, the views which had been unofficially expressed by the Chinese leaders were confirmed as the official position of the Chinese Government. It is my strong impression from my meetings with Chinese leaders that the Government of China will take necessary measures to terminate this Sino-Soviet treaty in April of next year.

Concerning the question of the Senkaku Islands, I explained the position of the Japanese Government in my talks with Vice-Premier Teng Hsiao-ping on the afternoon of August 10. In response, the Chinese side stated that as for the Chinese Government there should be no recurrence of incidents such as the earlier one.

65. Japanese Prime Minister Takeo Fukuda's statement on the Japan-China Peace Treaty, 12 August 1978 (Extract)

Since the Joint Communique between Japan and China was issued in September 1972, Japan-China relations have developed smoothly. Meanwhile, governmental working agreements in the fields of trade, aviation, shipping, fisheries, etc., were concluded, as was the more recent private long-term trade agreement between the two countries.

The Japan-China Treaty of Peace and Friendship, which was signed today, aims at placing these Japan-China relations which have so developed on a more stable basis and promises their further extensive development.

It is the basic position of Japan not to allow hostile relations to develop with any country and to seek peaceful and friendly relations with all nations. This treaty has been concluded fully maintaining this basic position, as is clear from its provisions. I firmly believe that this treaty will win the full congratulations of the nation. I hope this treaty will serve not only to strengthen and develop the peaceful and amicable relations between our two countries for a long time to come but also to contribute to the peace and stability of Asia and the world.

66. Premier Fukuda's speech in the Diet, 20 September 1978 (Extract)

The treaty of peace and friendship between Japan and the People's Republic of China was signed in Peking on August 12. Relations between Japan and China have undergone many vicissitudes in the course of history, and I consider it to be of profound significance that a solid foundation has now been laid for the relationship of long-lasting friendship and goodwill between the two countries based on the spirit of reciprocity and equality.

It is indeed a matter for congratulations that Japan and China have achieved an outcome satisfactory to both sides, in pursuit of our lofty ideals. I wish to rejoice together with all the people of Japan. With the conclusion of this treaty, the Government is resolved to exert its utmost efforts not only for placing Japan-China relations on a more stable foundation and thus strengthen the relationship between the two countries for many years to come, but also contributing to the peace and stability of Asia and thus of the world.

67. Premier Fukuda's speech on the occasion of the exchange of instruments of ratification of China-Japan Treaty of Peace and Friendship, 23 October 1978 (Extracts)

The normalization of diplomatic relations between Japan and China in 1972 has opened a new page in the history of continual close contacts and frequent exchanges between the two countries for the past two thousand years. The conclusion of the Treaty of Peace and Friendship has added an even brighter new page to the annals of Japan-China relations. It not only has far-reaching significance in strengthening and developing the relations of peace and friendship between Japan and China, but also has reflected the common aspirations of the two countries to contribute to peace and stability in Asia and in the world as stated in the treaty. . . .

I sincerely hope that the Governments and peoples of Japan and China, respecting the spirit of the treaty, will faithfully abide by all its articles so as to demonstrate once again our determination to strive for consolidating and developing the eternal relations of peace and friendship between our two countries.

As a result of the conclusion of the Japan-China Peace and Friendship Treaty today, I believe that all of you join me in looking forward to a rapid growth in the relations which have been developing smoothly between our two countries.

The relations of exchanges between our two countries have never been interrupted in our long histories. However, it is regrettable that our relations were beset by miseries in this century. Such a situation will never be allowed to recur. The Peace and Friendship Treaty between Japan and China is a mutual pledge for this purpose.

It is of great importance for leaders of the two countries to exchange views so as to develop friendly relations and contribute to peace and stability in the world in the spirit of the Japan-China Peace and Friendship Treaty.

68. Vice Premier Deng Xiaoping's statement at a dinner given in his honour by Prime Minister Fukuda, 23 October 1978 (Extract)

The conclusion of the treaty is a great event in our relations since their normalization. It is of immediate importance and far-reaching historical significance. It is a political summing-up of the hitherto Sino-Japanese relations as well as an important milestone marking a new starting point in the development of our good-neighbourly and friendly relations.

The treaty explicitly stipulates that neither China nor Japan should seek hegemony and that each is opposed to efforts by any other country or group of countries to establish such hegemony. This is the first time that such a stipulation is included in an international treaty. This stipulation is first of all a pledge of self-restraint on the part of China and Japan, which undertake not to seek hegemony. At the same time it is a heavy blow to hegemonism which is today the main threat to international security and world peace.

The conclusion of the treaty is heartily supported by the Chinese and Japanese peoples and well received by all the peace-loving countries and peoples of the world.

Our Treaty of Peace and Friendship is a continuation and development of our Joint Statement of 1972 and the normalization of our diplomatic relations. It has further consolidated the foundation of our good-neighbourly and friendly relations and opened up broader vistas for the increase of our exchanges in the fields of politics, economy, culture, science and technology. It will also exercise a positive influence for the maintenance of peace and security in the Asian-Pacific region.

Friendship and solidarity between the Chinese and Japanese peoples and harmony and cooperation between China and Japan are the common desires of the one billion Chinese and

Japanese peoples and represent a forward historical trend. Together with the Japanese Government, the Chinese Government
will steadfastly abide by and carry out all the provisions of the
treaty. Let us work together so that the Chinese and Japanese
peoples may live in friendship from generation to generation,
so that Sino-Japanese relations may have an even brighter
future and so that peace may prevail in Asia and the whole
world.

69. Vice-Premier Deng Xiaoping's Press conference in Tokyo, 25 October 1978 (Extracts)

The Vice-Premier expressed the hope that China and Japan will
strengthen their unity and mutual co-operation, implement and
uphold the principles of their Treaty of Peace and Friendship
and work tirelessly for the peace and stability of the Asian-
Pacific region.

He pointed out that the treaty was a major achievement of
the two Governments and peoples which was concluded by joint
efforts and by surmounting obstacles. It has further consolidated
the foundation of goodneighbourly and friendly relations between China and Japan and opened broader vistas for friendly
exchanges in the political, economic, cultural, scientific and
technological fields. . . .

Both China and Japan face the real threat of hegemonism.
The definite establishment of the anti-hegemony principle in
the China-Japan Treaty of Peace and Friendship is of great
significance in the present international situation. . . .

Answering a Japanese reporter's question, Vice-Premier
Teng stated that hegemonism was the basic cause of international insecurity and instability. He stressed that "anti-hegemonism is the nucleus of the China-Japan Treaty of Peace and
Friendship." . . .

We want to live on friendly terms with all countries. Unfortunately, there are some seeking hegemony in every part of the
world. This hegemonism is the root cause of insecurity and instability in the world, . . .

Vice-Premier Teng stated that he anticipated a substantial
growth in Sino-Japanese economic co-operation now that the
Treaty of Peace and Friendship had been implemented. He also

expected increased political, cultural, scientific and other civil and governmental exchanges between the two countries. . . .

"We have signed a long-term trade agreement between the two countries. But just one such agreement is not enough. The total business turnover involved in this agreement is 20 billion U.S. dollars. It will be doubled or trebled. The road will be even broader when our country is developed." . . .

"We have much to learn from Japan. There are many fields in which we can make use of Japanese scientific and technological achievements and even funds." . . .

"It is only natural that with the conclusion and implementation of the China-Japan Peace and Friendship Treaty, co-operation between the two peoples will be strengthened. Co-operation between the two countries in political, economic, cultural and scientific fields will all be increased. The exchanges between the two peoples including the dispatch of students and mutual visits of civilians will also grow. Meanwhile, governmental contacts will be increased. Of course, there is no need to have a fixed formula. In this respect, we shared the same view as Prime Minister Fukuda during our talks." . . .

Up to now China had not considered obtaining loans from the Japanese Government. "We will study this problem in the future," he said. . . .

Teng stated that it was wise for the Governments of China and Japan to put aside the question of Tiaoyu [Senkaku] Island. . . .

"Some people seek to pick faults on this kind of question in an attempt to hinder the development of Sino-Japanese relations." . . .

"It doesn't matter if this question is shelved for some time, say, ten years. Our generation is not wise enough to find common languages on this question. Our next generation will certainly be wiser. They will surely find a solution acceptable to all." . . .

Answering the question posed by a Japanese reporter that Korea and Viet Nam were the present centre of tension in Asia today, Vice-Premier Teng said: "We see no sign of tensions in Korea." As for Viet Nam, Vice-Premier Teng said: "People call Viet Nam the Cuba of the East. I agree with this view." . . .

"I frankly told Prime Minister Fukuda that as far as we know, there is no question of actions being taken by the north-

ern part of Korea. If south Korea does not take action, there
will be no tension. The question there is to create conditions
for north-south dialogue. That is, as President Kim Il Sung put
it, to negotiate peacefully and independently the question of
reunification between them." He pointed out: The United
States must withdraw its armed forces from south Korea. . . .

70. Vice-Chairman Liao Cheng-chih's report to the Standing Committee of the National People's Congress on Deng Xiaoping's visit to Japan, 4 November 1978 (Extracts)

The visit and the coming into force of the treaty opened
broader prospects for furthering friendship between China and
Japan and expanding exchanges and cooperation between them
in the political, economic, cultural, scientific and technical
areas. It would also favour the maintenance of peace and stability in the Asian and Pacific region and throughout the world.

It is a fact that the Japanese people everywhere feel close
and friendly to China. "Sino-Japanese friendship has become
an irresistible trend."

"During his visit, Vice-Premier Teng had wide contacts with
various circles, visiting old friends and making new ones, doing
a great amount of work, augmenting the treaty's effect in Japan
and the world over. This visit has furthered the friendship between the people of the two countries and promoted good neighbourliness and friendly cooperation between them. It also aided
the growth of the international united front against hegemony
and dealt a heavy blow at Soviet social-imperialism's attempt to
drive a wedge between China and Japan and isolate China. World
opinions generally hold that this is another major setback for
the Soviet Union, coming after Chairman Hua's visit to Romania,
Yugoslavia and Iran.

Vice-Premier Teng and Prime Minister Takeo Fukuda held
two talks on the international situation, bilateral relations and
questions of common concern. They exchanged views in a friendly and candid atmosphere, enhanced their mutual understanding
and broadened the area of common views.

Prime Minister Takeo Fukuda said that Japan would work
to establish enduring ties of good-neighbourly friendship with
China, in fact as in name. Japan would co-operate with China

in all fields except the military. He held that China's four modernizations were beneficial to prosperity and stability in Asia and the world over. . . .

Vice-Premier Teng stressed the significance of the signing of the China-Japan Treaty and of developing Sino-Japanese relations, pointing out that both China and Japan need Sino-Japanese friendship. "Vice-Premier Teng also took the initiative in proposing that the question of Tiaoyu Island be put aside pending a future solution and that the two countries should take the interests of the over-all situation into consideration. Our generation is not wise enough to find a solution. Our next generation will be wiser and will solve it satisfactorily."

Prime Minister Fukuda maintained that Japan was under a threat. He went on to stress that Japan's omni-directional, peaceful foreign policy was not equi-distant diplomacy. Japan wanted to be friendly with all countries but this was not a guarantee that other countries would not adopt a mistaken policy and invade Japan. Therefore, Prime Minister Fukuda pointed out, Japan must have sufficient self-defence strength to fight back and in the present circumstances, must rely on the Japan-U.S. Joint Security System.

"Vice-Premier Teng briefly expounded China's views on the general international situation, pointing out that a war is unavoidable and the danger of war mainly comes from the hegemonist policy of the Soviet Union. We desire peace. But if we want to postpone the war, we must heighten our vigilance and upset the strategic plans of the war launchers, and not practise appeasement."

Vice-Premier Teng also said: The Japanese government has set omni-directional foreign affairs as state policy. My understanding is that Japan will be friendly to all countries and this is beyond reproach. In this sense, China's foreign affairs are also omni-directional. But we add one point: We oppose anyone that practises hegemonism. Vice-Premier Teng said: We paid great attention to Prime Minister Takeo Fukuda's remark "Omni-directional foreign policy is not equi-distant foreign policy." China and Japan are in different positions and our views cannot be unanimous. Even where views are unanimous, the ways and the formulations may be different due to the

different situations. Vice-Premier Teng also said that some
people did not understand why China had formerly opposed the
Japanese-U.S. Security Pact but now found it possible to understand the relations between Japan and the United States. Likewise, why China opposed the revival of Japanese militarism
but now appreciates the fact that Japan has its own self-defence
forces. Viewing this in terms of global strategy, this helps to
postpone war, extending the period of peace. From this viewpoint, it is easy to understand.

On the Korean question, Vice-Premier Teng expressed
China's consistent stand of supporting President Kim Il Sung's
policy on independent and peaceful reunification of Korea,
which brooks no interference. The reunification of Korea is the
general and irresistible trend. The main thing to pave the way
for the independent and peaceful reunification of Korea is to
withdraw the U.S. troops from south Korea.

71. Deng Xiaoping's speech at the banquet given in his honour by Prime Minister Masayoshi Ohira in Tokyo, 7 February 1979 (Extracts)

Last October, I paid an official friendly visit to your country
and spent an unforgettable week here. We jointly accomplished
a historic mission—the exchange of the Instruments of Ratification of the China-Japan Peace and Friendship Treaty, and
solemnly declared the coming into force of this treaty. This
treaty has not only been warmly welcomed by the Chinese and
Japanese people, but also earned wide-spread support and
acclaim from various countries and peoples in the world. The
new year began with the establishment of diplomatic relations
between China and the United States. As Your Excellency Prime
Minister Masayoshi Ohira has stated, this series of diplomatic
activities will be a great contribution to peace and stability in
the Asian-Pacific region as well as in the rest of the world.

Today, we have had sincere and friendly talks with your
Excellencies, the Prime Minister and the Foreign Minister, and
there has been an exchange of views on the current situation
and on a number of questions of common concern. We feel
exceptionally happy at the reunion of old friends. The talks
have deepened our mutual understanding and trust. I am firmly

convinced that a frequent exchange of views between leaders
of our two countries is very beneficial. There is a solid foundation for the relations between China and Japan. The relations
of friendship and cooperation between our two countries will
surely develop enormously on the basis of the China-Japan
Peace and Friendship Treaty.

72. Statement by Foreign Minister Sonoda on China-Vietnam conflict, 18 February 1979

The Government of Japan expresses its deep regret over the
recent development along the Chinese and Vietnamese border.
The Japanese Government had repeatedly appealed to the
Governments of both China and Viet Nam to settle the problems by peaceful means. It had expressed deep concern that
continuing tension might escalate to a major military conflict.
However, the Japanese Government still retains a strong hope
that China and Viet Nam will come to settle their problems in
a peaceful way and that peace in Indo-China can be restored
as soon as possible.

73. Statement by Japanese representative Abe in the UN Security Council on China-Vietnam conflict, 25 February 1979 (Extract)

In our pursuit of restoring peace in the whole area of Indo-
China, we have asked the Government of Viet Nam to contribute to a peaceful settlement through an immediate cessation
of hostilities and the withdrawal of all its forces from Kampuchean territory. We have asked the Government of China to
contribute to a peaceful settlement through an immediate cessation of hostilities and the withdrawal of all its forces from
Vietnamese territory. We have asked the Government of the
Soviet Union to exercise caution and restraint for the sake of
peace and stability in Asia. In this connexion I should like to
add that my Government fully supports the statement made on
20 February 1979 by the Chairman of the Standing Committee
of the Association of South East Asian Nations (ASEAN)
appealing to all the parties in conflict in Indo-China immediately to cease all hostilities and to withdraw all foreign forces.

I should like to take this opportunity to appeal to all the
countries concerned to pay heed to the following two points,

and to express the fervent wish of my Government that these points will as the minimum requirement be incorporated in whatever type of action the Council may eventually decide to take.

First, all parties to the conflicts should immediately cease all hostilities; all foreign forces should be withdrawn from all the areas of conflict in Indo-China; and all parties concerned should immediately initiate talks to settle their conflicts peacefully, in accordance with the fundamental principles of the Charter of the United Nations, particularly those of non-interference in the internal affairs of another country and non-use of force. Secondly, all countries outside Indo-China, especially the big Powers, should exercise the utmost caution and restraint so that the conflicts will not be escalated and become a threat to the peace of the entire world.

I should like to add that my Government whole-heartedly welcomes the timely offer of good offices for a peaceful solution made by the Secretary-General on 22 February 1979. We hope that the parties involved will seriously consider the possibility of making use of his offer.

74. Statement by Japanese representative Abe in the Security Council on China-Vietnam conflict, 16 March 1979 (Extracts)

When I spoke in this Council on 25 February in order to voice the view of my Government on this issue, which is vitally important to the maintenance of international peace and security, I expressed the fervent wish of my Government that the following points would be incorporated in whatever form of action the Council might eventually decide to take. . . .

On the basis of this fundamental approach my Government has repeatedly called upon the parties concerned immediately to cease all hostilities, to withdraw all foreign forces, and to initiate, as early as possible, talks for a peaceful settlement of the conflict.

Particularly with regard to the conflict between China and Viet Nam. my Government has expressed its strong wish that any action leading to an exacerbation of the hostilities be avoided now that China has pledged the speedy withdrawal of its forces from Viet Nam, and that the Soviet Union exercise the utmost restraint so as to prevent the conflict from undergoing a further escalation and widening.

If one compares these points I have just quoted from my previous intervention with the draft resolution introduced by the Permanent Representative of Thailand on behalf of Indonesia, Malaysia, the Philippines, Singapore and Thailand (S/13162), all of them were in essence included in it. I may add, moreover, that many of the interventions made during the debate on this issue also underscore the importance of the same points as those contained in the draft of the five countries. I would argue, therefore, that the draft resolution embodies the fundamental and commonly accepted rules and norms which ought to be applied in cases of the sort that this Council is currently seized of.

The enormous efforts that the five countries have made to prepare this draft must be particularly commended, and I should like to express the sincere appreciation of my delegation to the five Governments for their initiative.

It is most regrettable, therefore, that, despite the efforts of the five countries, this Council was unable to adopt the draft resolution. It is hardly necessary to point out that its failure was not the result of a lack of majority support: on the contrary, more than two thirds of the members of this Council cast affirmative votes on this draft resolution. Surely I express the feeling shared by the great majority of the international community when I say that it is most regrettable that this Council was not able to apply such fundamental and commonly accepted rules for the settlement of interntional conflict.

Allow me to conclude by expressing the strong wish of my country that, even though this draft resolution was not adopted by the Council, all the parties concerned will pay maximum regard to the tenets of the draft so that peace and stability will be restored to Indochina as soon as possible.

75. **Speech by Deng Yingchao, Vice Chairman of the Standing Committee of the National People's Congress at a Press conference in Tokyo, 11 April 1979 (Extracts)**

We are glad to see that the conlcusion of the treaty not only has laid a solid foundation for strengthening and developing our amicable cooperation and led to closer relations, but also is exerting a positive influence for the maintenance of peace and security in the Asia-Pacific region. . . .

With the normalization of Sino-U.S. relations, quite a few Japanese and American friends have expressed concern over the future of Taiwan. . . . As far as our wish is concerned, we fully desire to see the matter settled by peaceful means, which will be in the best interest of our country and nation. However. this is not up to our side alone. Therefore, we cannot tie our own hands by committing ourselves to peaceful means. For that would make a peaceful settlement even more difficult. Acting, on the behests of the late Chairman Mao Zedong and Premier Zhou Enlai, we have repeatedly stated that in settling the question of China's reunification, the status quo on Taiwan and its present system will be respected and that fair and reasonable policies and measures will be adopted so as not to cause any loss to the people on Taiwan, or change their way of life, or affect the economic interests of foreign countries in Taiwan . . .

Some friends are worried whether the normalization of Sino-U.S. relations will affect the development of economic ties between China and Japan. Here I wish to say to you in all sincerity that China has already shifted the focus of its work to the programme for the four modernizations, and that the situation in China is stable, with the whole nation united in a drive to achieve the above goal. China's four modernizations policy will not change, nor will our policy on developing trade and economic relations with other countries. There are broad prospects for the expansion of economic exchanges and cooperation between China and Japan, which enjoy far more favourable conditions in their mutual relations than other countries. Difficulties of one kind or another may crop up sometimes, but they can be overcome all right. So you may feel assured and need not have any worries. . . .

Both our peoples ardently love peace. In the past the Chinese people suffered deeply from the scourge of war; we do not want any war. We fully understand the Japanese people's strong desire for peace. We firmly support the Japanese nationwide struggle for the recovery of their northern territory to its final success. One aim of our foreign policy is to delay the outbreak of a world war. However, the tree may prefer calm, but the wind will not subside. The hegemonists always reach out everywhere in an attempt to impose war on the people, thus seriously endangering world peace and international security. We must fully realize this danger and constantly remind the world's people of its existence, urging them to heighten their vigilance, close their ranks and upset the strategic plans of the hegemonists. This is the only way to secure a peaceful international environment of a relatively long period of time. It is our earnest hope that our friends in the Japanese mass media will regard this as their duty and do more work to this end. While China and Japan have their own independent foreign policies, we have much common ground in our approach to major international issues. We are sure that, on the basis of seeking common ground while putting aside differences, we will certainly be able to advance our friendly relations and cooperation in various fields and contribute to peace in Asia and the world.

76. "Defense of Japan," White Paper released by Japan's Defense Agency on 24 July 1979 (Extracts)

In the 1970s, China has brought about rapprochement with the U.S., joining the United Nations and normalization of diplomatic relations with Japan, thus opening its doors to Japan, the U.S. and western Europe and it is going to take a step toward the modernization of the country. On the other hand, it is considered that approaches by China toward the western countries seem to complicate relations with the Soviet Union, and the Soviets' reaction to it seems to be one of the background elements for change of situation in Asia in the areas surrounding China. . . .

Against such military reinforcement by the Soviet Union in the Far East the United States has clearly indicated its policy of respecting its commitments for the area and is making efforts to build up elastic preparedness for contingency by increasing strategic air transportation or air refueling capabilities as well as qualitative improvement mainly of naval and air combat capabilities.

On the other hand, the Sino-Soviet confrontation seems to have no perceivable possibility of reconciliation in the forseeable future in view of a series of such moves as the Sino-Vietnam conflict and notification of the non-extension of the Treaty of

Friendship, Alliance and Mutual Assistance between China and
the Soviet Union. However, the possibility that the relationship
between the two countries may be recovered in some form cannot be completely ruled out; therefore continuous attention is
necessary.

In the Korean Peninsula, although the dialogue was resumed between South and North, their objectives are parallel and
reported unilateral military build-up by North Korea becomes
an issue. Accordingly, military confrontation and tension between South and North continues to exist.

Maintenance of peace and stability in the Korean Peninsula
is not only closely concerned with Japan's safety but also is an
important factor for the peace and stability of the entire East
Asian area.

The U.S. seems to be holding in abeyance the planned withdrawal of its ground troops from South Korea. Japan has
constantly expressed its hope that the withdrawal would be
carried out carefully in order not to disturb the peace of the
Korean Peninsula. If the withdrawal plan were to be reviewed
in accordance with the new situation, effective supplemental
measures would ensure that peace and stability in the Korean
Peninsula was maintained and secured. It also accords with
Japan's national interest and Japan is strongly hoping so.

The U.S. responsibility for the defense of Taiwan will disappear because of the abolishment of the U.S.-Taiwan Mutual
Defense Treaty (to expire at the end of 1979) in accordance
with the normalization of U.S.-China relations. However, the
security of this area is expected to be maintained as the U.S.
will continue to take appropriate supplemental measures. Since
this area is near Japan and a major sea lane, Japan has a keen
interest in this situation.

77. Statement by Vice Premier Gu Mu at a Press conference in Tokyo, 6 September 1979 (Extracts)

China's Political Situation; Some friends are worried whether
the political situation in China would long remain stable. They
fear that another sudden 'violent outburst of political ideology'
would drown the present effort for modernization We think
that there is no such possibility. The basic reason is that the

Chinese people are against any political turmoil. They want stability and are determined to push forward the national economy.

Sino-Japanese Friendship: "Both our countries want to develop our friendly relations. This friendship is advantageous to the people of both countries and is conducive to the cause of opposing hegemonism and defending world peace." "An economically developed and technologically advanced Japan and a gradually prospering and modernized China working in close co-operation with other friendly countries in the Asia-Pacific region would in a very large measure ensure stability in the East."

Aim of Readjusting Economy: The problem that the present economic readjustment would affect China's import of foreign technology and use of foreign capital doesn't exist. China's economic readjustment is for the purpose of quickening the pace of modernization in the coming years, and the import of foreign technology and use of foreign funds are also for the same purpose. The two are not contradictory; in fact, they complement each other.

The Question of Loans: The funds needed in China's construction are provided mainly by ourselves while we seek foreign funds as an auxiliary. We will accept loans from all friendly countries as long as China's sovereignty is not impaired and the conditions are appropriate.

78. Statement by Premier Hua Guofeng at the banquet given in honour of Japanese Prime Minister Masayoshi Ohira in Beijing, 5 December 1979 (Extracts)

The current visit by Prime Minister Ohira "will deepen our mutual understanding, expand areas of friendly cooperation and contribute still more significantly towards opening up new vistas for the furtherance of Sino-Japanese relations in the 1980's."

"As the people of our two countries live in amity and friendship from generation to generation, it will be possible for us to make a major and lasting contribution to peace and security in Asia and the rest of the world." . . .

"Our traditional friendship over two thousand years and our common interest in world affairs today ensure a strong affinity between our two peoples and endow our growing bilateral relations with great vitality. While we each decide on our own policies independently, there is a common language between us on many major international issues.

"We in China are committed to developing our national economy on the basis of self-reliance; but in no way do we refuse exchanges and cooperation with other countries in accordance with the principles of equality and mutual benefit."

China and Japan could work cooperatively by supplementing each other's needs, and expanding and developing amicable relations and cooperation more substantially and effectively.

"This is not only in the fundamental interests of our two peoples, but also necessary for the cause of peace in Asia and the world." . . .

"We hope to have a peaceful environment in which to carry out our four modernizations programme. We unswervingly pursue a foreign policy of combating hegemonism and defending world peace. We have always held that peace can only be secured by struggle and and not by begging. We firmly believe that so long as all the peace-loving countries and people in the world unite and persevere in waging effective struggles as their circumstances prescribe, it is possible to deter aggression and expansion, postpone the outbreak of a new world war and win a relatively long period of peace."

"Having withstood severe tests and realized nation-wide stability and unity, the Chinese people have embarked on a new Long March. We are convinced that the development of friendly relations and cooperation between China and Japan in every field is conducive to China's modernization. We do not threaten each other, and our mutual understanding and trust are growing with each day.

79. China-Japan joint communique on Ohira's visit to China, 7 December 1979 (Extracts)

The leaders of the two countries exchanged their frank views on the international situation, particularly on the situation in the Asia-Pacific region. They affirmed their concern for the maintenance of peace and stability in this region and the determination of the two countries to make sustained efforts, on the basis of their respective positions to preserve and secure peace and stability in Asia and the world.

They expressed their deep satisfaction with the development of peaceful and friendly relations between the two countries since the normalization of relations in the autumn of 1971 and affirmed that they should, in the years to come, strive to firmly maintain and develop these relations on the basis of the China-Japan Joint Statement and the Treaty of Peace and Friendship.

They also emphasized that, while their political and social systems are different, there was the need to further promote exchanges at all levels so as to deepen mutual understanding and trust. The two sides held that the dialogue between the two governments should be strengthened and it was decided that, apart from consultations between the two foreign ministers whenever desirable, an annual meeting between high-level foreign ministry officials would be held alternately in their respective capitals.

Premier Hua accepted the invitation of Prime Minister Ohira and the Japanese Government to visit Japan in May next year.

"Prime Minister Hua expressed a desire to Prime Minister Ohira that China would like to strengthen economic cooperation with Japan and other countries in order to promote its economic construction.

"Prime Minister Ohira welcomed the policy expressed by Prime Minister Hua that China would strengthen cooperation with foreign countries in the process of its economic construction. Furthermore, Prime Minister Ohira explained Japan's basic policy for economic cooperation and Japan's readiness to conduct positive cooperation in response to the Chinese desire. Stating that the Japanese Government intended to extend the most possible cooperation to Shi Jiu Suo port construction, Yan Zhou-Shi Jiu Suo railway construction, Beijing-Qin Huang Dao railway expansion, Guang Zhou-Heng Yang railway expansion, Quin Huang Dao port expansion, and Wu Qiang Xi hydroelectric power plant construction, Prime Minister Ohira expressed the intention of providing up to 50 billion in yen credits for fiscal 1979.

"The two leaders agreed that cooperation for the projects

to be implemented after fiscal 1980 would be decided through consultations in working meetings with both countries to be held once every year. Those will consider project surveys, implementing conditions of projects, Japan's financial situation, etc.

"Prime Minister Ohira also stated that the Japanese Government intended to cooperate positively in the construction project of a modern hospital in Beijing and that Japan would soon conduct the surveys and consultations necessary for that.

"Prime Minister Hua highly evaluated the positive attitudes of the Japanese side."

The Japanese Government is making domestic arrangements so that China will be eligible for Japan's preferential tariff system for developing countries, with necessary adjustments, beginning in April 1980.

The leaders of the two countries agreed that negotiations would be initiated at the earliest possible opportunity in the next year for the purpose of concluding an agreement on cooperation in science and technology.

The leaders share the view that continued expansion of bilateral economic exchanges based on the principle of equality and mutual benefit is in the interests of both countries.

80. Foreign policy speech by Japanese Foreign Minister Saburo Okita in the Diet, 25 January 1980 (Extracts)

As Japan is dependent upon overseas sources for the vast bulk of its energy resources and for the majority of its main mineral resources and foodstuffs, maintaining and expanding free and diversified trade and economic relations is the basic means to protect the foundations of the people's livelihoods . . . .

During our stay in China, the leaders of our two nations held candid exchanges of opinions on the situation in Asia and on the Japan-China relationship in the 1980s. In these meetings, we indicated Japan's preparedness to cooperate positively with the building of the Chinese economy and, in so doing, we conveyed Japanese policy and obtained Chinese understanding that we will not cooperate in military areas, that we will not

sacrifice Japan's relations with the other countries of Asia,
especially our traditional relations with the ASEAN countries,
and that the Japan-China relationship is not an exclusive relationship but is a relationship of cooperation in concert with the
other advanced industrial countries.

81. "The present Asian situation and trends of development," article by the Observer in *People's Daily*, 27 March 1980 (Extracts)

Stepped-up Soviet aggression and expansion and the people's
struggle against this aggression constitute the basic factors
determining the general situation in Asia in the forseeable
years of the 80s. . . .

The Soviet Union regards aggression and expansion in
Southeast and West Asia as a major step in pursuing its global
strategy. Since the mid-70's Moscow has intensified its southward
drive into unstable and vulnerable Asia and Africa to outflank
Europe on two sides. Soviet support for Vietnamese aggression
in Kampuchea and its direct invasion of Afghanistan are apparent indications that the Middle East and the Pacific region are
linked together in its strategic plans. . . .

The Soviet Union is stepping up military deployments in
the far eastern part of its territory and on Japan's four northern islands in an effort to achieve strategic supremacy. Its use
of Danang and Cam Ranh Bay in Viet Nam and military bases
in the Middle East have enormously strengthened its strategic
position in the vast region extending from the Far East to the
Indian Ocean. Moscow is premeditating the seizure of the Strait
of Malacca at the right moment so as to place passage between
the Pacific and the Indian Ocean under exclusive Soviet
control. . . .

Being confronted with the overbearing threat of the Soviet
Union, more and more Asian countries are directing the spearhead of their struggles towards safeguarding national independence and sovereignty. The ASEAN countries are resisting the
threat by the big and small hegemonic powers and are resolutely supporting the Kampuchean people in their just struggle.
The Islamic countries, with only a very few exceptions, are

against the Soviet invasion of Afghanistan, as are most countries in South Asia. In order to cope with threats from the north, Japan is further strengthening its military alliance with the United States, beginning to strengthen its defence capabilities, intensifying diplomatic activities in the Middle East and the Pacific region, and strengthening friendly ties of cooperation with China.

In order to safeguard their interests, the United States and West European countries are further strengthening their military deployment in the Indian Ocean and the Pacific and seeking closer relations with Asian countries by increasing offers of support and aid. . . . In the Far East and the Southeast Asia, the United States is endeavouring to form a new line of defence to contain the Soviet Union through the strengthening of the U.S.-Japan alliance and the reaffirmation of the treaty between the United States, Australia and New Zealand.

It can be predicted that there will be more Soviet military forces deployed in the Indian and Pacific Oceans. U.S. and Soviet confrontation in the region will become more acute.

82. "Japan Looks to its Defence," commentary in *Beijing Review*, 31 March 1980 (Extract)

Speaking before the House of Councillors' Budget Committee on March 12, a senior official of the Defence Agency said that from 1972 to 1976 Soviet troop strength in the Far East had increased from 30 divisions to 34 divisions and that another two divisions had recently been assigned to the Far Eastern Command. Soviet naval strength had also grown around the four Japanese islands of Kunashiri, Etorofu, Habomai and Shikotan, and the addition of the aircraft carrier *Minsk* had strengthened the Soviet Pacific fleet.

Soviet air power in the Far East has been increased to over 2,000 combat aircraft with the addition of some 100 specially equipped Mig-27 fighter-bombers. The Soviet Union is also stepping up the pace of developing Pacific military bases on Sakhalin, the Kurils, and Kamchatka peninsula.

Apprehensions. Moscow's strategic gains in Viet Nam, such as the use of its ports and installations, are another source of uneasiness for Japan. When 16 or 17 Soviet naval vessels sailed from the South China Sea through the Strait of Malacca to the Indian Ocean during January alone, Japan became very concerned that in the event of a crisis, the maritime self-defence force would find it very difficult to give protection to Japanese oil tankers travelling to Japan from the Coral Sea and the Solomon Islands, so that Japan's economic lifelines would be cut.

Many Japanese have expressed the fear that should a crisis occur, the self-defence forces would not be able to fulfil their role. They feel that it is important to maintain an independent defence capability which can stand up to the Soviet military threat and that the urget task is to build up a defence capability able to face unexpected crises and uncertain situations in the 80s.

83. Statement by Chinese Vice Premier Yu Qiuli at the banquet given in his honour by Foreign Minister Saburo Okita, 3 April 1980 (Extract)

A closer friendly relationship and broader economic cooperation between China and Japan will not only benefit the economic development of the two countries but also contribute to the maintenance of peace in Asia and the rest of the world. This fully conforms to the fundamental interests of the two peoples.

The guideline for China's economic development is still to rely on its own resources while entering into extensive cooperation with other countries in the spheres of science and technology, economy and trade.

84. Joint Press communique on Chinese Premier Hua Guofeng's visit to Japan, 29 May 1980

1. Premier Hua Guofeng of the State Council of the People's Republic of China is paying an official visit to Japan as a state guest from May 27 to June 1, 1980. Among Premier Hua's party are Vice-Premier Gu Mu and Foreign Minister Huang Hua Premier Hua and his party will also visit Nagoya and the Kansai district in his tour of Japan.

2. Premier Hua was received by His Majesty the Emperor

at the Imperial Palace on May 27.

3. Premier Hua held talks with Prime Minister Masayoshi Ohira on May 27 and 28 and they had a frank and constructive exchange of views on a wide range of issues of common concern to China and Japan in a most friendly atmosphere.

Among those present at the talks on the Chinese side were Vice-Premier Gu Mu and Foreign Minister Huang Hua, and on the Japanese side were Foreign Minister Sabruo Okita and Chief Cabinet Secretary Masayoshi Ito.

The leaders of the two countries expressed satisfaction and deep appreciation of Prime Minister Ohira's China visit last December and Premier Hua's current Japan visit, regarding them as events of far-reaching significance in laying a new foundation for the relations of friendship and co-operation between China and Japan towards the 21st century.

4. The leaders of the two countries exchanged views frankly and in earnest on the international situation, especially the situation in the Asian-Pacific and Middle East regions since last December. They expressed deep concern over the new conflicts and tensions in these regions which endanger world peace and stability. They agreed that problems arising in these regions should be settled as soon as possible in accordance with United Nations Charter and the relevant resolutions adopted by the United Nations, They affirmed that China and Japan, each proceeding from their own positions, would continue to work for the maintenance of peace and stability in these regions and in the world at large.

5. The leaders of the two countries exchanged views comprehensively on bilateral relations, and they once again noted with satisfaction the fact that the bonds of peace and friendship between the two countries have undergone smooth development and consolidation through the conclusion of the China-Japan Treaty of Peace and Friendship, the visits paid by the leaders of the two countries to each other following the normalization of relations in autumn, 1972. They affirmed that China and Japan, their difference in social system notwithstanding, should constantly deepen their mutual understanding and mutual trust through a further increase in contact so as to develop and deepen their enduring and unshakable ties of peace, friendship and co-operation.

6. Premier Hua explained to Prime Minister Ohira the policy and progress of socialist modernization now under way in China and once again expressed the hope to strengthen economic co-operation with Japan and other countries on the basis of self-reliance and in accordance with the principles of equality and mutual benefit and mutual help and meeting each other's needs, with a view to promoting China's economic construction.

Prime Minister Ohira expressed welcome to China's policy as stated above and affirmed that Japan would adhere to her policy hitherto in force and carry on active economic co-operation with China.

7. The leaders of the two countries noted with satisfaction the restoration to the Chinese Government of its membership of the International Monetary Fund and the International Bank for Reconstruction and Development which they both believed. would have a salutary influence on China and the development of the world economic order.

8. The leaders of the two countries affirmed the importance of continued expansion of trade and other economic exchanges between the two countries based on the principles of equality and mutual benefit at the same time. Both believed that particularly in view of the critical situation in natural resources, energy resources included. it was desirable for the two countries to establish long-term and stable ties of co-operation in this domain, including the joint exploitation of petroleum and coal, in accordance with the agreements reached by the parties concerned of the two countries. They acclaimed the fact that the Chinese and Japanese parties concerned would soon conclude a contract on the prospecting and exploitation of oil in the Bohai Sea and that similar projects of co-operation are being undertaken in other parts of China.

9. The leaders of the two countries exchanged views on the present state of economic co-operation between China and Japan and expressed satisfaction over the exchange of notes in April 1980, on the instalment of a Japanese yen loan for fiscal 1979. They affirmed that the fiscal-1980 instalment of the loan would be decided through detailed negotiations at a meeting to be held between the government departments concerned of the two countries in autumn this year.

10. Regarding the project of building a modern hospital in Beijing, Prime Minister Ohira made it clear that the Japanese Government would co-operate in the form of gratis aid, and it was prepared to begin the project's designing in 1980, and was ready to co-operate technically in the training of the hospital's personnel.

Premier Hua expressed his deep gratitude for this positively co-operative attitude on the part of Japan.

11. The leaders of the two countries expressed satisfaction with the conclusion of the Sino-Japanese scientific and technological co-operation agreement during Premier Hua's visit in Japan. They expressed their readiness to further promote scientific and technological co-operation within the framework of the agreement. They also agreed to start as soon as possible the negotiations for a treaty on the preservation of migratory birds.

12. The leaders of the two countries noted with satisfaction the fact that Sino-Japanese cultural exchanges, which have a 2,000-year old history and tradition, have been going on more extensively and smoothly, with the conclusion of the China-Japan cultural exchange agreement last December as a new starting point. Above all, they deeply appreciated the smooth progress in the exchange of students between the two countries and the implementation, beginning in the coming summer, of the programme to advance the teaching of the Japanese language in China. It was decided that consultations between the two Governments, as provided for in the China-Japan cultural exchange agreement, would take place in July 1980.

13. The leaders of the two countries expressed deep appreciation of the extensive and smooth exchange of personnel between the two countries, and both believed that it is desirable for both sides to be better prepared for receiving visitors. In this regard, Prime Minister Ohira said that Japan was considering the construction of a multi-purpose building in Tokyo to promote Sino-Japanese exchanges. The leaders of the two countries affirmed that it was of special importance to explore ways of increasing the contact between the youth of the two countries.

14. The leaders of the two countries agreed that it was desirable for the two Governments to meet, when necessary, alternately in the capitals of the two countries at the level of

member of the Chinese State Council and member of the Japanese Cabinet, in order to facilitate wide-ranging consultations centred on bilateral matters. They decided to hold the first meeting in Beijing this autumn.

15. The Chinese side expressed heartfelt thanks to the Japanese side for the warm welcome and hospitality it accorded to Premier Hua and his party during the visit.

85. "Defense of Japan," White Paper released by Japan's Defense Agency, 5 August 1980 (Extracts)

No major progress has been seen in Sino-Soviet relations, although Sino-Soviet negotiations to establisha new relation ship have been held following China's declaration that the Sino-Soviet Treaty of Friendship and Mutual Assistance would not be renewed; thus relations between them have not been based on any treaty since the Treaty lapsed on April 11, 1980. Although there seems to be little chance that Sino-Soviet relations will be greatly improved in the future, the possibilities cannot be totally ruled out that the two countries may eventually achieve something in their attempt to improve bilateral relations, so that their talks will bear watching closely.

On the Korean Peninsula, although talks between the Republic of Korea and North Korea have been resumed, military confrontation and tension centinue between North and Sonth. While the danger of a full-fledged military clash appears to be effectively deterred for the time being thanks to the U.S. decision to freeze its withdrawal of U.S. ground forces until 1981 and other factors, this situation bears careful watching since the peace and stability of this area have an important bearing on the peace and stability not only of Japan but of all East Asia. . . .

Regarding Taiwan, the U.S.-Taiwan Mutual Defense Treaty was terminated at the end of last year with the normalization of U.S. relations with China, and the legal obligation of the U S. to defend Talwan directly based upon the Treaty expired. However, the U.S. Government has stated that it continues to be concerned over the peaceful resolution of the Taiwan issue and has enacted a law concerning Taiwan and is still providing weapons of a defensive nature to Taiwan, so the security of this region seems likely to be maintained. But, since the Taiwan area is near Japan and lies on important shipping lanes, Japan is also highly concerned with this area.

86. "Moscow's campaign of intimidation against Japan," Xinhua commentary, 19 September 1980

The 35th anniversary of the outbreak of World War II was used by Moscow as the occasion for a broadside of intimidation against Japan. The sabre-rattling statement of the Soviet Defence Minister and a spate of press articles exhorted Japan to give up its efforts to beef up its defence, an effort necessitated by the Soviet military buildup in the Far East.

Moscow warned Japan that to boost its defence capabilities "would only mean taking the path of national suicide." And to strengthen its ties with the United States and Asian-Pacific countries to meet the Soviet challenge would have the same consequences as that when Japan "joined the Axis". To press for the return of the 4 northern islands is an attempt to upset the pattern brought about by the Soviet victory in World War II. Therefore, Japan was told not to forget that the last battle of World War II was "the defeat of militarist Japan by the Soviet armed forces together with the allied forces."

In addition Japan was advised to conclude with the Soviet Union a "treaty of good-neighbourhood and cooperation" as was drafted by the Kremlin, while it should not hope to "commit itself to anything hostile to the Soviet Union" with impunity.

The motive behind all this insolent intimidation backed by massive dispositions of armed forces around Japan is obvious.

Japan, though one of the world's economic giants, possesses very limited military strength. Its armed forces amount to only one seventeenth of that of the Soviet Union. Its natural resources are meager and depends on imports for 90 per cent of the oil and the bulk of the raw materials needed by its industry. With the Soviet Union now relentlessly pushing to the East and South, Japan cannot possibly hope to safeguard its independence and security by relying on its own.

Both the late Japanese Prime Minister Ohira and the present Prime Minister Suzuki have stressed that Japan should

strengthen its own defence, solidify its military alliance with the
U.S. and upgrade its coordination with Asian-Pacific nations.
The Japanese Government believes that only by so doing can
the Soviet aggression and expansion in the Asian-Pacific region
be effectively checked.

However, this certainly cannot be tolerated by the Moscow
hegemonists. The Soviet intimidation and military threat to
Japan are precisely aimed at forcing Japan to give up its
necessary defence measures so as to leave the country in a help-
less state once war becomes imminent. Meanwhile, they are also
aimed at preventing the Asian-Pacific nations from framing
and developing a united strategy to counter the Soviet threat.

After all, intimidation and military threat cannot but arouse
strong discontent with and opposition to the Soviet Union
among the Japanese Government and public.

87. Xinhua report on the first high-level Sino-Japanese Minis-terial Conference, 3 December 1980 (Extract)

Representing China at this afternoon's meeting were Vice-
Premiers Gu Mu, Yao Yilin and Huang Hua, and 9 ministers
and Government members of ministerial level including Minister of Foreign Trade Li Qiang.

Representing Japan were Masayoshi Ito, Minister of Foreign Affairs, and 5 other ministers and members of their party.

According to authoritative sources, the two sides exchanged
views on issues concerning the current international situation,
diplomatic, economic and financial policies of the two countries as well as their cooperation.

They reviewed with satisfaction the smooth development of
Sino-Japanese relations. It was noted that the development of
Sino-Japanese friendly relations and cooperation had positively
contributed to peace and stability in Asia and the rest of the
world. Both sides stressed that they would strive to further expand, substantiate and strengthen these relations.

Referring to the international situation and Japan's foreign
policy, Masayoshi Ito said that the issues of Kampuchea, Indo-
Chinese refugees and the Soviet invasion of Afghanistan were
factors of instability. He said that the restoration of a lasting
peace in Kampuchea lay in the settlement of the Kampuchean

problem without outside interference.

Mr. Ito stressed that the establishment of good relations between China and the United States was an important factor for stability in Asia. "The Japanese Government is looking forward to the expansion of such good relations," he added.

"The prospects of Japan-China relations are exceedingly bright," the Japanese Foreign Minister went on. "Through our joint efforts and with mutual understanding difficulties on the road to advance can be overcome and relations between the two countries will expand in a down-to earth way," he added.

Chinese Vice Premier and Foreign Minister Huang Hua is said to have given an account of China's position on the current world situation. He was quoted as saying: "We should make a sober estimate of the Soviet Union's military capability and adventurism. Likewise, we should see its weaknesses and difficulties. The Soviet Union's southward-thrust can be frustrated and war can be postponed or prevented."

Huang Hua paid tribute to the Japanese Government for its positive foreign policy. "China and Japan have many common interests strategically and share converging views on a number of international issues ," he added.

The sources said that while discussing each country's economic and financial policies and cooperation between the two Yao Yilin briefed the Japanese ministers on the policies worked out by China, the measures adopted and results achieved in readjusting its national economy. He said, " the key link in the readjustment is to reduce capital construction and cut down other expenditures in a bid to achieve a balance in finances, credits and material supplies. After readjusting the proportional relationship between the various sectors of the national economy, China's economy will develop at a faster speed."

Director-General of the Japanese Economic Planning Agency Toshio Komoto explained the process of development of the Japanese economy and its orientation. He hoped that exchanges and cooperation between Japan and China would develop in the fields of trade, and energy, and natural resources.

Japanese Minister of Finance Nichio Watanabe explained Japan's financial policy and its policy on overseas investments. Japan's Minister of International Trade and Industry Rokusuke Tanaka expressed the hope that China would become Japan's

long-term and stable supplier of energy resources. Her Minister
of Agriculture, Forestry and Fisheries Takao Kameoka said
that he was pleased to see China had given priority to agriculture in the modernization drive and hoped for the expansion of
cooperation beween the two countries in agriculture. Japanese
Minister of Transport Masajuro Shiokawa said that he was
satisfied with the financial and technical cooperation between
Japan and China in the fields of railway and other means of
transportation. He hoped that Japan and China would cooperate
in ocean transportation.

Chinese Vice-Premier Gu Mu stressed: "In order to realize
the four modernizations programme, China's long-term strategic policy is, on the basis of self-reliance, to learn from the
strong points of other countries, expand foreign trade, introduce
advanced techniques, make use of foreign capital and to
increase technical exchanges and economic cooperation with
foreign countries.

"There are bright prospects for trade contacts and technical
cooperation in the economic field between China and Japan,"
he declared.

The Vice-Premier said he believed that on the basis of equality and mutual benefit, China and Japan could complement
each other in trade cooperation, which would make possible the
realization of the desired bright future.

Sources of Documents

1 *People's China,* 1 October 1951, 38-9.
2 Ibid., 16 May 1952, 4-6.
3 Xinhua News Agency, 9 October 1953, as reproduced in *News Bulletin* (Chinese Embassy, New Delhi), 21 October 1953.
4 *News Bulletin,* 24 March 1954, 10-2.
5 Ibid., 20 October 1954, 4-5.
6 Ibid., 27 April 1955, 8.
7 *People's China,* 16 August 1955, 5-6.
8 Ibid., No. 17 (1955), Supplement.
9 Xinhua News Agency, 17 October 1955. See also *Survey of China Mainland Press,* No. 1151.
10 *People's China,* 16 February 1956, Supplement, 5.
11 Ibid., 16 July 1956, Supplement.
12 Xinhua News Agency, 22 April 1957.
13 Chinese People's Institute of Foreign Affairs, *Oppose U.S. Occupation of Taiwan and "Two Chinas" Plot* (Peking, 1958), 128-33.
14 *China Today* (Chinese Embassy, New Delhi), 25 February 1958, 8-9 and 12.
15 *Peking Review,* 13 May 1958, 17.
16 Ibid., 25 November 1958, 10-1.
17 *International Affairs* (Moscow), January 1959, 78.
18 *Peking Review,* 24 March 1959, 18-9.
19 *China Today,* No. 17, 1959, Supplement, 57-8.
20 *Peking Review,* 1 October 1959, 28.
21 Ibid., 17 November 1959, 13-4.
22 *China Today,* 16 January 1960, 3.
23 Ibid., 16 April 1960, 5.
24 Ibid., 24 September 1960, 7-8.
25 *Peking Review,* 19 January 1962, 13-4.
26 *Survey of China Mainland Press,* No. 2860, 15 November 1960, 39-40.
27 *Peking Review,* 26 June 1964, 6-7.
28 Ibid., 1 January 1965, 17 and 19.
29 *Contemporary Japan,* June 1965, 464.
30 *Peking Review,* 8 October 1965, 12; also Foreign Lang-

uages Press, *Vice-Premier Chen Yi Answers Questions Put by Correspondents* (Peking, 1966), 18.

31 *Peking Review*, 7 January 1966, 8.

32 *Japan Report*, 20 November 1967, 9-10.

33 *Peking Review*, 19 April 1968, 26-7.

34 Ib'd., 27 December 1968, 20.

35 Ibid., 11 April 1969, 38-9.

36 *Japan Times*, 22 November 1969.

37 *Pacific Community*, January 1970, 335-6.

38 *Peking Review*, 24 April 1970, 31-3.

39 Ibid., 6 November 1970, 15-6.

40 *Pacific Community*, April 1971, 603.

41 *Peking Review*, 12 March 1971, 24-5.

42 Ibid., 9 July 1971, 20-1.

43 Ibid., 8 October 1971, 14-5.

44 Ibid., 22 October 1971, 17 and 23.

45 Ibid., 31 December 1971, 4.

46 Foreign Broadcast Information Service, *Daily Report*, 4 February 1972.

47 *Peking Review*, 21 April 1972, 17-9.

48 Ibid., 29 September 1972, 7-8.

49 Ibid.

50 Ibid., 6 October 1972, 12-3.

51 Ibid., 15.

52 Ibid., 8 February 1974, 3.

53 Ibid., 26 April 1974, 28.

54 Ibid., 29 August 1975, 12.

55 Ibid., 13 May 1977, 17-8.

56 *News from China*, 15 June 1977, 5-6; also *Peking Review*, 17 June 1977, 16-7.

57 Foreign Languages Press, *Chairman Mao's Theory of the Differentiation of the Three Worlds is a Major Contribution to Marxism-Leninism* (Peking, 1977), 56.

58 Japan External Trade Organization, *China Newsletter*, June 1978, 25-6.

59 Foreign Languages Press, *Documents of the First Session of the Fifth National People's Congress of the People's Republic of China* (Peking, 1978), 110-1; *Peking Review*, 10 March 1978, 39.

60 *Peking Review*, 17 March 1978, 44-5.

61 Ibid., 30 June 1978, 25.

62 Ibid., 18 August 1978, 7-8.

63 *News from China*, 14 August 1978, 7.

64 *Japan Review*, August 1978, 8-9.

65 Ibid., 7.

66 Ibid., September 1978, 9.

67 *Peking Review*, 27 October 1978, 3-4.

68 Ibid., 4.

69 Ibid., 3 November 1978, 14-6.

70 *News from China*, 7 November 1978, 2-4.

71 Ibid., 10 February 1979, 3.

72 UN Document S/PV. 2116, 11.

73 Ibid., 11-2.

74 UN Document S/PV. 2129, 52-6.

75 *News from China*, 14 April 1979, 3-5.

76 "Defense of Japan" (White Paper), as reproduced in *Strategic Digest*, October 1979, 641 and 643.

77 *Beijing Review*, 14 September 1979, 4-5.

78 *News from China*, 11 December 1979, 3-4.

79 *Beijing Review*, 14 December 1979, 3-4; *Look Japan* (Tokyo), 10 June 1980; and *News from China*, 11 December 1979, 5-6.

80 Japan, Foreign Press Centre, "Foreign Policy speech by Foreign Minister Saburo Okita in the Diet, 25 January 1980" (unofficial translation), 3 and 7; also see *Information Bulletin* (Tokyo), 15 February 1980, 5.

81 *News from China*, 1 April 1980, 2-3.

82 *Beijing Review*, 31 March 1980, 10.

83 *News from China*, 8 April 1980, 2.

84 *Beijing Review*, 9 June 1980, 8-9.

85 Japan, Defense Agency, *Summary of "Defense of Japan,"* 5 August 1980 (Foreign Press Center, Japan, August 1980, W-80-11), 8-9.

86 *News from China*, 23 September 1980, 6.

87 Ibid., 9 December 1980, 3-4.

Appendix 1

Exchange of Visits between China and Japan, 1972-1981

1 Prime Minister Kakuei Tanaka in
China   25-29 Sep 1972 P

2 Memorandum Trade Office delegation
led by Kaheita Okazaki in China   Oct 1972 E

3 Delegation of the Ministry of International Trade and Industry led by Yogoro
Komatsu in China   Nov 1972 E

4 Japan External Trade Organisation
(JETRO) delegation led by Kichihei
Hara in China   Dec 1972 E

5 Minister of International Trade and
Industry Yasuhiro Nakasone in China   Jan 1973 E

6 Senior Dietman of the Liberal Democratic Party Takeo Kimura in China   Jan 1973 P

7 A delegation of the Association for the
Promotion of International Trade led by
Tieji Hagiwara in China   Feb 1973 E

8 Government delegation in China   Mar 1973 P

9 China-Japan Friendship Association
delegation led by Liao Cheng-chih in
Japan   Apr-May 1973 P

10 A delegation of the Association for the
Promotion of International Trade led by
Aiichiro Fujiyama in China   Jun 1973 E

11 Memorandum Trade Office delegation
led by K. Okazaki in China   Jul 1973 E

12 Economic and trade delegation by Liu
Xiwen in Japan   Sep-Oct 1973 E

13 Memorandum Trade Office delegation
led by K. Okazaki in China   Nov-Dec 1973 E

14 Foreign Minister Masayoshi Ohira in
China   Jan 1974 P

15 Ministry of Foreign Affairs delegation
led by Michihiko Kunihiro in China   Mar 1974 P

16 Council for Promotion of International
Trade delegation led by Wang Yao-ting

in Japan	Jul 1974	**E**
17 A delegation of the Dietmen's League for Japan-China Friendship in China	Aug 1974	**P**
18 Komeito delegation led by Yoshikatsu Takeiri in China	Aug 1974	**P**
19 Council for Promotion of International Trade delegation led by Wang Yao-ting in Japan	Sep-Oct 1974	**E**
20 A delegation of the Association for the Promotion of International Trade led by A. Fujiyama in China	Nov 1974	**E**
21 Vice-Foreign Minister Han Nianlong in Japan to sign agreement on shipping	Nov 1974	**E**
22 Council for Promotion of International Trade delegation led by Wang Wen-lin in Japan	Nov 1974	**E**
23 Ministry of International Trade and Industry delegation led by Eguchi Hiro-michi in China	Dec 1974	**E**
24 Japan-China Friendship Association delegation led by Teruaki Sakata in China	Jan 1975	**P**
25 Japan-China Association on Economy and Trade delegation led by Yoshihiro Inayama in China	13-17 Jan 1975	**E**
26 Shigeru Hori, Speaker of the Lower House, in China	15-21 Jan 1975	**P**
27 A delegation of the Association for the Promotion of International Trade led by T. Hagiwara in China	Mar 1975	**E**
28 Council for Promotion of International Trade delegation led by Li Chuan in Japan	Mar 1975	**E**
29 Joint Trade Committee delegation led by M. Takashima in China	Apr 1975	**E**
30 Bank of China delegation led by Chiao Pei-shin in Japan	Apr 1975	**E**
31 Japanese Socialist Party delegation led by Tomomi Narita in China	May 1975	**P**
32 A delegation of the Association for the		

Promotion of International Trade led by
A. Fujiyama in China   May 1975 **E**
33 China-Japan Friendship Association
delegation led by Chu Tunan in Japan   Sep 1975 **C**
34 Former Foreign Minister Zentaro Kosa-
ka in China   Oct 1975 **P**
35 Federation of Economic Organisations
delegation led by Toshiwo Doko in
China   Oct 1975 **E**
36 Japan-China Friendship Association
(Orthodox) delegation led by Hisao
Kuroda in China   Nov 1975 **C**
37 Minister of International Trade and
Industry T. Komoto in China   Nov 1975 **E**
38 Foreign Trade Association delegation
led by T. Mizukama in China   Dec 1975 **E**
39 A delegation of the Association for the
Promotion of International Trade led by
A. Fujiyama in China   Dec 1975 **E**
40 Japanese Socialist Party delegation led
by Shoichi Shimodaira in China   Jan 1976 **P**
41 Japan-China Association on Economy
and Trade delegation led by Yoshihiro
Inayama in China   Jan 1976 **E**
42 Chinese People's Association for Friend-
ship with Foreign Countries delegation
led by Wang Ping-nan in China   Apr 1976 **P**
43 National Council for Japan-China
Friendship delegation led by Y.Miyazaki
in China   May 1976 **C**
44 Trade delegation in China   Aug 1976 **E**
45 A delegation of the Association for the
Promotion of International Trade led by
A. Fujiyama in China   Oct 1976 **E**
46 Permanent Adviser to Japan-China
Association on Economy and Trade K.
Okazaki in China   Oct 1976 **E**
47 Komeito Party delegation led by
Yoshikatsu Takeiri in China   Jan 1977 **P**
48 A delegation of the Japan-China

Association on Economy and Trade led
by Y. Inayama in China   Feb 1977 **E**

49 Ministry of Foreign Trade delegation led
by Hsi Yeh-sheng in Japan   Mar 1977 **E**

50 General Council of Trade Unions
(Sohyo) delegation led by M. Makeida
in China   Mar 1977 **E**

51 A delegation of Federation of Economic
Organisation led by Toshiwo Doko in
China   Mar-Apr 1977 **E**

52 A delegation of the Council for the
Promotion of International Trade led by
Li Chuan in Japan   Apr 1977 **E**

53 A 340-member delegation of Japan-China
Friendship Association (Orthodox) in
China   May 1977 **C**

54 Former Ground Self-Defence Forces
Chief of Staff M. Miyoshi in China   Jun 1977 **M**

55 Former National Defence Council
Secretary-General O. Kaihara in China   Jun 1977 **M**

56 A delegation of the Association for the
Promotion of International Trade led by
T. Hagiwara in China   Jun-Jul 1977 **E**

57 A delegation of the Japan-China
Cultural Exchange Association in China   Aug 1977 **C**

58 Vice Minister of Foreign Trade Liu
Xiwen in Japan   Sep-Oct 1977 **E**

59 A delegation of Association for the
Promotion of International Trade led by
A. Fujiyama in China   Oct 1977 **E**

60 Former Self-Defence Force General K.
Mitsuoka in China   Oct 1977 **M**

61 Former Chief Cabinet Secretary Susumu
Nikaido in China   Oct 1977 **P**

62 Yoshiro Inayama, Chairman of Japan-
China Association on Economy and
Trade, in China   25-30 Nov 1977 **E**

63 Japanese Military Academy delegation
led by T. Omuro in China   Dec 1977 **M**

64 A delegation led by Y. Inayama to

conclude long-term trade agreement   Feb 1978 **E**

65 Economic delegation led by Lin Hu-chia
in Japan   Mar 1978 **E**

66 A delegation of the House of Representatives Committee for Foreign
Affairs in China   Jul 1978 **P**

67 Foreign trade delegation led by Chang
Chun in Japan   Aug 1978 **E**

68 Foreign Minister Sunao Sonoda in China   Aug 1978 **P**

69 Association on Economy and Trade
delegation led by Y. Inayama in China   Sep 1978 **E**

70 Minister of International Trade and
Industry Komoto in china   Sep 1978 **E**

71 Deputy Chief of General Staff Chang
Tsai-chien in Japan   Sep 1978 **M**

72 40-member delegation led by Vice-
Premier Deng Xiaoping in Japan   22-29 Oct 1978 **P**

73 A 23-member delegation led by Yuan
Pao-hua, Vice-Minister of State Economic
Commission, in Japan   Oct-Nov 1978 **E**

74 12-member mission of Japan's House of
Councillors led by Upper House
President K. Yasui in China   Jan 1979 **P**

75 Vice Premier Deng Xiaoping in Japan
on his way back from the United States   Feb 1979 **P**

76 Bank of China delegation in Japan   Feb-Mar 1979 **E**

77 Vice Foreign Trade Minister Liu Xiwen
in Japan   17-30 Mar 1979 **E**

78 A delegation of Japan-China Asso-
ciation on Economy and Trade in China   Mar 1979 **E**

79 Chinese Minister of Railways Guo
Weichen in Japan   Mar 1979 **E**

80 A 25-member National People's Congress
delegation led by Madam Deng
Yingchao, widow of Zhou Enlai, in
Japan   8-19 Apr 1979 **P**

81 A 110-member goodwill mission from
Shanghai led by Chao Hsing-chin
in Japan   15-29 Apr 1979 **C**

82 Bank of China delegation led by Vice-

President and General Manager Pu
Ming in Japan May 1979 **E**

83 A 600-member friendship delegation on
board the ship Ming Hua led by Liao
Cheng-chih, Vice-Chairman of the
National People's Congress Standing
Committee, in Japan May-Jun 1979 **C**

84 Delegation of the Association for the
Promotion of International Trade led by
its Chairman, A. Fujiyama, in China Jun 1979 **E**

85 Japanese Diet delegation in China Jul 1979 **P**

86 Minister of Health and Welfare, Ryutaro
Hashimoto, in China Jul 1979 **C**

87 A 16-member delegation led by Vice-
Minister of State Economic Commission
Ma Yi in Japan Aug 1979 **E**

88 Vice Premier Gu Mu in Japan 1-12 Sep 1979 **P**

89 A 14-member Japanese government
mission led by Shinichi Yanai, Director-
General of the Foreign Ministry's
Economic Co-operation Bureau, in China
to conduct "pre-feasibility studies" on
China's major construction projects Oct 1979 **E**

90 Japanese Prime Minister Masayoshi
Ohira in China 5-6 Dec 1979 **P**

91 Governmental economic mission led by
I. Miyazaki, Deputy Director-General
of the Economic Planning Agency,
in China 14-25 Jan 1980 **E**

92 A 8-member Chinese delegation to study
joint ventures in Japan 14-28 Jan 1980 **E**

93 Minister for Foreign Trade Li Qiang in
Japan 22-30 Jan 1980 **E**

94 A delegation of the Foreign Investment
Commission of China led by Wang
Daohan, Vice-Minister of the Com-
mission, in Japan Jan 1980 **E**

95 A delegation of the Association for the
Promotion of International Trade led by
Shigeichi Koga, Vice-Chairman of the

Association, in China   Jan 1980 E

96 Vice Foreign Minister Han Nianlong in
Japan to attend the first session of
annual Vice Ministerial talks   12-20 Mar 1980 P

97 Xinhua delegation led by its Director,
Zeng Tao, in Japan   Mar-Apr 1980 C

98 Vice Premier Yu Qiuli in Japan   2-16 Apr 1980 P

99 Yoshitake Sasaki, Minister for International Trade and Industry, in China
                                      27 Apr-4 May 1980 E

100 Former Secretary-General of the Liberal
Democratic Party Nakasone, in China
                                      27 Apr-9 May 1980 P

101 Premier Hua Guofeng in Japan   27 May-1 Jun 1980 P

102 Vice Premier Geng Biao in China on
way home from USA   6-10 Jun 1980 P

103 A delegation led by Qiu Chunfu, Deputy
Chairman of the State Economic Com-
mittee, in Japan   Jun 1980 E

104 Premier Hua Guofeng in Japan to attend
Ohira's funeral   8-10 Jul 1980 P

105 A delegation led by Jiro Enjoji, Vice-
Chairman of Japan Atomic and Indus-
trial Forum, in China   Jul 1980 E

106 Foreign Minister Ito in China   2-4 Sep 1980 P

107 Vice Minister of International Trade and
Industry (MITI) Toshiko Yano in China   Sep 1980 E

108 Yoshimi Furui, Chairman of the Dietmen's League for Japan-China Friendship
in China   Sep 1980 P

109 A delegation led by Long Yiren, Chairman of the Chinese International Trust
and Investment Corporation, in Japan   Sep 1980 E

110 A delegation of the Chinese Institute of
Foreign Affairs led by its President Hao
Deging in Japan   Oct 1980 P

111 Energy Affairs group led by Coal Industry Minister Gao Yangwen, in Japan   Oct 1980 E

112 A delegation of the Japanese House of
Councillors led by its President Masa-

toshi Tokunaga in China — Jan 1981 **P**

113 A delegation of the Japanese House of
Representatives led by Vice-Speaker
Harano Okada in China — Jan 1981 **P**

114 Saburo Okita as Special Representative
of the Japanese Government in China to
discuss compensation for estimated loss
of 300 billion yen ($ 1.5 billion) suffered
by 26 Japanese firms as a result of cancellation and suspension of contracts — 10-12 Feb 1981 **E**

115 A Chinese delegation to discuss the
problem of compensation with Japanese
firms affected by cancellation of orders — Feb-Mar 1981 **E**

116 Aiichiro Fujiyama, former Foreign Minister
and presently Chairman of the Japan-China
Association for the Promotion of International Trade, in China — Mar 1981 **E**

117 Toshiwo Doko, President of Japan-China
Association on Economy and Trade, in
China. — Mar 1981 **E**

118 Kaheita Okazaki, Permanent Adviser to
Japan-China Economic Association, in
China — Mar 1981 **E**

119 Second China-Japan Foreign Ministry
working-level regular consultations in
Beijing — 10-11 Apr 1981 **P**

120 Vice Premier Gu Mu in Japan — May 1981 **E**

Agreements signed between China and Japan, 1971-1981

1	Agreement to transport Japanese air cargo to China via Hong Kong	6 Jan 1971
2	Memorandum trade agreement for 1973	29 Oct 1972
3	Trade agreement	5 Jan 1974
4	Civil aviation agreement	20 Apr 1974
5	Maritime transport agreement	13 Nov 1974
6	Insurance agreement for air traffic accident damages	2 Dec 1974
7	Agreement on forward exchange transactions between Japanese yen and Chinese renminbi yuan	16 Apr 1975
8	Fishery agreement	15 Aug 1975
9	Exchange of notes on setting up of consulates general in Shanghai and Osaka	15 Aug 1975
10	Agreement on establishment of private-level shipping offices in each country	25 Aug 1975
11	Agreement on meteorological cooperation	25 Sep 1975
12	Silk trade agreement	24 May 1976
13	Agreement on the establishment of a meteorological communication link connecting Beijing and Tokyo	25 Sep 1977
14	Agreement on trade-mark protection	29 Sep 1977
15	Long-term trade agreement	16 Feb 1978
16	Peace and Friendship treaty	12 Aug 1978
17	Contract on coking coal under the China-Japan long-term trade agreement	14 Aug 1978
18	Maritime arbitration protocol	9 Dec 1978
19	Japan-China liner service agreement	Jun 1979
20	Agreement providing for a Japanese loan of 50 billion yen to China	30 Apr 1980
21	Exchange of notes on construction of a China-Japan Friendship Hospital in Beijing	26 Jan 1981
22	Agreement on protection of migratory	

birds and their habitats   3 Mar 1981
23 Agreement by which Japan will provide
50 mn yen to China for use in education
and research work   20 Mar 1981

Appendix 3

Trade between China and Japan, 1934-36 to 1980
(in million US dollars)

Year	Chinese Exports to Japan	Chinese Imports from Japan
1934-36 (average)	103.0	171.0
1937	126.0	227.8
1946	3.6	3.6
1947	5.0	10.2
1948	24.8	4.1
1949	21.8	3.1
1950	39.3	19.6
1951	21.6	5.8
1952	14.9	0.6
1953	29.7	4.5
1954	40.8	19.1
1955	80.8	28.5
1956	83.6	67.3
1957	80.5	60.5
1958	54.4	50.6
1959	18.9	3.6
1960	20.9	2.7
1961	30.9	16.6
1962	46.0	38.5
1963	74.6	62.4
1964	157.8	152.7
1965	224.7	245.0
1966	306.2	315.2
1967	269.4	288.4
1968	224.2	325.4
1969	234.5	390.8
1970	253.8	560.9
1971	323.2	578.2
1972	491.1	603.9
1973	974.0	1039.5
1974	1304.8	1984.5
1975	1531.0	2258.6
1976	1370.9	1662.5
1977	1546.9	1938.6
1978	2030	3049
1979	2954	3698
1980	4323	5078

Appendix 4

Trade between Japan and Taiwan, 1947-1979
(in million US dollars)

Year	Japanese Imports from Taiwan	Japanese Exports to Taiwan
1947	.002	.009
1948	.017	.001
1949	2.5	5.9
1950	35.9	38.0
1951	53.0	50.6
1952	63.8	60.7
1953	64.0	60.9
1954	57.1	65.9
1955	80.9	63.8
1956	45.5	77.9
1957	67.3	84.3
1958	75.6	90.0
1959	71.5	86.9
1960	63.5	77.9
1961	60.9	104.0
1962	57.9	106.8
1963	118.4	97.1
1964	140.1	140.4
1965	151.6	206.1
1966	141.7	230.4
1967	134.8	314.7
1968	151.9	423.8
1969	178.9	489.2
1970	235.6	582.0
1971	267.0	767.4
1972	421.8	1090.6
1973	890.7	1641.7
1974	955.2	2009.0
1975	811.6	1821.7
1976	1189.8	2279.7
1977	1288.7	2552.7
1978	1750.2	3584.7
1979	2475.9	4366.8

Source: UN, *Direction of International Trade*; JETRO, *White Paper on International Trade*.

Select Bibliography

BOOKS

Bamba, Noyuya, *Japanese Diplomacy in a Dilemma: New Light on Japan's China Policy, 1924-1929.* Kyoto, 1978.

Barnett, A. Doak, *China and the Major Powers in East Asia.* Washington, D.C., 1977.

Borton, Hugh, et al., *Japan Between East and West.* New York, 1957.

Brezezinski, Zbigniew, *The Fragile Blossom: Crisis and Change in Japan.* New York, 1972.

Burnell, Alaine H, ed., *Asian Dilemma: United States, Japan and China,* Tokyo, 1969.

China, Foreign Languages Press, *Oppose the Revival of Japanese Militarism.* Peking, 1960.

———, *Support the Just Struggle of the Japanese People Against the Japan-US Treaty of Military Alliance.* Peking, 1960.

Coox, Alvin D. and Camoy, Hilary, ed., *China and Japan: A Search for Balance since World War I.* Santa Barbara, Calif., 1978.

Dunn, Fredrick S., *Peacemaking and the Settlement with Japan.* Princeton, N.J., 1963.

Endicott, John E., *Japan's Nuclear Option: Political, Technical and Strategic Factors.* New York, 1975.

Fukui, H., *Party in Power : The Japanese Liberal Democrats and Policymaking.* Berkeley, 1970.

Guillain, R., *The Japanese Challenge.* London, 1970.

Halpern, A.M., ed., *Policies Towards China: Views from Six Continents.* New York, 1965.

Harrison, Selig S., *China, Oil, and Asia : Conflic t Ahead ?* New York, 1977.

Helmann, Donald C., *Japan and East Asia.* London, 1972.

———, ed., *China and Japan: A New Balance of Power.* Lexington, 1976.

Herbert, Passin, *China's Cultural Diplomacy.* New York, 1962.

Jain, J.P , *China in World Politics.* New Delhi, 1976.

Jain, R.K., *Japan's Postwar Peace Settlements.* New Delhi, 1978.

———, *The USSR and Japan, 1945-1980.* New Delhi, 1981.

Jansen, Marius B., *Japan and Communist. China in the Next Decade.* California, 1962.

———, *Japan and China: From War to Peace, 1894-1972.* Chicago, 1975.

Japan, External Trade Organization, *How to Approach the China Market.* Tokyo, 1972.

Japan, Ministry of Foreign Affairs, *Major Policy Speeches of M. Shigemitsu,* Tokyo, undated.

Kahn, H., *The Emerging Japanese Superstate : Challenge and Response,* Englewood Cliffs, N.J., 1970.

Kajima, Morinosuke, *A Brief History of Modern Japan,* Tokyo, 1965.

Langdon, F.C., *Japan's Foreign Policy.* Vancouver, British Columbia, 1973.

Lee, Chae-Jin, *Japan Faces China : Political and Economic Relations in the Postwar Era.* Baltimore, 1976.

Leng, Shao Chuan, *Japan and Communist China.* Kyoto, undated.

London, Kurt, ed., *Unity and Contradiction.* New York, 1962.

Mendel, Douglas H., *The Japanese People and Foreign Policy.* California, 1961.

Mendl, Wolf, *Issues in Japan's China Policy.* London, 1978.

Morley, James W., *Soviet and Communist Chinese Policies toward Japan 1950-1957 : A Comparison.* New York, 1958.

———, *Japan and Korea: American's Allies in the Pacific.* New York, 1965.

———, ed. *Japan's Foreign Policy 1868-1941: A Research Guide.* New York, 1974.

———, ed. *Forecast for Japan : Security in the Seventies.* Princeton, N.J., 1972.

Mueller, Peter G. and Ross, Douglas A. *China and Japan—Emerging Global Powers*. New York, 1975.

Olson, Lawrence, *Japan in Postwar Asia*. New York, 1970.

Packard, G.R., *Protest in Tokyo: The Security Treaty Crisis* of *1960*. Princeton, N.J., 1966.

Reischauer, Edwin O., *Japan: Past and Present*, 3rd ed., New York, 1964.

Scalapino, Robert A., ed. *The Foreign Policy of Modern Japan.* Berkeley, 1977.

Scalapino, Robert A. and Masumi, J., *Parties and Politics in Contemporary Japan*. Berkeley, California, 1962.

Shaw, K.E., *Japan's China Problem: Marginal Position and Attitude during the Ikeda Period*. Tokyo, 1968.

Swearingen, Rodger, *The Soviet Union and Postwar Japan: Escalating Challenge and Response*. Stanford, Calif., 1978.

Weinstein, Martin E., *Japan's Postwar Defence Policy, 1947-1968*. New York, 1971.

Welfield, J., *Japan and Nuclear China: Japanese Reactions to China's Weapons*. Canberra, 1970.

Yoshida, Shigeru, *The Yoshida Memoirs*. London, 1961.

ARTICLES

Ahn, Byung-Joon, "The U.S.-Japan-PRC Triangle and the Balance of Power in Northeast Asia," *Korea & World Affairs*, Summer 1979, 163-82.

Albright, David E., "The Sino-Soviet Conflict and the Balance of Power in Asia," *Pacific Community*, January 1973, 204-34.

"Asian situation after conclusion of Japan-China peace and friendship treaty and Japan's foreign policy," *Japan Socialist Review*, October 1978, 14-23.

Baerwald, Hans H., "Aspects of Sino-Japanese Normalization," *Pacific Community*, January 1973, 195-203.

Barnett, A. Doak, "Peking and the Asian Power Balance," *Problem of Communism*, July-August 1976, 36-48.

Beer, Lawrence W., "Some Dimensions of Japan's Present and Potential Relations with Communist China," *Asian Survey*, March 1969, 163-77.

Brown, David G., "Chinese Economic Leverage in Sino-Japanese Relations," *Asian Survey*, September 1972, 753-71.

Buchan, Alastair, "Asian Balance of Power?" *Encounter*, December 1966, 62-71.

Bull, Hedley, "The New Balance of Power in Asia and the Pacific," *Foreign Affairs*, July 1971, 669-81.

Cheng, Joseph Y.S., "Sino-Japanese Relations, 1957-60," *Asian Affairs*, February 1977, 70-84.

Cheng, Tao, "The Sino-Japanese Dispute over the Tiao-Yu-Tai (Senkaku) Islands and the Law of Territorial Acquisition," *Virginia Journal of International Law* (Winter 1974), 14: 242.

Davies, Derek, "Will Japan's Accommodation with China Works," *Pacific Community*, April 1973, 340-45.

Eto, Shinkichi, "Post-War Japanese-Chinese Relations," *Survey*, Autumn 1972, 55-65.

———, "Japan and China—A New Stage?" *Problems of Commnnism*, November-December 1972, 1-17.

———, "Recent Developments in Sino-Japanese Relations," *Asian Survey*, July 1980, 726-43.

Fukui, Haruhiro, "Japan's New Relationship with China," *Current History*, April 1975, 163-8.

———, "Japan and China: Peace at least," *Current History*, November 1978, 149-53, 185.

Glaubitz, Joachim, "Balancing between Adversaries: Sino-Japanese Relations and Soviet Interference," *Pacific Community*, October 1977, 31-45.

Hellmann, Donald C., "Japan and the Great Powers to Post-Vietnam Asia," *Pacific Community*, July 1973, 588-601.

Haselkorn, Avigdor, "Impact of Sino-Japanese Treaty on the Soviet Security Strategy," *Asian Survey*, June 1979, 558-73.

Ho, Samuel P.S., "The China Trade: Recent Developments and Future Prospects," *Pacific Affairs*, Summer 1980, 269-89.

Hsiao, Gene T., "The Sino-Japanese Rapprochement: A Relationship of Ambivalence," *China Quarterly*, January-March 1974, 101-23.

———, "Prospects for New Sino-Japanese Relationship," *China Quarterly*, December 1974, 720-49.

Ikeda, Hayato, "Basic Foreign Policy of Japan," *Contemporary Japan*, November 1960, 611-15.

Inou, Shigenobu, "Communist China's diplomatic strategy and Japan's security," *Issues & Studies*, July 1978, 26-36.

Ishikawa Tadao, "Communist China's Policy towards Japan,"

Journal of Social and Political Ideas in Japan, December 1966.

Jan, George P., "Japan's Trade with Communist China," *Asian Survey*, December 1969, 900-18.

John, Chalmers, "How China and Japan See Each Other," *Foreign Affairs*, July 1972, 711-21.

Kamazawa Masao, "Japan and the Balance of Power in Asia," *Pacific Community*, October 1972, 71-8.

Kazuo, Ogura, "How the Inscrutables' negotiate with the Insrutables: Chinese negotiating tactics vis-a-vis the Japanese," *China Quarterly*, September 1979, 529-52.

Kennan, George F., 'Japanese Security and American Policy," *Foreign Affairs*, October 1964, 14-28.

Kim, Hong N., "Fukuda government and the politics of the Sino-Japanese peace treaty," *Asian Survey*, March 1979, 297-313.

———, "Sino-Japanese Relations since the Rapprochement," *Asian Survey*, July 1975, 559-73.

Kimura, Hiroshi, "Anti-Hegemonism and the Politics of the Sino-Japanese peace treaty: A Study in the Miki government's China policy," *Asia Quarterly*, no. 2, 1977, 101-20.

Klein, Sidney, "A Survey of Sino-Japanese Trade," *China Mainland Review*, December 1966, 185-91.

Lafeber, Walter, "China and Japan: A Matter of Options," *Current History*, September 1968, 153-8 and 179.

———, "China and Japan: Different Beds, Different Dreams," *Current History*, September 1970, 142-6 and 178.

Langer, Paul F., "Japan's Relations with China," *Current History*, April 1964, 193-8 and 244.

Lee, Chae-Jin, "Making of the Sino-Japanese Peace and Friendship Treaty," *Pacific Affairs*, Fall 1979, 420-45.

Li, Victor H., "China and Off-shore Oil: The Tiao-yu T'ai Dispute," *Stanford Journal of International Studies* (Spring 1975), 143-58.

Lowenthal, Richard, "The Soviet Union, China and Japan," *Survey*, Autumn 1972, 30-7.

Matsumoto S. "Japan and China: Domestic and Foreign Influences on Japan's Policy," in A. Halpern, ed., *Policies towards China* (New York, 1965), 123-64.

Mendel, Douglas H., Jr., "Sino-Japanese Relations in Crisis,"

China Report, July-August 1972, 18-27.

Mendl, Wolf, "China's Challenge to Japan," *World Today*, July 1979, 278-86.

———, "Japan and China," *Survey*, Autumn 1972, 66-73.

Miki Takeo, "Future Japanese Diplomacy," *Japan Quarterly*, January-March 1973, 20 and 22.

Miyoshi, Osamu, "How the Japanese Press Yielded to Peking," *Survey*, Autumn 1972, 103-25.

Morley, James W., "Japan's Position in Asia," *Journal of International Affairs*, no. 2, 1963, 142-54.

———, "Japan's Security Policy in Transition," *Current History*, April 1964, 200-6.

Murthy, P.A.N., "Japan's Changing Relations with People's China and the Soviet Union," *International Studies*, July 1965, 1-19.

———, "Japan's Defence Policies: Problems and Prospects," *International Studies*, January 1973, 1-56.

Okuhara, Toshio, "The Territorial Sovereignty over the Senkaku Islands and Problems on the Sorrounding Continental Shelf," *Japanese Annual of International Law*, 1971, 97-105.

Park, Choon-ho and Jerome Alan Cohen, "The Politics of China's Oil Weapon," *Foreign Policy*, Fall 1975.

Park, Yung H., The Politics of Japan's China Decision," *Orbis*, Summer 1975, 562-90.

Pi Ying-Hsien, "Impasse in the proposed Peiping-Tokyo treaty of peace and friendship and the anti-hegemony clause," *Issues and Studies*, March 1978, 73-85.

Ravenal, Earl C., "The New Strategic Balance in Asia," *Asia Pacific Community*, Fall 1978, 92-116.

Royama, Michio, "The Asian Balance of Power: A Japanese View," *Adelphi Popers*, No. 42, November 1967, 1-16.

———, "Why should Japan Recognize China," *The Japan Interpreter*, Summer-Autumn 1972, 255-68.

Sadako Ogata, "The Business Community and Japanese Foreign Policy: Normalizaton of Relations with People's Republic of China," in Robert A. Scalapino, ed., *The Foreign Policy of Modern Japan* (Berkeley, 1977).

Sakamoto Yoshikazu, "Sino Japanese Relations in the Nuclear Age," *Journal of Social and Political Ideas in Japan*, December 1966.

Scalapino, Robert A., "In Search of a Role: Japan and the Uncertainties of Power," *Encounter*, December 1966, 21-7.

————, "China and the Balance of Power," *Foreign Affairs*, January 1974, 349-85.

Simon, Sheldon W., "The Japan-China-USSR Triangle," *Pacific Affairs*, Summer 1974, 125-38.

Storry, Richard, "Options for Japan in the 1970s," *World Today*, August 1970, 325-33.

Takami Shigeyoshi, "Prospects for Trade with Continental China," *Contemporary Japan*, April 1958, 208-33.

Tanaka Kakuei, "Japan in the 1970s," *Contemporary Japan*, March 1970.

Tretiak, Daniel, "Sino-Japanese Treaty of 1978: The Senkaku Incident Prelude," *Asian Survey*, December 1978, 1235-49.

Tsurutani Taketsugu, "Japan, China and East Asian Security," *Asia Quarterly*, 1973, 221-42.

Wakaizumi, Kei, "Japan Beyond 1970," *Foreign Affairs*, April 1969, 509-20.

Weinstein, Martin E., "Japan and the Continental Giants," *Current History*, April 1971, 193-9.

Welfield John, "A New Balance: Japan versus China," *Pacific Community*, October 1972, 54-70.

Wrightnan, Alistair, "How China is Adapting to the Japanese Market," *U.S. China Business Reveiw*, July/August 1974, 30-3.

Yamamoto K., "Trade Problems with People's Republic of China," *Contemporary Japan*, September 1958, 363-98.

Yasutomo, Dennis T., "Sato's China Policy, 1964-1966," *Asian Survey*, June 1977, 530-44.

Yoshida Shigeru, "Japan and the Crisis in Asia," *Foreign Affairs*, January 1951, 171-81.

Young, Kenneth T., "Japan and the U.S. in Pacific Asia," *Pacific Community*, October 1972, 1-17.

Index

100, 103, 111-2, 144, 190, 201,
261, 263, 265, 287, 294-7,
301-3, 305
visit to China (Dez 1979), 188-9,
294-8
Oil
Chinese exports to Japan,
135-6, 138-9, 152, 160-72
declining production, 166-7, 171,
181
export of petroleum products, 171
failure to meet commitments
166-7
inland oil fields, 169-70
supplies under Long-Term Trade
Agreement, 164-7
see also Bohai Bay Development
project
Oil exploration, Japan-ROK-Taiwan,
off their coasts, 76
Okamur Neiji, 19
Okazaki Kaheita, 69
Okazaki Katsuo, 32
Okinawa, 6, 58-60, 97, 129, 266
Okinawa Development Agency, 127
Okinawa Reversion Agreement
(1971), 123, 248-9
Okita Saburo, 143, 189, 297-8, 300-1
Organization for Economic Coope-
ration and Development (OECD),
14
Organization of Petroleum Export-
ing Countries (OPEC), 170, 172
Ostpolitik, 100
Overseas Economic Cooperation
Fund, 144-5, 147, 151
Oyama Ikuo, 12, 210

Pak Jung Hi, 50, 252
Pakistan, 53, 193
Paracel Islands, 125
Peace and Friedship Treaty (Aug
1979), 98, 101, 107, 114-5, 149,
185, 212-3, 27 6-84, 286-8, 295,
301
and business community, 113, 116
and Japanese motives, 113-4

and Southeast Asia, 119
and US, 119
and USSR, 108, 118-9
Chinese motives, 113-4
intra-party debate in LDP on,
111-2
Japanese motives, 112-3
Peace Conference of the Asian and
Pacific Regions (1952), 10 n. 28
Peng Chen, 14, 50, 217
Peng Meng-chi, 92
People's Council for the Normali-
zation of Japan-China Relations,
104 n. 7
"People's diplomacy", 23, 49
People's Liberation Army (PLA), 229
Pescadores, 2, 4, 124
Philippines, 6, 45, 55, 290
Port Arthur, 2
Port Darien, 2, 164
Potsdam Declaration, 96, 106 n. 51,
125, 213-5, 262-3

Qinhuangdao port project, 145
Quemoy, 222

Red Cross Society of China, 19-20
215-6
Red Cross Society of Japan, 19-20
216
Red Guards, 56-7
Romania, 285
Rusk, Dean, 47
Ryukyu Island, 55

Saito Yoshida, 22
Sakhalin, 4, 299
Sasaki Yoshitake, 177, 179
Sato Eisaku, 50-1, 54-7, 59-61, 71,
74, 79, 84-6, 90-2, 240-1, 243, 245-
6, 284-9, 251, 255, 258
Sato Shoji, 110
Scalapino, Robert A., 203
Senkaku Island Incident (1978), 111,
126-9
Senkaku Islands dispute, 98, 110-1,
119, 122-30, 203, 284